MW00534947

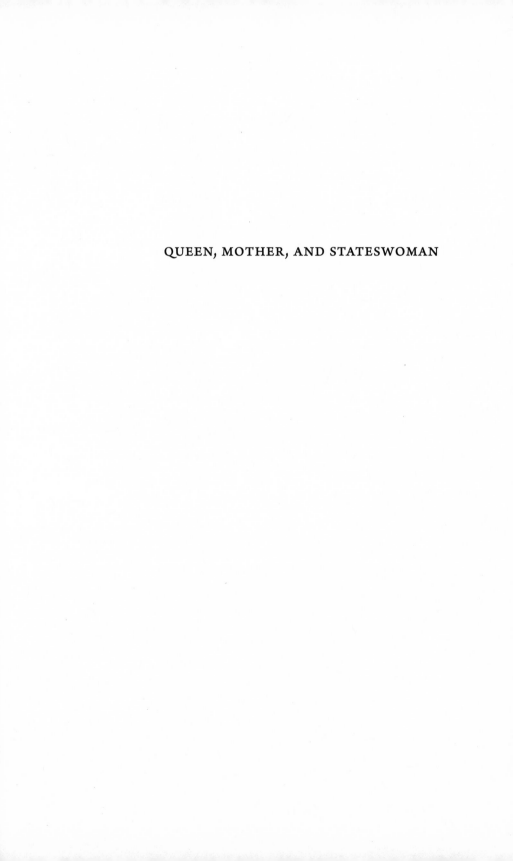

QUEEN, MOTHER, AND STATESWOMAN

Queen, Mother, and Stateswoman

Mariana of Austria and the Government of Spain

SILVIA Z. MITCHELL

The Pennsylvania State University Press
University Park, Pennsylvania

Library of Congress Cataloging-in-Publication Data

Names: Mitchell, Silvia Z., author.
Title: Queen, mother, and stateswoman : Mariana of Austria and the
government of Spain / Silvia Z. Mitchell.
Description: University Park, Pennsylvania : The Pennsylvania State
University Press, [2019] | Includes bibliographical references and index.
Summary: "A reassessment of the regency of Queen Mariana of Austria
(1634–1696) during the minority of her son, King Carlos II of Spain,
offering a new perspective on the Spanish monarchy in the later seventeenth
century"—Provided by publisher.
Identifiers: LCCN 2019001340 | ISBN 9780271083391 (cloth : alk. paper)
Subjects: LCSH: Mariana de Austria, Queen, consort of Philip IV, King
of Spain, 1634–1696. | Queens—Spain—Biography. | Spain—History—
Charles II, 1665–1700.
Classification: LCC DP185.9.M37 M58 2019 | DDC 946/.053092 [B]—dc23
LC record available at https://lccn.loc.gov/2019001340

The Pennsylvania State University Press is a member of the Association of
University Presses.

It is the policy of The Pennsylvania State University Press to use acid-free
paper. Publications on uncoated stock satisfy the minimum requirements
of American National Standard for Information Sciences—Permanence of
Paper for Printed Library Material, ANSI Z39.48-1992.

To Derek, Dominick, and Victoria

CONTENTS

Acknowledgments *(ix)*

Notes on Names *(xiii)*

Abbreviations *(xiv)*

Dynastic Chart *(xv)*

Introduction: The Historical and International Significance of Mariana's Regency *(1)*

1   A Habsburg Destiny, 1634–1665 *(19)*

2   Mariana's Court and Political System, 1665–1667 *(53)*

3   Resolving Philip IV's Legacy, 1665–1668 *(76)*

4   Consolidating Power at Home, 1668–1670 *(109)*

5   At the Pinnacle of Power, 1670 to November 5, 1675 *(141)*

6   The Politics of Motherhood, November 6, 1675, to 1677 *(170)*

7   Reconciliation, Vindication, Triumph, 1678–1679 *(199)*

Conclusion: Mariana's Historical Legacy *(227)*

Notes *(235)*

Bibliography *(265)*

Index *(283)*

ACKNOWLEDGMENTS

Writing a book requires training, resources, time, and support. It is therefore incredibly satisfying finally to be able to thank the many individuals and institutions that have supported me over the years it has taken me to write *Queen, Mother, and Stateswoman*. I first learned the fundamentals of early modern Spanish history and acquired the tools I needed to do historical research as an undergraduate and master's student at Florida International University (FIU) under the guidance of Noble David Cook, a distinguished historian of Latin America and early modern Spain. David encouraged me to pursue a PhD, and I am most grateful for his support and encouragement. Joseph F. Patrouch, who taught at FIU before leaving to become the director of the Wirth Institute for Austrian and Central European Studies at the University of Alberta, was also a key influence. Joe introduced me to the fascinating and complicated worlds of the Habsburgs, queenship, and court studies.

Guido Ruggiero—teacher, friend, mentor, and dissertation director at the University of Miami (UM)—has been my most important intellectual influence. He instilled in me not only intellectual integrity but also the confidence that allowed me to pursue a more difficult—and longer—path toward my goals. This book is better as a result. UM was, and is, an intellectual paradise populated by early modernists in various disciplines. I must next thank the Spanish literary critic Anne J. Cruz, whose teaching inspired me and whose conversations provided years of intellectual stimulation. I shall always treasure our marathon discussions about Spanish history and Habsburg women. Aside from Guido Ruggiero, other historians in the Department of History at UM—Karl Gunther, Mary Lindemann, Hugh Thomas, and Ashli White—as well as my fellow students, particularly Erica Heinsen-Roach (currently at the University of South Florida–St. Petersburg), have been critical to my development. Mihoko Suzuki, the inaugural director of the Center for the Humanities and professor of English, likewise provided invaluable support. My fellowship at the center in 2011 was a key moment in this project's development; feedback from Mihoko and the other members of the seminar was especially influential in shaping the chapters on Mariana of Austria's exile.

The Department of History at UM funded my first research trip to the archives, giving me an opportunity to survey the sources and begin to grasp the dimensions of the project that became this book. Additional grants from the department in 2008 and 2009 as well as a University of Miami College of Arts and Sciences Summer Research Fellowship in 2009 allowed me to complete my dissertation research. From 2006 to 2011, a McKnight Fellowship awarded to me by the Florida Education Fund made it possible for me to pursue doctoral studies free of teaching responsibilities. As a McKnight fellow, I also entered into a community of scholars. The foundation also granted me additional funding for research trips in 2007, 2008, and 2009.

Since 2013, the Department of History at Purdue University has been my home, and it is here that *Queen, Mother, and Stateswoman* was completed. I benefitted particularly from the Department of History and two Library Scholars Grants from Purdue in 2014 and 2016, which funded additional research for chapters 1, 3, and 5. Special thanks are due to Dr. Lawrence J. Mykytiuk, Department of History librarian, for supporting my applications. A series of ASPIRE grants from the dean's office of the College of Liberal Arts allowed me to present papers at several scholarly meetings in Europe and the United States. A junior leave in the fall of 2014 and a Summer Faculty Grant from the College of Liberal Arts in 2017 made it possible for me to finish the manuscript and complete the revisions in a timely manner. The dean's office of the College of Liberal Arts, in conjunction with the Department of History, provided a generous subvention to defray publication costs. I am particularly grateful to R. Douglas Hurt, head of the Department of History; Melissa Remis, associate dean for research, College of Liberal Arts; and the dean's office for their generous support.

My colleagues helped me face the challenges of completing the manuscript. Here I must single out Dawn G. Marsh, who made the long Indiana winter months both fun and productive; our frequent dinners were the focal point for intellectual exchanges. Rebekah Klein-Pejšová, David C. Atkinson, Ariel E. de la Fuente, and Yvonne M. Pitts have been incredibly supportive and have listened attentively as I thought my way through the implications of what I was discovering for the history of women, Europe, and Spain. My fellow early modern Europeanists—Jim Farr, Melinda Zook, and Charles "Charlie" Ingrao—provided feedback that sharpened the historical interpretations in these pages. In the Medieval and Renaissance

Studies (MARS) Program, Howard Mancing (in Spanish) and Michael Johnston (in English) also helped make Purdue a congenial intellectual home. My undergraduate student Abigail Nicole Frankovich (2018) helped me create the dynastic chart. I was also lucky to find three capable research assistants: Dr. Emilie Brinkman (history), Ana Maria Carvajal (Spanish), and Min Ji Kang (Spanish).

I have benefitted from many formal and informal conversations with a spectacular group of scholars currently working on queens, women's history, and courts, and I have had the privilege of participating in numerous conferences and workshops with many of them. Conversations about Mariana of Austria with Laura Oliván Santaliestra over the years have been critical in the development of my ideas. There are too many scholars to list individually, although I hope that this book honors their work. I thank all who shared references and documents found in the body of the text, but I must single out Renate Schreiber for generously sharing the letters the young Mariana of Austria wrote to her father.

Only the professional expertise of the archivists and staff in the Spanish archives made research on this book possible. Over the years, I have greatly profited from the vast knowledge of María Victoria Salinas at the Biblioteca Nacional de España and of Isabel Aguirre Landa at the Archivo General de Simancas. At the Archivo Histórico Nacional, Sección Nobleza in Toledo, Miguel F. Gómez Vozmediano was an excellent guide to the resources of a very rich archive. I am very grateful to the Fundación Medinaceli for allowing me to consult their catalog at the Palacio de Pilatos in Seville and for giving me access to the documents housed in the Edificio Tavera in Toledo before they were publicly available. The staff of these archives, as well as those of the Archivo Histórico Nacional, the Archivo General de Palacio, and the Real Academia de la Historia, patiently processed my innumerable requests.

Mary Lindemann has been a mentor since my graduate school days, a friend, teacher, and go-to person for many years now. She read the first draft of the entire manuscript as well as several iterations of the diplomacy chapters, for which her expertise was invaluable. Of course, any remaining errors are my own. The Early Modern Interdisciplinary Studies Group at the University of Miami read an early version of the first chapter and offered critical feedback. Noble David Cook and Alexandra Parma "Sasha" Cook, David C. Atkinson, and Anne J. Cruz also read early versions of my introduction. Martha Schulman has made this book much more readable than it once was, and I am very fortunate to have found her. The external readers for Pennsylvania State University Press read a long manuscript with critical but generous eyes, and their suggestions have much improved the final result. The executive editor of the press, Ellie Goodman, was an early supporter, and I repeatedly benefitted from her scholarly expertise as I moved from manuscript to published book. I am grateful to have found the perfect home for my manuscript.

My bilingual, transcontinental, and multicity family has been a critical asset in completing the book. My sister Érica Zisa housed me and fed me delicious and healthy Argentinian food during various trips to Madrid; she helped me navigate the city and made my stays productive and enjoyable. Our other sister, Nerina Soledad Zisa, did that and more by taking care of my daughter, Victoria, in summer 2014 while I worked in the archives. Although not physically present, the rest of my family in Argentina cheered me on and celebrated every milestone with me, and I am grateful for that. My now adult children, Derek A. Mitchell, Dominick F. Mitchell, and Victoria J. Mitchell, have grown up along with this project. They kept me busy, but they also kept me grounded all these years, contributing to my life in ways that they will never know. I dedicate this book to them.

NOTES ON NAMES

Names have been used in their anglicized forms when they are well known or are the most common spelling. I have used Philip instead of Felipe and Charles V rather than Carlos I (as he was known in Spain) or Karl V (in the Holy Roman Empire). Consistency in spelling women's names is almost impossible because the spelling changed from one court to another. Mariana, for example, was known as Maria Anna in Vienna and Margarita as Margarete Therese in Vienna; I have chosen the most common spelling here as well. Following convention, I have kept the Hispanicized spelling of King Carlos II to avoid confusion with his contemporary, Charles II of England. Names of cities have been used in their most common spellings for English speakers; when these do not exist, I have chosen the most common usage, such as Aix-la-Chapelle instead of Aachen. Don Juan José of Austria is referred to here as simply Don Juan, as this is what his contemporaries called him.

The conglomerate over which the Spanish Habsburgs ruled was known to contemporaries as *la Monarquía Hispánica*, which I translate here as "Spanish monarchy" and occasionally call Spain to avoid overwhelming the reader. All translations are the author's unless otherwise noted. I did not modernize Spanish grammar and spelling when quoting directly from sources.

ABBREVIATIONS

ADM	Archivo Ducal Medinaceli
Adm.	Sección Administrativa
AGS	Archivo General, Simancas
AHN	Archivo Histórico Nacional, Madrid
AHNSN	Archivo Histórico Nacional, Sección Nobleza
APR	Archivo del Palacio Real
APRDR	Archivo del Palacio Real, Descalzas Reales
BNE	Biblioteca Nacional de España
CODOIN	Colección de Documentos Inéditos para la historia de España
DBE	Diccionario Biográfico Español
doc.	documento
E.	Estado
exp.	expediente
fol.	folio
Hist.	Sección Histórica
leg.	legajo
ms.	manuscript
NL	Newberry Library
núm.	número
PTR	Patronato Real
r	recto (front folio page)
RAH	Real Academia de la Historia
RCII	Reinados, Carlos II
v	verso (reverse folio page)

The Spanish and Austrian Habsburgs

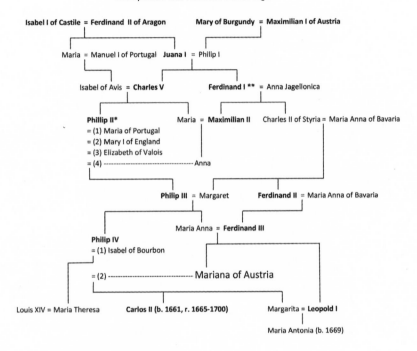

B	Rulers
*	Start of Spanish branch
**	Start of Austrian branch

Introduction

*The Historical and International
Significance of Mariana's Regency*

Millions of visitors to the Prado Museum in Madrid have encountered
Diego Velazquez's splendid portrait of Queen Mariana of Austria wearing
her signature hoopskirt or have seen her reflection in the background of
his masterpiece *Las Meninas*, yet few of those visitors, even specialists, are
aware of her historical significance. Arriving in Madrid as a fourteen-year-
old bride to King Philip IV, thirty years her senior and her maternal uncle,
Mariana began her sixteen years as queen consort of Spain in late 1649.
Despite dynastic and political crises, she immediately became the cultural
center of the Spanish court in one of its most glittering periods. Having
secured the succession and fulfilled her dynastic duties, Mariana was propelled to the highest level of political power when her husband died. On
September 17, 1665—the day of his death—she became the regent of the
Spanish monarchy on behalf of her three-year-old son, Carlos II (b. November 6, 1661). For the next ten years, she ruled the largest political conglomerate in Europe and had major political and diplomatic achievements.

Mariana was born to live and breathe high politics; hers was no rags-to-
riches story. From the age of eleven, when negotiations over her marriage
began in 1646, until her death from breast cancer in 1696, her life intertwined with some of the most important events in European history,
many of which she influenced directly. Her spectacular dynastic pedigree
as daughter, sister, wife, or mother of Holy Roman emperors, empresses,

and Spanish kings made her a conspicuous and influential figure. It was her regency, however, that elevated her to a position equal to that of Holy Roman Emperor Leopold I, Charles II of England, Prince William of Orange, and Louis XIV of France, each of whom benefitted from her political friendship or faced her as a political rival. An archipelago in the Pacific Ocean that bears her name (the Mariana Islands, now a commonwealth of the United States), eulogies published and delivered in the outposts of the Spanish monarchy in Europe and the New World, and a beatification proceeding that testified to her political and diplomatic influence are enduring symbols of her power. If her story has remained largely buried or distorted, this has less to do with her accomplishments or contemporary recognition and more with how the history of Spain has been written.[1]

The marriage of Isabel I and Ferdinand II in 1469 unified the kingdoms of Castile and Aragon, setting the political, institutional, and territorial foundation for the Spanish monarchy. By the time strategic marriage alliances and accidents of births and deaths allowed the Habsburgs to succeed to the Spanish throne in 1516, the monarchy was a global empire. Ruling over a dynastic conglomerate composed of an array of kingdoms with local political institutions and traditions, the Habsburgs—harnessing the legacy of the Catholic monarchs—developed an incredibly sophisticated bureaucracy that let them rule a global empire without modern technology. At its peak, the Spanish monarchy encompassed the Iberian Peninsula, large parts of Italy, the Low Countries, and territories in today's France. Their overseas territories included large areas of North America, all of Central and South America, the Caribbean, the Pacific, and during the period in which Portugal was part of the Spanish Empire (1580–1640), the Indian subcontinent and parts of East Africa.[2]

The history of Habsburg Spain is one of incredible power, expansion, and success but also exploitation and waste. To understand its contradictions, it must be remembered that Spain was, above all, a dynastic conglomerate built on and dependent on inheritance and succession and that the Habsburgs were called on to defend territories considered part of the family's patrimony, even if these lacked geographic continuity or political and cultural homogeneity. Conflicts with the French ruling dynasties (the Valois until 1589, then the Bourbons), for instance, forced the Habsburgs to mobilize enormous resources to keep their possessions, exacerbating internal challenges and external problems. Foremost among these were religious conflicts that were enmeshed with geopolitical ones. War was a constant drain on the economy, and despite the family's incredible riches, expenses consistently outpaced income. The deficit was borrowed by mortgaging future income: New World silver was often spent years and decades in advance.[3]

This patrimonial conception of the state—the idea that the inherited constitutive kingdoms of the monarchy had to be protected at all costs—largely explains Habsburg policies during the century and a half before Mariana came to power and the geopolitical issues that dominated her reign as regent. By the time Philip IV—Mariana's husband and predecessor—took power, the ability to sustain this level of expenditure was in doubt, yet the commitment to maintaining premier status in the continent was reaffirmed. The sixteen-year-old king succeeded to the throne after the pacifist reign of his father, Philip III (r. 1598–1621), and soon resumed an aggressive foreign policy intended to reverse what was seen as Spain's loss of position on the continent. The monarchy began to fight wars on an unprecedented scale. To move the state machinery, Philip IV—under the influence of his favorite / prime minister, the Count-Duke of Olivares—introduced a number of fiscal, military, and political measures that, while intelligent and ahead of their time, precipitated a major political crisis. The Catalonian revolt in 1640 came first, quickly followed by Portugal's before year's end. Multiple military commitments—in central Europe with the Thirty Years' War (1618–48), in the Netherlands against the Dutch, and on the frontiers with France with the Franco-Spanish War (1635–59)—made it impossible for Philip IV to put down these revolts swiftly. The so-called crisis of the 1640s brought a regime change in Madrid. Philip IV dismissed Olivares in 1643 and spent the rest of his reign trying to resolve these problems. This is the immediate context of Mariana's regency.[4]

Philip did address some of the most urgent problems. The Peace of Westphalia (1648) ended the religious conflicts that engulfed the continent since the sixteenth century and that deeply affected both branches of the dynasty, bringing some, although not total, relief for Spain. While the Franco-Spanish War continued its course, as part of the Westphalian settlement, Philip recognized the independence of the United Provinces, ending a war that had lasted eighty years. Philip successfully subdued the Catalonian revolt in 1652, twelve years after it started, which prevented the dismemberment of the Iberian territories. He also quickly put down a revolt in Naples in 1648. He was unable to do anything, however, about Portugal, which continued to prefer the Braganzas to the Habsburgs. Here the consequences of dynasticism are clear: the king considered it his prerogative and duty to bring the kingdom of Portugal back into the Habsburg fold no matter the cost. In 1659, he negotiated an important peace treaty with France—the Peace of the Pyrenees—ending a costly twenty-five-year war. Once the war was over, he could concentrate all of Spain's resources on the Portuguese problem. Two important decisions he made at this point directly affected Mariana's reign as regent. First, he agreed to the marriage of his oldest daughter, Maria Theresa of Austria, to King Louis XIV of France. Second, he launched a major military enterprise against Portugal. In combination, these decisions made for a military, fiscal, and strategic disaster.

When Mariana became regent, Spain had just lost a battle to the Portuguese in what turned out to be the last major battle of the conflict (Villaviciosa, June 17, 1665). Although the Peace of the Pyrenees (1659) was a major treaty, recognized as such by the parties and the international community, its collapse was imminent, as Louis XIV planned to attack the Spanish Netherlands to claim territories there for France. This threat materialized eighteen months into Mariana's regency; the enormous war expenditures on the Portuguese conflict meant that Mariana presided over a virtually bankrupt state with vulnerable frontiers and a much-diminished army. The dynastic configuration, however, made the military and fiscal crises infinitely worse.

A three-year-old king with no younger brothers succeeded to the Spanish Crown in an age in which children often died in childhood. Since the Spanish monarchy did not exclude women from the succession, Carlos II's older sisters were drawn into the politics of the succession. Although Philip IV set clear lines of succession in his testament, the marriages of his two daughters caused an international showdown between their husbands: the king of France, Louis XIV, and the Holy Roman emperor, Leopold I (Mariana's younger brother). Given the scope of the Spanish Empire, with its possessions spanning three continents, its partial dismemberment or complete dissolution (if the child died and the succession were contested) had the potential to upset the European balance of power and lead to a continent-wide war. Such was the high-stakes situation at the beginning of the regency.

From 1665 to 1675, Mariana's signature alone could move the Spanish government forward, and she led with a great deal of strength and single-mindedness. Despite the dire circumstances she inherited, the monarchy she passed on to Carlos II was virtually intact and in a stronger position than when she found it. Multipower coalitions against France, Spain's most dangerous enemy, put in place by Mariana and her diplomats had replaced the coalitions against the Habsburgs, typically led by France.

This is the first monograph dedicated to documenting Queen Mariana's substantial political agency and legacy during her regency and her temporary exile from court, during which she was still influential. Based on new sources and a reinterpretation of known ones, this monograph seeks to establish Mariana's rightful, preeminent place in Spanish history, a place denied to her for nearly three hundred years.

REVISIONING MARIANA'S REGENCY AS PART OF CARLOS II'S REIGN

In spite of her preeminence and extensive authority, Mariana has been dis-empowered in studies that focus on men and discuss her regency as part of Carlos II's reign. The historical record on Mariana tends to have it both ways. On one hand, the presence and subsequent fall of two figures closely associated with her—her confessor, the Jesuit Everard Nithard (1608–1681), and her protégé, the upstart Fernando Valenzuela (1630–1692)—gave rise to the idea that she surrendered power to her favorites. The ongoing conflicts with the late king's illegitimate son, Don Juan of Austria (1629–1679), as well as her exile from court (1677–79) further contributed to the notion of a disorderly court presided over by a weak and incompetent female ruler. On the other, in the typical double bind of powerful women, Mariana has been depicted as power hungry. Thus her execution of a Crown official without a proper trial, her decision to raise a three-thousand-man royal guard to safeguard her authority, and her unwitting humiliation of the king when she suppressed a coup to replace her have created the impression of a woman of unrestrained ambition. Mariana has been described as "weak," "unstable," and "ignorant" but also "Machiavellian," "scheming," "with a German outlook" (meaning foreign), at times "melancholic" because she suffered from migraines, and overly pious and uninterested in politics because she "dressed as a nun."[5]

None of these contradictory descriptions, often uttered in the same book by the same author, rests on solid archival research. Instead, they come from the account of the Spanish historian and politician Gabriel Maura y Gamazo (1879–1963). This important study of Carlos II's court during his royal minority—when the monarchy was ruled on his behalf by a regent until he came of age—reproduced the nineteenth-century paradigm of women uninterested in, or incapable of, ruling. Maura deeply shaped subsequent views of Mariana and her rule. Despite a few significant findings in the past decade, scholars still perpetuate Maura's basic premises about Mariana: that she was too young and inexperienced to rule a complex political entity such as the Spanish monarchy or, alternatively, that she had insufficient legal and constitutional prerogatives, or acceptance, in a society that rejected female rule. The idea that she surrendered power to her favorites has remained virtually intact.[6]

Mariana and her regency have also suffered because of the association of the period with the classic "decline of Spain" paradigm. Although the concept of decline extended to the entire century, the succession crisis that eventually plunged Europe into war has conditioned the way scholars have written the history of the Spain of Carlos II. His death in 1700 without descendants was a watershed for Spain and Europe: it precipitated the War of the Spanish Succession (1701–14), introduced the Bourbons as the new ruling dynasty in Spain, and established a new continental order. Until recently, teleological interpretations of Carlos II's reign that viewed his demise as the inevitable manifestation of a dynasty and monarchy in the last stages of decay have been the norm. Seen in this way, Mariana's difficulties during the regency—the coup of 1669 that resulted in Nithard's dismissal, the confederation of nobles that brought about the imprisonment of Valenzuela, and Mariana's exile—fit with the general narrative of doom.[7]

Research on the Spain of Carlos II is slowly emerging, however. Revisionist histories began to appear in the 1980s, but these were minor compared to the wave of studies that followed the publication of Luis Ribot's foundational essay commemorating the three-hundredth anniversary of Carlos's death in 2000. Newer approaches, like the excellent study by Christopher Storrs, emphasize the "resilience of the Spanish monarchy." As Storrs argues, the Spanish Empire not only survived virtually intact; it actually grew slightly during the closing decades of Habsburg rule, commanding substantial resources and utilizing them effectively. Likewise, characterizations of Carlos II as physically deformed, intellectually disabled, and unable to perform sexually stand in stark contrast to evidence showing a king who spent days hunting, was an accomplished musician and art connoisseur, and evidently had intercourse with his two wives. These studies form an important foundation for this present work; I have relied on many of their findings. Yet Carlos II's minority (one of the most difficult periods of this era to understand) has largely been left out of these important new trends or conflated with the rest of the reign in ways that obscure rather than illuminate its significance for the king and monarchy.[8]

Mariana has begun to receive some long-overdue scholarly attention. Although still limited—particularly given the many available documents and potential areas of research—archival-based studies have started to challenge some of the most outrageous claims about Mariana. The Spanish historian Laura Oliván Santaliestra has brilliantly deconstructed Maura's presentation of Mariana; made significant archival discoveries that document the existence of Mariana's extensive diplomatic networks as consort, regent, and dowager; and written about key diplomatic and political figures close to the queen. New studies on regency and postregency portraits by art historian Mercedes Llorente have once and for all eradicated some of the most ridiculous assumptions about Mariana based on her austere appearance. These studies are beginning to question some, if not all, of the most misguided claims about Mariana. But her regency should not be relegated to the study of gender, women, or queens.[9]

As long as the scholarship on Mariana as a female ruler and the revisionist scholarship on the reign of Carlos II inhabit different intellectual worlds, major interpretive problems will remain. Now that the reign of Carlos II has been set on a solid path of historical rehabilitation, scholars are beginning to go beyond the resilience paradigm, establishing the reign as a dynamic period of economic, demographic, diplomatic, and political transformation. Many of these changes, including fiscal reforms and foreign policy innovations, began during Mariana's regency. Often this has not been noted, and when it has, Nithard and Valenzuela are credited.[10]

The main obstacles to giving Mariana her due within the revisionist scholarship have been the persistent confusion about the political system in place during Mariana's regency, the assumption that she surrendered power, and not least, a resistance to seeing what is clearly there. Maura's paradigm of female weakness, though weakened, is not dead. This affects not only scholars working on Carlos II's economic, political, or military policies but also those working from gender and feminist perspectives. Mariana's regency will not be fully understood until the geopolitical aspects of Carlos II's minority and the making and implementation of foreign policy are also considered. A coherent analytical approach to Mariana's regency as an integral part of Carlos II's reign requires both gender analysis and an analysis of the strategies and policies of her reign and their effect on the European stage; the two areas must inform one another.

SOURCES AND METHODS

My analysis places Mariana's regency within the framework of a well-documented tradition of the Habsburgs' legally sanctioned, robust, and effective female leadership traceable to late medieval Iberian political traditions. While the fact that Mariana was born of, was married to, and gave birth to royalty certainly contributed to her preparation and access to the office, the institutional and legal frameworks of her regency were also connected to existing social traditions and practices that sanctioned multiple and conspicuous forms of female authority. These were an integral part of early modern Spanish society, including, but not limited to, the court and royalty. Grace E. Coolidge's study on female guardianship among the early modern Spanish aristocracy and Martha Hoffman's study of childhood in the court of the Spanish Habsburgs open the door to broadening the investigation of Mariana's regency by incorporating the social, legal, and cultural aspects of motherhood, widowhood, and childhood. This broader social approach is instrumental to my conceptualization of the office and my interpretation of the events that gave rise to Mariana's "black legend." This new conceptualization makes it clear that the nature and causes of the disorders of the court were not the result of a lack of authority or overt rejection of female rule; we must seek to discover them elsewhere.[11]

Mariana fulfilled all the tasks associated with sovereign rulers of Spain. The Spanish monarchy's political system was incredibly complex, based on councils that advised the monarch on different aspects of government and territories while also requiring the ruler to approve the final decisions personally. As governor of the monarchy, Mariana legalized, formalized, and completed all tasks of state administration; at any given time, she had three secretaries working with her and was directly involved in formulating and implementing foreign policy. This study is based on hundreds of documents from seven archival repositories in Spain and an array of published sources, including Council of State deliberations; diplomatic instructions; personal communications with secretaries, ministers of her court, and diplomats; and her royal decrees and her responses to the councilors of state. These papers provide a substantial body of evidence that highlights the inadequacy of previous theses about Mariana's regency and political agency during Carlos II's minority.

The Council of State deliberations, for example, held mainly in the Archivo General de Simancas, Valladolid, and the Archivo Histórico Nacional, include Mariana's actual signature (she rarely used royal seals) and her detailed responses and orders to the Council of State. The deliberations are particularly important for Mariana's regency, because under her, the Council of State became a powerful institution, overshadowing the Junta de Gobierno, or Regency Council, that Philip IV had instituted as a consultative body of government. The relevant documents are divided into several series—Estado España, Inglaterra, Alemania, Roma, Holanda, and Francia (or Estado K)—and in recent years, some of these series have been studied in their original organization, resulting in monographs on the Spanish embassies in Paris during the years of peace and in Rome and London. Although important, these studies have not substantially changed views of Mariana's regency because they are narrowly focused on the embassies. I have consulted documents from each of these series to understand Mariana's policies as a whole. The sources let us see how Mariana's political system worked and how she formed and managed it.[12]

I have given this archival material precedence over sources that obscure Mariana's political agency. Satirical political literature against her or about the controversies involving Nithard, Valenzuela, and Don Juan abound, for example, mainly in the Biblioteca Nacional de España (Madrid) but also in other repositories. These kinds of sources help in assessing the overall climate of the court during her rule, and I have consulted them when needed, but they reveal little about how Mariana actually governed. Likewise, the voluminous memoirs of her confessor, Father Nithard, can be problematic. His penchant for including state papers is invaluable to the researcher, and I have used them for this purpose. But they cannot and should not be read transparently—a mistake Maura made. Confessors of queens typically depoliticized the queens they confessed, and Nithard was no exception. He consistently showed the queen as removed and detached from politics in ways that are contradicted by other evidence.

The sources I favor in this study also provide a solid foundation for understanding the roles of the men typically seen as protagonists, particularly Nithard and Valenzuela. Initially I also assumed that these men had played a dominant role in her regime, but evidence of Mariana's strong and decisive personality and her extensive and consistent participation in all aspects of government suggests otherwise. The scholarship on favoritism as a European-wide political phenomenon—rather than as a sexual and/or emotional one—some of the best of which is dedicated to Spanish favorites, or *validos*, of kings who preceded Mariana, provides important ways to evaluate Mariana's political system. The existence of political partnerships with several other ministers of her court and her relationship with the Council of State challenge the idea that she ruled via a system of favoritism, or *valimiento*. It is my contention that the two political crises Mariana faced during her regency—the first, in 1669, resolved by her dismissal of Nithard; the second, between 1675 and 1677, ended by Valenzuela's fall and her exile—must be seen in larger contexts of policy and politics. The idea that she surrendered power to favorites is not supported by the evidence available in the state papers.[13]

Finally, the role played by the ad hoc committee—the Junta de Gobierno—that Philip IV established for the duration of the regency has also led to misunderstandings of Mariana's regency, including the nature of her constitutional prerogative to rule and the inner workings of her regime. Although the papers of the Junta de Gobierno are no longer extant, the many state documents that do exist provide a more than adequate foundation to reconsider its role. Aside from the state papers, the royal household records, held in the Archivo del Palacio Real (Madrid), for example, reveal Mariana's extensive, sanctioned, and legitimate authority. These documents also provide a means of challenging key claims about Philip IV's testament, the document that set the legal and constitutional foundation of Mariana's regency. Once we look at the court system and the composition of Mariana's regime, the decision-making process, and her policies, the roles of Nithard, Valenzuela, and the Junta de Gobierno emerge in a completely different light.[14]

The concrete issues that Mariana faced on the international stage, however, drive this analysis. Mariana's rule did not take place in a historical vacuum, and the making and implementation of policy must be examined to understand the politics of the court during her regency. Philip's death in 1665 reopened the traditional rivalry between the Habsburgs and the Bourbons. Rumors that Louis XIV was only waiting for Philip IV's death to invade the Spanish Netherlands began circulating immediately after the Peace of the Pyrenees was signed in 1659. By 1663, observers considered the renewal of hostilities between Spain and France almost inevitable, yet Philip IV remained focused on reconquering rebellious Portugal. By committing the bulk of the monarchy's financial and military resources to what became, in the later years of his reign, a futile enterprise, he left the monarchy in a dangerously exposed situation. He also left Mariana a court that was split on which course to follow: whether to grant Portugal independence dominated the early years of the regency, which made it difficult for Mariana to implement policies needed to defend the monarchy from France. These early years were the queen's defining moment. It was foreign affairs that divided the court, and it is there that Mariana emerged as a highly capable ruler and stateswoman.

One of the larger arguments of this work is that it is impossible to study female rulers without the sustained focus on policy issues that is part of studies of their male counterparts. Mariana's regency, however, has not been considered in the context of international politics. Spain fought two wars with France during Mariana's regency—the War of Devolution (1667–68) and the Dutch War (1672–78)—and even in peacetime (1665–67 and 1668–72, although Spain officially entered the conflict in 1673), the monarchy engaged in diplomatic competition with France. Mariana's strategies and undertakings on behalf of Spain thus had implications not only for Spain but for Europe as a whole. While this study cannot provide a comprehensive history of late seventeenth-century European international politics, it nevertheless establishes that under Mariana's rule, Spain was instrumental in shaping Europe's course. Spanish secretaries kept copies of dispatches to foreign embassies, receipts of communications, copies of letters, translations of documents, and reports; this rich trove reveals the brilliance of the Spanish diplomats who worked under Mariana's directives.

Spain's diplomatic accomplishments during Mariana's regency were significant. Aside from concluding the peace with Portugal in 1668, strengthening Spain's defenses, and rebuilding the army of Flanders, Mariana forged defensive and offensive leagues and coalitions and made neutrality agreements with England, the United Provinces, the Holy Roman Empire, Sweden, Brandenburg, and Denmark. The queen was a key figure behind the alliances formed against France in the 1660s and 1670s, coalitions that should be considered precursors of larger ones in the latter part of the century. These developments, substantiated by significant archival documentation, underscore the necessity of reconsidering the period. This reevaluation is particularly important if we are to reincorporate Spain into the history of European international politics in the post-Pyrenees period, as Christopher Storrs has suggested we must.[15]

Finally, as we undertake the task of examining this critical period in Spain's history, it is imperative not to ignore the underlying rules and theories that shaped the way Mariana governed. The specific parameters of Mariana's political office—a regent during a royal minority—had enormous implications for the queen, the king, and the court.

MINORITY REIGNS AND THE PROBLEM OF REGENCY

The burgeoning field of queenship studies has generated an intellectual transformation. No longer considered exceptional women whose privileged positions made them irrelevant to womankind or as incidental to the power of kings, queens are now firmly at the center of a historiographical turn that is transforming understandings of monarchy, the court, and kingship, along with war and diplomacy. A generation of scholarship on queens accentuates the importance of beginning an analysis of queens' rules with a consideration of the type of office they occupied. Proprietary or regnant queens—women who inherited sovereignty through their own succession rights—for example, faced a very different situation than did consorts. Aside from the specific historical and regional contexts shaping their rules, these structural differences dictated the way the women exercised their offices; the starkly different documentary records that consorts and proprietary queens left behind have also shaped the way we study them.[16]

By definition a temporary office, regency provided an interim solution when a king (or queen if she was the titular ruler) was incapable of exercising sovereign authority because of absence, illness, or age. Although the office could be exercised by a variety of figures—uncles, aunts, grandmothers—or a government body, it was associated with queens. Regency, therefore, became a special form of queenship, and a queen regent's position differed fundamentally from that of a queen proprietary. Both exercised formal political authority, but one did so as the titular ruler, the other one *on behalf of* the ruler. Regency during a royal minority forms an even more specific category with its own rules and regulations. Legal definitions of childhood, for example, shaped the length of the office, which could last from a few months to more than a decade. The constitutional rules of the monarchy determined whether queens were chosen for the task and, if so, the extent of authority they enjoyed. In the French monarchy, for example, political theorists argued that queen mothers were ideal for the task because of their maternal love. This was contrasted with male regents, who almost invariably tried to usurp the power they were supposed to protect, sometimes with disastrous consequences for the monarchy. Salic Law, which barred women from all aspects of royal succession, provided additional reassurances that no usurpation of power would take place. These two aspects of female regency—maternal love and political exclusion—increasingly meant that French queens were seen as the most suitable candidates, making the office essentially a feminine one. In contrast, the Habsburgs saw female regency as part of the traditions that sanctioned women's access to all sorts of political authority.[17]

Regency in the Spanish monarchy was part of a wider range of formal political functions allocated to Habsburg women, who were especially instrumental in the early sixteenth-century rise of the dynasty's global conglomerate. Habsburg women were far more than rich heiresses or pawns in the famously successful Habsburg marriage diplomacy. They proved critical in cementing power and administering this unprecedented collection of territories, and they regularly exercised guardianships over younger members of the family, including males. Women's formal political participation among the Habsburgs can be traced back to the institutions of queen lieutenancy in the Crown of Aragon and the governorships women held in Castile and the Netherlands. Titles such as that of lieutenant or governor were appended to those of queen, empress, princess, or duchess. In addition, the almost ubiquitous practice of allocating the guardianships of Spanish aristocratic children to women provided extra support for a female regent. Mariana represented both governorship exercised by Habsburg women and the guardianship assumed by her aristocratic counterparts; these provided the legal framework that Philip IV used in his testament. Regency in Habsburg Spain, therefore, was a multivalent proposition resulting from practices of the dynasty in combination with Iberian social, legal, and political traditions.[18]

These two distinct approaches to female regency explain important differences. Queen mothers in France, for example, received tutorship rights (control over the king) and only gradually gained governorship rights; in most cases, their political prerogatives were limited, at least juridically. In contrast, Mariana had both tutorship *and* governorship rights, and this authority was sanctioned by the laws of the realm and her husband's testament. Although Philip IV established a special government body for the duration of Mariana's governorship, he also ensured that she retained indisputable executive authority. This extraordinary constitutional right to rule unencumbered stands in stark contrast to conditions in France. Whereas French queen regents had control over the king, their formal authority over the government was limited; Mariana exercised a unified regency with no limits to her governing authority. I am not suggesting that French queen regents did not enjoy power and influence; they did and copiously. Yet comparing Mariana's extensive and legally sanctioned political prerogatives to the French situation is not merely a rhetorical exercise. It reveals the layers of legitimacy and entitlement that bolstered Mariana's regency. Any difficulties she faced cannot be attributed to lack of constitutional authority or personal deficiencies; we must look elsewhere.

What is missing in the analysis of regency? One obvious answer is the other major component of a regency during a royal minority: the king. Although only a child and with no direct impact on policy, the king was nonetheless central to the polity's functioning. To understand this, it is useful to look at royal transitions of power. The death of a king was a ubiquitous problem in medieval monarchy: it could lead to anarchy until the next ruler was anointed or elected. To minimize the potential for violence, political thinkers developed the theory of the king's two bodies. As historian Ernst Kantorowicz has observed, although the king dies physically, the political body of the king—the monarchy—never perishes. While some scholars have questioned aspects of Kantorowicz's theory, it nevertheless helps explain the implications of a royal minority for the institution of monarchy. It explains, for example, why royal minorities required two distinct authorities: a tutor to care for the physical body of the king and a single person or special council to care for his political body—the monarchy. Even if the same person had both roles—as Mariana did—the functions were still considered different aspects of government. This political separation reveals a great deal about the theoretical underpinnings of medieval monarchy that continued well into the early modern period. Although the system helped sustain a royal transition of power without a descent into chaos, the insecurity of a royal minority never completely disappeared: until the king came of age, his "two bodies"—the physical and the political—were temporarily out of joint. Even allowing that the Spanish monarchy was composite, corporate, gendered, and not absolute, it was the king who linked all its components. A royal minority, therefore, was potentially problematic in and of itself.[19]

The highs and lows of Mariana's regency were largely dictated by Carlos II's position as king and his own personal development, which, by definition, was also a political development. To keep its territorial integrity, the monarchy was dependent on the survival of a three-year-old. In the early years of the regency, Carlos II's youth contributed to Mariana's difficulties on the international stage. Once he had survived the most dangerous period in an early modern child's life, anxiety over succession subsided in Spain and in Europe more broadly. Likewise, when he began to assume a more active role in the rituals and ceremonies of the court, a new stability suffused the court as well. Mariana achieved the pinnacle of her power after weathering the political crisis of 1669; she remained dominant until the end of her regency in 1675. Such power resulted from the king's increasing participation in court activities as much as from her well-thought-out policies at home and abroad.

Nonetheless, as the king's legal emancipation approached, the anxiety of the court revived. This reminds us that when analyzing the rule of women during royal minorities, we must pay close attention to the specific parameters of the office *and* the political culture of the court. A minority regency was the only type of royal political regime where the end had a set date: the day of the king's legal emancipation. In Spain, that was the king's fourteenth birthday, while in France it began when the king entered his fourteenth year of life—that is, on his thirteenth birthday. The French monarchy had rituals in place to help provide a smooth transition of power from minority to majority rule. Scholars who have studied these special ceremonies—or *lits*—generally agree that they have been designed for the benefit of queen mothers, whose authority extended symbolically into the reign of the now adult king. Spain did not have these ceremonies. Philip IV's testament dictated the end of the formal period of the regency, but it was not clear how Carlos II's postminority rule would be shaped and what role, if any, Mariana would play. Philip IV had designated a role for Mariana as curator, or *curadora*, of the king, a less stringent form of guardianship intended to begin after her tutorship and governorship ended. But the king was not legally bound to accept Mariana as his curator. And indeed, he did not.[20]

Carlos II's fourteenth birthday on November 6, 1675, began with a coup against Mariana. Although she quickly ended it, the event inaugurated a political crisis that led to her exile from court a little more than a year later. Historians have interpreted this political crisis in terms of the ambitions of Don Juan of Austria (1629–1679), the king's illegitimate son, and discontent about Mariana's protégé, Valenzuela. The crux of the political crisis, however, was Carlos II and his position as king. Reading the events and the texts produced during these years with an attentive focus on the king and kingship leads to a new interpretation of the difficult events that began with Carlos II's legal emancipation. And new archival evidence demonstrates that although Mariana was no longer at court, she continued to play a key role in the political life of the king and the monarchy. The events preceding Mariana's exile, the exile itself, and her reincorporation at court are essential aspects of the overall history of Carlos II's reign and his kingship and are treated in detail in this book.

ORGANIZATION AND THEMES

In order to achieve the goal of analyzing Mariana's regency within the context of her political trajectory—from archduchess to queen consort, regent, and dowager—as well as the history of Spain and Europe in the later seventeenth century, I have organized the chapters chronologically and thematically. Chapter 1 covers the longest period and discusses Mariana's trajectory from her birth as the oldest daughter of a ruling emperor to becoming regent of the Spanish monarchy. It charts Mariana's youth and education at the imperial court of Vienna and her sixteen years as queen consort. Because her own life intertwined with the historical events that played a dominant role during her regency, the chapter provides the foundation needed to understand both Mariana's preparation and access to the office of regent and the internal and international situation she faced as governor. The structural framework of Mariana's regency is analyzed in chapter 2, beginning with an in-depth discussion of Philip IV's testament. The court underwent a substantial restructuring in the areas of etiquette and ceremony as well as political administration that is key to understanding Mariana's political system, including her elevation of the Council of State as the premier political body of the monarchy and diminution of the role of the Junta de Gobierno.

The discussion of the policies of Mariana's regency begins in chapter 3 and covers the first three years—the most difficult period—of her reign. The resolution of the war against Portugal with the Peace of Lisbon (1668) and her responses to the War of Devolution set the stage for Mariana's diplomatic accomplishments. Her court was deeply divided, and these divisions are key to understanding the first political crisis of her reign (1669). Chapter 4 reinterprets the political confrontation in 1669 between Mariana and Philip's illegitimate son, Don Juan, which resulted in Nithard's dismissal, and evaluates Don Juan's position as an illegitimate royal son. This chapter also reassesses Nithard's role in Mariana's regime compared with contemporaneous—and, I argue, more significant—political partnerships. One figure of interest to specialists will be the Marquis of Aytona, who came closest to becoming a favorite / prime minister in the style of Olivares but whose spectacular career was cut short by his sudden death in 1670. But even with such an influential figure, it is clear that Mariana was always actively in control. By midregency, she had shaped her political regime, bringing in a new generation of statesmen. While some of her strategies were controversial, including her decision to keep a permanent guard in the city of Madrid, she consolidated her position and had for the rest of her regency the kind of stability that had eluded her during the regency's first half.

The second stage of Mariana's foreign policy is discussed in chapter 5, which explores the diplomatic accomplishments she built on the foundation of her first three years of rule. She persistently sought to work with her relatives in Vienna, but when those efforts failed, she aggressively courted England, the United Provinces, and the princes of the north (i.e., Sweden, Denmark, and Brandenburg) to help neutralize France. In the Quadruple Alliance of 1673, Mariana linked Spain, the United Provinces, the Holy Roman Empire, and the Duke of Lorraine, who had been dispossessed of his estates but contributed a sizeable army. This offensive coalition was the culmination of seven years of unrelenting diplomacy. This victory was followed by her mediation of the peace agreement that ended the Third Anglo-Dutch War in 1674 and left France facing a coalition of major powers. Her success as head of state was accompanied by complete command of her court. As her regency came to an end, Mariana enjoyed what appeared to be unchallenged power.

Chapter 6 offers a new interpretation of the yearlong crisis that led to Mariana's exile, arguing that Mariana's powerful maternal influence interfered with Carlos's effective exercise of the office of king and was the main reason for the unprecedented confederation of twenty-three noble families demanding the permanent separation of mother and son. Mariana's unwitting emasculation and infantilization of her son exacerbated the situation. Carlos II's separation from his mother—and thus her exile—was a sine qua non for his political coming of age. Chapter 7 investigates the personal relationship between the two during Mariana's exile, looking at the renegotiation of their political relationship. The chapter is based on their never-before-studied personal letters as well as a close reading of the Council of State's voluminous deliberations on the king's marriage, which lasted from 1674 to 1679, a time when Spain was also at war. The chapter argues that Mariana's reconciliation with her son was negotiated before and was independent of Don Juan's death in September 1679.

After a two-and-a-half-year absence, Mariana returned in triumph to Madrid on September 27, 1679, received, as one gazette reported, "by the hearts of everyone." Her warm reception was the unofficial end of Carlos II's minority as well as the public recognition of Mariana's political and diplomatic contributions to her son and the monarchy. Her absence from the historical record lasted much longer than her short absence from court; I hope that her many contributions will finally emerge from historical obscurity.[21]

CHAPTER 1

A Habsburg Destiny, 1634–1665

The Habsburg dynasty shaped Mariana's life and political trajectory at so many different levels that it can be said without exaggeration that advancing dynastic interests was her *raison d'être*. She was born in Wiener-Neustadt on December 23, 1634, to Ferdinand of Styria (1608–1657) and Maria of Austria (1606–1646), the king and queen of Hungary and Bohemia. Although no real political power adhered to these titles, they indicate the couple's status as the son and daughter-in-law of Holy Roman Emperor Ferdinand II and their almost certain elevation to the imperial Crown. Mariana was only two years old when her father was elected king of Romans and, a few months later in February 1637, Emperor Ferdinand III. Her maternal lineage was just as prestigious: her mother, the Infanta-Emperatriz Maria, was the daughter and sister of two Spanish kings, Philip III (r. 1598–1621) and Philip IV (r. 1621–65), the man Mariana eventually married. Born into the Austrian Habsburg branch, Mariana had a strong Spanish descent through her mother, and the intricate connections produced by several generations of Habsburg marriages made Mariana the granddaughter, great-granddaughter, and great-great-granddaughter of three Spanish Habsburg kings.[1]

Marriage diplomacy had played a key role in the rise of the family to premier status in Europe. Emperor Charles V split his inheritance between his son, King Philip II of Spain (r. 1556–98), and his younger brother, Emperor Ferdinand I (r. HRE 1558–64), establishing two independent branches, the senior Spanish Habsburg branch and the junior Austrian Habsburg line. These two sides ruled over two distinct political entities: the Spanish monarchy and the Holy Roman Empire. But a strong connection between the two Habsburgs was considered essential for the interests of each branch and the dynasty's position in the continent. Intradynastic marriages, therefore, continued to be considered an essential diplomatic tool, more so than an exchange of diplomats. By the time Mariana was born, these marriages had occurred in every generation of Habsburg rulers, beginning in 1548 and repeating in 1570, 1598, and 1629. Like her predecessors, Mariana was destined to play a role in the intense marriage diplomacy of her family. Her double Habsburg pedigree and important position as oldest daughter of a ruling emperor meant her marriage would be a premier match, thus increasing the likelihood that she would have a major political role. Any analysis of her regency, therefore, must begin with her dynastic ties, her Habsburg identity and upbringing, and the circumstances that led to her becoming head of state of the largest territorial conglomerate in Western Europe.[2]

THE EDUCATION AND TRAINING OF A QUEEN

Children represented major dynastic capital for the Habsburgs, who expected all their members to contribute to the dynastic enterprise. The training of the younger generation of rulers, therefore, formed as essential a part of the family's strategy as marital strategies. After Ferdinand III's election, Mariana and her family lived mostly in Vienna, traveling periodically to their palaces in Linz, Graz, and Prague. Habsburg children lived at court, near their parents, surrounded by a large household of aristocratic attendants. The physical proximity of children to their immediate family fostered strong emotional bonds with parents and siblings, relationships that helped the family effectively navigate difficult matters of state. Habsburg children were educated for their future roles according to their gender and birth order. Mariana's older brother, Ferdinand (b. 1633), for example, was expected to become their father's successor; her younger brother, Leopold, on the other hand, was prepared for a career in the church, although he eventually succeeded their father as emperor. Mariana was the oldest and only surviving daughter of an emperor and as such was destined for a major dynastic marriage, probably royal. The double portrait of Mariana and Ferdinand done at the time of their father's election foreshadows the children's future political roles (fig. 1). Mariana's grandmother, Queen Margaret of Austria, had introduced the practice of having children wear amulets during

FIGURE 1 Frans Luycx (1604–1668), *Double Portrait of King Ferdinand IV and Mariana of Austria*, 1636. Oil on canvas. Kunsthistorisches Museum, Vienna, Gemäldegalerie, inv. GG3214. Photo: KHM-Museumsverband.

their nursing period as a form of protection. The amulets around Mariana's neck thus indicate that she was still nursing; the flower crown she holds points to her future as queen.[3]

Mariana was exposed from birth to the ways Habsburg women exercised authority over the younger generation and influenced dynastic and state matters. Her first and principal role model was her mother, who played a conspicuous political and diplomatic role as empress consort. Empress Maria's influence was publicly recognized by the emperor, who consulted with her regularly and left her in charge of the government during his absences. Mariana's stepgrandmother, the Empress Dowager Eleonora Gonzaga (1598–1655), the second consort and widow of Emperor Ferdinand II, was also a towering figure in the imperial court and another important model for the young archduchess. Mariana's brothers grew up under the authority and influence of older Habsburg women as much as she did.[4]

Traditions of female authority were not limited to empress consorts; aristocratic women at court also took on executive positions in the court hierarchy. Victoria de Toledo y Colonna, Countess of Siruela, for example, occupied the highest post in Empress Maria's household—that of *Oberst-hofmeisterin*, or mistress of the robes. Because she belonged to a prestigious Spanish aristocratic lineage and had traveled to Vienna with Empress Maria, the countess offered a living example of Spanish political ties and traditions. Susanna Veronika von Trautson, a German aristocrat from one of the empire's most prestigious lineages, became *Hofmeisterin*, or governess, after the birth of the first royal child in 1633 and supervised the upbringing and education of Mariana and her two brothers. Although young, the unmarried ladies of the court—the *Hofdamen*—also assumed political functions, reinforcing the ties of patronage and loyalty with the imperial princes and the Spanish court while helping to create a multilingual, multinational, and youthful environment. Royal children had daily contact with their parents, were incorporated into this rich web of patronage ties, and soon took on politico-familial roles. While still a child, Mariana became godmother to several aristocratic children and acted as amanuensis for her younger brother, Leopold, in writing to their father, the emperor.[5]

Even though they were introduced to their political responsibilities at a very early age, the lives of the Habsburg children included appropriate childhood activities. There was tobogganing, hunting, and daily games and walks in the gardens, along with enjoyable indoor activities. Mariana was raised in one of the most sophisticated cultural environments in Europe. She was exposed to the Spanish cultural traditions imported by Ferdinand I, who, though he founded the Austrian branch of the dynasty, was born and educated in Spain. By the time Mariana was born, the imperial court's preference for Italian culture had taken hold, due in part to the influence of two generations of Italian empresses. Opera and ballet, for example, had become favorite art forms. Ferdinand III, one of the most accomplished musicians and composers among a long line of musically talented Habsburg emperors, maintained one of the best orchestras in Europe and supported a wide range of musical and theatrical performances. Mariana both observed and participated in court ballets, rituals, and ceremonies; her dance master, Santo Ventura, was highly regarded. Boys received this kind of instruction as well. Leopold I, for example, was an avid consumer and practitioner of theater and music as emperor. And far from being superficial, these pastimes provided Mariana the proper training and skills to assume her future political role as consort. At the age of seven, for example, Mariana publicly greeted her parents on their return from the Diet of Regensburg in 1641 by saluting her mother in the Spanish style and her father in Latin. When the fourteen-year-old performed a similar greeting in Trento, this time as queen of Spain, she had had at least seven years of practice.[6]

Not many specific details of Mariana's academic education are available, but we know that Mariana and her brothers Ferdinand and Leopold had a comparable primary education under Trautson, the *Hofmeisterin*. Mariana could read and write by the time she was seven. Her primary language was German, but she had a basic command of Latin and Spanish, which she had been taught since early childhood. Extant letters written by Mariana at eleven and twelve years of age confirm her language skills. The correspondence she maintained in Spanish as an adult displays flawless grammar and a complete mastery of the language, even though she also spoke and wrote German to the end of her life. In 1647, after Trautson retired, Mariana received, as did the other Habsburg children, a Jesuit tutor from the University of Graz, the emperor's birthplace. This is how Mariana first met Father Everard Nithard (1607–1681), who became her teacher and confessor and accompanied her to Spain. The Jesuit curriculum emphasized languages, history, geography, and religion.[7]

Mariana's early instruction in international politics was part of internalizing her Habsburg identity. The process entangled religious, dynastic, and political history in such a way that it is difficult, if not impossible, to separate one from the other. Mariana's father, for example, introduced the Feast of the Immaculate Conception of Mary to the empire in 1645, proclaiming the Virgin as the "special ruler of Austria." The belief in Mary's Immaculate Conception characterized the *Pietas Austriaca*, the dynasty's particular religious identity, which emphasized the Eucharist, the cult of the saints, and the Virgin. This religious innovation, however, was also political; it took place as a Protestant Swedish army stood at the city walls of Vienna. The occasion, therefore, functioned as a commentary on international politics, war, and dynastic interests. Women and girls were not excluded from these important lessons.

War was a constant factor in Mariana's childhood, a permanent part of her family's past and present. Though she did not participate in military training with her brothers, she was exposed to war in ways that had personal meaning to her and her family. Indeed, in a letter written on October 8, 1647, she reported to her father that the Jesuits had held a forty-hour vigil for the success of the war; she had participated, along with Empress Eleonora and her brothers. Frequent journeys to Mariazell, the most popular pilgrimage destination in Austria, and regular visits to convents to see female relatives were not merely family outings; they were also religious, dynastic, and political activities. Portraits, rituals, buildings, and material objects constantly reminded Mariana of the history she was part of, providing an ongoing and omnipresent form of education.[8] All Mariana's activities and role models imparted political lessons, lessons that became even more important when the dynasty needed her to take on a political role more directly.

DYNASTIC AND STATE POLITICS

Mariana's political destiny was, to a large extent, determined before she was born. During the early decades of the seventeenth century, an almost simultaneous shift in the leadership of the two branches of the dynasty pushed both the Habsburgs and the continent toward war. Among the Austrian Habsburgs, the election of Mariana's paternal grandfather, Archduke Ferdinand of Styria—from a cadet branch of the Austrian Habsburg line—as king of Bohemia (1617) and Hungary (1618) portended the return of a staunch and unbending Catholicism that provoked the Bohemian Revolt. Ferdinand was confirmed as Ferdinand II, the Holy Roman emperor, in 1619, but the Bohemian estates picked the Calvinist elector palatine, Frederick V, as king of Bohemia. Ferdinand II's decisive victory at the Battle of White Mountain in 1620 swiftly ended the elector palatine's rule, but the century's most devastating conflict—the Thirty Years' War (1618–48)—had begun. As Ferdinand II began systematically reversing the policy of religious toleration that had lasted more than six decades, the conflict escalated from civil war into a continental conflict.[9]

The Spanish Habsburgs had avoided entanglements and followed a pacifist policy since 1598, but events in central Europe made military intervention almost unavoidable. The Austrian Habsburg women in Madrid, his queen consort and the residents in the Royal Convent of the Descalzas Reales, wielded significant influence in the court of Philip III. They helped create the shift toward more active intervention in European affairs that became palpable in the waning years of Philip III's reign. The succession of the sixteen-year-old Philip IV after his father's unexpected death in 1621 accelerated the path toward war. The Twelve Years' Truce (1609–21) between the United Provinces and Spain expired ten days into his reign; within weeks, Spain had committed to a full-scale war against the Dutch rebels in the Low Countries and to supporting the emperor against the Protestant rebels. By 1622, the successes of the Austrian and Spanish Habsburgs marked the renewal of a strong dynastic bloc.[10]

The marriage of Mariana's parents—Archduke Ferdinand, the oldest son of Emperor Ferdinand II, and the Infanta Maria, the sister of King Philip IV—was part of a deliberate policy that sought to join the two Habsburg branches for diplomatic and military purposes. Negotiations started not long after the failed "Spanish match" of the *infanta* to the Prince of Wales, the future Charles I of England. The intra-Habsburg union marked the beginning of a golden age of dynastic collaboration in which Maria played a central role. Working with her capable confessor, Fray Diego de Quiroga, Maria skillfully advanced the interests of the Spanish Habsburgs in Vienna. Her consort, Ferdinand, was equally critical: he replaced Albrecht von Wallenstein as supreme commander of the imperial army in 1634, leading the army to a string of victories. The height of Habsburg dominance came with the victory of the combined Catholic armies under the command of Maria's younger brother, the Cardinal-Infante Fernando, and her husband over the Protestant armies at Nördlingen (September 5–6, 1634). This strong dynastic bloc soon emerged as a major threat to other continental powers, particularly France. Louis XIII's chief minister, Cardinal Richelieu, warned that unless concerted action was taken, "the brunt of the power of the House of Austria [would] fall on France." The victory of Nördlingen was therefore, in a sense, a Pyrrhic one because it spurred the creation of a major coalition against the Habsburgs. This series of events led to a difficult juncture for the Spanish monarchy; the consequences were still reverberating when Mariana assumed the regency in 1665.[11]

The Franco-Spanish War (1635–59) began a year after the victory of Nördlingen, transforming the Thirty Years' War into a pan-European conflict fought mainly against the Habsburgs. After forging an alliance with the Dutch and the Swedes, France declared war against Spain, instantly multiplying Philip IV's military commitments. The war with France worsened internal problems in Spain. Under the influence of and in collaboration with his principal minister and favorite/*valido*, Gaspar de Guzmán, the Count-Duke of Olivares, Philip IV implemented institutional and political reforms aimed at centralizing royal power. Among the better known and more controversial was the "Union of Arms," which sought to spread the military burden of the Spanish monarchy more equitably across its territories. If successful, it would have created a standing army proportionally supported by all the territories. But the political traditions on which the monarchy was based made success impossible. Although ruled by one king, the monarchy was a composite state, made up of different kingdoms with independent political traditions. The king of Spain was expected to uphold the rights of each kingdom to self-determination, and the union affronted "the traditional rights and liberties" of Philip IV's subjects. The war with France, which was contiguous to Catalonia, became a testing ground for the policy and ultimately for royal authority. The Catalans—some of Philip's most recalcitrant subjects—deeply resented the Union of Arms and refused to comply with their military obligations under it.[12]

The riots in the kingdom of Catalonia began in early 1640; by August, they had become revolts. On December 1, in a bloodless coup, the kingdom of Portugal installed the Braganzas as the new ruling dynasty. In the summer of 1641, the 9th Duke of Medina Sidonia orchestrated a plot that would have proclaimed him king of Andalucía; this one, however, was discovered and suppressed. Nevertheless, war expenditures reached unprecedented levels, and internal problems in Spain weakened the Habsburgs, bringing them to the negotiating table by 1643. The Westphalian congress revealed serious rifts in intra-Habsburg relations, as each side looked out for its own interests. Empress Maria, who had played such a critical role in reestablishing a strong Spanish faction in the imperial court, became even more important now. More than the diplomats, it was she who kept the collaboration and ties between the two branches alive during the difficult peace negotiations. Her unexpected death on May 13, 1646, was a major personal blow to her husband, the emperor, and her brother, the king, as well as a political one. Indeed, the Habsburg cause was imperiled. Only eleven years old, Mariana was called to keep the dynastic ties alive.[13]

Within these changed political and international circumstances, the two branches of the Habsburg family decided to conclude a marriage alliance between the next generation of Habsburg cousins. As soon as he heard of his sister's death, Philip IV requested Mariana's hand in marriage for Prince Baltasar Carlos (b. 1629), the Spanish heir. Emperor Ferdinand III immediately accepted the proposal. Concluded within the time it took the letters to cross the continent, the union seemed to offer advantages for the peace negotiations by preserving and cementing a united Habsburg front. Contemporary comparisons between Mariana and her mother, the former said to be the "exact likeness" of the latter, should be read as much for their political symbolism as for their reality. Philip IV's ministers thanked their sovereign "a thousand times over for the singular grace bestowed on these kingdoms," while in Vienna the marriage was strategically announced after the elaborate obsequies in Empress Maria's honor had concluded. The eleven-year-old bride and sixteen-year-old groom seemed eager. Baltasar Carlos explained to Sor María of Ágreda, his father's spiritual confidant, that he had wished since an early age that his cousin would one day become his wife, even though he had never met her in person: "I am the happiest man in the world with my engagement," he wrote on July 20, 1646. "There can be no better choice for a bride than the archduchess." But the engagement was short-lived. In October, Baltasar Carlos was traveling with his father to the Catalonian warfront when he became sick and quickly died. His death precipitated a serious dynastic crisis that catapulted Mariana into an even more important role in the politics of family and state.[14]

Since Spain's laws did not preclude women from inheriting the throne, Philip's only surviving child, the eight-year-old Infanta Maria Theresa of Austria, became the heir apparent to the Spanish monarchy. Philip IV, a widower since 1644, had felt little need to remarry, since his son was of age and about to marry his cousin. Now, however, it was clear to all that he needed to remarry immediately in order to sire more children, ideally a male. Sor María, with whom Philip maintained a prolific epistolary relationship, urged the king to choose a bride and "take care of a business as urgent as this one." The emperor immediately suggested that Philip marry

Mariana—so immediately, in fact, that he made the offer in the same letter in which he extended condolences on Baltasar Carlos's death. By January 30, 1647, the marriage was confirmed and announced. The marriage capitulations, or *capitulaciones matrimoniales*—an important legal document that established the dowry, counter-dowry, and pension the bride would receive in widowhood—was ratified early in 1647, even before the necessary dispensation from Pope Innocent X arrived. Within eight months of her mother's death, Mariana's path was set; she would marry a ruling sovereign and immediately become queen. At her father's request, Mariana dutifully composed several letters in Spanish to practice the language of her future subjects. She was not yet thirteen years old.[15]

Although there was some controversy, neither the close degree of consanguinity nor the age difference was an impervious obstacle. Endogamy was by no means exclusive to the Habsburgs; Spanish aristocratic families also practiced it, albeit not as frequently or for as long as the Habsburgs, who had done so for generations. The thirty-year age difference was also not uncommon in early modern marriages, particularly among the nobility; it was especially common in Italian societies. Still Mariana's age was a concern, because as bride to the king rather than the prince, she would have to assume the responsibilities of a queen consort immediately, and the succession depended on her. A disquisition presented to Philip IV's chief minister offered a well-considered opinion against Mariana's candidacy. It came from an agent of Claudia de' Medici, regent of Tyrol, who had a particular interest: she had two daughters—the Habsburg Archduchesses of Innsbruck, Maria Leopoldina of Austria (1632–1649) and Isabella Clara of Austria (1629–1685)—who might be candidates to marry the king. Although unsuccessful, it reveals the concerns about Mariana's youth: the author invoked Galenic medical theory that viewed women younger than fifteen as likely to become infertile, give birth to defective children, or even worse, die during childbirth.[16]

During her engagement, Mariana's body was under great scrutiny. Reports about her physical readiness for childbearing were sent through both private and diplomatic channels to Madrid, revealing the anxiety over the future of the succession. Philip IV learned of Mariana's first menstrual period in May 1648 and was upset at finding out such important news indirectly. In a letter to his friend, the Countess of Paredes, the king made a vague reference to it, but his close attention to Mariana's development is confirmed by his June 9, 1648, letter, which explicitly affirmed that Mariana "was a woman in every respect." The play written to celebrate Mariana's fourteenth birthday and staged in the Spanish court clearly artic- ulated the expectations put on the young body of the queen: her arrival would make Spain "The New Olympus," particularly now that she had crossed the threshold into childbearing age.[17]

The marriage negotiations continued in spite of the bride's youth and the disappointing progress in the Westphalian peace congress. The Spanish delegation to the peace congress, led by Gaspar de Bracamonte y Guzmán, Count of Peñaranda, was concerned that the empire might abandon Spain—that is, that the Austrians would settle with France without Spain. The Spaniards were undeterred. In April 1648, Francisco de Moura Corter- real, 3rd Marquis of Castel Rodrigo, delivered the customary present from the groom, the jewel (*joya*) worth eighty thousand ducats, to the bride. The proxy ceremony went forward even though it failed to prevent what the Spaniards most feared: Ferdinand III signed a separate peace with France on October 24, 1648, agreeing not to provide military support to Spain against the French Bourbons. That the marriage concluded in spite of the major diplomatic split between the two Habsburg lines indicates the bride's value to both branches. Mariana's departure from Vienna on November 13, 1648, was celebrated with lavish entertainments in Madrid.[18]

QUEEN CONSORT OF SPAIN

Mariana left her father's court facing the formidable task of becoming queen and assuming the host of responsibilities that went with that position; she stepped into her role, however, deftly and with confidence. Even with her forceful personality and individual skills, Mariana's success is largely attrib- utable to her upbringing in Vienna. In Trento, the first stop in her long journey, she greeted the Habsburg Archdukes of Tirol in the language of her new country, the first of many rituals over which she would preside. The household provided by the emperor to accompany his daughter consisted of Mariana's older brother, now King Ferdinand IV of Hungary and Bohe- mia, and a substantial German-speaking entourage that included Father Nithard and four of the women who had made the journey to Vienna with Empress Maria in 1630. The enormous machinery of the Spanish Habsburg court was put in motion for the new queen: Mariana's new

Spanish household left Madrid to meet the young queen midway through her journey. Having inherited her mother's attendants when the empress died, Mariana was already accustomed to being the center of a large household. But the mixing of the two households proved complex, and even before her arrival, Mariana was introduced to the ways the Spanish court competed for access, influence, and place. A number of tense incidents among members of the two courts became serious enough that Philip IV dismissed and exiled the Spaniard in charge of Mariana's journey to Spain. The young queen, who would have to adjudicate similar conflicts later on, wisely remained neutral through the entire episode.[19]

The yearlong journey fulfilled political functions for the queen and both sides of her family. It brought imperial, Spanish, and Italian elites together, giving the Habsburgs the opportunity to display their unity after the Westphalian settlement that had ostensibly split them. It was no coincidence that Mariana's entry into Milan, a strategic Habsburg post, was so spectacular. To the sound of cannons, the Spanish household and no fewer than six Spanish *tercios*—the famous and feared Spanish military unit—escorted the young queen in the elaborate procession through the city. Operas, fireworks, plays, and at least one horse ballet—where nobles and horses displayed their equestrian skills in a choreographed sequence of movements—were performed in her honor. With considerable aplomb, Mariana visited churches and convents, greeted noblemen and noblewomen, and received dignitaries from Rome, Naples, and Florence during her nine-week stay. Before journeying on, she saw her brother and the returning members of the imperial entourage off with splendid presents. When she arrived in Spain, an additional two-week round of entertainments awaited her in the Port of Denia in Valencia; only then did she undertake the final trek through the Castilian plateau to Madrid. In spite of the deep political implications of her trip, Mariana enjoyed it with a youthful sense of adventure, at least when remembering it three decades later. In a letter she wrote to Carlos on October 28, 1679, when he was on a similar journey to meet his first wife, she wrote, "At your age [Carlos was seventeen years old], everything is cause for celebration; the same thing happened to me when I came here: the worse our accommodations, the greater my cause to celebrate."[20]

Mariana and Philip IV saw each other for the first time in the small city of Navalcarnero on October 7, 1649, where they were wed in a modest ceremony presided over by the archbishop of Toledo. The city would receive permanent tax-exemption status for hosting the event. After a few hours, the newlyweds left for San Lorenzo for the most striking Habsburg residence of them all—El Escorial, the architectural marvel built by the king's grandfather, Philip II, in the sixteenth century. On November 19, 1649, a year after leaving Vienna, Mariana traversed the principal streets of Madrid mounted on a beautiful white horse. Hundreds of members of her royal household surrounded her, and the city was ornately decorated for the occasion. A spectacular event from the viewpoint of the history of baroque festivals, it was a significant political moment for the queen, replacing a coronation ceremony, which the Habsburgs did not observe. The procession culminated with Mariana's arrival at the Alcázar, as the royal palace in Madrid was referred to, where she would reside, signaling the official beginning of her reign.[21]

The Viennese court had been influenced by Spanish Burgundian etiquette traditions, and Mariana must have been familiar with the ceremonial style and organization of her adopted court. The royal couple lived on the upper floors of the Alcázar in separate apartments that wrapped around two side-by-side courtyards, respectively called the *Patio del Rey* and the *Patio de la Reina*. Mariana's household was independent but organized much like her husband's. The queen's household was specially adapted to care for the royal children, who remained in their mother's quarters until they were given an independent entourage. Eleven-year-old Maria Theresa, therefore, became part of Mariana's household; not only physical proximity but their blood ties and closeness in age contributed to a lasting friendship. The queen's household was smaller than the king's and, in spite of a great measure of autonomy, ultimately subordinate to his authority. Nevertheless, allocating an independent household for the queen institutionalized the queen's authority and meant that a number of executive offices were reserved for women.[22]

The court of Madrid was notoriously more rigid than the one in Vienna, but everything indicates that Mariana adapted exceedingly well to her new environment and, indeed, influenced it. She played the lead in weekly public meals, kissing-of-the-hand ceremonies, official functions with foreign diplomats and local political figures, and a host of entertainments in which the royal family were both spectators and protagonists. Although portraits of Mariana as consort depict her with an impassive expression, her enjoyment of the comic actors, dwarves, and fools who populated the court is well documented; she was occasionally criticized for laughing too openly. Her public meals too, rather than being the solemn and carefully choreographed events they were supposed to be, became a "mêlée of servants, dwarves, onlookers, intermingling in an atmosphere of general abandon." These occasions indicate a lively and youthful personality and demonstrate a strong sense of self; the latter became even more evident later.[23]

Mariana's presence stimulated a cultural revival in the Spanish court, which had seen a temporary loss of luster as a result of the political crises and the deaths of Mariana's predecessor in 1644 and the prince's in 1647. Philip IV ordered a number of repairs to the Buen Retiro Palace in anticipation of his wife's arrival, and the palace did not have the negative connotations it had had for Queen Isabel, during whose reign it had been built amid controversy. In fact, the Buen Retiro became Mariana's favorite palace, and court spectacles staged with *tramoyas*, or stage machinery designed by expert Italian engineers, resumed after a ten-year hiatus. The queen's household had its own chamber orchestra and presented splendid theater productions, to the point that the companies had difficulty meeting their obligations in public theaters, or *corrales*. Mariana's pursuits were indicative of her formative years in Vienna but blended well with Spanish styles. This is important because her gift-giving practices, her passion for collecting, her tastes in fashion, and her love of theater gave her a centrality at court that she did not yet possess in the political realm.[24]

Mariana's position as consort coincided with Luis Méndez de Haro's period of influence, which started in 1644 and only ended at his death in 1661. Haro was the nephew of the figure he succeeded, Gaspar de Guzmán, the Count-Duke of Olivares. Although Haro is slowly emerging from historical obscurity, this latter period of Philip IV's reign is less understood than the first half. While the relationship between a queen consort and a *valido* was potentially dangerous for both, there is no evidence that Mariana and Haro were hostile. This formative period in Mariana's trajectory had a concrete impact on the politics of the court when she presided over it as regent.[25]

Indeed, local and international political networks began to coalesce the moment she arrived at court. Although German-speaking members of the court did not dominate Mariana's household, ties with Vienna were kept alive by the arrival of young women who accompanied imperial ambassadors. Johanna Theresia Lamberg (1639–1716), daughter of the Count of

Lamberg, for instance, served in Mariana's household during her father's embassy (1653–60); she returned during Mariana's regency with her husband, Ferdinand Bonaventure I, the Count of Harrach, who was chosen as imperial ambassador to Madrid in 1673 precisely because of Johanna's ties to the queen. Leonor de Velasco, a Spanish-born aristocrat who came to Vienna in the entourage of Empress Maria, returned to Spain with Mariana. Deeply involved in politics and with significant political skills, Velasco ended up occupying an important position in Mariana's court, especially during the regency. Mariana developed lifelong friendships with the resident nuns at the Descalzas Reales, the Convent of the Encarnación, and other religious institutions. Her friendship with her cousin (and now stepdaughter) the Infanta Maria Theresa started immediately when they met in El Escorial. All these connections had political consequences later on. Ties with Spanish elites also began quickly. Maria Magdalena Moncada, the sister of the Marquis of Aytona and one of the most important figures in Mariana's regency, was, according to diplomatic reports, already close to her during her tenure as consort. In many ways, Mariana's future regime began forming as soon as she arrived at court, though the consequences of this formative era only became apparent later.[26]

In the short term, however, Mariana had a specific responsibility: to give birth to an heir. Philip IV made no secret of his desire to "fill the house with children" as soon as possible. In a letter to his friend, the Countess of Paredes, he deemed his niece "well-developed for her age, but still very young [*bien niña*]." Despite the thirty-year difference in age, Mariana and Philip IV had what appears to have been an affectionate relationship. Philip IV was impressed with Mariana: "The petition about my happiness has already been granted as I find my niece with a better disposition than I have ever imagined possible," he wrote to Paredes shortly after Mariana's arrival. Although Philip IV had had his share of extramarital affairs in his youth, with Mariana, he was by his own admission "a changed man" and "free of temptations," and he remained a faithful husband—most if not all of the time—calling himself her *galán*, or admirer. He reportedly indulged her in anything she wanted. Mariana, in turn, according to the Venetian ambassador, worked to establish a good relationship with Philip IV, relying on "her natural kindness." The king, perhaps because of the bride's youth, or so they could get to know each other, waited to consummate the marriage until the arrival festivities were over.[27]

Philip IV's correspondence with Paredes allows us to deduce that intercourse began during Mariana's first royal vacation to Aranjuez— that is, sometime between March 8 and May 24, 1650. In mid-August, the midwife announced the queen was pregnant. Fearful of being disappointed—doubting, as he said, "like Saint Thomas"—the king refused to celebrate until he could "see it [the pregnancy]" with his own eyes. By December, the pregnancy had been confirmed, but Philip IV remained skeptical: "The belly does not correspond to a five-month pregnancy, even though the midwife has assured me of it and the old ladies believe it as well." He was partially correct—Mariana was pregnant, but not as far along as the midwife supposed. Mariana's slim figure probably contributed to the confusion. By March 11, 1651, Philip IV commented hopefully but with restraint that the "belly does not deny it, although I have felt no movement yet." Finally, a few weeks later, he excitedly assured Paredes that everything was fine: "I felt the creature myself and I am a witness that there can be no doubt on the matter." An unprecedented number of wet nurses (amas de lactancia)—thirty-two—were hired in anticipation of the birth, signifying the importance of the event.[28]

Expected in June, the birth took place on July 12, 1651. It was a dangerous ordeal for the sixteen-year-old queen; Philip IV, who was present, feared for Mariana's life. It took weeks for Mariana, who was left "too thin," to recuperate fully. The king was enthralled by the new addition to his family, calling her "gorgeous and so splendid that she looks more like a sister of her mother than a daughter." Maria Theresa was equally taken with the baby, whom she called "my daughter." "We will baptize her today," Philip IV wrote to his friend, and "call her Margarita Maria." Even though the child was not the desired male heir, Mariana had achieved a major political milestone in a queen's life: she was a mother.[29]

The first official portrait of Mariana as queen consort, painted by Diego Velazquez, was completed shortly thereafter, in 1652 (fig. 2). Here Mariana is shown wearing the famous guardainfante, which became her signature. Its name derived from the pregnancies with which it was associated. In the 1630s, the guardainfante was controversial: reformers found it "lascivious" and claimed that it "could provoke infertility and abortion" and the "inflammation of carnal desires due to its excessive hips." Philip IV imposed a ban on the garment in 1639, but to no avail. Amanda Wunder has shown how the guardainfante became a fashion craze during Mariana's reign as

FIGURE 2 Diego Rodríguez de Silva y Velazquez (1599–1660), *Queen Mariana of Austria*, 1652–53. Oil on canvas. Museo del Prado, Madrid, inv. P001191. Photo © Museo Nacional del Prado / Art Resource, New York.

consort. The way Mariana wore it became its most recognizable style, with an exaggerated geometric shape, elongated on the sides, rather than the rounded and more flowing style of its previous incarnation. The queen and the young princesses in their swollen gowns became memorable symbols of the Spanish court of the seventeenth century thanks to Diego Velazquez, most famously in the image of the Infanta Margarita in *Las Meninas* (fig. 3). Laura Oliván Santaliestra has perceptively suggested the multiple benefits a *guardainfante* afforded its royal wearers: it brought gravitas because it required measured movements, social distance by forcing a deeper reverence when men kissed their hands, and political centrality because its wearers occupied significant space. The Dutch ambassador to Madrid in 1660 calculated that the queen's skirt was six feet in diameter. Without a doubt, the association of the garment with fertility was the strongest political message at play. After all, the monarchy's future depended on Mariana's ability to *guardar infantes*.[30]

Although Mariana had produced a live child, pressure to give birth to a boy mounted. The monarchy now possessed two *infantas* who could inherit the throne, but the lack of a male heir limited Philip IV's ability to use their marriages effectively to benefit the monarchy. A Franco-Spanish marriage had been suggested at various points during the Westphalian negotiations, but as long as Maria Theresa remained the presumptive heiress, Philip IV could not allow her to marry, especially into France. In the 1650s, some of Philip IV's ministers suggested that Maria Theresa should be married to the Portuguese Braganza prince, which could potentially reunify the two crowns and resolve Portugal's rebellion. Before the Iberian Union, which brought Portugal under the Habsburgs, Hispano-Portuguese marriages had been the norm, but this was no longer an option because the Braganzas were considered subjects and rebels. Predictably, Philip IV did not even consider this practical solution. A French match for Maria Theresa came up a second time in the early 1650s as an alternative to the Portuguese option, but to no avail. As long as Maria Theresa was the heiress, Philip IV rejected the French match. If Mariana gave birth to a son, peace with France would be possible. With the solution to the monarchy's predicament requiring her body, Mariana's marital life became a matter of public concern. The amount of time the king spent with his wife fulfilling his marital duties or whether the queen had experienced a late period became matters of court gossip and public speculation, conveyed through the weekly *avisos*, or "news,"

FIGURE 3 Diego Rodríguez de Silva y Velazquez, *Las Meninas* or *The Family of Philip IV*, 1656. Oil on canvas. Museo del Prado, Madrid, inv. P001174. Photo © Museo Nacional del Prado / Art Resource, New York.

published by Jerónimo Barrionuevos, the court's official gossip columnist. News of this kind was read aloud in the streets, talked about, and avidly consumed by Madrid's inhabitants (*madrileños*) of all sorts.[31]

Mariana had five recorded pregnancies and births during her sixteen years as consort, plus several miscarriages. After Margarita's birth in 1651, no children were born for several years. The king was in good health, but he was forty-six years old, and his ministers pressured him to officially designate his oldest daughter as heir apparent in the traditional swearing-in ceremony. Rumors that the ceremony was about to take place circulated in Madrid in 1653, 1655, and 1656 but faded away with the news of the queen's latest pregnancy. Another consideration, perhaps the most important, was that Philip IV needed to keep Maria Theresa available for an advantageous diplomatic marriage. A match with France, for example, could not take place if the *infanta* was first in line to the Spanish throne. Maria Theresa's marriage, and later Margarita's, became the subject of intense debate from 1652 until 1665, with the negotiations and outcomes of the two marriages dominating the international scene during Mariana's regency. To understand why, it is necessary to consider how issues of inheritance and succession intertwined with specific political and diplomatic situations.[32]

HEIRESSES, HEIRS, AND INTERNATIONAL POLITICS

By 1655, Maria Theresa still had not been sworn in, Mariana had not given birth to a son, and the war against France continued. These issues were connected. Portugal's revolt became Philip IV's main priority after he had successfully returned Catalonia to the Habsburg fold in 1652. Resolution in Spain's favor would mean the empire of his grandfather, Philip II, would be fully restored. Desire for this blinded Phillip IV, leading him to a string of decisions that endangered other territories. To resolve the Portuguese problem, he needed to end the war against France. At this time, France was just as interested in peace as Spain. During the summer of 1656, Hugues de Lionne, the French representative, and Luis de Haro, Philip IV's principal minister, met more than two dozen times to negotiate. Haro offered France the Roussillon and some small territories in the Low Countries and hinted that Spain was willing to cede Perpignan and Arras. In return, the Spaniards wanted assurances that France would stop supporting the Portuguese bid for independence. They also demanded that the French king pardon the Prince of Condé, who had become Spain's ally during the war. France eventually agreed to these conditions, but negotiations stalled largely because Philip IV would not consider marrying his oldest daughter to Louis XIV. In October 1656, Lionne left Madrid empty handed.[33]

In order to break the stalemate and end the war in their favor, both sides sought alliances with other powers. France signed a commercial treaty with the Cromwell regime, while Philip IV formed an agreement with the exiled king of England, Charles II. This damaged diplomatic relations between Spain and England. Philip IV tried to secure an offensive and defensive league with the United Provinces, but the Dutch continued to side with France, their traditional allies. A number of Spanish ministers urged the king to conclude the Franco-Spanish marriage under the condition that Maria Theresa renounce all rights to the Spanish throne, but Philip did not budge. In March 1657, England and France formed an offensive and defensive league against Spain, exacerbating Spain's difficulties.[34]

All these issues were aggravated after Emperor Ferdinand III's death in 1657, when France challenged the Austrian Habsburgs over the imperial Crown. Ferdinand IV, the emperor's son (and Mariana's older brother) had been designated emperor-elect when he became king of the Romans in 1653, but he died unexpectedly from smallpox in 1654. His younger brother, Archduke Leopold, was elected king of Hungary and Bohemia in 1655 and 1656, respectively, but his father died before he could secure Leopold's election as king of the Romans. This left the door open for an alternative candidate. The designation of the new emperor lay in the hands of the seven prince electors of the empire, composed of the spiritual electors (the archbishops of Mainz, Trier, and Cologne) and the secular electors (the Duke of Saxony, the Count Palatine of the Rhine, the Margrave of Brandenburg, and the Duke of Bavaria). Nevertheless, major foreign powers saw it as an international matter and felt free to intervene. Representatives from Spain, France, Sweden, Denmark, Poland, Savoy, Mantua, Modena, and the Papal See attended the Electoral Diet of Frankfurt (1657–58). During the meetings, Cardinal Mazarin protested that the imperial Crown should not be considered the "patrimony of only one House, dictated by the will of Spain as it has been the case until now": in coalition with Sweden, he proposed Duke Ferdinand Maria of Bavaria as the next emperor. The ongoing negotiations of Leopold's marriage to the Infanta Maria Theresa posed additional difficulties. The possibility of Leopold moving to Castile if the marriage took place made the imperial princes extremely apprehensive about his candidacy.[35]

When Mariana gave birth to a boy, Prince Felipe Próspero, on November 28, 1657, the international situation immediately changed. Letters announcing the birth were sent everywhere, while the court began preparations for lavish celebrations. Ferdinand Maria of Bavaria pledged his vote to Leopold and withdrew his candidacy, leaving the French and Swedes without a viable candidate. Leopold I was elected Holy Roman emperor on July 18, 1658. But most importantly, the birth of Prince Felipe Próspero made peace with France a much stronger possibility. To the newly crowned emperor's chagrin—he had been very clear about his desire to marry Maria Theresa—Philip IV abruptly terminated marriage negotiations with the Austrian branch of the family. The *infanta*'s groom would be the king of France, as this marriage meant that peace with France could be pursued. Philip IV's representative arrived at the French court on August 21, 1658; negotiations officially began four days later. The good fortune of the Spanish Habsburgs became a windfall when on December 21, 1658, Mariana gave birth to another boy, Fernando Tomás, further securing the succession.[36]

Peace with France was only a matter of time. The Portuguese watched the shifting alliances apprehensively: they were fully aware that Philip IV's main motivation for concluding peace with France was to pursue the reconquest of their kingdom. Portugal offered France four million ducats and the opening of commerce in Portuguese colonies if they prolonged the war against Spain. Alternatively, they proposed granting France one million ducats and the same commercial advantages in the colonies if France mediated a truce between Portugal and Spain. Mazarin rejected the deal and continued to pursue peace between France and Spain.[37]

During the twenty-four sessions conducted from August 13 to November 7, 1659, Haro and Mazarin—with their armies of diplomats, geographers, and legal experts—drafted 124 public articles and 7 secret provisions and agreed to the marriage of Louis XIV and Infanta Maria Theresa. The Treaty of the Pyrenees was a major international event, both because it included almost every major and minor sovereign prince of Europe and because it sealed the Westphalian settlement of 1648, the international treaty that resolved the religious conflicts between Protestants and Catholics. Nineteenth-century historians described the treaty as a humiliation for Spain, but this view is no longer accepted. In fact, both sides were forced to compromise. Philip IV granted France the same commercial advantages the United Provinces received in 1648, while France gave up many of its war gains. Spain renounced claims to territories in the Pyrenees and some territory in Artois and the Spanish Low Countries, but not all territory on French soil. Louis XIV agreed to pardon the pro-Spanish Prince of Condé, to restore to the Duke of Lorraine his territories (albeit in substantially reduced form), and to accept the Spanish enclave in Llívia—on the French side of the Pyrenees—as permanent.[38]

The Franco-Spanish marriage was one of the most important cultural events of the century and an episode of major diplomatic and political significance. Yet the motivations for the two parties were diametrically opposed, setting the stage for the next round of conflicts between the dynastic rivals that would dominate Mariana's regency. France saw the marriage as a major part of a policy, adopted under Richelieu and maintained during Mazarin's ministry, that entailed a systematic expansion and consolidation of France's frontiers via "ancient" seigneurial rights acquired through marriage. Maria Theresa had actually renounced those rights before marrying the French king, but France still planned to use them to secure the territories it desired. The government in Madrid, in contrast, no longer saw Maria Theresa's position in the Spanish succession as a reason to bar the marriage; she had made an oath of renunciation (as Anne of Austria had when she married Louis XIII), and there were now two male heirs to the throne. For Spain, the peace and the marriage brought the monarchy closer to waging war against Portugal and reestablishing the famous Iberian Union of 1580, a project that eventually created the difficult international situation Mariana faced as regent.[39]

PRELUDE TO MARIANA'S RULE

The last five years of Philip IV's reign were punctuated by some good news but many more disappointments. There was another succession crisis not long after the Franco-Spanish wedding. Felipe Próspero, whose birth had facilitated the diplomatic negotiations of the previous three years, became ill in the fall of 1661 and died on November 1, a few weeks before his fourth birthday. It was a terrible blow, particularly because Mariana's second son, Fernando Tomás, had died in October 1659, before reaching his first birthday. This made the Infanta Margarita the presumptive heiress, but Mariana was in the last stages of another pregnancy (her final one), and once again, she "saved" the monarchy by giving birth to her third son, Carlos, on November 6, 1661, just five days after Felipe Próspero's death. The event was considered almost miraculous. Waiting to nurse the royal child were no fewer than sixty-four wet nurses. This unprecedented number—double the number hired for Margarita's birth—reflects the court's intense anxiety about the succession. The child was baptized on November 21, 1661; in spite of Felipe Próspero's death, it was a lavish event.[40]

Amid these personal and dynastic tragedies, Philip IV vigorously pursued the reconquest of Portugal. To procure an army, the king defaulted on his creditors and devalued Spanish currency by 50 percent. In 1663, he named his illegitimate son, Don Juan of Austria, "Captain General of the Conquest of Portugal" and placed him in command of twelve thousand infantry and six thousand cavalry. Early success in 1663 was followed by embarrassing losses later that year; it was already clear that the undertaking was headed for disaster. Philip IV recalled Don Juan to Madrid, subjected him to an investigation, and replaced him with the Marquis of Caraçena. Meanwhile, his continued focus on Portugal put other parts of the monarchy at risk.[41]

Portugal had powerful allies in England and France. Charles II of England, now restored to the throne, abandoned his standing agreement with Spain and established one with Portugal in 1662; it was cemented with his marriage to Catherine of Braganza. Catherine brought substantial commercial privileges for England in Portuguese India, North Africa, and Brazil, as well as a very large dowry. In return, the Portuguese obtained military and diplomatic support against the Habsburgs. Louis XIV, in violation of the Treaty of the Pyrenees, provided clandestine military support to Portugal. Rumors that he intended to press claims to territories in the Spanish Low Countries through his consort when her father died had been circulating since 1663.[42]

Rather than pull back from the war and begin reinforcing the army of Flanders in anticipation of a French attack, Philip IV resorted to a traditional Habsburg strategy: a marriage alliance with the Austrian Habsburgs. Margarita turned twelve in April 1663 and was now legally marriageable; negotiations to marry the *infanta* to her uncle, Leopold I, began immediately. This inaugurated a new and critical stage of diplomatic relations between the two branches, with Franz Eusebius, Count of Pötting, beginning his embassy in 1663. Leopold I also sent an extraordinary ambassador to Madrid, Ferdinand Bonaventure, Count of Harrach, husband of Mariana's friend Johanna Theresia of Lamberg. The shrewd Franz Paul, Baron of Lisola, was also enlisted to advance the emperor's marriage to the *infanta*. All these figures played major diplomatic roles during Mariana's regency, and thus the marriage negotiations also indicate Mariana's intervention in foreign affairs. She worked for the successful conclusion of the marriage in this early stage and was, in fact, responsible for bringing it to fruition. Margarita's marriage to Emperor Leopold I made the familial connections even more intricate than they were already: Mariana and Leopold were siblings, while Philip IV and Leopold's mother were also siblings, and thus Philip IV was Leopold's uncle. But for the Spaniards, the main goal of the marriage was to ensure the joint defense of the Low Countries. The intricacies of the succession also played a role; marrying a potential heiress to the Spanish Crown within the dynasty was seen as a necessity. In a consultation over the marriage drafted as a joint statement, councilors of state pointed out that Leopold I was in the best position to guarantee "the rights of the Lady Infanta to this Crown [of Spain]" and had the best claim to the "title of son of Your Majesty."[43]

The marriage capitulations were ratified on September 7, 1663, but even after the marriage had been agreed to, both sides had misgivings. The Spaniards expected Leopold I to shoulder the responsibility of defending the monarchy in case of a French attack and thus were unhappy at the emperor's slow recruitment. For the Austrians, the postponement of Margarita's departure was problematic, especially as Philip IV had deployed similar tactics during the failed negotiations between Maria Theresa and Leopold I. Although the situation was dramatically different than in 1654–57, the misgivings were not unfounded. Throughout 1664, the Spaniards stalled on sending the *infanta* to Vienna. Councilors advised Philip to extend the formalities to keep the emperor "dependent and secure in the knowledge of his impending marriage." The emperor, facing a succession crisis of his own and in desperate need of an heir, was increasingly alarmed by the delays. He personally pleaded with Philip IV to arrange Margarita's immediate departure. Spain's ongoing war with Portugal was another source of disagreement, as Leopold I insisted that the conflict be ended immediately. Although Philip was obviously keenly aware of the strong possibility of war against France—not only despite the marriage but because of the marriage—he made no preparations for it. The war with Portugal dragged on; the army of Flanders continued to languish; the frontiers with France remained unprotected.[44]

Even before Mariana's regency began, the split over the monarchy's direction was clear, indicating deep divisions within Madrid's ruling elite.

Duke Medina de las Torres, Don Ramiro Núñez de Guzmán, emerged in this period as a lone advocate of a truce with Portugal. The Count of Peñaranda, another powerful voice in the Council of State, was the leading voice of the general consensus that the reconquest of Portugal should not be abandoned. The general expectation was that Emperor Leopold I should receive subsidies, rather than the *infanta*, and that he should be ready to help Spain in case of a French attack. Medina de las Torres had a clear grasp of the gravity of the situation: negotiating a truce and arranging for Margarita's departure was the only way to protect the monarchy, but he was unable to convince the king. At least Medina de las Torres's impassioned plea caused Philip to set his daughter's trip for August 1665. Nevertheless, Philip remained more focused on the Portuguese. With an army of 13,000 infantry and 6,500 cavalry, the new Spanish commander made a last heroic effort but could not outlast a combined Portuguese, English, and French force of 25,000. The Battle of Villaviciosa on June 17, 1665, was a stunning defeat for Spain. The Spanish-born French queens—Philip IV's sister and daughter—sent urgent messages to Madrid via the Spanish ambassador in the summer of 1665, warning that an attack on the Low Countries was certain. Near death, Philip IV did not harken to the advice to send his daughter immediately to Vienna to secure an alliance with the emperor or take steps to protect Spanish frontiers. Mariana would be left to deal with these policies and their results.[45]

By Philip IV's death, Mariana held a central position at court. The birth of three male heirs, despite the early deaths of two, had made her an increasingly powerful figure. Her position, and the reconfiguration of the royal family after Felipe Próspero's birth and Maria Theresa's marriage, was represented visually. A mural inside the Convent of the Descalzas Reales, for instance, which showed Mariana and Philip IV praying with their daughter and son, symbolized dynastic stability—a precondition of creating the same in the political realm. Mariana was about to earn her spot in the dynasty's mausoleum in El Escorial, which contained the tombs of all the Spanish Habsburg rulers and queen consorts who were mothers of kings.

Philip IV drafted the testament that established Mariana's regency between late 1663 and early 1664. Although he continued to preside over the councils, meeting personally with the secretaries, and remained in charge of policy to the end of his life, Mariana increasingly assumed many public functions traditionally exercised by the king. She thus combined her role as queen consort with an expanded political role made more significant by Philip IV's frequent absences. Archival evidence strongly suggests that Mariana was privy to state papers before her husband died and had begun to assume some administrative tasks. In August 1665, for example, she ordered the Council of State to consult her about a report sent by Vicente Gonzaga from the northern frontiers with France. Mariana's decisive and immediate assumption of all government matters began behind closed doors when Philip IV first fell ill and became public mere hours after her husband's death.[46]

TRANSITION OF POWER

Transitions of power from one reign to another are loaded with political symbolism, particularly in early modern monarchies, where rituals and procedures were important in establishing the legitimacy of the next regime. This was even more true during a royal minority, with its inherent confusion about who is in charge. Although there were no recent precedents of royal minorities—all Habsburg kings of Spain succeeded as adults—there were no difficulties at the time of the royal succession. The spectacularly orderly transition of power from Philip IV to Mariana on behalf of her son itself contradicts the weak regency thesis.

Philip IV was unable to get out of bed on Sunday, September 13, 1665; everyone could see the end, and a transition of power began immediately. On Monday, the king received the viaticum—the communion administered to those near death. The same day, Don Blasco de Loyola, the principal royal secretary, supervised the strict legal procedures required for the final deposit of the king's testament. The presidents of the Councils of Castile and Aragon, a representative of the Council of State, the king's *summiller de corps* (chief gentleman of the king's chamber), his *caballerizo mayor* (master of the horse), the most senior of his *mayordomos* (in lieu of the master of the king's household, a post that was vacant at the time), and his confessor witnessed the document's deposit. Although completely lucid, Philip was unable to sign, and Secretary Loyola commissioned the president of the Council of Castile, Don García de Haro, Count of Castrillo, to sign in the king's name. Everybody then signed in order of precedence, with Castrillo signing a second time, this time for himself. The testament and an addendum containing important provisions for the next regime were sealed and locked. The queen held the keys.[47]

The following day, Philip IV received extreme unction and bid farewell to his family. Reportedly, the king talked to the three-year-old Prince Carlos, wishing that "God may make you happier than He made me." He urged his fifteen-year-old daughter, Margarita, to be "obedient" to her mother, the queen. The royal couple spoke privately for about an hour. After the somber farewells, the queen and children retired to their quarters while the king remained in his chambers surrounded by his male attendants. Philip addressed those present for the last time as their sovereign, his thoughts conveyed by Fray Antonio del Castillo, one of several religious figures tending to Philip's spiritual needs:

> His Majesty has asked me to tell you that he has loved you all very much and that he feels the love and the service that you have given him. If any of you have fallen short of his obligations, His Majesty forgives you. He also requests from all of you to work out any differences or dissension in your midst, and to reconcile with each other, always striving to serve God and the public good. *In particular, he charges all of you to serve and obey the queen, our lady.* He has told me other things, but the tears and emotions caused by this moment make it difficult for me to repeat them.[48] (emphasis mine)

Philip's final words thus laid the basis for a transition of power. Courtiers and ministers then performed the kissing-of-the-hand ritual, surely knowing that this was the last time they would do so for this king.[49]

Another significant political episode took place just before the king's death. According to several witnesses, on three different occasions the king refused to see his illegitimate son, Don Juan of Austria, who had journeyed to Madrid to see his dying father. Philip reportedly stated that "this was a time to die" and insisted that Don Juan leave Madrid at once. Even if the words were apocryphal, Philip IV's public snub confirmed his intention to exclude Don Juan from the regency government and succession, intentions made public when the testament was read. Philip IV drew his final breath on Thursday, September 17, at 4:15 a.m. Those in surrounding areas entered the royal chamber as the final moments approached.[50]

There was no hesitation, confusion, or disorder. As if performing a well-choreographed dance, the royal guards marched immediately to the queen's side of the palace, where the new king slept. Father Nithard, who had assisted Philip IV in his final days, immediately went to the queen's chamber. If she was asleep at this early hour, she was surely awakened by the church bells that began tolling across the city. Surgeons and attendants were already cleaning and embalming the king's body while a mass was recited at the head of the royal bed. Messages summoned any ruling elite not already present at 9:00 a.m., and Don Blasco de Loyola, Duke Medina de las Torres, and the Count of Castrillo were admitted into Mariana's antechambers. She granted them permission to open the testament and gave them the keys.[51]

By 10:00 a.m., the men had retraced their steps to the west side of the palace, entering a room next to where the king's body lay, now cleansed and dressed in full royal regalia. An all-male audience seated in strict order of precedence observed as they unsealed the document, recorded the king's death, and authenticated the signatures. Secretary Loyola read the lengthy document aloud; the process took about two hours. Mariana's central role was now established: she had been named head of the interim government established for the minority (clauses 21 to 53), named one of the king's heirs (clauses 20 and 56), and designated an executor of the testament (clauses 77 to 79). So critical was her role that numerous clauses (37 to 50) addressed alternative forms of government if she died. For the time being, however, "the two principal clauses of the testament," vice-chancellor of the Council of Aragon, Cristóbal Crespí de Valdaura, noted in his diary, were the designation of Carlos as universal heir to the monarchy and of Mariana as his tutor, governor, and curator.[52]

As the testament was being read, Mariana was already dispatching her first royal decree, placing the monarchy's premier political body, the Council of State, under her direct supervision. While the court prepared for the next day's public rituals, the councils of government and administrative bodies adopted the new formulas to be used in official documents: Carlos II's name would appear first, but the documents would be addressed to his mother. The councils met to officially note the change of regime. On September 18, Mariana received the keys to the king's chamber from Medina de las Torres, the *summiller de corps*, unmistakably demonstrating that the court was under her authority. On the same day, the ruling elite gathered in the palace to pay its respects to the dead king and kiss the hands of the new sovereigns, the young king and his mother. Members of the ad hoc committee established for the regency—the Junta de Gobierno—were sworn in. In a sequestered room on the ground floor of the palace, a small group of men witnessed the breaking of the royal seals and making of new ones.[53]

Barely a day after her husband's death, even before his burial, Mariana's signature had the legal force enjoyed by proprietary rulers of the realm; the king's household had been transferred to her authority; and the government bodies had formally pledged allegiance and loyalty to her. On Sunday, September 20, Philip's body was taken to El Escorial for burial. Spain did not have coronation ceremonies; Carlos II's proclamation, the formal marker of his de facto enthronement, took place without incident on October 8, 1665, under the directorship of Medina de las Torres. The royal exequies, or funeral ceremony, celebrated on October 30 and 31, proclaimed Philip's greatness but also the "promotion of the new regime." The smooth transition of power was not lost on witnesses from foreign courts. The French ambassador pointed out that Spaniards had received the news of Philip IV's death with "indifference," observing, with a hint of scorn, that they had "greater love of the State than the Monarch." The French ambassador may have been shocked by the Spanish penchant for legal and constitutional formalities, but these did not indicate a lack of love for Philip IV. Spaniards simply preferred to love a king who was alive.[54]

HABSBURG WIDOW AND GOVERNOR

For Mariana, this moment was the culmination of her lifelong training. Although her becoming regent was not a given, the possibility had always been there. Her upbringing, like that of other Habsburg daughters, had assumed she would take on major political tasks. At every stage of her life, Mariana had been an integral part of dynastic, state, and international politics. As a Habsburg archduchess, she replaced her mother as a link between the two branches of the dynasty. As a Habsburg bride on her journey through Italy and at the Spanish court, she embodied dynastic might. She wielded her considerable dynastic capital as the daughter of the emperor and a Spanish *infanta* as well as the bearer of potential fertility that was at the family's service. As a Habsburg consort and mother, she ensured the succession into the next generation. Although her life was largely determined by the conjunction of events and long-existing traditions, within those limits, Mariana asserted multiple forms of agency. She influenced the personality of her court, stimulated cultural and fashion trends, established her own networks of patronage, and took on important political tasks as consort. All these activities, including motherhood, prepared her for the task of being regent.

When Mariana's life is seen in its historical and political contexts, the thesis that she was too young and inexperienced to rule the Spanish monarchy is unsustainable. Mariana was thirty years old when Philip IV died. While this may seem young to assume the reins of a global empire, in early modern culture, Mariana's maturity was gauged by factors besides her age. First of all, she was a widow. Even if young—many women were widowed in their twenties—widows in early modern Spanish society were considered matriarchs. Further, she had sixteen years of experience as queen and two children, one of marriageable age. And there were precedents: the daughter of Emperor Charles V, Princess Juana of Austria, ruled the Spanish monarchy on behalf of her father and her brother for five years (1554–59) when she was only nineteen. Her mother, Empress Isabel of Avis, ruled the Spanish monarchy as "lieutenant and governor" when she was in her twenties and early thirties during the emperor's frequent absences. In this context, Mariana was already middle-aged and would have appeared anything but inexperienced to her subjects.[55]

Nor was her gender an obstacle. Habsburg women had habitually ruled the Spanish Netherlands, had taken over the guardianship of minors, and had assumed the government of the monarchy. These practices were also widespread among the Spanish aristocracy, who overwhelmingly preferred naming women to administer large landed states during minorities. Most of the members of the court either had been under the tutorship of their mothers or had chosen or were predisposed to choose women as guardians of their heirs and heiresses; many women of Mariana's court had performed these tasks. The one difference between Mariana, her Habsburg predecessors, and her aristocratic counterparts is that she exercised all these prerogatives at once and ruled over a major global empire for a decade at a critical juncture for her dynasty and the monarchy. The extent of her power was surely exceptional, but the conditions that placed her in her position were not. To her seventeenth-century Spanish subjects, Mariana was the ideal choice and fully prepared to preserve the monarchy and its most prized possession: the king.[56]

Mariana's transition from consort to regent was accompanied by a dramatic change in her demeanor and appearance. First and most obviously, she adopted the type of dress worn by Habsburg widows. Mariana's image has caused some confusion in narratives of her reign because, as figure 4 shows, her widow's garb resembled a nun's habit. But though it was associated with the Franciscan habit, the widow's garb was not specifically religious, since not all Habsburg widows took the veil. In fact, Mariana's clothing, featuring princely folds on the sleeves and skirt, was one of the most fashionable examples of widow's weeds among her Habsburg counterparts. Color was also important, and Mariana's garment was composed of abundant white silks and lavish materials (figs. 4 and 5). Mariana's appearance was austere, particularly in comparison to her fashion style during her consortship period, but it was also elegant and in no way indicated a desire to enter a convent or to renounce or avoid politics.[57]

Widowhood was considered a specific moment in the life cycle of early modern women. The Spanish humanist Juan Luis Vives advocated the ideal of seclusion or retirement in widowhood, and this ideal was current among the Spanish aristocracy and the Habsburgs. But it was an ideal, not a reality. A large body of research has shown that Spanish widows had both ample legal prerogatives and social approval when they played active roles in their communities. Habsburg widows also continued to be politically active. Mariana's hybrid style—combining the austerity of widows weeds with a decisively fashionable style—let her project the austere demeanor suitable for a queen governor while looking splendid enough to preside over a royal court.[58]

Mariana's swift and assured transition to a new political role bring to mind her extensive training in the performing arts, which started with ballet lessons and participation in public rituals when she was very young. The vice-chancellor of the Council of Aragon, Cristóbal Crespí de Valdaura, recorded one of the earliest impressions of Mariana as widow and governor. He was received in her antechambers with the rest of the court on September 18, 1665, literally a day after her husband's death. He observed Mariana's calm and "majestic" bearing, calling her words brief "but of great substance, *revealing talent*" (emphasis mine), a signal of his confidence in Mariana's ability to lead the monarchy. Early modern politics, it should be recalled, was highly performative, and though in Spain it was an administrative and decision-making enterprise as well, Mariana literally fashioned herself into a queen governor overnight. But though the symbols were important, she still had to exercise her office. Along with the widow's garb emerged her

FIGURE 4 Juan Bautista Martínez del Mazo (ca. 1613–1667), *Queen Mariana of Austria in Mourning*, 1666. Oil on canvas. National Gallery, London. Presented by Rosalind, the Countess of Carlisle, 1913 (NG2926). Photo © National Gallery, London / Art Resource, New York.

forceful and decisive personality and the juridical authority to shape the court. As Mariana began shaping her regime, she worked with those of the elite who could adjust to the new situation while seeking to replace those who were recalcitrant. In the ensuing period of transformation, some political careers ended and others were launched.[59]

CHAPTER 2

Mariana's Court and Political System, 1665–1667

When Philip IV wrote the testament that set Mariana's regency on a strong footing, he based the clauses dealing with Mariana's political prerogatives on both well-established dynastic traditions and Iberian political and legal precedents. Habsburg women often ruled with or on behalf of their male relatives over the entire monarchy or Habsburg territories such as the Netherlands. These practices were reinforced and expanded by Iberian political traditions of strong medieval queenship. Titles such as "governor" in Castile and the equivalent "lieutenant" in Aragon were often appended to the titles of queens and royal women. Mariana's regency also paralleled the widespread practice among the Iberian nobility of choosing mothers as guardians for minor heirs or heiresses. Although we have no first-person statement on Philip's motivations, clearly he had tremendous confidence in his wife's ability to rule. With unequivocal language, Philip IV essentially made Mariana a substitute king.[1]

The authority that Philip IV's testament established, however, must be evaluated within the context of the court in Madrid—more specifically the royal palace, or Alcázar, the residence of the ruler and his family as well as the principal location of government. Court offices in the households of the king and queen were important sources of royal patronage because they came with salaries and emoluments and gave the holders access to additional royal favors. This was particularly important for the titled nobility and even more so for the grandees, the great magnates who enjoyed additional privileges because they were considered "cousins" of the king. The ruler authorized the rights of *mayorazgo* (primogeniture) and approved marriages among the nobility at court. The palace also hosted the councils that met several times a week, tended by an army of secretaries and bureaucrats who acted as mediators between the king and his councilors. Not all organs of government were located in the Alcázar, naturally, but it was the center of the Spanish monarchy, the place where the Habsburgs administered their global empire. As the center of royal patronage and policy making, which often overlapped, the court was a brutally competitive environment, and Mariana had to find a way to create loyalty, control discontent, and manage the expectations of all who felt entitled to appointments and royal grants.[2]

To understand the making of Mariana's court and political system, we must consider Philip IV's testament, which affected the court's organization and functioning and the terrain of Mariana's political authority. But we must also understand Mariana's strategies to shape her regime—structurally, by developing her own system, and personally, by bringing in the people with whom she felt comfortable working. The spatial organization of the Madrid Alcázar, the center of the court system, offers a useful approach. The royal households on the upper floors of the palace provided the backbone for the court's ceremonial aspects; the councils of government, on the ground floor, administered the Habsburg global empire. This chapter follows this model and looks at the power dynamics of the two levels of the court separately.

MARIANA'S LEGAL AND CONSTITUTIONAL AUTHORITY

Regency was not a foreign word in seventeenth-century Spain, and it is a useful term to refer to Mariana's position. However, Mariana's authority rested on concrete powers enshrined in specific juridical prerogatives related to the titles Philip IV gave her when he named Mariana "tutor and curator" for Carlos II. These titles reflected the two types of guardians recognized by the Spanish legal system: tutors (*tutores*) for girls under twelve and boys under fourteen and curators (*curadores*) for children older than twelve or fourteen and younger than twenty-five. The tutorship in particular carried enormous political power beyond the responsibilities associated with the care and education of the child because it granted its holder control of the court's most important commodity: the king. After Carlos achieved legal majority on his fourteenth birthday, Mariana would become his "curator." The inclusion of the curatorship in the testament indicates Philip IV's desire for Mariana to play an active political role even in the postminority period, but this prerogative was not solely Philip's to give: when the time came, Carlos would have to confirm it. Mariana also received the title of "governor" of the monarchy during Carlos II's minority; this title indicated her political authority over the monarchy's administration and was independent of her position as tutor and even her status as queen. Her tenure as regent was strictly delineated by temporal limits associated with the juridical definitions of her titles. She served concurrently as queen "tutor and governor" from September 17, 1665, the day Philip IV died, until November 6, 1675, the day of Carlos II's fourteenth birthday. Yet a large amount of the official correspondence included all three titles. Everyday memoranda and royal decrees to her ministers were addressed to and signed *La Reina Gobernadora*, or the queen governor.[3]

Mariana's authority as guardian gave her control of the king, and the combination of Habsburg child-rearing practices and the way Philip IV had set up the tutorship led to a restructuring of the court. Habsburg children saw their parents regularly but lived in the queen's side of the palace and grew up under her direct supervision. An entire hierarchy of court offices, from the highest executive office of *aya*, or head governess, down to the temporary *amas de leche*, or wet nurses, cared for the royal children within the framework of the queen's royal household. Philip respected this tradition during his son's minority, decreeing that the child-king would continue to live in his mother's household and be served by its members until he received his own royal household, a decision that Philip left in Mariana's hands. After Philip's death, there was no king's household at the Spanish court until Mariana reestablished it on April 14, 1675. As the king was usually the foundation of the court system, Mariana undertook an administrative overhaul to adapt the court to the terms of Philip IV's testament.[4]

Governorship was a gender-neutral political office, frequently allocated to Habsburg women but also to royal men (younger brothers, for example) as well as nonroyal men. Yet in Spain, the office was typically associated with the king, who was often referred to as the "king governor," or *el Rey Gobernador*. The idea of the king as governor indicates the consultative nature of Spanish kingship. Spanish kings had executive power, but they ruled with the aid of government councils that advised the kings through written *consultas* (consultations or deliberations). The choice of word is significant: *consejo* means "counsel" and can be used as a verb (*aconsejar*, or "to counsel") or a noun (*consejo*), which also refers to a government body or council. The conciliar system allowed the Habsburgs to divide their vast holdings into territorial councils (i.e., Castile, Aragon, Italy, the Indies, etc.) and special-task councils (Councils of State, War, Finance, etc.), and it required tremendous quantities of paper. The twice-weekly consultations from the Council of State ran from five to more than one hundred sheets of paper, depending on the topic and the situation. All the other councils produced enormous quantities of documents as well. The king did not see all of them, but so intimately associated were Spanish kings with administrative duties that they were often portrayed holding a sword and a document. Mariana, in turn, adopted this symbol in her regency portraits (figs. 4 and 5).[5]

Philip IV incorporated the characteristics of Spanish kingship into the testament with language that explicitly and painstakingly enumerated Mariana's duties: "The state papers that I often and I usually sign, the queen should also sign in the same manner and place"; "the resolutions that she would take in consultations, whether they be in matters of peace, or in those of government, grants and justice, as well as the orders that she may give should be executed in the same way as when I was the one resolving them." Philip left no room for misunderstanding: "I do not hold back any of the faculties that I have [as king] and that she assumes as tutor, curator, and governor, even if that entails to make and proclaim new laws or revoke them." He clearly stated his intention to "give her as much power as it resides in me for everything that is necessary and convenient so that she is able to use the greatest prerogatives and royal power (*regalías*) that belong to the Dignity [of kingship]." She could "provide for all the viceroyalties, governorships, and other offices of peace and war" and was expected "to do her will in everything that may be necessary and convenient." In short, Philip IV envisioned Mariana as a complete substitute for himself until Carlos II came of age on November 6, 1675. Although queen mothers in other monarchies were often chosen as regents during their royal children's minorities, rarely do we see them having this level of political entitlement.[6]

Within this governing structure, which included the special consultative body—the Junta de Gobierno, or Regency Council—that Philip IV instituted for the duration of Carlos II's minority, Mariana began shaping her political regime by implementing her preferences and identifying trusted advisors and collaborators. She had on her side the extensive authority granted in Philip IV's testament and a system that, though complex, was adaptable. And adapt it Mariana did, deftly maneuvering through the Habsburg system, adding her own people, and shaping a new ruling style. But even with all her options, authority, and the strength to implement her will, the process was not smooth or simple.[7]

MARIANA AND THE REFORM OF THE KING'S ROYAL HOUSEHOLD

Mariana's first major task was to implement Philip IV's mandate regarding the royal households. He requested that the chapel section of his household, which had its own hierarchy of preachers and royal musicians, remain intact. The rest of the household underwent substantial changes. With the young king now served by officers of the queen's household, much of Philip's household was out of work. And since the king's royal household served the entire court, it had the largest number of courtiers and employees and functions that were not replicated elsewhere, like the *botica real*, or royal pharmacy; there would be major disruptions if Mariana handled the changes badly. Court offices were granted for life: Mariana had to allocate pensions or find employment for every member of the king's household. It was not just a matter of making practical decisions. As posts in the king's household went to the most powerful members of the court, eliminating that household posed a major political problem. Mariana had to proceed with extreme caution to avoid disenfranchising some of the most powerful members of the ruling elite.[8]

To understand the scope of the problem, we must recall that the Spanish Habsburg court was a huge enterprise built on an intricate system of patronage and exchange that extended over all of Madrid. By 1665, the bureaucratic machine that was the court had almost 1,800 employees, 1,300 of whom were located in the king's household. Every day, the royal kitchens prepared twenty-seven dishes for the king's table and another twenty-two for the queen's. And those meals fed many more than the people at the table. Leftovers formed an integral part of the court's exchange economy, with courtiers often using food from the royal table to pay their personal servants. Employees also received emoluments (*gajes y raciones*) as part of their salaries. They might receive bread, wine, ice, foodstuffs, and/or clothing, depending on the positions they held. These obligations—some distributed daily, some seasonally—increased the court's expenses and contributed to its overall economy. Unlike monetary compensation, they could not be in arrears. Day in and day out, carriages loaded with goods, sellers, buyers, and ministers converged in the palace's ground floors to conduct business. Provisioning these goods and services for the royal family and all their courtiers increased the court's economic ties to the city. The title of the book *Solo Madrid es corte* (Only Madrid is court), which went through several editions in the 1670s, indicates the intimate relationship between court and city.[9]

Mariana had to find ways of dismantling a significant portion of this patronage exchange without losing political loyalties, provoking disaffection, or fostering a climate of discontent. One of her first acts as regent was to commission Medina de las Torres, Philip IV's final appointment as *summiller de corps*, or "chief gentleman," and thus the principal courtier in the king's chamber, to prepare a report on the king's household. His investigation produced comprehensive data on active and inactive personnel, salaries, outstanding commitments, and expenses. This document is critical to understanding the organization and function of the court before and during Mariana's regency, as it formed the basis for the "1666 reforms," the term used in household documents to describe the court's reorganization. Luis Guillermo de Moncada Aragón, 7th Duke of Montalto (1614–1672), implemented the reforms in his capacity of *mayordomo mayor* of the queen's household. A man of high lineage and with a long history of service, he was also a controlling personality who immediately clashed with Mariana. Montalto's brother-in-law, Guillén Ramón de Moncada, 4th Marquis of Aytona (1618–1670), was a member of the Junta de Gobierno and the *caballerizo mayor* of the queen's household. It was he who ended up engineering the reforms needed to comply with the testament while keeping the system from collapsing. His intervention does not appear in the official royal household records but can be found in his papers. Aytona's memoranda to Mariana reveal how the reforms were devised and implemented and underscore his role as their author.[10]

Many of the gentlemen of the royal table (*caballeros de la boca*) and of the chamber (*caballeros de la cámara*) remained on the court payroll, receiving not just salaries but the emoluments that came with the office. These obligations meant that the kitchen of the king's household could not be closed, even though Mariana and Carlos II were now served from the queen's kitchen. The royal pharmacy and those responsible for the maintenance of furniture, tapestries, and art also continued to perform their previous duties, as did the chief household administrators (*oficiales mayores*), including the treasurer, procurer, accountant, and secretary (*tesorero, contralor, grefier,* and *secretario*).[11]

There were efforts to reform the king's royal household in the previous reign, but they went nowhere, so this was a chance to reduce costs and clean up corruption. Reducing the numbers on the court payroll was a major priority, and many members of the king's household became part of the entourage accompanying the Infanta Margarita to Vienna, a ploy that allowed Mariana to shift costs from the king's household to Margarita's. This let her avoid incurring new costs while still covering those for which she was responsible. Although modest, the cost-cutting measures had an impact on overall spending patterns and reduced abuses. Mariana and Aytona left vacant posts unfilled and began keeping a tighter accounting of personnel—no easy task, given the court's size and complexity. Members of the court drawing double salaries were identified and forced to give up one, and the dead were removed from the payroll. Although commonsensical and relatively limited, in aggregate these strategies proved successful. By 1667, expenses associated with the king's chamber were cut in half, and the reforms were the basis for the more extensive and radical reforms implemented during Carlos II's reign.[12]

Mariana's way of handling the new statuses of the royal households was most visible in the chain of command. The queen's *mayordomo mayor* (instead of the king's *mayordomo mayor*), for example, now slept in the palace to respond to any emergency; he also supervised the *porteros de cadena,* the gatekeepers who monitored entrances and exits from the palace grounds. Mariana's *mayordomo mayor* assumed the responsibilities of the king's *mayordomo mayor* and *summiller de corps* and presided over the tribunal that disciplined court personnel. With unfettered access to the queen, the *mayordomo mayor* was the regency's most important masculine court appointment until Mariana established an independent household for Carlos II.[13]

Two other court offices in the queen's household emerged as powerful positions during the regency, both held by women. The *camarera mayor* governed the queen's household almost entirely, with a ceremonial supremacy unmatched in the court hierarchy. Always powerful, the position gained additional prerogatives when Mariana became governor. For example, the *camarera mayor* received and delivered all state papers to the queen and handled Mariana's correspondence and scheduling, which gave her an enormous amount of power. Only five days into the regency, Mariana decreed that the *camarera mayor* was the designated person to carry state documents so that they "arrive in my hands with all the necessary security." Although the actual motivation to issue this order is not clear, it confirmed the central position and new power of the *camarera mayor*. The imperial ambassador recorded punctiliously in his diary his visits to Mariana's *camarera mayor*, on whom he depended to see the queen.[14]

A similar situation occurred with the office of *aya*, or governess, another prestigious political appointment with substantial authority. Although subordinate to the *camarera mayor*, the *aya* exercised authority over all the personnel caring for the children within the queen's household. Mariana's tutorship thus propelled the *aya* to a much more powerful position; since she now served a king rather than a prince, she gained preeminence in all court rituals and ceremonies. The women who filled these positions belonged to the upper crust of the nobility. As all the principal offices within the queen's household grew in power, the stage was set for tense and difficult situations.[15]

WOMEN AND MEN IN MARIANA'S COURT

The conflicts in the Spanish court during Mariana's regency reflect, on one hand, the perennial competition between personnel serving the inner chambers (with intimate access to the ruler) and those serving outside the chamber or house. In the sixteenth century, this chamber/house opposition was seen in the factional struggles between the *albistas*, followers of the Duke of Alba, and *ebolistas*, followers of the Prince of Éboli, who occupied the posts of *mayordomo mayor* and *summiller de corps*, respectively. At the court of Philip II, these struggles were largely ideological in nature. In Mariana's court, struggles arose from the gendered nature of the queen's household, which meant that women served the more powerful inner chamber, while men were relegated to the outer offices of the house. The personalities of the people involved exacerbated the situation; none of these powerful women was inclined to yield her preeminence, and Mariana was not interested in disempowering them.[16]

Doña Mariana Engracia Álvarez de Toledo, Marquise of los Velez, entered the queen's household as lady of honor in 1657 and became the *aya* of Mariana's children in 1659. A woman of an austere demeanor with considerable administrative experience from managing her son's inheritance during his minority, she was the first and only *aya* of a ruling king in Habsburg Spain. Doña Elvira Ponce de León, Marquise of Baldueza, the *camarera mayor* from 1654 on, belonged to an important lineage and, like Velez and Mariana herself, had been the tutor and curator of her minor daughter, the heiress to the family's title and fortune. Baldueza, who served the queen until 1691, had the rare distinction of being addressed as "Her Excellency," a social recognition coveted by, and usually given to, men. These women had the necessary experience and confidence to claim and use the preeminence afforded by the court's new organization.[17]

Mariana expected the Duke of Montalto, the *mayordomo mayor*, along with the rest of the male leadership at court to abide by her authority and that of the *camarera mayor* and the *aya*. Clashes during the household reforms soon made it clear that Montalto was not the right man for the job. He refused to follow the protocol Mariana wanted him to apply in dealings with the officials of her late husband's household. Unpleasant exchanges followed, culminating in Mariana's unambivalent command that Montalto act "in the manner in which you have been told." After this episode, Montalto complained about not being consulted about two appointments in the queen's household and the resistance he claimed he encountered everywhere. Later, he explicitly identified the *camarera mayor*, the Marquise of Baldueza, as the source of "the repeated setbacks and humiliations that I have suffered." By exercising her own authority over the queen's household, Baldueza, as Montalto put it, "prevented me from complying with the obligations of my office."[18]

Discomfort turned into hostility when Montalto issued a private memorandum to Mariana accusing women in her entourage of inappropriate behavior during the practice of *galanteos*, the Spanish version of the courtly love tradition. *Galanteos* was a sanctioned, institutionalized form of flirtation that allowed young males to openly declare their love for ladies in the queen's entourage. The *galanes*, or heartthrobs, provided a colorful addition to public processions, following the women they loved. Everyone participated, including the king, who had called himself Mariana's *galán*. Occasional controversies arose, leading the king to restrict participation to unmarried men and those who owned horses, but it remained a popular pastime.[19]

Montalto claimed that the young unmarried women in Mariana's entourage were flirting inappropriately and that with so many young men present, her court had become a place of improprieties. Most damningly, he claimed that flirtation between Mariana's ladies and the *galanes* had moved out of the realm of the platonic. A young nobleman who was romancing two ladies at once had purportedly consummated the relationship with one. Meanwhile, one of Mariana's lower servants had given birth in the palace clinic, another indication that the queen's household was not properly monitored. "The palace guards," Montalto complained, ignored his position as the one who should be told when infractions occurred "either because they think I am so utterly base that I would not care to do anything about them, or because they know that *I do not have the backing of Your Majesty*" (emphasis mine). Montalto scolded Mariana about the political danger—"a monarchy could be lost"—if these kinds of activities went unchecked.[20]

Mariana took the charges seriously and dealt with the situation swiftly. She ordered Montalto to reprimand the *galanes* in question and instructed Baldueza and the *guardamayor*—who was in charge of the unmarried ladies—to do the same with the women Montalto accused. She also ordered a strict watch over her quarters to control who entered and when; servants were prohibited from leaving the palace premises altogether. The *meninos grandes* (older boys) were prevented from contact with the young ladies of her court, and the woman who had reputedly given birth in the palace was sent to the galleys "for two to three years." It was an exemplary punishment that left no doubt that Mariana would not tolerate even the appearance of impropriety. As she was issuing these orders, she was also taking steps to replace Montalto.[21]

Mariana had to manage the situation with skill and diplomacy. Court appointments were held for life, so absent a major transgression, she could not dismiss Montalto. Instead, she accelerated Montalto's promotion to a cardinalate working with the Council of Italy, the papal nuncio, and her representatives in Rome, making it look like a sign of favor. When

Pope Alexander VII confirmed the appointment in March 1667, Mariana requested Montalto's resignation from his court office, arguing that it was incompatible with his new position. Further, she issued an order for Montalto's immediate departure to Rome. Montalto resigned shortly after his appointment but delayed leaving the court on account of his health. In late 1668, still in Madrid, Montalto pleaded with the queen to let him remain in Madrid given his "deplorable mental and physical health"; his tone was much humbler than it had been in his memoranda.[22]

Montalto was not alone in pushing back against the women now in charge of the court. On November 20, 1668, for example, Mariana ordered Aytona—then the *mayordomo mayor*—to discipline her treasurer, Baltasar Molinet. The man had refused to follow orders from the "*camarera mayor* and the *aya* of the king, my son," to release funds to buy traditional departing gifts for a diplomat from Florence. "The treasurer," Mariana reminded Aytona in clear terms, "is subordinate to both women [*subdito de ambas*]," and "he must obey them both." Mariana ordered Aytona to "warn and reprimand him for not having done what he was told" and to "ensure that from now on he does not fail to carry out his duties on any occasion that may present itself in the future." When interrogated by Aytona, the treasurer responded that it was the *mayordomo mayor*'s job to approve these types of requests. Aytona quietly ensured that Mariana's orders were carried out. Here we can see the role personality played in the power dynamics in the queen's household. Montalto was forced out, while Aytona became Mariana's most trusted counselor.[23]

The *mayordomo mayor* remained the most important court position held by a man during the regency, but the conflicts of the first year and a half of Mariana's regency diminished substantially. The selection of her *mayordomos mayores* was an important aspect of Mariana's regime-building process. Her first appointment was highly symbolic: she replaced Montalto with Fernando Álvarez de Toledo y Mendoza, 6th Duke of Alba. The Albas had one of the most powerful lineages of Castile and boasted a long history of high court office. Three earlier dukes had served as *mayordomos mayores* in the households of Charles V, Philip II, and Philip IV. The current duke was a member of the Council of State and one of its most conscientious participants during the latter part of Philip IV's reign. The appointment of someone of Alba's stature lent prestige to the office, indicating that the queen's household was now atop the political hierarchy. It was a strategic and smart decision on Mariana's part, one that no one criticized. His tenure in office, however, lasted only six months owing to his untimely death.[24]

By the time Mariana replaced Alba with Aytona, the political circumstances had altered dramatically. Aytona had held an important position in Mariana's court since the death of Philip IV, but he had gradually taken on more responsibility, including devising the reforms of the royal households. More importantly, Aytona was actively involved in military recruitment at the most critical time for Mariana, when Spain faced an attack from France with inadequate forces. Aytona's appointment to the highest court position was one of the earliest examples of Mariana's policy of rewarding military service. When Aytona died in 1670 and Mariana required a new *mayordomo mayor*, conflicts had essentially disappeared. The Duke of Pastrana served in the post until his death in 1675. After Pastrana's death, Mariana did not immediately appoint a new *mayordomo mayor*; the establishment of the new king's royal household meant that the position of *mayordomo mayor* of the queen's household returned to its previous place in the hierarchy.[25]

Mariana's strategies with the royal households were implemented quickly. By 1667, the new hierarchy of the court was firmly in place and did not cause additional conflicts. When it came to exercising her governorship, Mariana also had to adapt the terms of the king's testament to the existing government structure of the Spanish court. To understand her political system, we must begin with Philip IV's testament and, in particular, his decision to establish a special government body.

MARIANA AND THE JUNTA DE GOBIERNO

While many Habsburg women had ruled as governors in Spain and its territories, Mariana was the only one who ruled without the presence of an adult king, which meant that her decisions had additional weight. As we have seen, Philip IV envisioned Mariana as his substitute and left no room for dispute, and Mariana ruled as Philip had, adopting the political traditions of consultative rulership. Yet all was not the same, because Philip IV created a special government body for the duration of his son's minority, and the Junta de Gobierno presented Mariana with a political dilemma. In clause 22 of his testament, Philip gave Mariana political advice, a dynastic political tradition going back to Charles V. He charged her with keeping the conciliar system of government of their ancestors and recommended that the queen "pay attention to the election of ministers [and] rule, paying particular attention to the consultations of the Councils." Finally, he asked her to remit all political matters to the "Junta de Gobierno [Regency Council] that I want and is my volition to form and that should be attended by the president of the Council of Castile, the vice-chancellor [presiding minister] of the Council of Aragon, the Archbishop of Toledo, the Inquisitor General, and a grandee." A separate clause made a provision for an additional member to be appointed to represent the Council of State.[26]

Philip's motivation for instituting the Junta de Gobierno has caused major misunderstandings about Mariana's regency. It was Gabriel Maura y Gamazo, in his two-volume study of Carlos II's minority, who first advanced the thesis that Philip limited Mariana's sovereignty with the junta because he lacked confidence in her ability to govern. Subsequently, in his pivotal study of Spanish favorites, Francisco Tomás y Valiente echoed this idea. Also, Antonio Domínguez Ortíz, in his introduction to his transcription and edition of Philip IV's testament, argued that the king followed tradition (by making Mariana governor, tutor, and curator) against his own inclinations. Although these esteemed historians have made enormous contributions to our understanding of seventeenth-century Spain, their error comes out of their misreading of the evidence. Both Tomás y Valiente and Domínguez Ortíz, for example, recognized that the king invested Mariana with full sovereignty. When explaining Philip's institution of the Junta de Gobierno, however, they both concluded that Philip had done so in order to circumscribe Mariana's political authority tightly because she was incompetent.[27]

The thesis that the Junta de Gobierno limited Mariana's authority does not stand up when the testament is analyzed from a legal perspective. Philip IV repeatedly ensured that Mariana possessed the fullest political authority—short, of course, of inheriting the throne in her own right. Clauses 21 and 35 clearly established Mariana's sovereignty and preempted any possibility of a legal challenge to her position; the categorical language explains why the transfer of power was so smooth. The legal historian María del Carmen Sevilla González has recently argued that Philip IV's intention to endow Mariana with *plenitudo potestatis*, or complete political power, was so clearly stated that no portion of the testament, even the clause in which he recommended that Mariana follow the advice of the Junta de Gobierno, contradicted it. Indeed, Mariana had the legal authority to dissolve the group.[28]

These claims are confirmed by Mariana's contemporaries. The Council of Aragon's secretary, for example, recorded in the minutes, "Philip IV died in Madrid on September 17, 1665." Immediately underneath, he wrote, "[The king named] the Queen, our Lady, governor, with very extensive powers, *with the same authority as the king*, without need to submit anything for referendum, and as tutor of the king until he is fourteen years of age" (emphasis mine). Cristóbal Crespí de Valdaura, vice-chancellor of Aragon, Junta de Gobierno member, and eyewitness to all that transpired at Philip IV's death, made similar notes in his diary. The court of Vienna received a report on the conditions of Mariana's regency that points to the same reading: "Her Majesty the queen remains absolute governor, tutor and curator of her son, and [rules] with the committee of ministers that the king named in his testament; they only have the right of consultation." Finally and most importantly, all state papers that passed over Mariana's desk end with the customary "and Your Majesty will order what is more convenient to Her royal service," exactly the same language used when addressing male proprietary monarchs. It is clear that none of Mariana's contemporaries doubted her legal and constitutional authority to rule as a king.[29]

It then makes sense to ask why Philip IV established the Junta de Gobierno. There are several issues to consider. To begin with, he was acting within well-established traditions. The Habsburgs had long ruled with ad hoc committees, or juntas; these were temporary and intended to address a specific task or problem. Philip II relied on them, particularly in the latter part of his reign, as did Philip IV, first under his principal minister/*valido*, the Count-Duke of Olivares, who used juntas to control recalcitrant councils. After the death of Don Luis de Haro, Olivares's successor, in 1661, Philip relied on a three-member Junta de Gobierno to dispatch government matters. Two of its members were appointed to the junta for Mariana's regency.[30]

This continuity has led to the thesis that Philip IV was attempting to prevent the rise of a favorite and wanted Mariana to rule as he had during the last few years of his reign. Maura was the first to propose this hypothesis, which Sevilla González confirmed in 2006. This reading makes some sense, given that two members of Philip's junta were named to Mariana's. Yet the hypothesis does not explain the different composition of Mariana's Junta de Gobierno, which had six members rather than the three that aided Philip IV. Moreover, a new dating of Philip IV's testament by Cristina Hermosa Espeso reveals that the idea of establishing the Junta de Gobierno for Mariana's regency was initially discussed during Luis de Haro's lifetime. Haro, of course, was the king's principal minister, or *valido*, for nearly twenty years.[31]

Additional precedents for the Junta de Gobierno can be observed in the several governorships Queen Isabel of Bourbon (r. 1621–44), Philip IV's first consort and Mariana's immediate predecessor, exercised on several occasions. In 1626 and 1632, when she was temporarily left in charge of the government, the Junta de Gobierno was composed of three ministers—a grandee, a member of the Council of State, and the president of the Council of Castile. During her three brief regencies between 1642 and 1644, when Philip IV was at the Catalonian front during the revolt and simultaneous Franco-Spanish War, Isabel was assisted by another Junta de Gobierno, this one composed of six members, including a cardinal, the president of the Council of Castile, three councilors of state, and the *mayordomo mayor* of the queen's household. The composition and the very existence of these committees suggest a desire to appoint a larger sample of the ruling elite. This is another indication that the junta's existence cannot be explained by the desire to prevent the rise of a favorite, since *validos* were in power during all of Isabel's governorships.[32]

Philip IV's appointment of a Junta de Gobierno for Mariana's regency reflected a method he had employed for several decades. The institution of the Junta de Gobierno was a politico-institutional development and not, as the previous explanations imply, a mechanism to undermine Mariana's authority or a reflection of Philip IV's supposed doubts about his wife's political skills. The terms of the testament were unequivocal; if he had any concerns about her naming a favorite, it did not affect the authority he granted her.

Although there were many precedents for the Junta de Gobierno, Mariana's regency was unique because it took place during a minority. During the governorships of Queen Isabel, the king was alive, just absent. Furthermore, in her last series of brief governorships, Prince Baltasar Carlos was in Madrid and near the age of majority. Mariana, in contrast, would be the sole ruler for a long time and would rule on behalf of a child. These considerations led Philip IV to request legal counsel. Between late 1663 and early 1664, the lawyer José González advised the king on how to organize the government during a minority. Aside from the fact that Philip IV was getting old and that Spanish kings considered drafting testaments a priority, there were other, more concrete international and dynastic considerations.[33]

Rumors that Louis XIV intended to claim a portion of Carlos II's lands in the Low Countries raised concerns that parts of the inheritance would be contested. Protecting those territories thus became a major consideration. Using the Spanish legal code—the Siete Partidas, or Seven Divisions of Law—as the juridical model, González deemed the Junta de Gobierno necessary to preserve the unity of all the monarchy's territories, legitimize the regency government, and build loyalty. Since the Spanish monarchy was a composite state with each constitutive kingdom owing allegiance to one monarch, transitioning from one reign to another always raised fears of instability. This is why each kingdom pledged allegiance to the new king individually. Although the Habsburgs commanded substantial loyalty, Portugal and Catalonia (and, briefly, Naples) had revolted in the previous decades. Indeed, according to González, when faced with the recalcitrant Crown of Aragon and the danger of France, the Catholic monarchs Isabel and Ferdinand had also established similar juntas in their respective testaments. These considerations explain the representation on the Junta de Gobierno, which included the president of the Council of Castile and the vice-chancellor of the Council of Aragon, the territories whose original union of Crowns birthed the Spanish monarchy. It also included the two highest religious officers of the realm—the archbishop of Toledo and the inquisitor general—and a grandee and a councilor of state as representatives of social and political hierarchies.[34]

Even with ultimate executive power over policy, Mariana still had to establish a working relationship with this special government body in order to govern effectively. Philip IV's statement that "it would be best that the queen is in conformity with the opinion of all or the majority of the Council" should be understood as what it was: not a limit on Mariana's executive capacity but a political mandate to protect the territorial integrity of the monarchy during Carlos II's minority. It was establishing this modus operandi, not dealing with limitations to her authority, that posed difficulties for Mariana. The political culture of the Spanish court was characterized by great loyalty to the Crown as well as a highly enhanced sense of the notion of self-government embodied by Renaissance political theorists. The famous dictum *obedezco pero no cumplo*, or "I obey but do

not comply," invoked by members of the ruling elite in councils, governorships, viceroyalties, and other middle levels of government in overseas or
pan-European possessions, illustrates this principle quite eloquently. The
motto simultaneously recognized the theoretical power of the king (*obedezco*, "I obey") while asserting the right of subjects not to consent to that
authority (*pero no cumplo*, "but I do not comply"). Strong kings, including
Philip II and Philip IV, were not exempt from this principle and had faced
problems when trying to implement unpopular or unreasonable mandates.
Like her predecessors, Mariana would have to find the right balance with
her ministers.[35]

The Junta de Gobierno was a consultative organ of government but
nevertheless emerged at the beginning of the regency as a key political body.
Its initial strength came not just from the principles behind its existence
but from the individual accomplishments of its members. The junta was
essentially a gerontocracy, and each member's substantial service record
made his opinions count and added to the junta's collective power. The two
oldest members were Don García de Haro Sotomayor y Guzmán, Count
of Castrillo (1588–1670), in his eighties, and Don Gaspar de Bracamonte,
Count of Peñaranda, in his seventies. Both younger sons of prestigious lineages, the two men had risen politically and socially through education,
ability, and strategic marriages. Castrillo had been a member or presiding
officer of the most important councils of the monarchy, including those of
the Indies, Italy, Finance, and Castile. He served as viceroy of Naples, in the
Juntas de Gobierno instituted for Queen Isabel, and in the three-member
junta for Philip IV. He was also the president of the Council of Castile, the
most prestigious political office of the monarchy; if no member of the royal
family was available, he could replace the king.[36]

Peñaranda was a senior member of the Council of State and president
of the Council of Italy. He was also the most experienced diplomat in Mariana's court: his spectacular career took off in 1645, when he was named
plenipotentiary to represent Spain in the negotiations that led to the Peace
of Westphalia, and his intervention at Münster was legendary. He participated in the Imperial Diet that elected Leopold I as Holy Roman emperor
in 1657. Although he was staunchly anti–Austrian Habsburg, his sterling
qualities as a statesman explained why Philip IV selected him to represent
the Council of State in the Junta de Gobierno. Mariana was not a docile
woman and expected these powerful men to submit to her, but Castrillo

and Peñaranda had independent standings at court and were not easily swayed. Mariana relied particularly on Peñaranda, whose expertise she respected. Yet both men ended up at odds with her. Peñaranda completed his term, but Mariana forced Castrillo to resign in 1668.[37]

Cristóbal Crespí de Valdaura, in his sixties, was a well-known jurist and an accomplished scholar. As the vice-chancellor of the Council of Aragon since 1652, he had a lengthy history of service to the Crown. He generally worked well with Mariana but maintained his independence. At forty, Cardinal Pascual de Aragón was the youngest member of the group; he had just been nominated as inquisitor general. He had extensive political and diplomatic experience, however, as viceroy of Naples and ambassador to Rome, and as a cardinal, he also represented the church. Although he was a second son, he belonged to one of the most prestigious lineages of the realm: his mother, Catalina Fernández de Córdoba, Duchess of Cardona, took over the viceroyalty government of Catalonia from her husband and mediated between the Catalan rebels and Philip IV. Aragón became an important figure in Mariana's regime; his ecclesiastical office and diplomatic skills allowed him to survive the difficult political struggles at the end of the regency unscathed.[38]

In his midfifties, Aytona represented the grandees. His selection by Philip IV was a surprise; everyone assumed that Duke Medina de las Torres, a longtime friend and important figure in Philip IV's regime, would be selected. The circumstances of the appointment remain obscure; perhaps Mariana influenced Philip IV, as Aytona was the brother of one of Mariana's longtime confidants, Magdalena Moncada. But Aytona was accomplished in his own right. The author of an important military treatise, he had held generalships, viceroyalties, and prestigious court offices, and he long enjoyed the king's confidence. He was uncompromisingly loyal. All these men seemed well disposed to Mariana's regency, but it remained to be seen how much power the queen was going to grant them.[39]

MARIANA'S STRATEGIES

Mariana's rule began in the midst of an international crisis and in a deeply divided court. She inherited a group of older men whose vision of Spain did not allow for the adaptations needed to deal with the crisis. To find consensus and implement her policies without opposition, Mariana needed

to either make the Junta de Gobierno her instrument or diminish its influence. In the end, she did both. Her first opportunity to make an appointment came just hours after taking office: the archbishop of Toledo died
immediately after Philip IV, creating a vacancy. To replace him, Mariana
nominated someone already on the junta, Cardinal Aragón, forcing Aragón
to choose between the two positions, either one of which would give him
membership in the junta. Predictably, he picked the more lucrative arch-
bishopric, leaving the office of inquisitor vacant. Mariana delayed choosing
a replacement for the office of inquisitor for several months. During the first
year of the regency, until Cardinal Aragón returned from Naples in the
summer of 1666, only four members of the junta were at court. The expectations for the junta were high, but the queen's lukewarm attitude toward
it soon became evident. As early as January 1666, the Marquis of Aytona
protested to Mariana that the Junta de Gobierno lacked the authority that
Philip IV had intended, reminding the queen that her late husband had
instituted it to "serve and lighten Your Majesty's burden."[40]

Mariana's intention, which soon became clear, was to appoint her confessor, Father Everard Nithard, to the office of inquisitor, which would
automatically make him a member of the Junta de Gobierno. Mariana first
named Nithard a state councilor on January 24, 1666, as part of a cluster
of appointments to the Council of State. Confessors of kings had been
appointed to the Council of State before, so Mariana did not go against
tradition. She then appointed him, along with Peñaranda and Medina de
las Torres, to the three-member ad hoc committee negotiating peace with
Portugal. By the summer of 1666, Mariana started dealing with two potential obstacles for Nithard's greater role in her government. As a foreigner,
Nithard was prevented by Philip IV's testamentary mandate from becoming
a member of the Junta de Gobierno; further, the Jesuit order required their
members to have papal permission to hold political office. She quickly dispatched both, ordering the Council of Castile to request individual cities
to grant Nithard citizenship and personally requesting permission from
Pope Alexander VII, which he readily granted. The other junta members
tried to dissuade Mariana from appointing Nithard, but on September 21,
1666, she named him inquisitor general, an appointment that automatically made him a member of the group. With Nithard's appointment, Mariana was closer to having control over the Junta de Gobierno, but the process
was far from complete.[41]

In the first year of the regency, the Junta de Gobierno became a battle-
ground, with power struggles among its members, those who wanted to be
members, and those who wanted the junta dissolved. Duke Medina de las
Torres had been expected to be a member and was a strong pro-Austrian
Habsburg, which recommended him to Mariana. He approached Nithard
with the idea of forming a two-person committee to advise the queen.
While negotiating this behind the scenes, he circulated a paper advancing
the position that Mariana had the right, perhaps even the obligation, to dissolve the Junta de Gobierno. The disquisition, which presented a positive
view of female regencies, indicating that the author sought Mariana's favor,
was published anonymously, but everyone knew Medina de las Torres was
the author. He was eager to be part of Mariana's inner circle, either in the
junta or with the elimination of the junta.[42]

We do not know Mariana's reaction to the proposal, but while she could
have dissolved the Junta de Gobierno, it would have been unwise to undermine Philip IV's testament, which was, after all, the main source of her
authority. Nithard's appointment shows Mariana's strategic thinking, but
it also required a measure of serendipity. The office of inquisitor was vacant
because of a death, and this office was suitable for Nithard—his foreignness
aside—as he was a theologian and lawyer. Ultimately, Mariana's ability to
control the composition of the junta was limited. She orchestrated a resignation in 1668, but it would have been unwise to replace everyone by
scheming and impractical to wait for people to die in office.

This left the other option: diminishing the junta's power. A crucial institutional shift in Mariana's regency involved the Council of State. Although
still considered the monarchy's premier political body, its influence had
significantly diminished during the age of the great minister favorites, or
validos. The *valido*'s ability to control the Council of State was an indication
of his power. Over the six decades of the rise of the *valimiento* (favoritism) system, the council had lost most of its decision-making power. King
Philip III's favorite, Francisco Gómez de Sandoval, 1st Duke of Lerma,
enjoyed carte blanche to preside over the council, and from 1612 to 1618, his
signature equaled the king's. During Lerma's *valimiento*, the number of ministers grew substantially, but while an appointment as councilor of state was
prestigious and sought after, it was mostly honorific, and the council had
limited influence. Olivares, who endeavored to present himself as the king's
minister rather than his favorite, appropriated the Council of State's right to

counsel the king on foreign affairs and undermined the group by instituting juntas that were under his direct supervision. Don Luis de Haro, who succeeded Olivares in 1643, was more discreet than his uncle/predecessor but still controlled the council: special meetings were held in his house. During the later years of Philip IV's reign, even after the last *valido* had left the scene, a mere handful of men—usually two to six—attended council meetings. Although it regained some footing, the council was never as dominant as it became during Mariana's regency.[43]

Mariana placed the Council of State under her supervision on the very first day of her governorship. Five days later, she ordered the council to send their consultations to her rather than the Junta de Gobierno, a procedure that, she insisted, "must be observed with inviolability." This was within established practice—the king had always presided directly over this council. (Other councils had presiding officers who met with the king regularly; the meeting with the president of the Council of Castile, for example, was scheduled for Fridays.) It is not clear if she originally intended to rely on the Council of State so heavily, but in late January 1666, she took the drastic measure of packing the council by appointing no fewer than seven new councilors, including Nithard. She then began sending all governmental matters requiring debate to the council. The influx of new councilors altered the internal dynamics of the existing group and reinvigorated it, and soon everyone was attending meetings. Charged with debating and consulting with Mariana on all matters of state, and newly influential, the council began meeting more frequently. Indeed, the number of extraordinary meetings increased so much that the Council of War, which shared a room with the Council of State, complained. Mariana apologized and told the Council of War she would not usurp their meeting times. It is not clear how she dealt with the space problem (a long-standing one), but the council now had real decision-making power.[44]

These changes in the government system—the Council of State's enhanced role and the addition of the Junta de Gobierno—exponentially augmented the work of the secretaries, which made them more important politically. The secretarial staff belonged to a different, albeit privileged, social class: the *letrados*, or university-trained men. Like the Council of State, secretaries had seen their heyday in the sixteenth century, particularly under Philip II, who relied on them heavily. During the seventeenth century, their role became purely bureaucratic, as the *validos* took over the function of consulting with the king face-to-face orally, or *a boca*. But the secretarial staff became central in Mariana's regime. Although there were at least a dozen secretaries in staff, Mariana worked closely with three at any given moment. She had inherited her secretarial staff from the previous reign, but during her regency, she appointed a total of twelve secretaries and promoted several within the existing ones. The highest secretary was the *despacho universal*: when Mariana took on the reins of power, the post was occupied by Don Blasco de Loyola. This role was critical: Loyola was the medium of communication between the queen and her councils. He attended the meetings personally and reported their proceedings to the queen; he put Mariana's decisions in writing and communicated the queen's orders to the men who would carry them out. Loyola's responsibilities pertained to the Junta de Gobierno meetings, some of the Council of State meetings, and the important ad hoc committees, including the Junta de Inglaterra, which handled peace negotiations with Portugal.[45]

Two additional secretaries divided the work of the Council of State: one handled negotiations pertaining to Italy, the other matters of the north. The career of Don Pedro Fernández del Campo, who was charged with communicating with the ambassadors in London and The Hague and attending and reporting on the most important Council of State meetings, highlights the secretarial staff's preeminent role in Mariana's regime. He became one of her most trusted advisors, and in 1673, she gave him the title of Marquis of Mejorada. In 1676, when the shape of Carlos II's regime was still unclear, Mejorada almost became the next *valido*.[46]

MARIANA'S POLITICAL SYSTEM

Mariana adapted the system to her political interests, and members of the court also adapted. She succeeded in streamlining the functioning of the court and implementing needed reforms. While gender played a role, personality did as well. Aytona's input was critical in the royal household reforms, and this initial collaboration soon moved into other areas of government. Montalto, who could not or would not adapt, was soon gone.

At the level of political administration, the establishment of the Junta de Gobierno introduced significant changes in the conciliar system of government. Although she had to uphold and work within the conditions and appointees set by her husband's testament, Mariana quickly identified capable and loyal men and appointed them to government councils, court posts, and the diplomatic corps. These men became part of her inner circle, a circle from which she excluded figures who had been well positioned to assume prominent roles but whom she found unsuitable or difficult to work with.

During Mariana's regency, the trajectory of the educated elite, or *letrados*, was significant. They could not, however, completely eclipse the influence of the nobility, which was concentrated in the Council of State and the royal households. While Mariana significantly changed the conciliar system of government, certain appointments were divisive and created jealousy and controversy. Her appointment of Nithard to various political offices was a source of conflict even though he was never really in charge of policy. Her court was transforming, but during the early years of the regency, the larger issue was political strife connected to the broader context of European and international affairs. None of these issues were new, but they became crises when Philip IV died. It is in this context, and in the realm of foreign affairs, that Mariana's political acumen can best be seen.

CHAPTER 3

Resolving Philip IV's Legacy, 1665–1668

Philip IV bequeathed Mariana the war against Portugal, already essentially lost by the time she took power, and a monarchy hobbled by debt. His decision to marry Maria Theresa, his daughter from his first marriage, to Louis XIV, not only did not bring the hoped-for stability; it created more difficulties. Louis XIV blatantly violated the terms of the Treaty of the Pyrenees by providing military and financial support to Portugal. Most troubling, despite Maria Theresa's renunciation of her Spanish inheritance, Louis XIV intended to claim the Spanish Netherlands through her. Louis XIV's intentions to proceed with this plan after Philip died had been known in the Spanish court since 1663. These rumors were confirmed in the summer of 1665; the two Spanish-born queens of France—Anne of Austria, Louis XIV's mother, and Maria Theresa, his wife—wrote Philip warning that an invasion was imminent. They urged him to cede those territories to France in order to avoid the renewal of war between the Habsburgs and the Bourbons. Philip IV died three weeks after the letter was sent, and it is not clear if he read it. (It took about a month after Philip's death for the Spanish ambassador to receive official notice of the king's death, and he continued to address correspondence to Philip IV until late October 1665. However, the Spanish court may have been deliberately slow in sending the news to France.)[1]

The army of Flanders was in no position to defend the Spanish Netherlands, as it had been substantially reduced after peace with the Dutch (1648) and with France (1659). The war with Portugal made the problem worse. When Mariana took power, the army counted only 2,904 officers and 8,394 soldiers. Her problems were compounded by Spain's lack of allies: her only possible support was from Leopold I, as this was the only agreement Philip IV had undertaken to secure the Spanish Netherlands. But the agreement stood on shaky ground. The marriage of the emperor and the Infanta Margarita had been confirmed in late 1663, but despite Leopold's pleas and Philip's promises, the *infanta* still had not left Spain.[2]

Louis XIV's attack on the Spanish Netherlands not only initiated the War of Devolution (1667–68) but acted as a catalyst that allowed Mariana to implement new, more successful policies. Although the major loss the Spanish army suffered in the Battle of Villaviciosa on June 17, 1665, suggested that the war with Portugal was essentially lost, the idea of accepting the inevitable—Portugal's independence—was a highly divisive and contentious issue. Indeed, the divisions of Mariana's court must be seen within the context of Portugal's future. The Council of State's deliberations are an important source to understand the issues Mariana dealt with on the international stage, her policy decisions, and her leadership skills and political agency. While this chapter focuses mainly on policy matters, a connecting thread with the previous and the following chapters is the composition and dynamics of her political regime.[3]

By the early months of January 1666, the Council of State had been transformed into Mariana's principal advisory committee, subordinating the Junta de Gobierno to a secondary role. During this period, the records of the deliberations came to her in the form of individual votes; Mariana's responses—crafted with the secretaries—were very specific and detailed. Mariana's correspondence with her diplomats and the governor of the Spanish Netherlands—or the Low Countries, as this territory is referred to in the sources—is also critical. The instructions and communications were mediated by the royal secretaries, who dispatched the queen's instructions and maintained a parallel communication with the diplomats. The active participation of the royal secretaries; the ambassadors in London, Paris, and The Hague; and the governor of the Spanish Netherlands nurtured political partnerships that explain the composition of Mariana's regime in the years to come. The personal papers of the Marquis of Aytona also reveal the beginning of Mariana's most important collaboration. These detailed records make it possible to examine how Mariana navigated dissent, how she rose above it, and which measures she implemented to extricate the monarchy from its dire predicament.[4]

DYNASTIC AND GEOPOLITICAL CONSIDERATIONS

The dynastic configuration after the death of Philip IV explains why Carlos II's minority reignited the dynastic rivalry between the Spanish Habsburgs and the French Bourbons. Thus to understand Mariana's predicament, we must examine the specific dynastic configuration created by Philip IV's death and the testamentary clauses that established the lines of succession. The naming of the three-year-old Carlos II as universal heir was unproblematic and widely anticipated. The designation of the Infanta Margarita as Carlos II's successor if he died without issue confirmed Maria Theresa's exclusion from the succession, based on her renunciation and her father's wishes. Philip IV also established a third line of succession through his younger sister (Mariana's mother), the Infanta-Emperatriz Maria (who married Emperor Ferdinand III in 1629). Maria's only surviving son, Leopold I, was third in line to succeed, after Margarita. The Habsburg marriage alliance between Margarita and Leopold I meant, therefore, that the Austrian Habsburgs had unquestionable precedence over the French Bourbons in the succession.[5]

The rest of the clauses further underscore Philip's goal of excluding France. He instituted an additional line of succession via the Savoyard dynasty, going back a generation to name the descendants of his aunt, the Infanta and Duchess consort of Savoy Catalina Micaela of Austria (1567–1598), daughter of Philip II and Isabel of Valois. Thus there were multiple lines of succession between the Spanish Crown and the French Bourbons. Still France had two generations of Spanish *infantas*—Queen Anne and Queen Maria Theresa—in its lineage. Both were oldest daughters and thus born with precedence in the succession (the first over the Infanta-Emperatriz Maria and the second over the Infanta Margarita); both had renounced their rights upon their marriages to Bourbon rulers. Excluding the French descendants was so important that Philip IV dedicated an entire clause—the longest in the testament—to legalize it.[6]

The justification had to be carefully crafted. Spanish laws, as we have seen, respected female inheritance rights. Philip IV circumvented the law by claiming his "absolute royal power" as king of Castile, explaining that, like his predecessors, he could use his royal prerogative to alter the order of the succession when required by the public good. The potential unification of Spain and France was, he said, against the public good. Although his sister, Anne of Austria, was named in the clause, it mainly focused on his daughter, whose potential succession rights were stronger because younger generations had precedence over the older. Philip made it clear that as long as she remained queen of France, Maria Theresa forfeited her rights to the Spanish Crown "in perpetuity." Her children would be considered "as if they had never been born." To reinforce the legality of the exclusion, he reinstated her rights if her ties to France no longer existed—that is, *if* widowed *and* childless, she could return to Spain and become queen proprietary, or if she remarried, she could pass on succession rights to her descendants. Provisions for the regency reinforced the thrust of these succession and exclusion clauses. Aside from appointing Mariana tutor and governor during Carlos II's minority, Philip IV also named her governor if Margarita and Leopold I inherited and were not in Castile. As a result, Mariana was called to protect not just her son's inheritance but also that of her daughter and brother.[7]

The clauses establishing the lines of succession were so critical to the future of the continent that they were copied, printed, sent to foreign courts, and commented on in diplomatic circles. Louis XIV, of course, was particularly interested, since the testament gave precedence to the Holy Roman emperor over the king of France: Leopold was about to be married to Carlos II's sister, the next in line to the Spanish Crown. Louis XIV's goals when Philip IV died were twofold. First, he sought to establish a claim to at least some of the Spanish inheritance in the event that Carlos II died before marrying and producing children. Second, he wanted to press inheritance claims through his wife immediately. Although he had already begun planning for these potential scenarios, implementing his plans required utmost caution. The Treaty of the Pyrenees had settled territorial disputes between Spain and France; it had been witnessed by almost the entirety of the international community. Louis XIV had the military capacity to invade the Spanish Netherlands, but doing so would risk the major diplomatic gains made by his brilliant teacher and minister, Cardinal Mazarin, and likely alienate his diplomatic partners. Nonetheless, he quickly began maneuvering.[8]

Louis tried to convince everyone that he would respect the existing peace treaty with Spain, but few believed him. When the Spanish ambassador, the Marquis de la Fuente, notified the French royal family of Philip IV's death, Louis began his deceptiveness. Queen Anne made him promise that he would not break the peace while she lived. The king ostensibly agreed and swore to guard the new king, Carlos II, as carefully as his own son. But as a diplomat observed, his mother's breast cancer was in an advanced state, and his promise would soon be invalid. Perhaps more tellingly, the campaigning season had ended, and he could wait until spring. He used the time to recruit an army and prepare a campaign, all the while insisting he was committed to preserving the peace. He also exploited the anxiety felt everywhere in Europe by periodically spreading rumors that Carlos II had died.[9]

EARLY DEFENSIVE STRATEGIES

Mariana's policies reveal no hesitation. Only five days into her reign, Mariana ordered a series of fortifications built in Catalonia, Aragon, and Navarre, enjoining her officials to proceed swiftly (*con celeridad*). She combined the Sicilian and Genoese galleys and placed them under General Pagan Doria's command. They arrived in Cadiz in October. She instructed the 7th Duke of Medinaceli, the captain general of the coasts and the ocean of Andalucía, to prepare the Andalusian coast for a French attack. Reinforcement of the Army of Flanders started immediately: a three-hundred-strong Castilian infantry force left for Flanders in October, and another several hundred Italian recruits left around the same time. She sent seventy thousand *escudos* to Flanders in October and another eighty thousand in December. The viceroy of Navarre, Francisco de Tuttavilla, Duke of San Germán, sent Spanish agents to Toulouse, Avignon, and Perpignan upon learning that France had dispatched five thousand infantry soldiers and a one-thousand-man cavalry force to Bayonne, close to Spain's northern frontier. Mariana sent money and men to the province of Guipúzcoa, in the Basque Country, as well. These were modest efforts as a result of the deficit, but they show Mariana's determination to respond quickly to the French threat.[10]

At the same time, Mariana entered a vertiginous period of diplomatic negotiations to confirm the marriage alliance with the Austrian Habsburgs. At the first formal meeting of the Junta de Gobierno, just one day after Philip's death, she asked the ministers to confirm Margarita's marriage to Leopold I, which they did. Five days later, Mariana sent her brother letters announcing her regency and urging him to raise an army to be deployed in case of a French attack. She included 152,625 *escudos* to raise a twenty-thousand-man army; Leopold I received an additional fifty thousand from Sicily. Mariana's regency was received very positively in Vienna. Count Johann Maximilian of Lamberg, one of the emperor's ministers, wrote to the governor of the Low Countries, the Marquis of Castel Rodrigo, that the imperial ministers "think that the death of the king of Spain brings more good than bad." They expected the Portuguese issue to be resolved, freeing up the men, matériel, and money being wasted "in such a useless pursuit" to go to Flanders. They also expected the Infanta Margarita's departure to take place sooner than it would have if the king were still alive.[11]

Leopold and his imperial ministers may have been positively inclined to Mariana's governorship, but they did not make the commitment Mariana hoped for. Answering her letters of September 1665, Leopold expressed pleasure at Mariana's dedication to the tutorship and the governorship, acknowledged her "exhortation" to protect their common interests, and thanked her for the money. He said Mariana should be secure in the "firmness of my affection," as "the causes of our Houses are one and the same," but he remained vague about military support, stating only, "I will assist Her Majesty and her son, with all that is in my power to protect the estates of Spain." He also asked for larger subsidies. The war with Portugal was another impediment to a military alliance, as Leopold feared he would have to shoulder the military burden in the Low Countries alone, since Spain was tied down on the Portuguese frontier. Mariana became frustrated: having sent money and seen no results, she requested an accounting of the "dispositions that the emperor has made on building a force, the number of troops, where they are located, and whether or not they would be ready, if necessary, to march to Flanders and Italy." Although Mariana and Leopold collaborated actively and effectively in the diplomatic arena, militarily he offered little.[12]

Whether Mariana had a grand design or simply recognized that a change of course was essential, she did not hesitate to act. She abandoned the effort to reconquer Portugal and began looking for new allies. Her diplomats had reported that most, if not all, Italian princes were pro-French and no alliances could be expected there. France had diplomatic advantages in the north as well. The League of the Rhine of 1657—a defensive coalition of dozens of German princes that limited the emperor's ability to assist Spain militarily—had isolated Spain diplomatically. Mariana took on the task of dissolving France's diplomatic advantages over Spain one by one.[13]

The first treaty of her regency, the Treaty of Peace and Commerce, was with England. Drafted by December 1665, it was modeled on one signed in 1630—before England's attack on Jamaica in 1655 placed the monarchies at war. Aside from confirming peace between the countries and granting English merchants permission to conduct limited trade with Spanish cities in Europe, secret clauses also designated King Charles II of England the mediator in a truce between Spain and Portugal. (Mariana needed an intermediary to negotiate a truce with the Portuguese because Spain could not establish direct diplomatic talks with rebel subjects.) Her choice of England was a deliberate move against Louis XIV, who was negotiating an offensive alliance with Portugal. The treaty with England, however, failed at the last moment because Charles II refused to ratify it on a technicality—the treaty was written in Spanish. The actual reason Charles II changed his mind is not clear; surely it was not the language. But Mariana continued to rely on Charles II as the potential mediator between Spain and Portugal. She offered the Portuguese a generous thirty-year truce.[14]

An alliance with the United Provinces was also a priority for Mariana, which she pursued despite many obstacles. The Peace of Münster (1648) ended the Eighty Years' War (1568–1648) between Spain and the Dutch, resulting in the United Provinces' independence. Friendly relations were established, but the Dutch were still suspicious of Spain. To make matters more difficult, the United Provinces traditionally allied with France and had a standing treaty with them. The future of the Spanish Netherlands had figured prominently in the last treaty between France and the United Provinces (1662), negotiated between Louis XIV and Johan de Witt, the grand pensionary of Holland and the United Provinces' highest official. De Witt made Louis XIV promise that no incursions in the Spanish Netherlands would take place unless both Philip IV and Carlos II had died. The Dutch were interested in keeping the status quo in areas affecting their own frontiers, but their negotiations with France also indicate the centrality of the Spanish succession in European politics. Mariana was concerned about whether the Dutch would remain neutral if Louis XIV invaded or enforced the terms of the Franco-Dutch treaty of 1662. She aggressively sought an alliance with the Dutch; aside from the existing difficulties, her efforts were further complicated by Spain's incipient collaboration with England.[15]

England and the United Provinces were at war. The Second Anglo-Dutch War (1665–67), fought over the control of trade routes and colonies, put Mariana in the delicate predicament of trying to make simultaneous alliances with rival powers. The Dutch learned, for example, that Charles II had requested permission to disembark in Spanish ports to attack them, and they begged Mariana not to allow it. "If we concede on the point, we risk angering the king of England, and perhaps lose him," Mariana noted in her instructions to her ambassador in The Hague, Don Esteban Gamarra, but "if we refuse," the Dutch would increase their suspicions. She instructed Gamarra to tell the Dutch regents—members of the United Provinces' oligarchy—that she was only collaborating with England to end the Portuguese conflict. She insisted that "Spain had for a very long time held a great desire to establish a league with the Dutch." She did not allow England to use Spanish ports, and although she had initially thought that the Anglo-Dutch War had benefits for Spain and instructed Gamarra to support the peace publicly but boycott it in secret, by January 1666, she had changed course.[16]

Mariana's choices about where to focus Spain's diplomatic strategies were good, but the initial results were mixed. The English ambassador, Sir Richard Fanshawe, returned from Lisbon in March 1666 with news that not only had Portugal rejected Spain's offer of a thirty-year truce, but it also demanded that negotiations take place "king to king"—that is, from the king of Spain to the king of Portugal. From the Spaniards' point of view, this was unconscionable: if Mariana agreed, Portugal's position as an independent kingdom would automatically be legitimized. The Council of State insisted that this could not happen. The Count of Peñaranda, with all his knowledge of foreign affairs, seniority in the council, and membership in the Junta de Gobierno, was categorical: "Your Majesty cannot even consider negotiating with Portugal from king to king." The Duke of Montalto, Mariana's beleaguered *mayordomo mayor*, referred to the proposal as "a monstrosity and an abominable sound to the ears of a subject." The council advised Mariana to share copies of Portugal's proposal with the imperial ambassador, anticipating that Leopold would not want Mariana even to "listen to such an indecent proposal." In a very real sense, Portugal's counteroffer brought Mariana back to where she started.[17]

Although Mariana could not resolve the Portuguese issue as swiftly as she had hoped, she could at least accelerate her daughter's departure to

Vienna. She had instituted an ad hoc committee to collect the enormous amount of money needed for the journey, which allowed her to expedite the departure. Shortly after the Portuguese counterproposal sent the court into near chaos, the marriage was celebrated by proxy on Easter Sunday, April 25, 1666, in the Madrid Alcázar; the entire court watched the historic ceremony. While Margarita's position as universal heiress of Carlos II raised the stakes of her marriage, Mariana saw her daughter's departure as a tool to secure Leopold I's military support in case of a French attack. Although she would miss her daughter "because I was so used to having her close to me at all times," Mariana did not hesitate. Margarita left for Vienna a few days after the ceremony.[18]

Despite the many benefits the marriage promised, sending the universal heiress outside Castile when the succession was not fully secured in the next generation was a controversial decision. It tied the future of the monarchy to the Austrian Habsburgs and thus incontrovertibly cast the politics of Madrid onto the international stage. With Margarita in Vienna, the theoretical scenarios of Philip IV's testament were closer to reality. It explains why Louis XIV began secret negotiations with Leopold I to split the Spanish inheritance between France and the empire if Carlos II died. Louis XIV had the military superiority and Leopold I the upper hand in terms of succession rights, so they needed to act in concert. But it was the women who had the actual succession rights. From this point of view, keeping Margarita in Madrid would have been preferable: Mariana was gambling that Leopold I would cooperate with Spain if France attacked.[19]

Margarita's marriage and subsequent departure highlighted Spain's tremendous anxiety about succession. Despite what has been assumed, Carlos II was not suffering from serious ailments; nonetheless, everyone knew children could die suddenly. Nithard noted in his memoirs that Spaniards loathed the thought of accepting a foreign ruler, even a Habsburg emperor, who was "deeply despised." Aside from these international considerations, many felt that the cost of Margarita's journey—1.5 million *escudos*—should have been spent on the army of Flanders or given to the emperor to raise an army to help his relatives. Leopold I may have been despised as a potential king of Spain, but he was expected to come to the defense of Spain if the French attacked. Mariana's gamble would pay off if Leopold offered substantial military support or if Margarita and Leopold had enough children to secure both the Spanish and the Austrian successions. In 1666, however, Margarita's departure from Madrid, together with Portugal's demand to negotiate peace "king to king," split Mariana's court and her government, inaugurating a bitter period of division.[20]

A DIVIDED COURT

On the Portuguese matter, Mariana was in favor of finding an immediate solution even if this meant negotiating "king to king." She was joined in this by men of stature: Duke Medina de las Torres, who, as the most senior member of the Council of State, had the right to speak first, and the well-respected Marquis of Aytona, a member of the Junta de Gobierno, were the most important. As a stateswoman, Mariana understood the necessity of resolving the Portuguese issue. As regent, however, her main task was protecting her son's inheritance. Indeed, the main obstacle to making peace was whether she had the right to forfeit such an important portion of her son's inheritance. To address this, Medina de las Torres suggested that if Carlos II wished, upon his majority he could reverse Mariana's decision, because it was signed on his behalf rather than by him. The solution was not sufficient to appease those—the majority of the court—who thought that conceding on this issue compromised Spain's reputation. This principle of foreign policy led to massive military commitments and overseas expenditures to maintain Spain's position as the leading state. It had been the driving force of the Spanish Habsburgs, particularly during Philip IV's reign, when the Count-Duke of Olivares was a major influence.[21]

Mariana's first move was to create a three-member ad hoc committee—called the Junta de Inglaterra because of England's role as mediator—to handle the negotiations with Portugal. The members were Medina de las Torres and Peñaranda, the leaders of each side, and Nithard. The committee's first meeting with the English ambassador took place on July 9, 1666. Their reports were sent to Mariana, who periodically forwarded them to the Council of State. The extensive deliberations for and against independence produced an enormous amount of paperwork, indicating what a divisive—and dominant—issue it was. Although some of the arguments against peace were sound—Peñaranda was adamant about losing commercial ties with the East Indies—the reality was that the war was lost, and prolonging it was reckless. Thus the issue was when to accept the inevitable.[22]

The debate took place in the Council of State but was not secret or contained within the council. Individual opinions, such as that of Medina de las Torres and Aytona, who was not even a member of the Council of State, circulated as manuscripts and were widely read by members of the court and foreign dignitaries. To this already semipublic debate were added the voices of the men married to Carlos II's sisters, Leopold I and Louis XIV. Imperial and French representatives lobbied individual ministers of the Council of State, the first advocating peace, the second war, which is why proponents of the peace are sometimes referred to as pro-Habsburgs and those opposed as pro-French. But this oversimplistic division obscures the real ideological battle inside the Council of State and the rest of the councils, which were involved in the debate because Mariana requested general votes on the matter. The Councils of Castile, War, Aragon, Flanders, Portugal, Knighthood, and Finance voted against the peace; the Council of Indies was undecided; the Council of Italy was divided; and except for Medina de las Torres and the Duke of Alburquerque, the majority in the Council of State was also against independence.[23]

Ministers of the Council of State were asked to write memos recording their position and its rationale. Medina de las Torres's opinion stands out because the approach he articulated was a significant shift from that of the previous four decades. Mariana was under no obligation to recover a kingdom that was effectively lost, he said; her responsibility was to *conserve* the rest of the territories. She should not, therefore, "risk all to regain a part." A policy based on *reputación* (reputation) had led the monarchy to near ruin; moreover, it was based on faulty logic. As Medina de las Torres put it, "The real reputation of monarchies does not consist of appearances based on vanity" but on "the actual security of subjects, the conservation of kingdoms, the expansion of power, the respect with which other princes look to its authority, as well as the fear its armies inspire." Many great kingdoms—the Roman Empire and medieval Castile, as well as contemporary powers such as France, the papacy, and the Holy Roman Empire—had tolerated great losses in order to preserve the bulk of their estates without losing prestige. His lengthy opinion was persuasive, but his opinion was only shared by the Marquis of Aytona. Nonetheless, it was this approach that reverberated in Mariana's policy in the coming two years, not Nithard's, who was actually against a permanent peace with Portugal.[24]

Mariana's insistence that the matter be debated suggests that she expected the reports that Louis XIV had mobilized large infantry and cavalry forces to change opinions. Such reports arrived regularly in Madrid between July and December 1666. While Mariana's councilors stalled and pursued other diplomatic solutions, she was engaged in a diplomatic battle with Louis XIV over who would have the support of England and the United Provinces. Louis XIV tempted Charles II with subsidies and territorial gains if he joined or remained neutral while France attacked the Spanish Netherlands. But Mariana's diplomats, including the Spanish ambassador in London, Antonio de Tobar y Paz, Count of Molina, and the imperial ambassador in London, Baron Franz Paul of Lisola, cultivated parliamentarians. Charles II and Parliament were at odds over what course to follow. If England allied with France, a war with Spain was likely, and with it the loss of the commercial concessions to English merchants. The pro-Spanish senior secretary of state, Henry Bennet, 1st Earl of Arlington, and a network of support from members of Parliament greatly helped Mariana's cause. From Brussels, the governor of the Spanish Netherlands, the Marquis of Castel Rodrigo, supported the Spanish faction in England, cultivating the support of Sir William Temple, who played a decisive role in the ensuing diplomatic maneuvers.[25]

Nevertheless, it was not easy for Mariana and Charles II to come to an understanding. He wanted more commercial concessions than Mariana was willing to grant, and she wanted more diplomatic concessions than he was willing to offer. If he acquiesced to Spain's request for neutrality, England would be in opposition to France, and Louis XIV was offering Charles II subsidies and potential conquests. Molina pled, "So long as Your Majesty refuses to sign the treaty, the king will listen to France's propositions." Rumors of a planned Anglo-French attack on Santo Domingo reached Mariana in March 1667; they made her reconsider. The Treaty of Peace and Commerce that had failed in December 1665 was finally signed on May 23, 1667. It allowed English and Spanish merchants to navigate, buy, sell, and exchange goods without fear of confiscation in their respective maritime jurisdictions in Europe. The treaty did not stipulate anything about American waters, a topic on which it was purposely silent. The secret clauses that stipulated that neither party could assist their respective enemies—that is, Charles II's neutrality—were a major victory for

Mariana. England began mediating a new round of negotiations between Spain and Portugal. Independence was not on the table, and neither was the concession of negotiating "king to king," but Mariana was now offering Portugal a forty-five-year truce.[26]

Mariana's efforts to win the United Provinces to Spain's side were equally intense. At the same time she was negotiating the treaty with Charles, the imperial and Spanish ambassadors in London, the Baron of Lisola and the Count of Molina, were planning a secret journey to The Hague to end the Second Anglo-Dutch War in order to get the warring parties on board to defend the Spanish Netherlands. Lisola carried a personal letter from Charles II to the grand pensionary stating that the English monarch had already accepted the emperor's mediation; he urged de Witt to do likewise. "I believe Your Majesty will be well pleased," Molina wrote to Mariana in April 1667. "From this journey we can expect all advantages," the principal one of which was "disrupting the Most Christian King's primary aims."[27]

Meanwhile, Mariana received good news from Vienna. Margarita's royal entry was spectacularly staged. A Hungarian guard of 1,500 horsemen, a German one of 1,000 men, all the gentlemen of the bedchamber, ministers of state, members of the Order of the Golden Fleece, and Margarita's Spanish and German entourages followed the imperial couple. According to the newly appointed Spanish ambassador to Vienna, Baltasar de la Cueva, Count of Castellar, the *infanta-emperatriz* was adapting well. The couple was clearly compatible; within months of her arrival, by March 1667, Margarita had stopped wearing the *guardainfantes* and was being carried on a chair. Although associated with pregnancies, the garment's waist was so constrictive that it was dangerous for pregnant women, so this change essentially announced Margarita's pregnancy. Given the testamentary clauses and the dynastic configuration, this was an international event. The elaborate display upon Margarita's arrival, coupled with the resurgence of Spanish plays and culture and Margarita's pregnancy, showed Europe that the two Habsburg lines shared a single future.[28]

After eighteen months in power, Mariana's small victories meant that the future looked brighter than might have been expected at the start of her regency. Margarita's pregnancy advertised the closeness of Spain and the empire and vindicated Mariana's decision to send her to Vienna. The Treaty of Peace and Commerce with England had been signed, and a new round of negotiations with Portugal was under way. Major progress had been made in ending the Anglo-Dutch War, a critical step in negotiating a coalition with both powers. Yet before Mariana could be ready, Louis XIV showed his cards.

THE FRENCH THREAT BECOMES REALITY

During the spring of 1667, the Spanish ambassador in Paris, the Marquis de la Fuente, sent unequivocal reports indicating that the opening of hostilities was imminent. With the death of the queen mother, Anne of Austria, in January 1666, Spain had no sympathizers in the French court. De la Fuente explained that the queen consort, Maria Theresa, could not be asked to intervene, as it would put her in a severely compromised position. Hoping to stir public protest against the war or perhaps even trigger an uprising, de la Fuente commissioned and distributed two publications written with "venom in each point" and made to look as if they had originated in France. But the war was unstoppable. His last dispatch before war broke out estimated the number of French troops at between seventy and eighty thousand. If Mariana hoped to come to an agreement with Portugal before the attack, Louis XIV had effectively put an insurmountable obstacle in her path. He concluded a ten-year offensive and defensive league with Portugal, which ended hopes for a truce between Spain and Portugal. Worse, he invited "all princes who want to enter it, particularly the king of England," to do so.[29]

On May 17, 1667, the French ambassador in Madrid, the archbishop D'Embrun, went to the palace with a mission so contrary to what he had been adamantly saying for months that he felt the need to apologize before his audience with the queen. "You must think that I am the most despicable clergyman and the most wretched man," he told the Duke of Alba. "Two days ago I zealously defended my king against accusations of his intentions and today here I stand with a declaration of war [in my hand]." He presented Mariana with two letters—one from Louis XIV and one from Maria Theresa—and a treatise expounding the legal justification of the claim to Habsburg territories in the Low Countries: the opening salvo in what history calls the War of Devolution (1667–68). The treatise argued that as the oldest daughter of Philip IV's first marriage, Maria Theresa was the rightful heiress to the Duchy of Brabant and other territories in the Low Countries. The duchy's laws gave inheritance precedence to children of the first marriage over all children born of a subsequent marriage, and therefore the territories had "devolved" to Maria Theresa. The document also stated that her renunciation was caused by paternal and royal pressure and had been against her will.[30]

Louis XIV demanded that Mariana cede the territories or face an attack by the end of the month. The notice was much shorter than the six months specified in the Treaty of the Pyrenees; he justified the violation by saying that the messages his mother sent to Madrid in the summer of 1665 when Philip IV was terminally ill counted as having warned the Spanish court. It was Mariana who had received those communications and rejected the proposition to cede the territories upon Philip IV's death. Mariana later argued that this exchange had occurred between family members and could hardly qualify as an official announcement of war. Nevertheless, this is exactly what Louis XIV did, stating that Mariana had been informed of his intentions but had refused to consider his claims. He also stated that she had provoked him by extracting an oath of allegiance to Carlos from subjects in the Low Countries. The entire justification of the war was an affront to Mariana's position as wife and mother, suggesting as it did that the children of her husband's first marriage had precedence over her own children. Despite all her work to prepare for a "wicked, hateful, and ill-timed attack," as the Council of State described it, Mariana had not achieved a truce with Portugal and now faced the possibility of fighting two simultaneous wars. But the positive outcome of Louis XIV's declaration was that her court was now wholly behind her, freeing her to lead without fear of repercussions.[31]

"I HAVE FOUND HER MAJESTY NOT AT ALL DISTURBED"

Mariana convened an extraordinary meeting of the Council of State, which met all day on May 18, 1667, to devise military and financial strategies. Aside from Louis XIV's declaration of war, with the accompanying treatise, they considered seven letters penned by Castel Rodrigo from April 29, two from de la Fuente from May 1 and 5, and two from Gamarra from April 28. The divisions over Portugal had evaporated overnight. Peñaranda, the most vocal opponent of granting Portugal its independence, stated that it was the "only means to face this challenge" and should be pursued "at any price and in any form." Montalto, another vocal opponent, reminded his colleagues,

"It is most fitting of great monarchs to accommodate to the times." He pointed out that a similar solution had been found in Münster in 1648, when Spain granted the United Provinces independence.[32]

Concluding that the onset of hostilities was "unequivocal and certain," the councilors expressed complete loyalty to Mariana and her son. The great military general who had led the Spanish armies against Portugal, the Marquis of Caraçena, stated that Mariana possessed not just the justification but actually the "obligation to defend the rights of the King, Her son." He pledged his person and his wealth to this endeavor: "I would not refuse to serve with a pike in my hand, in whenever place would be of the greatest service of Your Majesty." Montalto denounced Louis XIV's actions as despicable acts of ambition, stating that instead of respecting "the widowhood and saintly mission of Your Majesty," as a Christian prince should, he "found in both incentives to implement his grandiose designs." Medina de las Torres advised "fearless resistance" (*gallarda resistencia*) against France.[33]

This was a critical moment for Mariana. She was facing the much larger armies of Louis XIV with inadequate forces and without major allies. On the other hand, now she could implement her policies without the Portuguese dilemma blocking her efforts. She rose to the occasion without hesitation, making difficult decisions about military, financial, and diplomatic strategy swiftly. Her councilors provided expert advice, and she followed it as she saw fit. "I have found Her Majesty not at all disturbed," Pötting reported after seeing her on May 18. He was shocked by Mariana's seeming indifference, not realizing that she had been preparing for this moment from the regency's beginning.[34]

Mariana's response to the Council of State was clear: "With an accident of such magnitude, it is imperative to spare no efforts to respond to the Most Christian King's so utterly unjust and untimely action." After stating that she had ordered fervent prayers to call for divine intervention, she laid out her strategies. She rejected Peñaranda's proposition to use the pope as an intermediary, stating that Charles II's mediation was "the most expedient way" to conclude the treaty with Portugal. She declared her intention to seek alliances with the English and Dutch "with particular application" and said she would seek alliances as well with princes of the empire and the king of Sweden. She hoped that Leopold I would lead an army against France through Alsace with Swedish troops as reinforcements and affirmed that "no efforts will be spared" to further that goal: "My brother and the Marquis of Castel Rodrigo," she said, "will be assisted with the maximum amount of money possible as this important matter requires."[35]

The question of how to finance the war posed dilemmas, but Mariana was quick to resolve them. Medina de las Torres and Peñaranda, seconded by others, had suggested that she convoke the Cortes, or parliaments, to request funds. This was a common procedure, but it was slow, and Mariana rejected the idea, calling the process "expensive, inconvenient, and of little benefit." In order to procure "all possible [financial] means in substantial quantities and at once," she continued, "I have requested all councils to prepare a report without any delay on the means that can be used in this difficult moment."[36]

She requested donations from cities, particularly Madrid, and anyone with means, including "grandees, ministers, and rich vassals," urging everyone to collect as much money as possible. Cardinal Aragón and Father Nithard sided with her, both expressly opposing the levy of additional taxes through the Cortes, but so did Aytona. Her opposition to the levy has been seen as a sign that she was dominated by her confessor, but it reflects a policy she put into action at the beginning of her reign to spread the fiscal burden more equally. Mariana had been streamlining expenditures via a gradual reduction of personnel and elimination of corrupt practices since 1666. In a context of war, additional reductions of expenses became much more imperative. Mariana announced that they were "working ceaselessly" to rebuild the army of Flanders, which required money. Promising "to lead by example," she indicated that "the first reforms will take place in the royal households, for which a special committee has been formed." She eliminated nonessential expenses such as double salaries and "excessive emoluments and gifts." Additional monies came from the silver fleets that began to arrive more regularly and with larger cargoes, but it is no small matter that war was fought without levying additional taxes through the Cortes.[37]

Other early initiatives also paid off. Mariana had sent companies to the Low Countries from August 1666 to February 1667 to form the first Spanish *tercio* for the army of Flanders since 1659. Aytona had been recruiting since January 1666 in Castile. Additional efforts were ongoing in Italy; recruits from Naples and Milan embarked for Flanders in January and February despite transportation delays (a problem Mariana resolved a few months later); they arrived by May 1667. She placed the viceroys of Sicily and

Cerdeña under the command of the viceroy of Naples and ordered them to better coordinate their actions. The Spanish force was still much smaller than France's, but Antonio José Rodríguez Hernández's 2008 study shows that Castel Rodrigo had about twenty thousand infantry and seven thousand cavalry by 1667, double the number of the army of Flanders at the beginning of the regency.[38]

Mariana began developing effective rhetoric to defend her cause, depicting herself as a mother trying to defend Carlos II's rightful inheritance. She presented Louis XIV's actions as inexcusable and called for the international community to support her. "The Most Christian King's resolution," she wrote, "requires that all representatives" of other powers at her court "should be informed of the unjust attack [*atentado*] against this monarchy." The word *atentado* has a very negative connotation, suggesting that Louis XIV's attack was reprehensible in the extreme. In addition, she had her ministers draft letters to the pope, the College of Cardinals, and other European rulers protesting the French king's actions.[39]

Mariana's response to Louis XIV was firm, making it clear that she would not be intimidated. She acknowledged the correspondence in which he put his claim and threat to attack if she did not acquiesce to his demands, stating, "I did not want to delay responding to the said letter to express the great shock that such a scheme has caused me" (*no sin gran admiración de la novedad que me ha hecho semejante designio*). She contested Louis XIV's excuse to launch an attack before the conventions of the treaty allowed: "For even though Your Majesty suggests that the Most Christian Queen, my sister, now in God's glory, hinted to the Marquis de la Fuente, and I indeed recall that he wrote to me about that. . . . I only attributed it to a domestic and confidential conversation that was never made with the proper formality of ambassador or minister of Your Majesty, nor in his royal name." (Mariana was Queen Anne's niece; their mothers were sisters. But as queen consort to Philip IV, conventions in letter writing among fellow monarchs made her Queen Anne's "sister.") "Clause 90 of the Peace Treaty [of the Pyrenees]," she pointed out, "requires that such matters were to be resolved in the court of law, not with arms, and through amicable means of justice." She hoped that he would follow this procedure and was ready to accept such a judgment, knowing that she would have won such judgment. Although her response had conciliatory moments, she made it clear where she stood. If Louis XIV was not willing to use legal mediation to resolve the problem, she said, "I will be obligated by my conscience and the ministry of the Royal Tutorship of the King my Son to defend his rights with the same [violent] means [you employ]." The monarchy may not have been ready to wage a full-scale war on France, but Mariana was not ready to accept defeat.[40]

France's declaration of war was a litmus test for evaluating where intra-Habsburg relations truly stood. Had Mariana been right to rely on her brother? The Council of State met on June 21 to discuss a report from the Spanish ambassador, the Count of Castellar, describing the general mood of the imperial court as war became ever more certain. Whereas Leopold I was concerned about Spain's interests, "there [were] other reasons that incline[d] him to keep the ... peace [with France]." There was little chance the emperor would intervene unless Mariana sent two hundred thousand *escudos* and an additional twenty-five thousand monthly in subsidies. It appeared that all the money Mariana had already sent counted for nothing. Worse yet, although he controlled a force of twelve thousand men, Leopold was reluctant to mobilize it for the current year's campaigning season. Castellar concluded, "It will be difficult to expect reciprocity on his part unless Mariana sent all that was promised and all that is necessary."[41]

This news immediately reopened the divisions within the Council of State. Medina de las Torres argued that sending money to the emperor was imperative, but Peñaranda countered that money had already been sent, and still the emperor showed no signs of action. It was at this moment that Mariana invited Philip IV's illegitimate son, Don Juan of Austria, into Council of State deliberations. He had extensive military experience, and while Mariana had earlier refused his requests to reside permanently in Madrid and attend Council of State deliberations, the war required all hands on deck. Don Juan's presence on the council was helpful. He counterbalanced Peñaranda's strong criticisms of the emperor and supported sending additional funds. Although Mariana had taken a chance at the beginning of her regency with Leopold—sending him money and her daughter to cement the alliance—she hoped to change his mind without additional concessions. The funds she had at her disposal—seventy-thousand *escudos*—Mariana sent to Castel Rodrigo for the army of Flanders, not to Leopold. Mariana exerted pressure on Leopold, relying on Cardinal Aragón to present her case to the Count of Pötting, hoping to prompt Leopold to action. She also resorted to the Habsburg practice of writing of "her own hand" to her brother. These special kinds of letters were believed to be effective to obtain a desired diplomatic outcome, which is why councilors had suggested Mariana write to Leopold personally. Mariana utilized all the diplomatic tools available to her to get Leopold on board.[42]

Castellar's subsequent report from Vienna was even bleaker. Empress Margarita had "burst into tears" upon learning that Louis XIV had declared war on her brother, Carlos II, indicating that she was aware of the gravity of the situation. Emperor Leopold and his ministers had a very different reaction, actually doubting the accuracy of the reports. This indifference was infuriating but made worse when Castellar discovered that the reality of the war was accepted in the imperial court only when French representative Chevalier Jacques Bretel de Grémonville confirmed it upon receipt of letters from France. Within days, Castellar discovered that Louis XIV had told the emperor that helping Spain would be considered an act of war against France. The ambassador launched an intense writing campaign that accused Leopold and his ministers of "indifference during the most dangerous moment for the monarchy." Although he was a fierce advocate for Spanish interests, Castellar's confrontational style caused considerable difficulties for Spain. Leopold repeatedly asked Mariana to recall him, but Castellar remained in Vienna until 1670.[43]

Castellar's discouraging account inaugurated a new wave of controversy in Madrid. Peñaranda delivered a scathing reproach of the emperor, saying, "The lukewarm attitude with which this critical business has been received in the imperial court is nothing new." The truth was that "ministers of the emperor [were] not, and never [had] been, for many years . . . , inclined to defend the interests of the August House of Habsburg but only interested in their own positions." His list of grievances against Mariana's German relatives went back to the election of Leopold I in 1657–58, which had been pushed through by Philip IV. In Peñaranda's view, Leopold's lack of gratitude was outrageous, since Philip IV had ensured the election by paying "enormous amounts of money to the electors of Saxony, Treveris, Bavaria, and Brandenburg." He added that though it was "an extremely delicate proposition" to declare war on behalf of someone else, Philip III had done just that in 1619, when Spain came to the aid of the Austrian Habsburgs after Bohemia revolted at the onset of the Thirty Years' War. Nor could Leopold complain about money, given that Mariana had sent him money for the army and "spent 1.5 million [escudos]" to pay for Margarita's journey. Even listening to France's proposal of neutrality was "insolent," and it was beyond

Peñaranda's understanding why the French envoy had not been expelled from Leopold's court. He concluded by advising Mariana to demand the immediate expulsion of Louis XIV's representative in Vienna and to write to the emperor "in the strongest possible terms that Her Royal Prudence would allow."[44]

Diplomatically, this was the lowest point of Mariana's regency, as it made it clear that her decision to send Margarita to Vienna had not achieved what had been expected. Mariana acknowledged that Spain had incurred enormous "expenses in support of the empire" and hoped that the emperor would "show the reciprocity that I expect of him in this present state of affairs." She announced her intention to write to her brother in "her own hand" but admitted that other than emphasizing the need for cooperation, not much else could be done. It took Mariana five more years to forge the kind of alliance she had expected in 1667.[45]

In the meantime, Mariana worked on other fronts. The news from Vienna meant that the Portuguese issue was, she stated, "the principal and most important business of the moment and [one that] must be placed above all others." While Peñaranda had indirectly chastised Mariana for her brother's lack of action, Mariana vented her frustration about the Council of State's and Peñaranda's hard-line Portugal policy. She admitted, "[To] voluntarily alienate a kingdom, and to attract with that action disrepute, is extremely painful, and in spite of the necessity and the risk of losing it all, I can hardly be satisfied with the final decision." But "if we had given them hope two years ago," she lamented, "we would be in a much better position now" and would probably have avoided the "costs, difficulties, and risks that we are currently facing." By this she meant Portugal's offensive alliance with France, indicating that to settle with Portugal, she would have to break that alliance.[46]

Mariana was unrelenting in her drive to defend the Spanish Netherlands from Louis XIV's claims. She used her jewels to secure loans to rebuild the army of Flanders and liquidated other royal jewels to pay for domestic expenses. Reprisals and embargoes on incoming French goods as well as the confiscation of the property and goods of French subjects in "all the ports of these kingdoms" commenced on August 27. Fortunately, as mentioned, the size of the silver remittance from the New World increased substantially in 1667 and 1668, reversing the prior downward trend. The governor of the

Low Countries received seventy-thousand *escudos* with the last ordinary courier in May 1667; the embassies of London and The Hague received an immediate cash remittance of sixteen thousand *escudos*. And as Mariana informed her councilors, "We are endeavoring to conclude *asientos* of much greater quantities": she was in the midst of negotiating a loan of two million pounds from the United Provinces for the war efforts and "to assist Gamarra and other ministers in foreign courts."[47]

The same resolve marked Mariana's military strategies. She needed to allocate her funds where they would yield the best results. She charged her ministers to find out what, if anything, "my brother would be able to do if we supplied the funds, whether we did so fully or partially, and if he was, in one case or the other, willing to break with France." "We will decide the most appropriate course," she said, "depending on his response." Rejecting the suggestions of the Council of State that Cadiz be the embarkation point for troops, she noted that Cadiz had proven inefficient in transporting Italian recruits and moved military operations to the north. Also for expediency, she hired privateers, "men with smaller ships but very knowledgeable of the north seas," to attack enemy ships immediately; this strategy turned out to be quite effective.[48]

The frontiers with France needed immediate attention. The viceroy of Navarre had already predicted a long siege in Fuenterrabía and attacks in San Sebastian; Mariana sent money to reinforce fortifications and ensure a steady supply of men. By levying troops directly in the north, the Basque Country and Galicia, Mariana reduced transportation delays. These areas, particularly Galicia, which was "very densely populated" and as such critical for recruitment, also became essential in intelligence gathering and shipbuilding. While the initial campaigns in the summer of 1667 had been overwhelmingly advantageous for Louis XIV, Spain's mobilization of men and arms and rapid responses ended the string of French victories in September 1667. The Marquis de la Fuente informed Madrid that Spain's armies in Flanders had caused France to lose at least five thousand "of its most flowering youth and up to fifteen people of higher rank."[49]

But these successes did not mean that Spain could win on its own. As it prepared to fight what Peñaranda eloquently described as a hereditary and perpetual war against the French, who "will always be the sworn enemies of this Crown," Mariana endeavored to find allies.[50]

IN SEARCH OF COALITION PARTNERS

From the war's beginning to the end of her regency, Mariana's main goal was to form a multipower coalition against France. When she eventually succeeded with the Triple Alliance of April 25, 1668, among England, the United Provinces, and Sweden, it was instrumental in ending the War of Devolution. While Spain was not a signatory, the alliance came out of Mariana's coalition-building efforts with England and the Dutch. Its formation began to take shape with the unofficial suspension of the war in September 1667. As the armies took a break for the winter, diplomatic maneuvers in anticipation of the coming campaigns intensified. The War of Devolution was a major reason that England and the United Provinces concluded the Peace of Breda, ending the Second Anglo-Dutch War on July 31, 1667.

Spanish and imperial diplomats had done everything in their power to push for Leopold I as the official mediator of that peace to prevent Louis XIV from taking the role. Being a mediator in a peace congress provided many advantages and prestige, as the prince who took on the role could establish a collaborative relationship with the powers under his mediation. While England and the United Provinces rejected the emperor's mediation, they also rejected Louis XIV's, instead choosing Sweden as the intermediary; the Queen Regent Hedwig Eleonora took over the mediation. This was considered a small diplomatic victory for Spanish and imperial diplomats.[51]

As soon as England and the United Provinces concluded the peace, Spain and the United Provinces began discussing the possibility of creating a defensive alliance against France with England as the third party. De Witt, the Dutch grand pensionary, indicated his willingness to come to the defense of the Spanish Netherlands. Talks started in The Hague, eventually moving to London. Mariana broached the prospect of expanding the neutrality agreement Spain currently had with England—part of the secret clauses of the Treaty of Peace and Commerce of 1667—into a more active military collaboration. In the ensuing talks, Mariana's diplomats began to articulate Mariana's wish for Charles II to become "[her] friend of friends and [her] enemy of enemies" (*amigo de amigos y enemigo de enemigos*), which meant that she wanted a defensive and offensive league against France. Although the two monarchies had as long a history of diplomatic collaboration as of rivalry, an offensive alliance was unprecedented in Anglo-Spanish relations. The new scheme entailed a military alliance with a Protestant king against a Catholic one, and Mariana had to find the right justification. She appointed Nithard to lead a Junta de Teólogos, an ad hoc committee of nine theologians, plus Peñaranda, the only secular member, to consult on whether she could take such a step. The committee produced a long, learned, and convoluted argument that gave Mariana the justification to "ally with heretics." The paper contended that an alliance with the "heretics" of England would save Catholicism because only a territorially integral Spain could save the Catholic cause on the continent and in the colonies. But even before Nithard submitted the final consultation, Mariana had already asked the Councils of Finance, Indies, War, and State to decide just how much Spain could offer to Charles II in subsidies and under what conditions; in the meantime, Molina negotiated with Charles II's senior secretary of state, the 1st Earl of Arlington.[52]

Although Nithard's theological disquisition focused on England, Mariana sought alliances with many Protestant powers, including Brandenburg, Sweden, Denmark, and Norway, and small principalities in Central Europe. As she told her councilors in November 1667, it was the "best security that we could conceive of to defend the Low Countries." Castel Rodrigo concluded an agreement with the elector of Brandenburg in early November: the bishop-elector pledged eight thousand infantry and four thousand cavalry for the 1668 campaigns, which meant the French would not win all next years' campaigns as easily as they had in 1667. Mariana had not been able to get Leopold's military support, but she could count on his diplomatic help. Leopold I approached Sweden, stating that an alliance would be "of utmost convenience for the two august lines." Mariana quickly gave plenipotentiary rights to Castel Rodrigo in Brussels, Molina in London, and Gamarra in The Hague to negotiate "a league with the king of Sweden." In the next years, she began active diplomatic negotiations with Denmark and Norway as well. All these powers—Sweden, Brandenburg, the United Provinces, and England—had been France's allies. Mariana's strategies, therefore, marked a shift in Spain's foreign policy and on the continent more widely.[53]

These alliances, however, depended to a large extent on Mariana's ability to resolve the conflict with Portugal. The United Provinces as well as other potential allies were skeptical about Spain's ability to contribute to its own defenses, since its resources were tied up in the Portuguese conflict. By the summer of 1667, Mariana was ready to resolve the situation. Negotiations—with independence now on the table—began behind

France's back. A coup in Lisbon, however, delayed the process. On September 3, Peter, Duke of Beja, the younger brother of King Afonso VI, in conjunction with the queen consort, Maria Francisca of Savoy-Nemours, who
accused her husband of impotency, declared the Portuguese king incapable
of ruling. Not much is known about this episode or whether France was
behind it, but it resulted in annulment proceedings and the establishment
of a regency government under Peter. It was not clear how the new regime
would align on the war issue.[54]

Working with the Earl of Sandwich, Charles II's representative at the
peace congress and his ambassador in Madrid, Mariana continued to push
for peace between Spain and Portugal. The queen "intensely desires a final
accommodation with Portugal," the secretary noted in the instructions for
Spain's representative in the congress. Sandwich received the draft of the
peace settlement, in which Mariana stated that the "difficulties of the past
had been overcome" and that she was now ready for a permanent resolution of the conflict. He also had a copy of the plenipotentiary rights dispatched for the Marquis of Carpio (Medina de las Torres's son), who was
held in Lisbon as a prisoner of war. Carpio had free reign to grant Portugal
unconditional independence; he also had instructions to seek an alliance
between Spain and Portugal against France. By December, reports from
Lisbon indicated that peace was almost a foregone conclusion; pro-Spanish
members of the Portuguese court were expected to prevail over the pro-
French faction in the forthcoming convocation of the Portuguese Cortes,
or parliaments.[55]

With peace with Portugal now a concrete possibility, the defensive
and offensive alliance Mariana wanted with England and the Dutch could
move forward. Negotiations to forge a Triple Alliance among England,
the United Provinces, and Spain began in October 1667. The Spanish and
imperial ambassadors in London, Molina and Lisola, began negotiations
with the two extraordinary—the special title given to ambassadors sent to a
foreign court for a specific purpose—Dutch ambassadors de Witt had sent
to London: John Meerman and John Boreel. They held five conferences
with Charles II's representatives between October and December 1667.
Well informed about these maneuvers, Louis XIV sent his own diplomats
to London, led by the Marquis of Ruvigni. London soon became the stage
of a diplomatic war between the French and Spanish as they raced to bribe
and entertain members of Parliament; despite the monarchy's financial

difficulties, Mariana kept the Spanish embassy in London well provisioned. It was not clear who would prevail in the diplomatic war, especially since neutrality was all France needed to derail Mariana's plans.[56]

Spanish diplomats may have been the ones who leaked the content of the conferences to the French ambassador, hoping to sow discord between France and the United Provinces. If so, the price Spain paid for this move was high. When he realized that a coalition was potentially forming against him, Louis XIV preempted it by proposing a path to peace later known as the "alternatives." He offered Spain two options: either accept all French conquests made during the previous campaign or cede equivalent territories, such as Luxembourg or Franche-Comté, as a condition for ending the war. Although his demands were substantially diminished from the initial purpose of the war, in either case, Louis XIV still wanted Mariana to recognize Maria Theresa's legal rights to these lands. The introduction of a solution based on one of the "alternatives" derailed Mariana's scheme for an offensive league against France with England and the Dutch on her side. Charles II initially refused the "alternatives" proposition, dismissing it as dishonorable. But the Dutch took a more conciliatory stance, viewing the "alternative solution" as a path out of the war that was acceptable to them. When the Dutch officially presented the alternatives to Mariana, they told her that they wanted Spain to accept the solution proposed by France. According to Molina, the English king did everything in his power to bring the Dutch back to the original project of a Triple Alliance with Spain but was unsuccessful.[57]

Mariana found the demand preposterous, protesting that the Dutch regents were imposing "such unequal conditions on both parties." She reminded them that it was the "Most Christian king who . . . violated the faith and rights of the poor people who inhabit those states, and, shockingly [escandalosamente], invaded the territory [the Spanish Netherlands] that belong to a minor king [Carlos II]." The Dutch remained firm, but so did she. In early 1668, she rejected the proposal outright, stating, "I'd rather lose the Low Countries with the sword in hand, than submit to the ignominy of French law." She also refused a two-million-pound loan from the United Provinces, as she found the conditions—de Witt wanted Spain to pawn the Port of Ostend and other towns, allowing the Dutch to occupy them until Spain discharged its debt—unacceptable. Mariana's refusal of Louis XIV's "alternatives" proposal prompted the king to invade the Franche-Comté in January 1668. Military action was unusual in winter, and Louis explicitly said it was done "to incline Spain to conclude the peace." Louis XIV easily occupied the duchy, but Mariana did not move from her initial position.[58]

Mariana's stubbornness was a matter of principle but also a response to the way her situation had improved. In January 1668, Mariana sent six hundred thousand *escudos* in letters of credit and one million *reales de a ocho* worth of silver bars to Castel Rodrigo in Brussels for the army of Flanders. This substantial amount portended well for the next campaign season. Recruitment increased substantially early in 1668, allowing for a constant flow of troops to the north. Furthermore, while Louis XIV invaded the Franche-Comté in February 1668, Mariana's plenipotentiaries were concluding the Treaty of Lisbon. Portugal was now independent, and Spain was free of a war. The cessation of hostilities allowed Spain to redirect resources and made Mariana's potential allies more favorably disposed toward her regime. Mariana also counted on Brandenburg's commitment of a twelve thousand-man army for the next year's campaign. Leopold was also expected to finally make good on his obligations.[59]

Emboldened by these positive developments, Mariana launched a new initiative to bring the Dutch to her side. As soon as news of the Portuguese peace reached her, she urged Gamarra "to negotiate more forcefully and influence the outcome of the pending negotiations." But the alliance Mariana sought did not turn out. Neither England nor the Dutch wanted an alliance with Spain because it would mean war with France. There was a desire to stop Louis XIV's invasion of the Spanish Netherlands—no one wanted to see him too powerful—but there was also a desire to do so with the least possible military intervention. Mariana was unable to get Spain as a named partner in an alliance against France, but the Triple Alliance of 1668—among England, the United Provinces, and Sweden—was an effective alternative, as we will see.[60]

The Triple Alliance originated with the governor of the Spanish Netherlands. The Marquis of Castel Rodrigo began maneuvers by working with Sir William Temple, the English resident in Brussels and a major figure in the conclusion of the agreement. Temple left Brussels on a secret mission to The Hague; the key to understanding the subsequent events lies in the reports of a private audience Temple had with Castel Rodrigo immediately before his departure in late December. When he got to The Hague, Temple, following Castel Rodrigo's plan, began ultrasecret negotiations with de Witt, obtaining de Witt's approval to conclude an alliance between England and the Dutch. Under the guise of family business, Temple traveled to London and returned to The Hague with plenipotentiary rights from Charles II. On January 23, 1668, in a matter of weeks, de Witt and Temple concluded an alliance. Castel Rodrigo described the maneuvers preceding Temple's mission as part of a *"coup de grâce* that [they had] been plotting."[61]

England and the United Provinces agreed to join forces to "procure peace between the Catholic monarchs and the Most Christian King." The confederation foresaw a peace based on these conditions: Spain would accept one of the "alternatives" proposed by France. France would abide by Spain's choice, return territories that were not part of the agreement, and commit to an immediate cease-fire. If Spain did not agree to the conditions, it would be compelled by military force to do so. France was prevented from attacking the Low Countries. The two allies also agreed to guarantee the peace to prevent the resumption of hostilities.[62]

Although it appeared that Mariana had lost this round and would have to accept one of the alternatives, the reality was different. The most critical part of the agreement was in the separate, supposedly secret, clauses: England and the United Provinces (and later Sweden) agreed to join forces *with Spain* and *against France* if Louis XIV continued the war and insisted on the legality of Maria Theresa's claims. If he did, the allies (England, the United Provinces, and Sweden) would join the king of Spain to secure the return to Spain of all conquered territories that had existed when the Treaty of the Pyrenees was signed.[63] In short, England and the United Provinces would let Louis XIV keep some of his conquests or gain the "alternative" territories, but the *status quo ante* of the Treaty of the Pyrenees—Maria Theresa's renunciation and the preservation of the Spanish Low Countries—remained intact. Negotiations to incorporate Sweden in the league began a week later, when the Swedish envoy, Count Christopher von Dohna, arrived in The Hague on January 31.[64]

Spain and France now had to be brought to accept the treaty's terms—terms they did not fully know. The negotiations moved from London to The Hague, where English and Dutch diplomats began revealing the content piecemeal to Spanish and French diplomats. The confederation latent in the separate clauses was precisely the alliance Mariana had been seeking all along, and the attitudes of the parties changed as the actual terms became known. Louis XIV was furious with the Dutch. de Witt argued that his intention had only been to facilitate peace and force Spain to accept one of the alternatives, but as the content of the secret clauses emerged, he could hardly conceal the treaty's implications. For the moment, however, unaware of the separate clauses, Mariana rejected the "alternative" solution, causing a diplomatic stalemate.[65]

This changed when, on March 4, Castel Rodrigo accepted the first "alternative." His plenipotentiary rights meant he could do this, but he acted before receiving instructions. He saw an opportunity and took it, stunning everyone. Although it was not clear whether Mariana would confirm Castel Rodrigo's bold move, the acceptance of one of the "alternatives" totally altered the situation. Now Louis XIV had to accept or reject the terms imposed by the confederates. Because he had originally made the proposal, he was not in a strong position to reject it. In Molina's estimation, Castel Rodrigo's acceptance "turned the league of The Hague [the Triple Alliance] . . . completely in our favor and against France, which now finds itself with no alternative other than peace—against its will and against its designs—and with the prospect of all of Europe against it."[66]

Once clear on the secret provisions, Mariana approved Castel Rodrigo's choice on April 7, 1668. She presented herself as an agent of peace, reminding the Dutch regents that she now possessed the means to take vigorous action against France's "unjust invasion." On April 9, Mariana accepted the two million pounds from the United Provinces, after the Dutch modified the terms of repayment. The money was used to continue to build the army of Flanders. This was key because unlike the previous treaties Spain had signed with France, this one would not be followed by disarmament. On the contrary, Mariana intended to secure the area more.[67]

During the peace congress in the city of Aix-la-Chapelle, Mariana secured the future of the monarchy in several ways. First, she demanded a declaration in the treaty stating that she had surrendered the territories only "for the public benefit of peace and *not for any other motive*"—that is, she did not accept Maria Theresa's inheritance rights and wanted her renunciation confirmed. In addition, she wanted the agreement to be applied to "the rest of the Spanish monarchy" and to indicate that the peace was "general on land and sea." This way, she preempted the possibility that France would find another excuse to reopen hostilities against Spain in other territories or by other means. Finally, she demanded that the Triple Alliance be transformed into a league of guarantee after peace was concluded, which meant that Spain would be protected by the Triple Alliance if Louis XIV found another excuse to break the peace. When she obtained these guarantees on April 20, she agreed to surrender the towns and fortresses Louis XIV had conquered before September 1667.[68]

Mariana seconded Castel Rodrigo's decision to accept the first alternative (a series of fortress cities in the northern frontier with France) rather than the second (the Franche-Comté). This was strategic: the fortresses and towns lay deep within Spanish territories close to the Dutch Low Countries. The Spanish anticipated that if Louis XIV made hostile movements in the area, it would spur the United Provinces into action more reliably than if Spain gave up the Franche-Comté. The last step in the process was to confirm Sweden's inclusion in the Triple Alliance by setting the amount it would receive in subsidies in war or peace. The subsidies for Sweden were to pay for the Swedish army that would come to the defense of Spain if Louis XIV went back on his agreement and attacked the Spanish Netherlands or any other Spanish territory. Confirmed the same day as the agreement among the three powers, the subsidies were negotiated and guaranteed by Charles II but were to be paid by Spain. That the subsidies were paid by Spain is another indication that the Triple Alliance was formed principally against Louis XIV. The Triple Alliance among England, the United Provinces, and Sweden was finally signed on April 25, 1668, at Westminster Palace. Thus the Spanish Netherlands were preserved for Carlos II.[69]

DIPLOMATIC AND POLITICAL OUTCOMES

Mariana and Louis XIV agreed to the terms of the Treaty of Aix-la-Chapelle on May 2, 1668, thus officially ending the short but significant War of Devolution. Article 8 of the treaty specified, "Nothing contained in the Treaty of the Pyrenees has been revoked (except regarding what pertains to Portugal, with whom the said Catholic King has made peace)." "The ceding of the said *plazas* [towns and fortresses]" had been done "without the parties having acquired new rights, for which in all the cases there was no express mention in the present agreement." The language was moderate, but no doubt existed in anyone's mind that the renunciation stood. Louis XIV put on a brave face or perhaps even deceived himself. In his *mémoires*, he explained that he had accepted such modest gains despite his military superiority and conquests because he had obtained the principal goal: the invalidation of Maria Theresa's renunciation. "The Spanish implicitly abandoned by a voluntary treaty the renunciation that was their only claim to exclude the Queen from her succession." This statement would have amused Mariana: neither she nor the international community recognized these claims.[70]

If he was referring to the Secret Partition Treaty he signed with Leopold I in January 1668, this was a clear attempt to present the results of the war in a positive light, but it was hardly accurate. Louis XIV and Leopold I had drafted an agreement that divided the monarchy between them. This treaty, however, pertained to the future of the Low Countries, not the present—that is, if Carlos II died without a child to succeed him. This was fundamentally different from what Louis XIV sought in the War of Devolution: Spanish territories in the Netherlands upon the death of Philip IV as a claim against Carlos II's inheritance when Carlos inherited, not when or if he died. The Aix-la-Chapelle settlement of 1668 successfully preserved the status quo in the Spanish Netherlands until 1700. Carlos II indeed died without descendants on November 1, 1700. By then, other treaties and a different international situation, as well as the specifics of his testament, determined what would happen not only in the Low Countries but in the entire monarchy and its overseas possessions.[71]

Mariana and her ministers in Madrid were unaware that Leopold I and Louis XIV had negotiated such a treaty and only learned of it about a year later. Had it been known in Madrid during the maneuvers leading to the Peace of Aix-la-Chapelle, it would have caused tremendous difficulties for Mariana, likely a major scandal. The loss of the towns of Charleroi, Binch, Ath, and Dovay and the fortresses of Scarpa, Tornay, Audenarde, Lille, Armentieres, Courtrai, Bergues, and Furness was no doubt painful, but they were not major territorial losses. Considering the dire situation Mariana faced at the beginning of the regency, her ability to end the war so quickly and without losing the principle of the renunciation should be considered a victory.[72]

After three years in power, Mariana had resolved Philip IV's legacy and built a strong military and diplomatic foundation. In the military realm, Mariana's major accomplishment related to the army of Flanders. By 1667, she had doubled the number of infantry and cavalry forces, which started with a meager 2,904 officers and 8,394 soldiers. By 1668, the army was a 53,000-infantry force, and it gained an additional 10,000 soldiers by the end of that year. Mariana accepted losses, but she was no longer in a reactive mode. Rather, she was in the process of strengthening Spain's military capacity and defenses. Also important is that the War of Devolution inaugurated a number of innovations in recruitment and the composition of the army, which saw much higher—indeed, almost unprecedented—levels of recruitment inside the peninsula, especially in Galicia. Last but not least, the way Mariana had funded the war spread the burden of supporting the military more equally between the upper and lower classes.[73]

To resolve the Portuguese rebellion, Mariana had to rise above the fray in her court; she did so by patiently waiting for the right moment to act while continuing to negotiate with allies. Her patience did not mean inaction; by the time conditions were conducive to her strategies, she could act because she had put in place all the necessary groundwork. As painful as it was to let go of the riches of Portugal and forfeit the Iberian union achieved in 1580, the resolution of the conflict was a reasonable and far-sighted decision. Spain had not enjoyed the benefits of the Iberian Union since 1640. Mariana's handling of this controversial issue reveals the political skills she had acquired during a lifetime of exposure to, and experience in, court politics. As she navigated the difficult early years of the regency, she quickly became adept in her role as head of state. Indeed, her diplomatic and political skills developed rapidly precisely because of the initial difficulties she faced. In the end, Mariana viewed the peace with Portugal as another diplomatic victory over France, much as Philip IV saw the 1648 peace with the United Provinces.[74]

The peace with Portugal was a sine qua non for concluding alliances against France. It is the principal reason she chose England as the intermediary in negotiations with Portugal. Her decision to develop and then strengthen ties with England was not always popular but became a key to her diplomatic successes. She put Anglo-Spanish relations on a collaborative course that proved critical to preserving Spain's power. While she could claim many successes with England in the prolonged and convoluted negotiations, her ability to bring the Dutch over to Spain's side proved more limited during the early years of her regency, but she did not abandon her goal.[75]

Diplomacy, therefore, was Mariana's—and Spain's—greatest success. When she became regent, Spain's only standing alliance was with Emperor Leopold I, who proved of little use when Mariana needed him the most.

Under Mariana, Spain overcame its diplomatic isolation and broke the alliances that France under Mazarin had so efficiently woven. Several traditional French allies—the United Provinces, Brandenburg, Sweden, and Portugal—turned against France to support the Spanish cause. By 1668, power had substantially shifted in the relationship between Spain and France: France still had military superiority, but Mariana had started shaping a solid grid of anti-French alliances.

Court dynamics—particularly in the Council of State, but in the other councils as well—also shifted significantly during the regency's first three years. The declaration of war unified the Council of State but led to an irreparable confrontation with the late king's illegitimate son, Don Juan of Austria. During the summer of 1667, when French victories seemed to portend the loss of the Spanish Netherlands, Mariana had invited Don Juan to join the deliberations. He had military expertise, and she planned to appoint him governor of the Spanish Netherlands and the head of the army of Flanders. During the convoluted negotiations with diplomats in The Hague, London, Brussels, and Madrid, Don Juan accepted Mariana's offer but kept delaying his departure to Brussels. Now, with the War of Devolution behind her, Mariana could deal with his defiance.

CHAPTER 4

Consolidating Power
at Home, 1668–1670

On June 2, 1668, Joseph Malladas, an Aragonese captain and tax collector working for the Crown, was apprehended at his temporary residence in Madrid, taken to the palace prison, and after a summary process, garroted in his cell. Because this occurred in the palace and did not go through the city's legal channels, it was obvious that the queen had arranged the hasty execution. The news leaked immediately, and within twenty-four hours, the Junta de Gobierno condemned the incident, which soon became a major scandal. But the suspiciously rapid "trial" and execution did not mean that Mariana had acted impulsively; rather, she was quite deliberately sending a warning to Don Juan of Austria, who had allegedly hired Malladas to assassinate her confessor, Father Everard Nithard. But her action was considered an abuse of power, and it evoked waves of repulsion and shock. Worse yet, this incident triggered a public confrontation between Mariana and Don Juan. Although centered on Nithard, their conflict started boiling a few months prior to the events of June 2, when Don Juan refused to take up the governorship in the Low Countries.[1]

The rivalry between the two was the catalyst for the most serious political crisis in Mariana's regency, in the winter of 1668–69, less than a year after the Malladas incident. Under pressure from ministers who feared violence as Don Juan marched toward the city with a small infantry, Mariana acquiesced to his demands to dismiss Nithard from court. This event has cast a long shadow on subsequent interpretations of Mariana's regency. Scholars describe the events as a coup d'état. While I agree with this assessment—marching on Madrid with an armed force, even a small one, and demanding that the ruler abide by specific demands certainly qualifies—I challenge the interpretation of the events and the main actors. At first glance, Don Juan seems a familiar figure—yet another male relative of a minor king, often if not always an illegitimate older brother or uncle, who tries to unseat a female regent. But this is a misreading: Mariana's legitimacy was too well established for Don Juan to take power or even impose himself and his presence on her. His actions were unplanned and haphazard and, as we will see, a reaction to Mariana's threats to his freedom and even, as he may have feared, his life. This chapter reconstructs the events leading to the "coup" of 1669, analyzing them from a variety of viewpoints, while taking into account the larger political context at court and on the international stage.[2]

As part of the analysis, I reassess Nithard's role in both the events that led to his dismissal and, more generally, Mariana's regime. The fact that Nithard was at the center of the controversy has led to the assumption that he had great or even undue influence on Mariana's government. But when Nithard's performance is analyzed based on archival evidence and within the context of the important body of work on favoritism, the notion that he was Mariana's *valido* is hard to sustain. He did not meet the two principal litmus tests to be considered a *valido*: (1) the management of royal patronage and/or (2) the development of domestic and foreign policy for the monarchy. The deliberations of the Council of State, of which Nithard was a member, as well as diplomatic correspondence and papers of key members of the elite, all reveal that he was rather marginal in matters of state. I have not found evidence that he controlled things—or Mariana—behind the scenes; in fact, the opposite is true, with many figures commenting on his shortcomings. Mariana patronized Nithard from the beginning of her tenure, but she was also developing political partnerships with other figures at the same time. Of these, the Marquis of Aytona, who had significant influence in shaping Mariana's court and foreign policy, stands out. Indeed, Aytona played a key role in helping Mariana consolidate her position in the aftermath of the 1669 crisis. This chapter analyzes Mariana's regime from the reconfiguration that occurred between 1668, when she ordered Malladas's execution, and 1670, after Aytona's death.[3]

THE DON JUAN PROBLEM

The first step in disentangling and analyzing the events of February 1669 is understanding Don Juan's status as an illegitimate—though recognized—member of the royal family. The product of Philip IV's affair with the famously beautiful actress María Inés Calderón, Don Juan emerged from the shadows in 1641 after the death of the king's last surviving brother, the Cardinal-Infante Fernando. The timing indicates that Philip IV intended to rely on his son politically, as the monarchy was facing revolts in Catalonia and Portugal. Illegitimate Habsburg children like Don John of Austria (1547–1578), the victor of Lepanto; Margaret of Parma (1522–1586), twice governor of the Netherlands; and Sor Ana Dorothea of Austria (1612–1694), the unofficial representative of the Austrian Habsburgs in the Descalzas Reales, had each played key military and political roles.[4]

Indeed, Philip IV appointed Don Juan as general of the army of Portugal just a week after officially recognizing him. Since he was only thirteen, the post was largely symbolic, but it inaugurated what was to be a prestigious political and military career. Philip granted Don Juan a position in the church as the prior of San Juan, which offered both income and administrative responsibilities. But the restrictions on Don Juan indicate the conflictive space illegitimate children occupied. He could not participate in public events with the royal family, live permanently at court, or enter the royal palace through the main door. Although protocol limited Don Juan's contact with Mariana and the two *infantas*, they were by no means strangers, as he occasionally joined the family during royal vacations.[5]

Philip IV granted Don Juan significant privileges, including the title of "His Serene Highness" (Su Serenidad), but short of *infante*.[6] He would be addressed as "my brother" by Prince Baltasar Carlos—Philip's son by his first consort—and as "my son" by Queen Isabel. Don Juan's presence was a delicate matter for Queen Isabel, as it forced her to acknowledge her husband's infidelity. There is a record of Philip's mandate regarding the queen's treatment of Don Juan but no evidence that she actually followed that mandate. If she had, it might have set a precedent for Mariana, who never considered him her son. Mariana addressed him as "my cousin" (a biological truth, as Don Juan's father and Mariana's mother were siblings), but this is the same form of address she used for the grandees—the crème de la crème of the aristocracy and considered cousins of the king—and it was far from being the queen's son. Forms of address were highly regulated and extremely important for the royal family in its correspondence with heads of state and for titled elites. Mariana acknowledged that he was the son of her late husband but did not grant him the distinction of calling him her son.[7]

By the time Mariana was regent, Don Juan had accumulated a substantial record of military and political service. He had been general of the Spanish armies on several occasions and viceroy of Sicily (1649–52) and Catalonia (1653–56), as well as general of the army of Flanders and governor of the Low Countries (1656–59). He had successfully crushed revolts in Naples and Catalonia. Despite these accomplishments, his failure against the Portuguese armies in 1663 drove a wedge between father and son, evidenced by Philip IV's refusal to admit him to his deathbed. And of course, Philip did not give Don Juan a role in the regency government. Instead, he requested that the queen "protect and favor him, employ his services, and assist him financially" so that he could live "according to the quality of his person." These vague requests meant that Mariana could decide Don Juan's future. Anticipating her role, Don Juan wanted to gain her confidence: the imperial ambassador reported that Don Juan had learned German to speak with the queen in her native language. According to an admiring Pötting, he was fluent after only two years of study.[8]

After Philip's death, Don Juan's future depended on Mariana. Already dismissed as the general of the Portuguese armies, he had no official assignments when his father died. The king's final snub surely contributed to what was reported as Don Juan's subsequent melancholy. During the regency's early months, he turned for help to Nithard and the imperial ambassador, Pötting, asking them to intercede on his behalf with Leopold I and the queen. He sought a marriage with the Habsburg archduchess Claudia Felicitas of Tyrol and, whether he was married or not, asked Leopold—through Pötting—to put him forward as a candidate to the king of Poland, which was an elective office at the time. The ambassador entertained these projects so as to not alienate Don Juan, but Leopold never considered them seriously. Nithard had an excellent relationship with Don Juan and wanted to help him, but he did not obtain anything on his behalf from the queen.[9]

Mariana and Don Juan had very different ideas about his role in the government, and she initially denied his requests to attend meetings of the Junta de Gobierno and reside in Madrid. His unrelenting quest to obtain a permanent political position became a nuisance for Mariana, who continued to deny him despite Nithard's intercession. Everything changed for Mariana, however, when the War of Devolution began. Within a month of Louis XIV's declaration of war, Mariana invited Don Juan to attend Council of State meetings. Philip IV had appointed him to the council in the 1650s, but he was not allowed to attend meetings because Philip wanted to avoid seeming to give him either too much or too little recognition. Once again, the question of titles and forms of address emerges as an important practical and symbolic matter in early modern political culture. The timing of Mariana's reversal of her husband's prohibition indicates her desperation at the start of the war. Even though she had men with military experience working with her, Don Juan's military career and expertise were too sterling to ignore. It is possible that she already intended to name Don Juan to the governorship of the Low Countries; she appointed him only a few months later. Mariana needed all hands on deck, and it was this, not his continued requests, that changed her mind about Don Juan.[10]

The troubled later relationship between the queen and Don Juan has obscured their period of cooperation. Don Juan's initial performance in the Council of State was excellent, and Mariana benefitted substantially from his military and diplomatic recommendations. He proposed the offensive alliance between England and Spain that eventually led to the formation of the 1668 Triple Alliance, and Mariana put him in charge of negotiating with the English ambassador in Madrid. A close reading of the Council of State deliberations from June through August 1667 reveals that Don Juan's opinions were well regarded by his colleagues and the queen.[11]

The seriousness of Spain's military situation also challenges the idea that Mariana appointed Don Juan governor of the Low Countries to banish him from Madrid. First, she appointed him September 21, 1667, following a string of alarming French victories. Second, appointing a member of the royal family to the governorship of the Spanish Netherlands was traditional; all Mariana's predecessors, from Charles V to her husband, had done the same. Third, Don Juan's appointment immediately affected the course of the war and the negotiations. Mariana's correspondence with her ambassador in The Hague, Esteban Gamarra, and the governor of the Low Countries, Castel Rodrigo, makes clear that the expectation was that Don Juan's arrival in Brussels would be a coup for Spain. Indeed, his appointment worried Louis XIV, who feared that the presence of a member of the royal family could rally the local populace behind the Spanish Crown. Mariana's letter to her subjects in the Netherlands suggests as much: she lamented that Carlos II's "tender age prevented him from going personally to the defense of his subjects" but stated her hopes that Don Juan's presence, as well as the "rightfulness of our cause," would facilitate a positive resolution. She praised Don Juan's piety and his immense service to the Crown and expressed deep appreciation that they would now "benefit the monarchy in one of its most difficult hours."[12]

Don Juan accepted the appointment. Everything indicated that he was going to follow through: while preparations for his household and papers were under way, he left to the north of the peninsula, stopping in Galicia, where military recruitment was ongoing. Mariana granted him the same enormous concessions in the governorship enjoyed by the Cardinal-Infante Fernando and Archduke Leopold Wilhelm, legitimate members of the royal family who governed the Spanish Netherlands in 1634–41 and 1647–56, respectively. She provided Don Juan with a splendid entourage and a substantial army, as well as extensive powers to make leagues, grant titles, and mortgage cities and territories to obtain loans and cement alliances. "With the trust I place in your person, secure in the knowledge of your obligations that require you to perform this service for the king, my son, and for me," Mariana wrote, "you can be assured that nothing will be wanting and that I will consider myself well served [by you]." Although the governorship, with such enormous prerogatives, could have relaunched his political career, his ambition to stay in Madrid and play an active role in Mariana's government prevailed in his judgment. He started to make excuses for delays in his departure for the Low Countries while increasing his demands for money and men. Important members of the Council of State and the Junta de Gobierno tried to persuade Don Juan to take up his new post, but to no avail.[13]

The delay began to drive a wedge between Mariana and Don Juan that eventually escalated into open confrontation. Mariana replaced him on January 22, 1668, with Don Íñigo Fernández de Velasco, Duke of Frías and constable of Castile, Castile's highest military title. He had been deeply involved in recruitment efforts, and the appointment rewarded him for his energy and activity. When Don Juan heard that he had been unceremoniously replaced, he sought to be reinstated. He apologized to the queen, stating, "I am moved by my desire to serve the King our Lord and the desire to avoid the slightest aggravation to Her Majesty." Given the advantages of placing a member of the royal family in charge of the Low Countries, Mariana accepted the apology and wrote an open letter to the Low Countries announcing his imminent arrival. Don Juan arrived at the Port of Coruña, on the northwest coast, in late March, weeks after pledging to depart directly. Rumors began to circulate at court, however, that he was merely waiting for the right moment to return to Madrid. As he continued to employ obvious delaying tactics, the Council of State unanimously affirmed the necessity of him going to Flanders even if the peace was signed.[14]

The peace was considered a momentary solution to the threat posed by France, which is why Mariana continued to insist on Don Juan's departure even after the treaty with France was concluded in May 1668. While peace treaties often led to military cuts, Mariana continued to recruit and spend money on the army of Flanders. Although numbers had improved substantially (it rose to sixty-three thousand members by the end of 1668), Louis XIV's armies were still larger (about seventy thousand) and expanding. The peace between Spain and France was considered highly unstable, and while the Triple Alliance stood between Louis XIV and the coveted Spanish Netherlands, he was actively trying to dissolve it. Mariana and her councilors were well aware and doing their part for the preservation of the alliance. The advantages of having a member of the royal family as governor of the Low Countries were often enumerated in diplomatic dispatches and formed a major part of her decision to rescind her appointment of the constable (which deeply offended him) and reinstate Don Juan. The reason for the execution of Malladas—a month after the peace—had been the discovery of an assassination plot Don Juan supposedly orchestrated against Nithard. However, this seems a little farfetched. Whether this was fabricated or was real is unclear; Don Juan adamantly denied it. The message Mariana sent to Don Juan *was* clear. This was a technique of intimidation, an attempt to bend Don Juan to her will as well as retaliate for his refusal to take over the governorship at a moment of desperate need.[15]

THE CONTOURS OF ROYAL AUTHORITY

The event also illustrates the power dynamics of Mariana's court. The queen's ability to have someone apprehended, tried, and executed within twenty-four hours demonstrated that she had both the will and the means to exercise her power. Mariana—who by the time of the execution had endured Don Juan's excuses for nine months—had been patiently preparing to assert her authority over him. She started by replacing the president of the Council of Castile, a strategically important office because the council controlled the judicial administration in Madrid and the rest of the kingdom. If Don Juan were to be brought to justice, it would be through the Council of Castile.[16]

The president she replaced was Don Garcia de Haro Sotomayor y Guzmán, Count of Castrillo; he had been part of the Spanish ministerial class since the early years of Philip's reign and had been very close to Queen Isabel. But he did not work well with Mariana. He was the oldest member of the Junta de Gobierno and an octogenarian, but the problem appeared to be not ill health but uncooperative behavior. When Mariana requested all the councils to vote on whether the monarchy could or should grant Portugal its independence, Mariana sent a royal secretary to Castrillo's house to collect the vote in case he did not attend the meeting, which suggests that this was not the first time he had dragged his feet. As the tension regarding Don Juan's departure built and she could not get enough institutional support to punish Don Juan, Mariana held a private audience with Castrillo. He resigned his position as president of the Council of Castile shortly thereafter. Although records of the meeting have not come to light, the court assumed that Mariana forced Castrillo's resignation, as it was unprecedented to see so high a minister step down from office. An anonymous chronicler described it as "the most singular event, one that will remain unique in the annals of posterity."[17]

Mariana filled the vacancy with Diego Riquelme de Quirós, bishop of Plasencia, who was ready to clean house, eliminate corruption, and work for the queen's regime. But his unexpected death a little more than a month later required Mariana to select another president. She chose an energetic, loyal, and competent man willing to act on her behalf and carry out unpopular measures if necessary: Diego de Valladares Sarmiento, bishop of Oviedo. Valladares quickly became a central figure, intercepting the letters that led to Malladas's execution. Events moved quickly: Valladares took over the presidency on a Thursday, and on Saturday, the mayor of the palace—a lawyer named Don Pedro González de Salcedo, later an important figure in the regency government—executed a warrant, written in the queen's hand, for Malladas's arrest and execution.[18]

The Alcalde de Corte carried out royal orders inside the palace, and thus the execution was not technically illegal. Nevertheless, it was perceived as an abuse of royal power. Members of the Junta de Gobierno, who had not been consulted, protested vigorously; even the normally loyal and supportive Aytona was appalled. In a paper presented in the Junta de Gobierno and circulated in manuscript form among members of the elite, Nithard, who reproduced it in his memoirs, defended the execution's constitutionality. He explained that Mariana had observed due process by appointing three judges to conduct a summary trial. The episode remained shrouded in mystery and speculation. Leopold asked his ambassador for details, but the usually well-informed Pötting had no information. The English ambassador reported that Mariana had ordered Malladas to poison the Duke of Alba, who during his tenure as *mayordomo mayor* had supposedly reprimanded Nithard for entering Mariana's chambers while she was abed. Another rumor said that Malladas had sent Louis XIV a copy of the secret instructions Mariana gave her diplomats about the peace with Portugal. The number and variety of rumors illustrate the event's significance; it became a cause célèbre in local and international circles.[19]

The timing clearly indicates that Mariana was asserting her authority over Don Juan, who quickly arranged for his departure to Brussels. But the backlash against Mariana's actions encouraged him to resume his defiance. Don Juan now claimed that bad health prevented him from taking the governorship in the Low Countries. His reluctance to go to Brussels has to be interpreted within the values of early modern political culture, and this applies to other monarchies as well: the allure of the court was simply too great, as the center of power near the king and the queen in this case. Don Juan's refusal to leave indicates that he expected to have an active participation in the regency government, but he completely misjudged Mariana. The queen once again lost patience and ordered him to send all official papers pertaining to the governorship to the constable, whom she reappointed as governor. She banished Don Juan to the city of Consuegra "to await my orders" and prohibited him from coming any closer to the court than twenty *leguas* (about sixty miles). In a deliberate attempt to humiliate him publicly, Mariana sent the news of his banning from Madrid and the constable's reappointment to the governorship as a circular letter. The letter stated that Don Juan had refused the governorship even though the resources granted him had not been seen since the time of Charles V.[20]

The constable traveled to the Low Countries with plenipotentiary powers to negotiate treaties and alliances. Mariana did not, however, abandon the idea of placing a member of the royal family in the governorship, designating the constable's governorship as provisional, lasting only until she could appoint a person of royal blood. Her willingness to negotiate with Don Juan (he was the only person she could have appointed) is further indication that putting him in the governorship was a matter of state, not just a political ploy to get him out of Madrid. Tensions at court continued to escalate. The loss of Portugal, the prospect of war with France, and especially Malladas's execution weakened the regency government. The turmoil gave Don Juan an opening, and he launched a war of words against Mariana and her regime. In a series of letters to key members of court, Don Juan accused Nithard of tyranny and Mariana, in collusion with her confessor, of transgressing the traditional boundaries of political and religious power as confessor and minister. Circulating in manuscript and printed forms throughout Spain and at foreign courts, these writings amounted to pasquinades—political satires against the government. It was an attack on Mariana but was directed against her confessor as a matter of decorum. These writings were feared to stir a popular revolt, and that is why they became a weapon that Don Juan deftly deployed.[21]

In the midst of the scandal, Mariana deployed her most powerful weapon: the king. A series of public processions provided a welcome distraction from Don Juan's calumnies. Processions in the capital city occurred frequently, but this was the first time in Carlos II's reign and thus a major event: On July 2, 1668, residents of Madrid, or *madrileños*, of all classes lined the streets to witness Carlos II perform a traditional act of Habsburg devotion—a visit to the Virgin of Atocha. Dances greeted the young king and his mother as they passed through densely thronged streets and plazas, and an eyewitness described seeing "clear signs of happiness." When the sovereigns "returned to the palace at eleven at night, the shouts of 'long live the king' were accompanied by widespread popular jubilation; those who saw Carlos counted themselves as the most in love with their king." Pötting also noted the "low approval of Mariana's government" but did not explain how that was evident. Mariana's greatest asset, however, was the king, and this is why she chose to show him publicly at such critical time. Everything indicates that the strategy worked: Carlos was greeted exceedingly well, "acclaimed by his subjects during the procession, who competed to show their love of the monarch."[22]

Over the next days and weeks, the young king made outings to other devotional sites in Madrid, the Descalzas Reales, the Convent of the Encarnación, and other convents. During one day trip, a mysterious visitor arrived at the palace and asked for a private audience with the queen. Mariana reportedly learned from this shadowy figure that Don Juan was once again plotting against Nithard. This time the conspiracy was to be carried out by a man named Bernardo Patiño, the brother of Don Juan's secretary and thus more closely associated with him than Malladas. The plan was to abduct Nithard with a cavalry force of sixty after the customary weekly meeting of the Junta de Gobierno. While the kidnappers drove Nithard to the northern frontiers, Don Juan would seize control of the palace. Other rumors suggested that Don Juan's intention was to assassinate Nithard. The more sinister variations on the alleged plot may have been invented to discredit Don Juan; nevertheless, the Marquis of Aytona and Don Blasco de Loyola, the main royal secretary, gave the rumors credence.[23]

When Valladares learned of the plot, he had Patiño and two servants thrown into the palace jail; when the news came out the next day, "everyone was bewildered," and the court plunged into "a deep state of turmoil." The Malladas incident had taken place only a month before, and everyone feared a repeat. Mariana and her collaborators, however, exercised restraint this time, going no further than imprisonment. Patiño too had learned from the previous incident: he quickly confessed, openly implicating Don Juan. Mariana was eager to hold Don Juan accountable, and she enjoyed significant support. With the backing of most Junta de Gobierno members, she dispatched a fifty-man mounted force to seize Don Juan and bring him to the royal palace of Segovia, where political prisoners were traditionally kept. Warned in advance, Don Juan fled.[24]

Although ordering the arrest of her late husband's illegitimate son showed Mariana's determination and boldness, her decision precipitated the final confrontation with Don Juan. Having seen Mariana's behavior and her determination to bring him to justice, fearing for his freedom, and perhaps for his life, he fled. Don Juan left behind a letter—addressed to the queen but appealing "to all those who read it"—that was nothing short of a political manifesto. In it, he justified his flight, scathingly critiqued

Mariana's regime via an attack on Nithard, and demanded that Mariana banish her confessor. A serious challenge to Mariana, it is worth quoting at length:

> The tyranny of Father Everard and his execrable malice, which he focused against me when he imprisoned the brother of my secretary and with other actions, such as attacking my honor with abominable words, have led me to flee in order to secure my person. Although this action may seem at first an admission of guilt, it is nothing more than the act of a loyal subject of the King, my Lord, for whom I always will give all the blood in my veins. And I declare today to Your Majesty and to all who read this letter that *the actual reason that prevented my departure to the Low Countries* was my intention to separate from Your Majesty's side that beast so unworthy of occupying such a sacred place. God has inspired me to seek this goal as I see such horrific tyranny displayed, especially when I witnessed how that innocent man was executed in such violence. . . . I have long been meditating and had the intention of executing my plans without scandal or violence. . . . It was because of this, and not because I am afraid of staying in Consuegra [and being arrested], that I have decided to leave. And then only in order to protect myself from the perfidious designs of this vile man while Your Majesty reconsiders my humble representations. In short, my only desires are the expulsion [of Nithard], the reparations to my honor, and the liberation of these kingdoms of the calamities and the oppression of these poor subjects. . . . I beseech Your Majesty on my knees and with tears in my heart to not lend your ears to the perverse counsels of this poisonous individual. I protest in front of God, the King my Lord, Your Majesty, and the entire world that I will not be responsible for the potential consequences that may result in the absence of public peace. . . . October 21, 1668. The humblest subject and servant of Your Majesty, Don Juan.[25] (emphasis mine)

In this manifesto, Don Juan observed proper deference, assuring Mariana that he fled only because of his desire to secure the "expulsion [of Nithard] and nothing else." And he accompanied his threat with much "begging and imploring of Your Majesty," deploying his criticisms of Nithard as excuses for his refusal to take up the governorship of the Low Countries. Although righteous, his rhetoric was hardly convincing.[26]

Mariana was shocked by Don Juan's letter, reportedly falling ill with a severe migraine after receiving it. And the letter was just the beginning. Don Juan dispatched a flurry of letters to ministers of the court, viceroys, and government bodies; they were unsealed, which meant that everyone at the court would have had access to them. Mariana's ladies divided themselves into the *austriales* (followers of Don Juan) and the *gerardas* (supporters of Nithard); this was actually beneficial for Mariana's image, as it made her the adjudicator of the dispute. It was hard to conceal that Don Juan's attack was an attack on her, not just her confessor. Don Juan's ability to attract a following, his extensive military experience, and his semiroyal status raised concerns of disorders and violence. The situation was deteriorating, but Mariana was not ready to give in. Aytona proposed establishing a royal guard, but the idea languished in the Council of Castile; the Junta de Gobierno was divided on whether to support the mobilization of forces to defend Mariana's confessor. Nithard was not really hated; he lacked supporters, however, who would vouch for his position.[27]

A similar ambivalent attitude prevailed in the Council of State. State councilors regarded Don Juan's behavior—"his refusal to go to Flanders, his intention toward the Father Confessor of Her Majesty, and the letter of Consuegra"—as "enormously irreverent acts" that "lacked all explanation." Yet they adopted a conciliatory approach, explaining his actions as the result of "extreme grief." His problems had "the effect of alienating him [from Your Majesty and] making him forget his usual decorum, temperance, and good manners." Ministers pleaded with Mariana "to act as an angel of peace whose presence calms this tempest, reduces to tranquility these troubled times, and creates harmony within [competing] desires." The viceroy of Catalonia, Gaspar Tellez Girón, Duke of Osuna, charged with discovering Don Juan's whereabouts, could not say where he was or what he was planning.[28]

The last push in the storm against Nithard came from France in the form of support for Don Juan. Rumors that Louis XIV would support Don Juan with money and men and then take advantage of the internal disruption to pursue his plans in the Low Countries were confirmed in several letters Mariana received from the viceroy of Aragon and her ambassador in Paris.

These types of maneuvers were typical in early modern politics and had been used against France by the Spaniards, more recently during the civil wars in France known as the Fronde (1648–53). When internal disorders took place in a rival monarchy, it weakened them, and thus it was natural—if reprehensible—to take advantage of the situation. Aside from the potential intervention of France, the support of Aragon and Catalonia for Don Juan was also becoming a problem; the history of those territories greatly contributed to opinion turning against Nithard.[29]

In December 1668, the Council of Castile respectfully suggested to the queen that finding another occupation for the father confessor "may be of utmost service to Her Majesty as well as the public good of these kingdoms." The idea of naming Nithard to an embassy in Rome and perhaps nominating him to the rank of cardinal was presented as a way to avoid escalating the already precarious situation. This decision on the part of the ruling elite was a sin of omission rather than commission. It was done to pacify Don Juan and avoid the outbreak of violence, not retaliate against the Jesuit confessor. Nevertheless, it is clear that Nithard had become a convenient target, making this a good time to evaluate his role in Mariana's regime.[30]

THE QUEEN'S CONFESSOR

Nithard's role has been the subject of much historical debate and considerable misinterpretation, both stemming from his ten-volume memoirs. These are not the confessional and first-person accounts associated with memoirs; he provides some biographical information about his education and family, but the volumes are essentially a compilation of documents he had access to as a member of the Junta de Gobierno, interspersed with commentary. Nithard also left behind borradores, or drafts, in which he recorded his grievances with many of his fellow members of court. Both manuscripts are important, as much of the information we have about the Junta de Gobierno comes from Nithard, but there are important caveats.[31]

Nithard wrote the memoirs in Rome in the late 1670s, after his political aspirations had essentially been destroyed. In Nithard's telling, he was the innocent victim of Don Juan's ambition. More problematic for my purposes is that he wrote within the limits of decorum required of a confessor of a queen of Spain. Magdalena S. Sánchez has persuasively demonstrated that confessors and other religious figures writing about queens and Habsburg women emphasized their piety while diminishing their substantial political activities and influence. Nithard did exactly this with Mariana: he mentioned her as little as possible, and when he did, he made her saintly—pious, uncompromisingly kind, virtuous, and detached from cutthroat politics. Nithard cannot be faulted for following accepted rules of decorum, but his approach has had the unfortunate effect of depoliticizing Mariana and obscuring her active involvement in political matters. The combination of Nithard's text and the lack of Mariana-centric research have created the inaccurate but persistent image of Mariana as dominated by her confessor.[32]

In the early stages of her regency, Mariana patronized Nithard decisively. It was a happy coincidence that the post of inquisitor general, for which Nithard was qualified, had just become vacant, and Mariana seized the opportunity, swiftly demolishing any barriers to his appointment. She also appointed him to the Council of State and to key ad hoc committees, such as the Junta de Inglaterra. This was in line with both Viennese and Madrileño political culture: in the one, Jesuits often filled major political niches, and in the other, confessors did, although in the latter case, they had not been Jesuits. Jesuits had been associated with queens. The Dominicans, in particular, reacted against his appointment as inquisitor and member of the Junta de Gobierno. Mariana was not deterred; she needed to surround herself with trusted figures who depended on her, and she trusted and respected Nithard. But she did not surrender her power to him.[33]

The early years of her regency were a testing ground for the queen and her ministers, and it did not take long for Mariana to see that Nithard did not measure up. We know this both from contemporary descriptions of him and from her behavior. Contemporaries often described the Jesuit as an honest man lacking the necessary strength of character and personality to command the court. Pötting reported in his diary the "lectures" Medina de las Torres gave Nithard, exhorting him to action. Leopold—although his opinion should be taken with a grain of salt as well—had no faith in Nithard's abilities either and questioned his resolve. When Nithard was proposed as a possible replacement for the Spanish ambassador to Rome in 1671 (two years after his dismissal), Peñaranda said he would be no match for those who had "dedicated their lives to the quintessential study of people, politics, and diplomacy." Although he acknowledged Nithard's integrity, Peñaranda believed that his immersion in theology and philosophy would impede his ability to deal with "the most astute and skillful individuals." Peñaranda was not alone in his assessment of Nithard's lack of political savvy: when Nithard temporarily replaced the Spanish ambassador in Rome, his blunders frustrated, and at times infuriated, ministers in Madrid. His performance indicates that he lacked the skills to dominate, or even survive, either in Madrid or in Rome. In cutthroat environments like the papal and Spanish courts, he was a cat among lions.[34]

His recorded votes on most matters discussed in the Council of State were unexceptional, and it is abundantly clear that his opinions did not carry much weight with his colleagues or the queen. For example, like all members of the Council of State, Nithard voted on whether Spain should end the Portuguese War by granting the kingdom independence. Members had to justify their vote in writing: Nithard's first draft had 162 points of argument and counterargument, with his final recommendation—against peace—buried near the end. Written in Spanish with extensive quotes in Latin and numerous references to canon law and scripture, it was the kind of text that prompted the frustrated imperial ambassador to write in his diary that "Nithard wanted to solve political matters with theology." The final version was a disquisition of 265 points. For all his erudition, Nithard could not deliver a strong political message that could shape policy decisions.[35]

Mariana expressed respect for Nithard's opinions and utilized his scholarly talents when appropriate. She appointed Nithard to head the Committee of Theologians that justified a military alliance with England in which Spain allied with "heretics" against a Catholic prince. Nithard worked to reform the tax system, and while his role in this endeavor needs to be evaluated, he may have influenced Mariana's refusal to have the Cortes request war subsidies that would have affected the less fortunate. She requested donations from "grandees, ministers, and rich vassals" instead. Nithard was unusual in another regard: he did not accumulate significant personal wealth under Mariana's patronage and avoided many of the scandals usually associated with *validos*. Mariana could count on his honesty, and as a Habsburg and a queen, her closeness to her confessor had an important symbolic function. Her response to the Council of State following France's declaration of war on May 18, 1667, for example, opened with a statement that followed Nithard's recommendation to seek "divine intervention" to respond to this "utterly unjust and untimely action." Indeed, the language was exactly that of her confessor. But for military and diplomatic strategies, Nithard carried less weight than other figures in Mariana's regime.[36]

Had the regency been less besieged by crisis, her collaboration with Nithard would probably have been more productive. However, even before the crisis, she developed other fruitful political partnerships that made his policy role negligible. Since individual votes were recorded in the Council of State deliberations, it is possible to see which figures influenced Mariana and the council. Medina de las Torres was so influential on Portugal that at least two historians have called him Mariana's behind-the-scenes *valido*. This is perhaps exaggerated, but he was an important figure during the early years of the regency, as was the Count of Peñaranda, who had extensive expertise in diplomatic matters. Mariana also forged critical partnerships with figures outside Madrid, consolidating them during Nithard's supposed tenure as the favorite he never was.[37]

Nithard's role in Mariana's regime was rather undefined. He had access to the queen and was a central figure, but he never became a dominant policy influence. Influencing domestic and foreign policy was the first fundamental mark of a favorite/*valido* in the seventeenth century, which Nithard thus did not fulfill. Furthermore, he never controlled royal patronage, and this is, without a doubt, the other litmus test of a *valido*. Indeed, Francisco Tomás y Valiente, whose work on *validos* remains foundational, called Nithard a *valido frustrado*, or a frustrated favorite. Evidence suggests that his lack of support when Don Juan attacked can be traced to unfulfilled promises he made to, among others, Peñaranda and the Duke of Montalto, whom Nithard later identified as enemies in his memoirs. A similar pattern can be found with Don Juan. Early in the regency, Nithard tried to mentor the prince but was unable to broker any deals in Don Juan's favor with the queen or Montalto or Peñaranda. No one could survive the court environment without the ability to broker power, favors, and even financial gains and thus develop a substantial clientele, which Nithard evidently did not have. When he found himself in trouble in 1669, he had few strong supporters: those who opposed his dismissal did so out of loyalty to the queen.[38]

Nithard had no one to blame but himself. Not only did he fail to cultivate supporters, but his scholarly writing style was no match for Don Juan's sparkling, punchy, and persuasive prose. Nithard's point-by-point rebuttal was published soon after Don Juan's open letter; it was long, repetitive, pedantic, erudite, and boring. It made solid legal arguments that revealed Nithard's scholarly prowess, but his strong points—like the suggestion that Don Juan's behavior was treasonous—were buried. Nithard lost the battle against Don Juan to the power of the pen as much as to the power of the sword.[39]

If Nithard was politically incompetent, why did Mariana stand by him? Perhaps it was for personal reasons—he had been at her side since her childhood. More convincing, however, is the idea that Don Juan's demand that she dismiss her confessor put her authority in question. She would not tolerate such a thing, but the majority of her ministers had no desire to come to Nithard's defense to preserve Mariana's honor. Avoiding an outbreak of violence trumped defending royal authority. At the critical juncture of 1669, Mariana became painfully aware that she did not have enough support to preserve the prerogative to choose her ministers and exercise her right to royal patronage. The resolution of the confrontation was a key moment for Mariana as well as Don Juan and Nithard.

"THE COURT CALMED DOWN AND THE GOVERNMENT RETURNED TO NORMAL"

Don Juan was able to elude royal authority because some Catalonian cities were willing to protect him and because the effort to apprehend him was poorly organized. However, he lacked widespread backing. Many cities in Castile, Aragon, and Valencia forwarded letters sent by Don Juan to Madrid with the seal intact to show that they had not even opened them. He lacked the support needed to hold a principal role in Mariana's government and certainly could not have replaced her. How then did he accomplish his escape and Nithard's banishment? It was partly because of the international situation. The possibility that Louis XIV would support Don Juan, arming him, and/or take advantage of a civil war in Spain to invade the Low Countries or even the peninsula became real fears. This was the modus operandi of early modern politics, and although Castile was an incredibly loyal kingdom, Catalonia had a troubled history with the central government in Madrid. On the advice of the Council of State, Mariana sent instructions to the viceroys of Aragon, Catalonia, and Valencia on how to proceed if faced with a military attack from France.[40]

Pope Clement IX offered Mariana his support and volunteered to mediate between her and her illegitimate stepson, but she followed her councilors' advice and declined, downplaying the severity of the problem. She ordered the Duke of Osuna, the viceroy of Aragon, to investigate Don Juan's "designs" inside and outside of Spain and find him. Other than a vague idea that he may have been in the vicinity of Zaragoza in late November, not much was known. By late 1668, councilors feared the consequences if Mariana did not give in and had little will to defend Nithard, who stopped attending Council of State meetings.[41]

Don Juan had informants and was aware of the hesitation within the councils. Emboldened by the fear the court exhibited, Don Juan came out of hiding, repeated his demands that the queen dismiss Nithard, and marched toward Madrid with a small infantry force. Don Gerónimo de Quiñones, the Spanish ambassador in Paris, reported that Louis XIV had sent officers to support Don Juan's coup. The viceroy of Navarre informed Mariana that the French king was moving men and arms to the Spanish frontier in the Pyrenees. Don Juan did not accept France's help, which would have amounted to treason, but the possibility of losing the gains already made on the international stage with the peace settlement that had prevented the loss of the Spanish Netherlands, coupled with the looming fear of disturbances, sealed Nithard's fate. Citing the "vast designs of that [French] Crown," the Council of State emphasized to Mariana the consequences of Don Juan entering Madrid with an army. Although his force numbered just several hundred, his arrival was expected to provoke riots and uprisings. Another vote was held to decide Nithard's fate: the Junta de Gobierno and the Council of State were divided, but the Councils of Castile and Aragon favored dismissal. As the days passed, there was an increasing consensus that immediate dismissal was the best, most practical solution.[42]

Mariana did not have the support to gather armed forces to face Don Juan, and she was unwilling to risk violence. She discharged Nithard of all duties on February 24, 1669, even prohibiting her lifelong teacher and confessor from coming to the palace to bid her farewell. The phrasing of the decree safeguarded Nithard's honor, but everyone knew that "license to retire" meant exile. She promised to make him an extraordinary ambassador to Vienna or Rome, "whichever he chooses," and confirmed his retention of all "posts and privileges." Cardinal Aragón and the Count of Peñaranda delivered the difficult news and escorted the fallen confessor from Madrid that same day. Mariana did not want this to happen but was unable to protect her confessor. It was a prudent decision and likely saved many lives, perhaps including Nithard's, but it was a serious blow to her royal power. What started as Don Juan fleeing the queen's wrath in the summer of 1668 ended up as a coup against the regency government.[43]

However, it did not go any further, and this fact is as important as understanding that Mariana's hand was forced. Two days after Nithard's departure, Don Juan wrote to Mariana, throwing himself at her feet and informing her that he had abandoned his march on Madrid and was on his way to Guadalajara. The ruling elite may have turned a blind eye to his quasi-treasonous behavior, but they never gave Don Juan unconditional support for a coup against Mariana. Peñaranda, for example, cautioned him to moderate his behavior or the government would be forced to "condemn his actions." Don Juan could not ignore a reprimand from the Junta de Gobierno, particularly one voiced by a powerful councilor. The charge of treason was, after all, a capital crime. Grasping the situation, Don Juan limited his demands, satisfied with achieving Nithard's dismissal. He also requested that Mariana implement fiscal reforms to alleviate the plight of the poor. Although it appears that he took too many risks for a relatively small payoff, it is also useful to remember that the situation started with Don Juan escaping the queen's wrath. Mariana's legitimacy was too strong for him to challenge, and he evidently understood that the queen was not going to be pushed into accepting him into her government. Mariana had preserved the court's stability, and a gazetteer reported that she had done so easily: "After the quarrel [was laid to rest], the court calmed down and the government returned to normal."[44]

MARIANA'S STRATEGIES IN THE AFTERMATH OF THE CRISIS

Mariana did not let the lesson or the opportunity pass. She immediately began to implement measures that would prevent such a situation from happening again. In a secret convocation about ten days after Nithard's dismissal, Mariana requested that the Council of Castile "consider the present situation and recommend the measures best able to maintain peace." The first measure was to find a permanent position for Don Juan: Mariana appointed him viceroy and captain general of the kingdom of Aragon. This was a necessary and acceptable, if not ideal, solution: it got her enemy out of Madrid gracefully. She went through the motions of establishing a committee to implement fiscal and social reforms—the Junta de Alivios—as Don Juan had demanded. She named Valladares, the minister who had issued the order for Malladas's execution and Patiño's imprisonment, president of the committee, surely as a provocation to Don Juan. (She also appointed him inquisitor general as Nithard's replacement.) The committee was then allowed to wither away after six months of ineffectual existence. Mariana had always been open to reform—she had already implemented many reforms in the royal households and the Council of Finance. Her sabotage of the committee was a rejection of Don Juan's imposition.[45]

In the aftermath of the crisis, Mariana significantly reduced long-standing royal pensions, targeting those at the top of the pyramid. Royal grants of up to two hundred *ducados* remained in order "to protect the poor." Those between two hundred and three hundred were reduced by a third. Pensions between four hundred and eight thousand were halved, and Mariana decreed that "no royal grant should exceed the sum of 4,000 *ducados*." She used the monarchy's need to "gather funds with which to assist the defense of these kingdoms and eliminate the need for the common folk [*pueblos*] to contribute to the support of the court" to justify the cuts. This was sound policy but also potentially controversial, as cutting benefits always was. No one protested, however. She also instituted two chairs of theology at the University of Alcalá de Henares filled by Jesuits, saying she was honoring Nithard's wishes. Mariana specifically stated that she followed the same principle that led Philip III to institute two chairs of theology—filled by Dominicans—at the Duke of Lerma's request. The Dominicans had been some of Nithard's most vocal critics.[46]

She had another change in mind as well. There had been discussions about establishing a personal royal guard as the conflict between Mariana and Don Juan escalated, but they had never gone anywhere. Aytona contended that if they had, Don Juan would never have challenged her authority. Shortly after Nithard's exile, Mariana and Aytona revived the idea, and in April 1669, the levying of troops commenced under Aytona's coronelship. Mariana and Aytona drew on older political traditions as well as more recent examples. The Spanish Habsburgs had inherited a number of royal guards from their Castilian and German ancestors and had incorporated them into the royal households. Others were formed during political upheaval to protect the king. Both King Ferdinand II of Aragon and King Carlos I (before becoming Emperor Charles V) had formed guards. Although their duties had become ceremonial, these guards provided both model and justification for Mariana's guard, which, per Aytona's suggestion, she called the "Regiment of the *King's* Guard." The name obscured the fact that the regiment protected Mariana and was her instrument, not the king's; it essentially amounted to having a standing army in the capital city.[47]

Aytona relied on recent precedents, using the guard Olivares had created for Philip IV as a model for salaries, rules, training, and organization of the new regiment. Like Olivares, Aytona intended his guard to serve as a military school to produce better-trained soldiers and officers. And in a policy reminiscent of Olivares's "Union of Arms" scheme, Aytona recruited soldiers from across the peninsula, including from the two Castiles, Galicia, Navarre, and Vizcaya. In both guards, the commander in chief was known as the coronel. In 1634, Philip IV had given orders to form a *coronelía*, an armed force, of between 2,500 and 3,000 infantry, and he had designated these as the king's guard. Philip IV's guard had a clear military purpose and had been created with the intention of integrating it into Spain's standing army. Closely associated with Olivares, who was appointed commander in chief with the title of coronel, the king's guard of the 1630s was nicknamed, scornfully, the "Guardia Guzmano" (Olivares's last name). It was not a popular measure, but Philip IV went ahead with the idea in spite of objections raised by the Council of War. After Olivares's fall, Don Luis de Haro succeeded his uncle as coronel. Carlos II's guard, like its most recent predecessor, was also called a *coronelía*, and the commander in chief bore the title of coronel.[48]

The city of Madrid strongly opposed the regiment's establishment. City officials expressed their "anguish" (*desconsuelo*) at seeing "a *tercio* raised in Madrid." Arguing that it trampled the city's traditional liberties and was without precedent, the city councilors claimed it would create confusion, render the roads dangerous, burden the tribunals, interrupt commerce, increase crime, and compromise the city's ability to care for its own inhabitants. The establishment of a standing army in Madrid fell under the jurisdiction of the Council of Castile, which was adamantly opposed to it. Councilors begged "at Her Majesty's feet to desist of the project." Mariana acknowledged their request and stated that she had carefully considered the matter with "all the attention that it requires." "I have decided," she wrote, "that the regiment will be formed in imitation to the one the King [Philip IV], My Lord, also so that the soldiers that found themselves without employment as a result of the peace find a form of sustenance." Lavishly dressed in red uniforms and heavily armed, the regiment mounted guard at the palace doors for the first time on July 19, 1669. Ten days later, the entire guard assembled in the Madrid Alcázar for Carlos II's review. This was symbolically important, as it hid Mariana's desire to protect her own authority under the rationale of protecting the king. The king provided still another justification for the guard's existence, as Mariana and Aytona framed it as a didactic tool for him. No one, surely, could object to that.[49]

The regiment's presence was a highly visible reminder of the queen's monopoly on violence. "King's guard" or not, its association with Mariana and the fact that one of its main purposes was to keep Don Juan at bay were common knowledge. The controversial decision was a stroke of political genius: Mariana now had a standing army, and she could use it for royal patronage. Housed, fed, clothed, and paid on time—unusual in a court where most salaries were in arrears—the guard offered work for soldiers and officers and nonmilitary personnel, including chaplains, Latin instructors, bureaucrats, and a teacher of mathematics. Captains were usually nobles, and they were soon competing for commissions, perhaps the greatest measure of Mariana's success. Although she trampled the ancient rights and liberties that Spaniards were so proud of and that had shaped the Habsburg political system, the "Queen's Regiment of the King's Guard" greatly consolidated Mariana's position.[50]

THE QUEEN'S TRUSTED COUNSELOR

The difficulties of 1668–69 tested the loyalty of all, and while many demonstrated their commitment to Mariana, none did so with the dedication of the Marquis of Aytona, whom studies of the period have tended to undervalue. After Nithard's fall, however, everyone in Madrid knew that Aytona was the most powerful man at court. It is he, not Nithard, who came closest to occupying the position of *valido*, but a more accurate description of Aytona's role would be that of the queen's most trusted counselor.[51]

Mariana and Aytona's political partnership developed gradually as Aytona rose through the ranks, working with and within the court system. In the regency's first two years, he moved mostly behind the scenes,

engineering the reforms of the royal households and devising and execut-
ing Spain's military strategy. He was Mariana's link to the Council of War,
advising the queen on fortification, defense, and distribution of arms and
soldiers. An extensive memorandum on foreign policy from February 1666,
signed and annotated by the queen, suggests that he advised on foreign
policy as well. Mariana charged him with projects in engineering, education, commerce, and finance. For example, he had permission to convoke
meetings in his house to form a commercial company that would stimu-
late Spain's trade and the economy. Mariana also gave him a free hand in the
king's education. His research on previous royal tutors probably served as
the basis for Mariana's decision to appoint Francisco Ramos del Manzano,
and he advised Mariana about Carlos's dance teachers and musicians. It was
Aytona who conceived of the king's regiment as a didactic tool and marshaled it for the seven-year-old to review. Aytona also oversaw the building
of a miniature fortress in the Casa del Campo; it looked like a playground
but was intended to arouse a love of martial activities in Carlos.[52]

Aytona had a solid institutional and patronage base and was the brother
of one of Mariana's closest female companions, Magdalena de Moncada.
Although chosen to accompany Margarita to Vienna, Moncada declined
the appointment, remaining in Madrid, where she was an influential figure
in the regime. Yet Aytona's central place came not from his family but from
his abilities, including being able to adapt to the queen's temperament. His
dedication to the queen's cause was uncompromising. The events that led
to Nithard's exile troubled him deeply: "Had I not been so sick," he assured
the queen, "I would have prevented [Nithard's exile] or I would have died
in the process." Mariana needed a skilled strategist to help her overcome the
political, logistical, and financial obstacles that had originally prevented
the establishment of a royal guard, and Aytona filled that role.[53]

By the second half of 1669, a recognizable shift had occurred. Aytona
had gathered the most important offices of the court, the government,
and the military. He was *caballerizo mayor* (master of the horse) and the
mayordomo mayor (grand master) of the queen's household, thus monop-
olizing the only masculine positions available in the royal households; he
was also member of the Junta de Gobierno and now coronel of the king's
guard. Particularly notable was the fact that he was the third larger-than-life
seventeenth-century figure to become coronel of the king's guard, following the Count-Duke of Olivares and Don Luis de Haro, Philip IV's two

successive *validos*. To the court, it appeared that a new *valido* had emerged, which provoked resentment—the court was soon flooded with anti-Aytona pasquinades. Even Aytona, not easily intimidated, felt compelled to defend himself, asking the queen to write a declaration saying that he received no salary. But Aytona's controversial role was short lived. Only fifty-five but with serious health problems and bearing great responsibility, he died on March 17, 1670. She lost an intelligent and loyal minister, but Mariana had a sizeable group of capable men at her disposal.[54]

THE RECONFIGURATION OF MARIANA'S REGIME

Mariana did not replace Aytona with a single figure but instead distributed his offices among several people, further evidence that there was no *valimiento* system in place. One reason is that Mariana had important partnerships with several figures and needed to reward them for their roles during the crisis. For example, the constable of Castile, who had assisted with military recruitment and replaced Don Juan as governor of the Low Countries, took Aytona's spot in the Junta de Gobierno representing the grandees. Barely forty, he also received the presidencies of the Councils of Military Orders and Flanders and became a member of the Council of State. The Marquis of Castel Rodrigo, who had orchestrated the Triple Alliance in 1668 and led negotiations with France, was rewarded with the post of *caballerizo mayor* of the queen's household. Castel Rodrigo became one of Mariana's most trusted councilors in the years to come. She appointed him to the Council of State, from where he played a key role in devising military and diplomatic strategy that Mariana followed in the second half of her regency.[55]

The Duke of Pastrana succeeded Aytona as *mayordomo mayor* of the queen's household, holding this important office until Carlos II's own household was established in April 1675. Pastrana died shortly after, but Mariana did not replace him; the office was not as symbolically or logistically central as it had been when the king was part of the queen's household. Cardinal Aragón was coronel of the king's guard until he moved to Toledo to take up his duties as archbishop. As a result of Cardinal Aragón's leaving Madrid for Toledo, the regiment remained under the effective command of the lieutenant coronel, the Count of Aguilar, another key figure in this phase of the regency. With none of these men did Mariana have the level of partnership she had had with Aytona, but they formed a cohesive group she could work with.[56]

By 1670, Mariana had established patronage networks across all power centers: the ruling classes (nobles, *letrados*, and ecclesiastical elites), institutions (household officials and councils of government), and diplomats outside the court. The Council of State was completely populated by her own men. When Medina de las Torres died in 1670, Peñaranda became the senior member and had the right to speak first. But from 1670 onward, Peñaranda shared the spotlight with two towering figures: the Marquis of Castel Rodrigo (former governor of the Low Countries) and the Marquis de la Fuente (ambassador to France before the war). Mariana had worked closely with both and had tremendous respect for their knowledge and experience.

The Council of State retained a principal role, and when the constable arrived from the Low Countries in 1670, he joined a cohesive group of loyal supporters. From then on, councilors usually drafted their opinions as a group rather than individually, perhaps the strongest evidence that the deep divisions of the previous years had been overcome. Mariana also streamlined the governing process. She began to dispatch state papers with the help of Don Pedro Fernández del Campo, who replaced Don Blasco de Loyola after his death in 1668 as the main royal secretary. He supervised the rest of the secretaries and became her right hand. He had an enormous workload and commensurate responsibility, which Mariana recognized in 1673 by giving him the title of Marquis of Mejorada.[57]

The second important shift came from changes Mariana made to the Council of Castile. She adopted the tradition of the kings' weekly meetings with the council president, a post now held by Don Pedro Núñez de Guzmán, Count of Villaumbrosa. (After the crisis, Valladares had replaced Nithard as inquisitor general, leaving the presidency open.) Villaumbrosa, an incredibly intelligent man, soon earned Mariana's complete trust. The Junta de Gobierno, of which Villaumbrosa was a member in his capacity as president of Castile, was also populated by most of Mariana's appointees. Meetings ceased to occur, but the junta's juridical status remained in place. Mariana kept the group as Philip IV's testament had established it, making the last appointment in 1671, when Melchor de Navarra y Rocafull, Duke of Palata, replaced Crespí de Valdaura, the vice-chancellor of Aragon, after his death. Mariana's political system consolidated into a predictable pattern:

Mejorada and Villaumbrosa were the two figures closest to the queen. Institutionally, she relied on the Council of State and individual figures within that council whom Mariana trusted and had been working with for the previous five years.[58]

The new stability can be seen in Mariana's regency portraits, which settled into a fixed iconography developed by court painter Juan Carreño de Miranda. He depicted Mariana seated at her desk in the act of dispatching documents as if she had just lifted her eyes from the task. The picture of the consummate governor, it was widely reproduced (fig. 5). Mariana's position as the king's tutor took on additional significance after the crisis of 1669 as well. The king's tenth birthday in 1671 marked a political milestone, the point when, according Philip IV's testament, he was to begin his formal political instruction "in order to be knowledgeable of all matters of state when the government [came] to depend on him." He began to take a more active role in court ceremonies, learning to order grandees to cover their heads in his presence and receiving diplomats, who commented on his precociousness.[59]

Carlos II's portraits also had their own iconography, using symbols from traditional representations of kingship while implicitly referencing Mariana's role. Around his tenth birthday, Carlos was shown standing holding a piece of paper, as was typical of Spanish kings (fig. 6). In his case, however, the paper alluded to his education rather than to actual government administration, which remained in his mother's hands. Looking at paintings of the two side by side shows that the representation of rulership during the regency minority was split between Carlos II and Mariana, with Carlos embodying sovereignty while Mariana exercised it. Neither could exist without the other (figs. 5 and 6).

The treatises celebrating the king's tenth birthday also emphasized Mariana's role in her son's education and political preparation, explicitly comparing Carlos II's education and the progress of his minority with those of earlier kings. His namesake, Emperor Charles V, who ruled Spain as Carlos I, offered a felicitous comparison. *Reynados de menor edad* (Minority reigns), written by Carlos II's teacher, Ramos del Manzano, and dedicated to Mariana, contained two engravings showing similarities between Carlos I and II. One depicted Charles V with his tutor and governor, Margaret of Austria; the other showed Carlos II with his tutor and governor, Mariana (figs. 7 and 8). The book reinforced Mariana's regency by

FIGURE 5 Juan Carreño de Miranda, *Carlos II*, ca. 1671. Oil on canvas. Museo del Prado, cat. 642. Photo: Erich Lessing / Art Resource, New York.

FIGURE 6 Juan Carreño de Miranda (1614–1685), *Queen Mariana of Austria as Governor*, ca. 1675. Oil on canvas. Museo de la Real Academia de Bellas Artes de San Fernando, inv. 640. Photo: Album / Art Resource, New York.

FIGURE 7 Pedro de Villafranca Malagón (ca. 1615–1684), *Engraving of Emperor Charles V and Margaret of Austria*. Plate (Estampa) 10 in Francisco Ramos del Manzano, *Reynados de menor edad* (Madrid, 1672). Biblioteca Nacional de España, Madrid. Photo © Biblioteca Nacional de España.

FIGURE 8 Pedro de Villafranca Malagón, *Engraving of Carlos II and Mariana of Austria*. Plate (Estampa) 1 in Francisco Ramos del Manzano, *Reynados de menor edad* (Madrid, 1672). Biblioteca Nacional de España, Madrid. Photo © Biblioteca Nacional de España.

comparing her son to one of the greatest monarchs of Habsburg Spain and exalting Mariana's role as comparable to that of Margaret. Readers were also reminded that Mariana was the direct descendant of Charles V.[60]

There were other instructive examples. King Ferdinand III of Castile and León also succeeded to the throne as a minor and went on to expand the Castilian frontiers into Muslim territory and become one of the most formidable warrior kings of the Reconquista. He was sanctified in 1671, thus making the connection between him and his successor even more compelling. Don Pedro González de Salcedo, the lawyer who ordered the execution of Malladas, wrote a treatise in 1671, *Nudrición Real* (Royal nourishment), that exalted Mariana's image as "the supreme royal maternity." History, therefore, augured exceedingly well for the monarchy, given that the king was in the same position as some of the Castile's and the Habsburg's most venerated rulers, and his mother was a model queen whose "saintly endeavor" and "royal nourishment" would ensure the king's greatness.[61]

By midregency, Mariana had successfully weathered major threats to her authority, fighting off the challenge of Don Juan, ending the difficulties caused by Nithard, establishing strong political partnerships, and setting up an armed guard. She had fully shaped the regime. Nevertheless, Mariana never lost sight of the international situation. The peace was unstable. Although the army of Flanders had regained its former strength, it was still smaller than France's; other areas, such as those in the Mediterranean and along the Pyrenees frontiers, remained unprotected, and the French king was still plotting against Spain. It was time to turn her attention back to the international stage, where Louis XIV's machinations would present the next set of challenges.

CHAPTER 5

At the Pinnacle of Power, 1670 to November 5, 1675

In spite of the settlement of the Peace of Aix-la-Chapelle (May 2, 1668),
the French still posed a major threat to Spain. Knowing that the renewal of
hostilities was only a matter of time, Mariana worked to prepare. Conscious
that France had its eye on the Spanish Netherlands and that Spain was still
in no condition to face a war on its own, she took a conciliatory line with
Louis XIV. The four years of peace (1668–72) gave her the breathing room
she needed to build up Spain's military power and reinforce its frontiers.
The newfound stability of the court greatly contributed to Mariana's ability
to accomplish these goals. She now counted on a cohesive, reliable group
of councilors. The deliberations of the Council of State indicate that it continued to be Mariana's principal organ of government until the end of her
governorship. We can also gauge through the deliberations that she adopted
the strategies presented to her by state councilors based on their individual
expertise. The Marquis of Castel Rodrigo, former governor of the Low
Countries, for example, was critical in formulating Mariana's strategies with
Scandinavian powers, the Holy Roman Empire, and the United Provinces;
the Marquis de la Fuente, former ambassador in France, became her principal advisor on the relationship with the French; the Count of Peñaranda,
the oldest serving councilor of state, took the lead on English policy. These
are some of the most important figures, but certainly not all of them. Mariana counted on a small army of diplomats, viceroys and governors, and
generals to do her bidding outside Madrid and to compile the reports

and recommendations she based her policies on. Mariana certainly did not act alone (few monarchs did), but she chose the policies she deemed most appropriate, often in situations with multiple options and risks.[1]

Even during peacetime, Mariana and Louis XIV engaged in a diplomatic war over the fate of the 1668 Triple Alliance. Louis XIV worked to dissolve it, Mariana to preserve it. When Louis XIV joined forces with England's Charles II to invade the United Provinces in April 1672, it ended the Triple Alliance, as England was now fighting its cosignatory, the United Provinces. This was a loss for Mariana, but in less than a year, she made Spain the head of a major anti-French coalition. Formed in August 1673, the Quadruple Alliance—an offensive coalition between the United Provinces, Spain, the Holy Roman Empire, and the Duke of Lorraine—transformed the Franco-Dutch War (1672–78) into a pan-European conflict now fought against France. In the next few years, Mariana also concluded defensive leagues with Northern European princes and negotiated Charles II's withdrawal from his alliance with France. These accomplishments marked the height of Mariana's power on the international stage.

As Mariana reached that pinnacle of power, she faced political pitfalls as her tenure in office was nearing the end. In anticipation of Carlos II's emancipation, she transformed the court, establishing the king's royal household. An explosion of theatrical productions, the resumption of hunts and royal vacations—the *jornadas*—to Spanish palaces, and a resurgence of building projects contributed to the court's splendor. These were orchestrated by Mariana's protégé, Don Fernando Valenzuela, a man of the theater with experience in the politics of representation. Valenzuela was starkly different from any of Mariana's other political partners, and even without influencing foreign policy, he had a tremendous impact on the court. Its new brilliance, for which he was largely responsible, helped mask the uncertainty of the queen's future as the process of surrendering power began. This chapter takes us through the second half of Mariana's regency, filled with accomplishments but also heartache, losses, and difficult political and diplomatic decisions.

AN UNSTABLE PEACE

After the peace of Aix-la-Chapelle, diplomatic relations between France and Spain were only slowly restored. Louis XIV sent an extraordinary ambassador, the Marquis Pierre de Villars, to Madrid in September 1668 to invite Mariana to become the godmother of Louis's newborn son, Philippe Charles, Duke of Anjou. Villars was charged with gaining Mariana's trust, a task complicated by Louis's continuing attempts to undermine the treaty. In the months following the peace, there were constant reports that Louis was moving men and arms near the Spanish frontiers in Catalonia, Navarre, and the Mediterranean. Convinced that "the peace was unstable," the viceroy of Navarre, Duke of San Germán, asked for reinforcements. Mariana pretended to accept Louis XIV's gestures of friendship, but everything indicated that war was on the horizon.[2]

Louis XIV was a constant source of concern. Mariana found out, for example, that he had influenced the Duke of Savoy, Carlo Emanuel II, to cede his succession rights to the Low Countries to France in exchange for the "ones that his Most Christian King had over the Republic of Genoa." While the Savoyard dynasty had been named in the succession in Philip IV's testament, the Duke of Savoy would only inherit—the entire monarchy, not just the Low Countries—if both Habsburg lines were extinct. The purported agreement between Louis XIV and Carlo Emanuel was therefore outrageous. Acts like these were provocations, but Mariana instructed her ambassador in The Hague, Esteban Gamarra, who had found out about the scheme, to ignore it.[3]

It was only after the peace that Mariana learned about the Partition Treaty of the Spanish monarchy that Louis XIV and Leopold I had signed in January 1668, agreeing that the Spanish monarchy would be divided between them if Carlos II died childless. This discovery was shocking and potentially explosive: not only was Leopold Mariana's brother, but he was married to the universal heiress to the monarchy, Empress Margarita, and was named directly in the succession. Mariana ordered her ambassador in Vienna, the Count of Castellar, to investigate, but she did not bring the matter to the Council of State. Mariana could be as shrewd as Louis XIV, and she continued to collaborate in the diplomatic realm with her brother as if nothing had changed. While Castellar was investigating, Spanish and imperial diplomats were working together to preserve the Triple Alliance and expanded it to include Spain and the Holy Roman Empire as named members.[4]

While she could shrug off the Savoyard claims and her brother's duplicity, she could not ignore conclusive reports from cities in Catalonia,

Navarre, and the Mediterranean that Louis XIV was moving thousands of men and matériel closer to the Spanish frontiers. The king claimed he was responding to pleas from the Republic of Venice for Christian rulers to help liberate the Duchy of Candia, as Crete was known when it was a colony ruled by the Venetian Republic, at this point under Ottoman siege. The viceroys of Catalonia and Navarre were convinced, however, that this was a ruse and that Louis was simply readying his attack.[5]

That threat did not materialize, but six months after the Ottomans had captured Candia, Louis XIV concocted another stratagem to penetrate Spanish waters. He requested permission for his ships to harbor in Spanish ports while he cleansed the Mediterranean of "Algerian pirates, who were infesting the area." This bold demand would have allowed twenty-six French vessels and thousands of men to remain along the Spanish coast or within Spanish ports, well within striking distance of Spanish territory. Mariana informed officials in the twenty-three Spanish port cities and presidios in the Mediterranean to be prepared to defend themselves but not to attack unprovoked. Relations with the fleets should be conducted courteously, but officials should allow no more than six vessels at a time within port waters. Even then, the French captains would have to agree to quarantine their vessels with the excuse that they were coming from plague-infested areas. These conditions were absolutely nonnegotiable. When the French ambassador protested, Mariana responded that a similar policy applied to English and Dutch vessels. While avoiding open confrontation, Mariana kept Louis XIV's threat at bay, and he found himself with no choice but to abide by her rules.[6]

Given Louis XIV's machinations, Mariana focused on preserving and, ideally, expanding the 1668 Triple Alliance between England, the United Provinces, and Sweden. This alliance had forced the settlement of the War of Devolution and protected Spain's sovereign rights in the Netherlands. As Mariana saw it, the Triple Alliance was "the only way to secure the dominions of the King, My Son, and to curb the ambition of the King of France." Mariana wanted Spain included in the alliance, and when her negotiators in The Hague ran into obstacles, she could not understand "why the Dutch would not want to include us [Spain] in a treaty that is for the common security and benefit." Spanish diplomats in London failed to include the emperor, and attempts to attract German princes into the alliance also met with failure. Indeed, the Triple Alliance itself was at risk. One major point of contention was the subsidies Spain was supposed to pay to Sweden. At first Mariana refused to pay, alleging that she had not been consulted on the amount and had not agreed that Spain would be solely responsible. This is hard to believe, since she received a copy of the agreement where this was clearly stated. This contentiousness did not bode well for the alliance's survival.[7]

Mariana continued to reinforce Spain's frontiers and expand its offensive capacity, but money, as always, was an obstacle. Silver shipments had increased significantly during the War of Devolution (1667–68), but they declined by 50 percent in 1669–70. Special taxes and a wider distribution of the fiscal burden helped offset the deficit. Naples, for example, shouldered a particularly heavy fiscal burden throughout the regency. Local cities bore a substantial portion of the cost of strengthening their defenses.[8]

Although relatively effective, these measures were not enough, and Spain desperately needed loans. Here too Mariana faced difficulties, as rumors that Spain contemplated a suspension of payments limited her ability to obtain them. Mariana assured individual bankers that the monarchy would meet its obligations; she also used her jewels as collateral. These strategies had a cumulative effect: between 1669 and 1671, Mariana secured loans worth 2.5 million silver *escudos*. Although the economic history of the period is still in need of further investigation, Sanz Ayán and Sánchez Belén indicate that there was an improved financial situation, which allowed Mariana to borrow as much as 6.5 million in 1672–73. The *Asiento de Esclavos*, or monopoly on the slave trade in the New World, which she established in 1674, yielded an additional 450,000 *reales de a ocho* yearly for the war effort.[9]

SECURING THE PEACE TO PREPARE FOR WAR

By 1670, Spain's military and defense capacity were still below the levels of Philip IV's heyday but were up dramatically from 1665 levels. The army of Flanders had sixty-three thousand men, and Spain's frontiers with France in Catalonia also received men and arms. On Mariana's orders, the Duke of Osuna, viceroy of Catalonia, oversaw repairs of the fortifications in multiple port cities in the Mediterranean and the southern Pyrenees and flooded the area with artillery, munitions, and military supplies (*pertrechos de guerra*).

Osuna also raised fifteen *tercios* who were "well-dressed, paid, and ready for combat." Working with the Duke of San Germán, Mariana also ensured that Navarre and the Basque region received men and arms, thus protecting the northwestern frontiers with France.[10]

Spanish outposts in the Mediterranean also received an influx of men and arms. The viceroy of Sardinia, the Marquis of Camarasa, was assassinated in 1668 as a result of a local political crisis. Mariana expanded the Sardinian fleet and gave its command to the Duke of San Germán, a man with proven military skills. These measures stabilized the political situation but also advanced her overall Mediterranean strategy. Mariana's decision to expel the Jews from Oran in 1669, for example, grew from the desire to impose royal control in the most important Spanish port in the area; at the time, the governor of Oran made a convincing case that the Jews posed a security threat, as they were thought to be allied with "Moors and Turks." Key coastal cities, including Gibraltar, Cadiz, and Ceuta, which Portugal returned to Spain in 1668, also received reinforcements. Mariana's ability to implement such a coherent policy was due largely to the fact that the councils in charge of these issues—State, War, Italy, and Castile—acted in concert.[11]

With the monarchy's defenses strengthened, Mariana began to crack down on illicit activities that affected Spain's commerce. She apprehended English pirates, Dutch smugglers, and French outlaws; confiscated merchandise; and imposed exemplary punishments on those who cut into Spain's trade beyond the terms allowed. She could be diplomatic when it suited her: she ordered the confiscation of the Dutch ship *Unicorn* for engaging in contraband, but she did so within the strict confines of the law in order to "not offend our allies." When the Dutch ambassador, Hieronymus van Beverningk, protested the "bad treatment that their merchants" received in Malaga, Mariana immediately ordered that the malefactors be punished "in order to satisfy the ambassador and show our [Spain's] genuine interest in observing the terms of the peace." Her vigorous defense of Spain's commerce sent a strong message to her fellow monarchs and allowed her to negotiate with potential allies from a position of strength.[12]

In spite of the advances in Spain's defenses, Mariana still needed the Triple Alliance. Accepting the impossibility of sharing the cost of Sweden's subsidies with England and the Dutch, Mariana authorized the governor of the Low Countries to negotiate the payment schedule. Before the money was delivered, the governor convened a conference in The Hague to determine the "assistance of men and navies to be given to Spain if France attacked the Low Countries." Mariana was willing to pay, but not before knowing exactly what she would get in return. The meetings began in March 1669 at the same time that Mariana sent remittances to Brussels, dangling the cash in front of Sweden and thus accelerating the process. After nearly eight months of intense negotiations, England, the United Provinces, and Sweden concluded the Act of Guarantee (*Acto de Garantía*) on January 31, 1670. It confirmed not only the Triple Alliance but the agreement's most important clause: all the members agreed to deploy military forces against Louis XIV if he failed to abide by the terms of Aix-la-Chapelle. This coalition could have mobilized a significant force against France: England and the United Provinces committed to contributing forty large, fourteen medium, and twelve small warships of thirty to eighty cannons each. The United Provinces promised a six-thousand-strong infantry and two thousand cavalry; England, a cavalry force of six thousand; and Sweden, eleven thousand men and five thousand cavalry.[13]

The conclusion of the Act of Guarantee intensified tensions between Spain and France. Louis XIV increased his provocations, while Mariana responded with astute strategies devised by the Marquis de la Fuente, former ambassador in France and now member of the Council of State. When Louis XIV added more warships in the Mediterranean with the excuse that he was clearing the waters of pirates, Mariana undermined him by harboring French subjects and arming them against France. It is not clear how many subjects of the French king she could turn against him or the actual effect this had, but the infuriated king protested to Mariana via his ambassador; Mariana denied the accusations. Louis banned Spanish correspondence from passing through his territories in late 1669; Mariana did the same for French correspondence, insisting that the king "failed to observe the terms of the peace." Next, Louis XIV manufactured a new claim against Spanish territories, saying that the "dependencies" of the cities ceded to him in the settlement of Aix-la-Chappelle should have been surrendered as well and threatening to take them by force. Mariana, who had just paid the subsidies to Sweden and was on excellent terms with England and the United Provinces, coolly responded that she would submit his claims to the Triple Alliance for arbitration. This stopped Louis: denying arbitration would activate the Triple Alliance, and the two agreed to evaluate his claims at a conference in Lille.[14]

With no real way to stop an arbitration he would most likely lose, Louis XIV found a way out of his predicament. He accepted the kings of England and Sweden as arbiters but rejected Dutch participation. He knew this would sow discord between members of the Triple Alliance, which had just concluded the Act of Guarantee, but Mariana protected the honor of the excluded party. Mariana refused to participate unless the Dutch were included, a refusal that put not only France but the alliance members on notice. If the matter was not resolved and Louis XIV pressed his claims, the Triple Alliance would have to respond to his aggression by deploying the forces agreed upon in the Act of Guarantee. A stalemate in Lille followed. Once again, Louis XIV shifted his tactics: he was now actively trying to turn the king of England away from the Act of Guarantee with a new scheme.[15]

Mariana and Louis XIV engaged in a new diplomatic contest, now in London and over the loyalty of the king of England. Louis XIV offered Charles II large subsidies to assist France in a joint campaign against the United Provinces, which would have automatically dissolved the agreement Mariana so badly wanted to preserve. Charles's sister, Henrietta of England, was married to Louis XIV's younger brother, the Duke of Orleans, and she traveled to London to help with the negotiations. The talks culminated with the signing of the controversial Secret Treaty of Dover in June 1670. In exchange for large subsidies, Charles II agreed to join France in an invasion of the United Provinces. He also promised to convert to Catholicism. The treaty remained secret but placed the Triple Alliance on life support.[16]

Meanwhile, Mariana was doing her utmost to counteract Louis XIV's enticements. She relied on the expertise of the Count of Peñaranda, the president of the Council of Indies. Working with the English ambassador in Madrid, Sir William Godolphin, Peñaranda negotiated a new treaty with England to prevent England's complete defection to France. The Treaty of Madrid—concluded on July 18, 1670—was the first treaty to establish peace between Spain and England in American waters. Although Spain did not grant English merchants permission to conduct commerce in Spanish colonies, it recognized their New World possessions, including Jamaica, a point of great significance for Charles II. The Spanish monarchy benefitted from the agreement because it confirmed all existing treaties and secret agreements between Spain and England and, most importantly, prevented the signatories from supporting the others' enemies. The Treaty of Madrid confirmed Spain's ongoing collaboration with England. The extent to which it granted Mariana a reprieve was relative. Charles II pressured his secret ally, Louis XIV, to resolve the stalemate between Spain and France. The Conference of Lille, to resolve Louis's claim of the dependencies, resumed in March 1671. It did because Louis accepted the arbitration of the United Provinces, which he previously rejected; upon the recommencing of the talks, an extension of the peace between France and Spain was agreed upon for another year.[17]

But barely three months later, news reached Madrid of a violent episode in the Caribbean that threatened to undo the understanding between Mariana and Charles II. English pirates, led by the infamous Henry Morgan, had attacked the port of Panama City in January 1671; the governor then torched the city to deny it to the invaders. When she heard the news, Mariana immediately imprisoned the English Consul in Cadiz; formed a *Junta de Represalias*, or Committee of Reprisals; and started preparing to "expel and punish the intruders." Juan Francisco de la Cerda, 8th Duke of Medinaceli and captain general of the coasts and the ocean of Andalucía, readied an armada of seven galleys and three thousand men.[18]

The Spanish captured and imprisoned forty Englishmen who were brought back to Spain with the silver fleet. When Godolphin pleaded for the release of ten of the men, Mariana told him that pirates did not deserve the king's protection. Although the understanding between Spain and England was at risk, the quarrel went no further. The invaders abandoned Panama City before any Spanish galleys were dispatched. Spanish and English diplomats in Madrid and London did their utmost to preserve the hard-won agreement, and Charles II replaced the governor of Jamaica and brought the intruders to justice (although Morgan was pardoned in 1675). Mariana accepted Godolphin's abject apologies and released some of the imprisoned Englishmen. By the end of the year, the situation had been defused.[19]

Having been thwarted in his ambitions to obtain Spanish cities in the Low Countries and pry England away from its admittedly lukewarm friendship with Spain, Louis XIV shifted his focus to the United Provinces. This move forced Mariana to once again adapt her strategies. Rumors that

France and England were planning a dual invasion of the United Provinces had circled for months; they were confirmed in October 1671. A French invasion would be bad enough; a joint invasion was far more worrisome, as Mariana's diplomatic gains in the previous years would be lost. Relying on her ministers' expertise, Mariana adopted a different policy with all the parties involved with the goal of keeping the English and the Dutch on the Spanish side.[20]

First, Mariana used the situation to conclude the type of military and diplomatic alliance with the United Provinces she had been seeking for years. The Dutch had supported Spain's claims to the Low Countries, but so far only indirectly, with the Triple Alliance rather than with Spain. As soon as the threat to the Dutch was known, Mariana offered them assistance. An extraordinary ambassador in The Hague, Manuel de Lira, had been sent to negotiate with the Dutch regents—the United Provinces' ruling elite. Lira, who was "shadowing" the elderly Gamarra in anticipation of his retirement (he died in 1671), became an important figure in Mariana's regime. Like Gamarra, he knew Dutch and possessed considerable diplomatic skills. Within months of his arrival, he had successfully negotiated the "Act of Reciprocal Assistance Against France," which stipulated that Mariana would place "all the troops and possible means available" at the Dutch's disposal for defense against France. The agreement was concluded on December 17, 1671. Although the alliance between Spain and the United Provinces meant a greater risk of war, Mariana considered it a diplomatic victory, one she had wanted since 1665. She purposely avoided offering help against England, but Lira began to advance Mariana's candidacy as an intermediary in the peace negotiations between England and the United Provinces even before the Third Anglo-Dutch War started.[21]

The Act of Reciprocal Assistance provoked strong reactions in London and Paris. Louis XIV wanted Mariana to remain neutral, and he began his usual combination of enticements and threats. He reached Mariana through his ambassador in Madrid and Leopold I, bombarding her with messages. Although Louis acknowledged that Mariana was entitled to provide auxiliary troops to the Dutch under the terms of the Treaty of the Pyrenees, he reminded her that these forces were supposed to be small. If she offered too much aid, he would consider her actions an act of war. He also tempted the queen with peace, promising to abandon his claims to the towns under litigation at the Conference of Lille if Spain remained neutral in the conflict.

Mariana did not even consider the proposals: she curtly informed the French ambassador that the agreement with the United Provinces had already been signed and ratified; there was nothing more to be done. She sent the message to Louis XIV through Vienna as well; the French resident in the imperial court, Chevalier Jacques Bretel de Grémonville, heard the same thing as the French ambassador in Madrid.[22]

Similar proposals came to Mariana from London, with Charles II proposing that Spain stop providing help to the Dutch and join England and France instead. He said England was committed to securing the peace between Spain and France and offered Mariana his help in negotiating an alliance with the empire and Sweden. Failing that, he asked for Spain's neutrality during the invasion. Mariana remained firm in her commitment to the Dutch, but rather than simply rejecting the king's proposals, she offered a counterproposal that set the stage for her eventual diplomatic victories. She warmly thanked Charles II for his membership in the Triple Alliance, reminding him that it was Louis XIV who had made the union necessary; confirmed her intention to defend the Dutch; and urged Charles II to abandon the Anglo-Dutch War, offering to act as a mediator if he did so.[23]

Mariana's approach allowed her to influence the two wars that were starting: the Third Anglo-Dutch War (1672–74) and the Franco-Dutch War (1672–78). Spain had finally reached a position of strength, as shown by England and France's eagerness to prevent a Spanish-Dutch alliance. For the past four years, Mariana had handled Louis XIV's constant provocations with caution and firmness. Using her expert councilors and her own experience, knowledge of international politics, and influence, Mariana navigated the international situation and emerged as a leading figure in the negotiations that led to the formation of an offensive coalition against France.

THE QUEEN AT WAR

Mariana approached the French and English threats differently. Assisting the Dutch against the French was a preemptive defense of Spanish territories in the Low Countries. With England, in contrast, she worked to save the alliance and end the conflict. These goals structured her orchestration of what ultimately became a wildly successful diplomatic campaign.

Spain's military aid to the Dutch started small and gradually increased: Mariana wanted more allies in the fight against France, particularly her brother, Leopold I. Although Leopold had not helped Spain during the War of Devolution and had signed the Partition Treaty with France, by 1672, relations between the two Habsburg lines had improved significantly. Her brother had dismissed and exiled his principal minister, Prince Johann Weikhard Auersperg, the man responsible for the treaty with France. News of his fall was received enthusiastically in Madrid, with members of the Council of State convinced that Mariana was behind the change. Mariana also replaced the Spanish ambassador to the empire, the volatile Count of Castellar, in 1670 with Don Pablo Spínola, Marquis of Balbases, who became an influential figure in Vienna. The possibility of Leopold I's military collaboration with Spain was already evident in the early months of 1672, reflecting the shifts in the imperial court. Balbases reported that princes of the empire had unanimously voted for subsidies for the imperial army and that recruitment had begun in earnest.[24]

But even as collaboration seemed secure, Balbases failed to extract an official confirmation from the emperor, worrying Madrid. Apprehension became anger when Mariana and her councilors learned that the emperor had signed a neutrality agreement with Louis XIV on November 1, 1671. This, it seemed, put everything back at square one. A mortified Pötting explained that his master was in no position to risk war with France—and Sweden, which was considering abandoning the Triple Alliance to join France—while dealing with a revolt in Hungary; Leopold also faced threats from the Ottomans on the empire's eastern frontier. Although Leopold I's neutrality agreement with Louis XIV caused outrage in Madrid, this time his fickleness did not have the negative impact it did in 1667.[25]

That was because, even with the agreement, the climate in Vienna was changing. On June 23, 1672, Balbases reported that Leopold I had concluded a league with the elector of Brandenburg to enforce a clause in the Westphalian settlement of 1648 that prohibited princes of the empire from allowing foreign troops into imperial territories without the emperor's express approval. This was clearly a move against the French and effectively nullified the neutrality agreement. In addition, the alliance expressly guaranteed the Pyrenees and Aix-la-Chapelle settlements, both of which involved the preservation of Spain's territories. The emperor's willingness to protect Spanish interests erased the anger the neutrality agreement had provoked. The Council of State (except for Peñaranda and Cardinal Aragón) suggested that Mariana allocate substantial subsidies to the emperor. With an increase in silver shipments, Mariana could send her brother 120,000 *reales de a ocho*, the equivalent of four monthly payments. From then on, generous subsidies poured into Leopold I's coffers to support his military contribution to the defense of the United Provinces. Adding her brother's armies to Spain's was both a practical matter (putting at her disposal a larger military force faster) and a strategic move (drawing another state openly to war against a common enemy, a strategy that Mariana's predecessors had used repeatedly). Mariana was on the brink of achieving what she had sought unrelentingly for some seven years: a military coalition that would revive the traditional military bloc of the Spanish and Austrian Habsburgs.[26]

Mariana and Leopold were moving into a greater stage of collaboration, but they were pushed together even more when Louis XIV announced his plan to attack Cologne. Louis claimed he was only seeking to "contribute to the universal peace and tranquility of the continent." The former ambassador to France, the Marquis de la Fuente, one of Mariana's most influential figures in the Council of State, described the statement as "foolish" (*desatinado*) and advised Mariana to ignore it—advice she followed. Instead of answering the king, she ordered the governor of the Low Countries, the Count of Monterrey, to "use all available forces for the defense of Cologne if France went forth with the plans." She urged Balbases in Vienna to "instill vigor and resolve on his Imperial Majesty and his ministers," and more concretely, she sent sixty thousand *reales de a ocho*, an advance of two monthly payments, to "encourage the Emperor." To the elector of Brandenburg, she sent a one-time payment of forty thousand. Monterrey was to send forces to supplement Leopold's if an attack on Cologne took place. But Mariana was not ready to openly enter the war. She clarified that the Spanish troops should only act as auxiliary forces. Conducting a shadow war—sending troops and money—was a proven strategy, which her predecessors had adopted "with much success for the empire and the August House of Habsburg." She also began negotiating to form a League of Guarantee with the emperor and Brandenburg, modeled on the Triple Alliance. The Franco-Dutch War gave Mariana the opportunity to implement a long-term goal: a diplomatic and military alliance against France with Spain as a named partner.[27]

For these reasons, Mariana saw a cease-fire or, worse yet, peace between the Dutch and French, as undesirable. When, in the face of French occupation of much of the Republic, the Dutch began considering a settlement,

Mariana instructed Lira to use the "art of dissimulation" and his utmost "sagaciousness" to prevent it, because "nothing could be as detrimental to the interests of the King, My Son," than a hasty peace between the two. "You should insist that my greatest desire is peace," Mariana said, but also "do your best to abort any treaty of peace, truce, or suspension of arms."²⁸

Riots and widespread political unrest in the United Provinces led to the rise of Prince William of Orange (the future William III of England) as Statdholder of Holland and the renunciation by Johan de Witt of the office of grand pensionary. What amounted to a lawful change of regime unfortunately did not prevent de Witt's and his brother's brutal assassination, during which they were assaulted by a mob and dismembered in public. Mariana had cultivated the prince's friendship since before the coup, and now she could establish a closer military collaboration. After a summer of deep political upheaval, there was an almost miraculous turn in the winter of 1672–73. Spain increased its military intervention in the fall of 1672, sending three thousand men and twenty-five companies of cavalry. Spanish armies played a key role in the battle won by the Dutch at Charleroi (February 1673), and the following month, a combined Dutch and Spanish fleet defeated a French squadron in the Strait of Gibraltar. But these victories were a double-edged sword, as they indicated that Spain's official entry in the conflict was imminent, a source of concern for Mariana because she had no additional allies. Brandenburg and the empire were only committed to a defensive war and only if it spread to Germany. As Spain's commitment escalated, a catastrophic family tragedy seemed to compromise matters for Mariana and the rest of the Habsburgs.²⁹

Margarita of Austria, Holy Roman empress and *infanta* of Spain, died on March 12, 1673, in her twenty-first year. She left behind a daughter, Archduchess Maria Antonia of Austria, who was only four years old. The devastating news reached Pötting in Madrid on April 4, and he went to the palace immediately to confer with the Marquise of Baldueza, Mariana's *camarera mayor*, about how to break the news. They waited until the following morning. Carlos II consoled his mother "like an angel," helping Mariana take the news with "perfect resignation." While her daughter's death was personally devastating, the matter was also a political crisis and required a cool head. Mariana needed to consider how to keep Leopold I engaged in the absence of his Spanish wife's presence. An extraordinary embassy was planned to deliver the royal family's sympathies to the emperor, but the delegation also had the diplomatic mission of concluding the offensive league with the emperor. So delicate was the situation that the instructions were redrafted three times.[30]

Margarita's death coincided with a critical period in the war. The Dutch ambassador in Madrid was pleading for help and urging Mariana to declare war on France. Official involvement in the war required deliberation in the Council of State, which met on April 18, 1673. The question was whether the monarchy should go to war before confirming the intervention of Leopold and the elector of Brandenburg. The contrast with the early years of the regency is worth noting. In spite of the issue's significance and the range of opinions, the councilors were not deeply divided: Mariana had created a reliable group of ministers who put their expertise at Spain's service. One main consideration was the undesirability of starting a war during Carlos II's minority that could last for years, if not decades. Yet as Castel Rodrigo noted—surely voicing Mariana's sentiment—war was the only way to "secure our [Spain's] peace and safety," although he cautioned against declaring it without the emperor's commitment. Mariana agreed that declaring war without the emperor's commitment would be a misstep, but she saw it as inevitable. "If the Emperor, the United Provinces, and other allies (whether Brandenburg is included or not) resolve to unite in waging war against France," she told her councilors, "I will also enter the conflict . . . with all the means that are at my disposal." "We will dissimulate," for the time being, "but prepare for total war."[31]

The Council of State was also concerned that Margarita's death had weakened Spain's position in Vienna. The mission to Vienna was absolutely critical, and Mariana split the task: she selected the Marquis of Povar to deliver the condolences and Don Pedro Ronquillo, a man of proven ability and extensive diplomatic experience, to carry on the political, military, and diplomatic negotiations. Mariana's instructions to Ronquillo reveal how, in moments of personal and dynastic crises, the Habsburgs simultaneously compartmentalized and conflated familial and state matters. Mariana instructed Ronquillo to be "her voice," telling him to start by inquiring about the emperor's health. This was not merely polite conversation; Ronquillo should explain to the emperor how critical it was that he take good care of himself, since the "good of Christendom and the succession of our House" depended on his survival. Mariana crafted her words fastidiously and instructed Ronquillo to observe the emperor's emotional state before introducing the delicate topic of his remarriage: "If you deem it appropriate then, or later if you think it better, you need to convey the necessity of ensuring the succession." She understood how the mere mention of Margarita's name "brings tears and sorrow," yet remarriage was "a critical business that could not be delayed." Indeed, Mariana's "greatest consolation would be to see him with sons [*hijos varones*]." By acknowledging his place in the succession, Mariana reinforced the idea that the ties uniting them were alive, even though Margarita was not. Only then was Ronquillo directed to begin discussing the offensive alliance; it was up to him to introduce all of these topics at once or over the course of several days. He was authorized to offer a monthly subsidy of fifty thousand *reales de a ocho*, a substantial increase from the previous thirty thousand.[32]

The dual embassy was successful on all counts. Leopold I married the Austrian archduchess, Claudia Felicitas, from the Tyrolean line of the Austrian Habsburgs, at the end of 1673. Good progress was also made in convincing the empire to intervene in the Dutch War. Indeed, Ronquillo's extraordinary embassy inaugurated a flurry of activity among Vienna, Brussels, and The Hague. Charles IV, the Duke of Lorraine, whose territories Louis XIV had confiscated in late 1669 and who had sought Mariana's protection in 1670, also participated in these talks.[33]

On July 1, 1673, the empire, Spain, the United Provinces, and the Duke of Lorraine signed a ten-year defensive alliance that included the provision that members could not negotiate separate peace agreements with France. Another alliance was concluded between Spain and the emperor on August 28, with both sides promising to defend each other's territories *and* wage war against France. On August 30, Spain and the United Provinces signed a comparable alliance, as did, separately, the empire and the United Provinces. On October 6, Spain, the empire, and the United Provinces concluded an offensive and defensive league with the Duke of Lorraine, who joined the confederates not as the head of a state but as the head of an army. These agreements were all directed against France—England's ongoing war with the United Provinces was not even mentioned. The elaborate array of agreements known as the Quadruple Alliance transformed the Dutch War into a pan-European conflict now fought mainly against France.[34]

Mariana declared war on December 11, 1673, in response to Louis XIV's declaration against Spain on October 19. Although more than ready, she let France take the initiative so that she could continue presenting herself as a proponent of peace. Now, however, she openly indicted Louis XIV even as she carefully observed rules of decorum, particularly in the version circulated in France. The term "the French" (*franceses*), for example, was substituted for the "Most Christian King" normally utilized in official correspondence. Pronouns were carefully chosen to avoid a direct reference to the person of the king. But the allegations were uncompromising. The text incorporated the opinions of the councilors of state as compiled by Mariana's secretary, but since she approved it before dissemination, it represented her views.[35]

The text announced her declaration of war and prohibited any type of commercial activities with French merchants under the threat of execution. It denounced the actions of Louis XIV with a long set of grievances that went back to the Peace of the Pyrenees (1659), which "Philip IV had sacrificed a great deal to conclude." Although "religiously observed on our [Spain's] side," Louis XIV paid it little regard, and "not even the blood and marital ties between the two crowns were sufficient to impede his thirst for conquest" (*estorvar la codicia de conquistar*). The French had "made a mockery [*hicieron risa*] of the renunciation of the Most Christian Queen" by refusing to register the document, the entire basis on which the peace and the marriage had been concluded, and by never intending to abide by it. They had, Mariana charged, barely concealed their "designs," inquiring about the health of the Spanish king "not as a form of charity but as if waiting for his death." France offered to help the Portuguese in express contravention of treaty terms and then formed with Portugal an offensive league against Spain. Such peace could not, the document continued, be considered real, as it was merely a "suspension of arms" purposely utilized by France as "an artifice to disarm us and attack us [Spain] by surprise." Indeed, while moving arms and men and making overt preparations for war, "they continued to dispel our [the queen's] suspicions," which she chose to accept "as a token of our ... sincerity and our ... trust in the royal word." But the events in the Low Countries opened Spain's eyes and simultaneously "banished our [Spain's] hopes." Indeed, Spain's desire to preserve peace was destroyed by France's desire to "provoke new wars." Their proposals had not only been false and "extremely prejudicial" but sought to rob Spain of "the most precious parts of our Crown."[36]

The duplicity of the French—or rather of Louis XIV—was contrasted with Mariana's efforts to bring peace to Christendom. But the French had taken advantage of her patience: the Peace of Aix-la-Chapelle had been nothing less than "ruinous, deceptive, and false." The Franche-Comté, "which was promised to be returned to us [Spain] in its original condition," came back as "a body without a soul," its fortresses dismantled, its walls destroyed, and its forests razed. Under the cover of peace, France had committed unspeakable acts of destruction against Spanish territories: "Not even respecting the most sacred, they had profaned churches, raped daughters and wives, pillaged and plundered those that are without defenses, doing so without restraint." The Act of Guarantee signed by members of the Triple Alliance—a cause of celebration among Europe's princes, as it confirmed peace in Christendom—had so incensed the French that "they decided to seek the total destruction of the United Provinces for daring to defend us [Spain]." Under the circumstances, it would have been unthinkable to "abandon those who had so generously exposed themselves for our defense." Although the Spanish had done everything they could to maintain peace, she said "we feel that our obligations to our subjects leaves us no choice," hence her decision—after so many outrageous provocations—to "use violence to repress violence." The elaborate declaration was designed to make Mariana's actions irreproachable. The text—sent to the French court and printed and distributed in France—reveals Mariana's long accumulation of grievances.[37]

Once war was a reality, Mariana used all the tools she had. She had letters drafted to the kings of Poland, Denmark, and England, as well as the Senate of the Republic of Venice, explaining her motives for waging war on France and calling for them to join Spain. She actively pursued defensive and offensive leagues or, if those failed, neutrality agreements, obtaining many. In her instructions to Lira, whom Mariana had chosen as Spain's representative in the peace congress that was taking place in Cologne, Mariana revealed her intention to prevent the peace in order to form that major coalition against France. Lira was supposed to fake her interest in the peace and impede it in private. Leopold, always prone to avoid conflicts with France, was warned against a move toward peace. Even the evidence of a cease-fire would be enough for Mariana to withdraw Spain's subsidies.[38]

Agreements multiplied. Mariana negotiated Spain's inclusion in an existing treaty between the emperor and the elector of Saxony: the three signatories promised mutual defense in case of an invasion. Mariana and Leopold concluded a similar defensive league with the elector of Trier in

December 1673, securing the passing of the Spanish and Austrian armies through the elector's territories by promising a monthly subsidy of six thousand *reales de a ocho* to help the elector sustain his troops. A secret clause stated that the Dutch would pay three thousand *reales de a ocho* of the subsidies, halving Mariana's and Leopold's contributions. Mariana also gave Balbases plenipotentiary powers "to propose, conclude, and Capitulate in Her Royal name offensive or defensive leagues" with the emperor and with "kings, republics, electors, and princes, to ensure their respective dominions."[39]

Another wave of alliances came in 1674 and 1675. After temporarily defecting to the French side, the elector of Brandenburg rejoined the league with Leopold and Mariana on July 1, 1674. Mariana, Leopold, and the United Provinces concluded a ten-year defensive league with the Duke of Brunswick-Lüneburg on June 20, which was ratified on December 5, 1674. Together with Brunswick-Lüneburg, Mariana, Leopold, and the Dutch concluded an additional league with the bishop of Osnabrück to "re-establish the peace and tranquility." Mariana and the Dutch concluded similar alliances with the Prince-Bishopric of Münster (October 1675) and the Elector Palatine-Neuburg (March 1676). Spain fueled this dizzying array of alliances by giving money to allies and the imperial armies. Leopold I received four hundred thousand and then another one hundred thousand *reales de a ocho* in June 1673 and continued to receive substantial amounts in the following years. Juan Antonio Sánchez Belén calculates that more than five million silver *escudos* were spent on the war between 1670 and 1676. Christopher Storrs calculates that Spanish armies in 1674 and 1675 totaled approximately 100,000 men. The armies of Louis XIV in 1672, for the Franco-Dutch War, were said to be around 120,000. This is why the military alliances Mariana forged were so important to Spain.[40]

Mariana's engagement with the Scandinavian powers was also crucial. Although embassies had been established in Denmark and Sweden in the aftermath of the Westphalian settlement, the collaboration with these powers became much more significant and meaningful under Mariana. In her quest to get one or the other to join the Habsburg cause, she sent extraordinary ambassadors to Copenhagen and Stockholm with instructions to play the two powers against each other. She had an agreement with Sweden from 1668 to 1673 until the Swedes went to the French side. It was a painful loss because Mariana had decided to pay the subsidies negotiated at the time of the Triple Alliance. These kinds of turns were not uncommon in early modern warfare, which was so dependent on mercenary forces even if kings or princes led the armies for hire. It did not make it less painful for Mariana to lose her investment. However, although Sweden never deployed its armies on behalf of Spain, its role as a deterrent cannot be underestimated. Castel Rodrigo noted that the 480,000 *reales de a ocho* "bought us four years of peace to recuperate and re-arm." After Sweden's defection to France, the Habsburgs concluded an alliance with Denmark in July 1674; the enemies of the Swedes thus joined the war on the Dutch/ Habsburg side.[41]

Although Mariana was unable to conclude or achieve to the fullest extent all the alliances she sought—she would have preferred, for example, offensive rather than defensive leagues, and she had lost Sweden to France—the outcome was nonetheless spectacular. The impressive cluster of agreements marked the culmination of years of negotiations requiring clarity of purpose, diplomatic skill, expert ministers, and money. And they were not all Mariana had accomplished.

"GUARANTOR AND JUDGE"

If Castel Rodrigo could call the 1668 Triple Alliance the "coup de grâce" of Spain's diplomacy, a similarly remarkable event occurred in 1674. Mariana had been working to "separate the king of England from France" since 1671, when she found out about England's and France's joint invasion plans. This is why she did not impose commercial sanctions on England, which the English king reciprocated by carefully avoiding Spanish territories when England invaded the United Provinces in April 1672. Mariana tried to influence the English king to end the conflict, but he was reluctant to withdraw. The peace congress then in session in Cologne posed additional difficulties for Mariana. It was mediated by Sweden, a fact Charles II used as an excuse to reject Mariana's offer of mediation, saying he did not want to offend the Swedes. After the conclusion of the Quadruple Alliance, however, Mariana intensified pressure on Charles II, offering to extricate him from "his compromise with France" and enticing him with promises of possible Dutch concessions.[42]

Unless England withdrew from the United Provinces, Spain and England would soon be drawn onto opposite sides of the conflict. Mariana made it clear to Charles that she was not bluffing; she had indeed promised the United Provinces she would wage war against England if she failed to bring it to the negotiating table. Her timing was impeccable. The possibility of a war with Spain had instilled "great fear" among Londoners. The Dutch were inflicting painful losses on England in American waters, taking New York and other important outposts. Charles II's secret treaty with France, including his intention to convert to Catholicism, became known at this point, causing an uproar in his court despite his denials. The king's only solution was to end the Third Anglo-Dutch War. Both Charles II and the Dutch agreed that Mariana should mediate, and after an intense period of secret negotiations that went on while the Cologne conference was still meeting, she obtained excellent terms for England. The Peace of Westminster was concluded on February 9, 1674, effectively ending the war between England and the Dutch fewer than two years after it had started.[43]

Mariana's mediation offered Spain several benefits. First, getting Charles II to conclude a separate peace left France to its own devices in what had become a pan-European war against it. Second, the treaty satisfied both the English and Dutch while simultaneously increasing their ties to Spain. Mariana, for example, extracted a payment of eight hundred thousand *reales de a ocho* that the Dutch paid to the English—not a small amount of money—which compensated for the loss of French subsidies. The treaty set forth rules and regulations for both parties on commercial activities in the East Indies, with a special conference convened in London to negotiate the terms; both sides named the queen as the adjudicator of differences in case of a stalemate. Charles II effusively praised the Spanish ambassador in London, the capable Marquis of Fresno, during the talks and thanked Mariana for having taken the role of "guarantor and judge" in the peace negotiations.[44]

Between 1673 and 1674, Mariana's reputation grew considerably. She continued to commit to the conflict with France single-mindedly, even as the war expanded to Catalonia and the Mediterranean in the summer of 1674, and a revolt in the Port of Messina on the island of Sicily was exacerbated when France supported the rebels. Mariana enjoyed a cohesive regime, and her system of alliances was working to offset Louis XIV's military superiority. Indeed, the United Provinces sent an armada commanded by the great naval commander Admiral Michiel de Ruyter to defend Messina from France; it was here that he lost his life.[45]

At home, her role was secure as long as she operated under the terms of the testament that sanctioned her right to govern. But Carlos II's emancipation was no longer in a distant future: he turned thirteen on November 6, 1674, and Mariana had to prepare the court for his new rule. The first step was establishing his royal household, which inaugurated, symbolically and literally, the beginning of the end of Mariana's regency. As the emancipation neared, Mariana had to carve out a new political role. In this, she was no different from other queen regents who ruled on behalf of their sons: surrendering power to an adolescent boy and retreating from the center of power required a new set of political strategies. The situation opened the door for the rise of a controversial figure with whom Mariana had a political partnership that was different than those she had before.

THE QUEEN'S PROTÉGÉ: A POLICY OF BREAD AND CIRCUSES?

Fernando Valenzuela is a controversial figure in the transition from Mariana's regency. Like Nithard, Valenzuela had no policy influence, but unlike him, his political role was quite significant. Once again, context is required. Mariana ruled on behalf of the king and *as* the king, signing documents and dispatching royal decrees as a sovereign monarch. Those prerogatives would end on November 6, 1675, and the queen had to think about how she would vacate her role and still exercise influence.

To prepare the court—inside and outside the palace—for Carlos II's long-anticipated majority, Mariana created a major program of display. Theater productions in the city, which had greatly declined during the regency's early years, increased exponentially after 1673. The royal theater returned to the court, soon matching its past splendor. The extended *jornadas* to royal palaces that took place about four times a year had been halted for nearly a decade. They began again; the first such journey to the palace of Aranjuez, which became Carlos II's favorite destination, took place from April 21 to May 21, 1674. Mariana's orders to begin preparations for the king's quarters, accompanied by her announcement of the members of the king's household on November 26, 1674, accelerated activities. Palace repairs, purchases, and a flurry of administrative tasks were needed to reestablish the king's household. A total of 150,000 *ducados de vellón* were budgeted just to furnish the royal table and supply the king's sleeping quarters—some 30,000 was spent on linens alone. Officials inventoried silver and gold tableware to see what was available and what needed to be purchased—just some of the innumerable preparations needed to return the king to the center of the court.[46]

The journeys required moving a large entourage of servants and material to offer the king entertainments suitable for the countryside, such as hunting expeditions, which delighted the young sovereign. These were the cultural, political, and institutional contexts in which Mariana's patronage of Fernando Valenzuela developed. Valenzuela was married to one of Mariana's ladies, Maria Ambrosia de Ucedo y Prada, and Mariana had granted the couple a pension so that they could get married. Valenzuela earned the queen's attention as a trustworthy figure, replacing Manuel de Lira as the supervisor of ambassadors in 1671. If Lira's political trajectory as a diplomat is an indicator, Valenzuela could have followed in his footsteps.[47]

But Valenzuela remained in Mariana's circle instead. His first significant appointment was in 1673, when Mariana appointed him to one of the executive offices within the queen's stables. He became the *primer caballerizo*, an office just below the *caballerizo mayor*, or master of the stables. This position gave him direct access to the monarchs during hunting expeditions and the royal vacations. Next Mariana made him *juez conservador* (commissioner) in the Council of Italy in 1674; the post had no policy responsibilities—only administrative and secretarial—but it provided an income and more access to the bureaucratic machine of the court. Valenzuela's rise coincided with the explosion of court entertainments.[48]

Valenzuela was ideally suited to managing these entertainments: he had extensive experience hiring acting companies, selecting plays, managing stage machinery, distributing roles, and organizing entertainments during intermissions. One of the many *relaciones* (news sheets that circulated independently or were published in gazettes) widely consumed in seventeenth-century Madrid identifies him as responsible for "the dispositions of the plays, amenities, hunting, and ultimately everything that had to do with sportsmanship and the break needed from the burden of governing." Mariana appointed Valenzuela *alcalde*, or mayor, of the royal palace of El Pardo. The position was usually occupied by nobles, which he was not, but it also involved staging theatrical events. Valenzuela undertook, with Mariana's support, a program of renewal across the city. Among the projects were the reconstruction of the Plaza Mayor, or the Main Square, of the city, which had been badly damaged during a fire in 1671, and the construction of two bridges over the Manzanares River. He also helped stabilize the price of basic commodities and started a building program inside the palace as well. Last but not least, he ensured sufficient funds for theatrical projects by selling offices; this was not necessarily uncommon, but the practice reached new levels under his leadership. This became a source of criticism not only because of his methods but because the practice gave him tremendous power and influence; he controlled who would be given the opportunity to purchase these offices.[49]

An *arbitrista*, the seventeenth-century equivalent of a political pundit, described Mariana as exerting "tyranny with sweet and artificial methods" to prevail over the will of her son and her subjects (*"intenta la Reina usar de la biolencia y aquel aquien esta rendida venciendo la voluntad del Rey con alagos al Pueblo y los basallos esclarecidos con los terminos de una tirania dulce y artificiosa"*). This policy of bread and circuses, quite different from the ways the queen had proceeded in the previous decade, highlights the growing anxiety about Carlos II's emancipation. Valenzuela's ascent was commented on, as were Mariana's methods, with a tinge of criticism, but behind this criticism was the anticipation that a change of regime was coming one way or another. A sense of unease was unavoidable, and the queen was just as anxious as everyone else was about the future. Mariana was evidently working hard to ensure the stability of the city at the time of the transition. From this perspective—at least before the regency ended—she was successful. Thanks to Valenzuela, the court sparkled and the population was content.[50]

As her regency neared its end, Mariana appointed Valenzuela to supervise renovations of the Madrid Alcázar. He remodeled the colonnade that surrounded the internal plazas of the Alcázar—called the Queen's Gallery—and connected them to the royal stables. He imported no fewer than two hundred marble sculptures from Italy to complete the project, which ultimately was an ode to the queen. Valenzuela also oversaw the renovations of the palace facade. Construction had started during Philip's reign, but now the work became a theater for symbolism as the end of Mariana's regency neared. Nothing was more telling than the transfer of an imposing equestrian statue of Philip IV to the Alcázar, where Valenzuela placed it above the principal doorway. This monumental feat, requiring support capable of bearing nine tons, reminded the court that Philip's testament gave Mariana the right to participate in governance during Carlos's reign.

As if to further underscore the connection, the statue was relocated in April, near the date that Carlos II moved into his own chambers.[51]

Valenzuela had no role in formulating policy; Mariana ruled as she had before. His centrality in matters of the court, however, was undeniable. His selling of offices and knowledge of the palace gave him significant control over royal patronage. His boldness made him even harder to ignore. On Carlos II's fourteenth birthday, for example, Valenzuela made a spectacular entrance, following the Dukes of Medinaceli and Alburquerque in the procession and standing to the right of the Duke of Infantado's oldest son, a display that did little to endear him to the proud and status-conscious aristocracy. Valenzuela had only become a noble days before, when, in one of her last acts as governor, Mariana granted him the marquisate of Villasierra, presumably to secure him a prominent place in Carlos II's regime. But major changes were coming, and neither Valenzuela nor Mariana could stop the political avalanche that came with the king's fourteenth birthday.[52]

THE COURT AT A CROSSROADS

Carlos II's majority had been preceded by the establishment of his royal household, thus ending the monopoly the queen's household had exercised over court politics. The formation of a new household always meant a shuffling of political centers of power. The arrival of a foreign household with a queen or empress, for example, usually brought major political shifts—so much so that entourages of consorts were often the subject of intense negotiations. In Carlos II's case, the stakes were higher because he was a ruling monarch. All the king's activities—dressing, eating, and recreation—were performed as part of the rituals of the court with the etiquette rules dictating the roles that members of the king's household perform in each, from holding the basin so the king could wash his hand to the handing of his shirt and all other details of his existence. The move into his own quarters with his own entourage, therefore, became a political milestone by determining who had direct and daily contact with the king. As Carlos's mother and a queen, Mariana still had access to him, but she lost the monopoly she had enjoyed on the court's most important commodity: the king.[53]

In the meantime, she had the power to make appointments to the king's household. Mariana rewarded the men who had been important to her, men with appropriately noble backgrounds. The admiral of Castile received the position of *caballerizo mayor*, the Duke of Alburquerque became *mayordomo mayor*, and the Duke of Medinaceli *summiller de corps*. The admiral was loyal to Mariana during the Nithard controversy, was a member of the Council of State, and was married to the daughter of the Marquis of Baldueza, Mariana's *camarera mayor*. The 8th Duke of Alburquerque, Francisco Fernández de la Cueva, had supported Mariana's wish for peace with Portugal and was a strong advocate for Habsburg interests; he had escorted the Infanta Margarita to Vienna. The 8th Duke of Medinaceli, Juan Francisco de la Cerda, like his father before him, had taken on the naval defense of the monarchy from their family base in Andalucía, most recently in 1671 during the Siege of Panama. All three had proved their worth and been steadfast in their support of Mariana.

There were many assignments to distribute: six rotating *mayordomos* to manage Carlos II's household, nine gentlemen of the bedchamber (*gentiles hombres de cámara*), and thirty-six gentleman of the table (*gentiles hombres de la boca*). These were the new appointments; an additional six *mayordomos* and fourteen gentlemen of the bedchamber and the table, as well as hundreds of lower level officials, who had been members of Philip IV's household, were reinstated in the new household. Mariana's appointments were meant to place her men in critical positions without, if possible, slighting other important families and groups. Nonetheless, many elite families—including the Albas, the Aragón brothers, and the Count of Talara, all of whom later plotted against Mariana—were unhappy. In early 1675, however, Mariana still had the court under tight control; any criticisms were muted, which, in the context of the Spanish court, counted as a victory.[54]

By Mariana's decree, Carlos II moved to his own quarters on April 15, 1675. In spite of her precautions and efforts to mold his entourage, the establishment of his household created endless political competition and jostling for power. The more than five hundred notes and letters that the Aragón brothers—Cardinal Pascual Aragón and Pedro de Aragón—exchanged with those involved in the aborted coup of November 1675 and the successful one in December 1676 illustrate the types of maneuvers that occurred. The correspondence runs from July 1675 to March 1677, when Mariana left the court in her retirement qua exile to Toledo. This incredible source of evidence—all original, many encoded—reveals the dangers that lurked in the rooms of the Alcázar.[55]

The men who participated in the plot of 1675 had patronage ties to Mariana but saw advantages in promoting a new political regime around the king. The tight circle of Medinaceli, Alburquerque, and the admiral of Castile that Mariana set up around Carlos II would not have been easy to penetrate, however, had it not been for two men who enjoyed almost unrestricted access and significant influence over the young sovereign: his teacher, Francisco Ramos del Manzano, and his confessor, Father Pedro Álvarez de Montenegro.

The question is why. Ramos del Manzano belonged to the class of *letrados*, or university-trained figures, that held central positions in Mariana's regime. Although he had received honors and favors from the queen, he competed with the Count of Villaumbrosa, the president of the Council of Castile and one of Mariana's most trusted advisors, who had similar social status. Both had officially responded to Louis XIV's justification for the War of Devolution and written and published educational treatises to mark Carlos II's tenth birthday. Mariana, however, obviously preferred Villaumbrosa's political advice to that of Ramos del Manzano, naming the latter Carlos's teacher and the former the president of the Council of Castile, with regular access to her and the Junta de Gobierno. Villaumbrosa became one of the most trusted and influential figures in Mariana's regime. This kind of competition and jealousy—brewing for years—was the typical fare in the court environment.[56]

Montenegro appears to have been driven in part by greed. He demanded thirty thousand *ducados* for participating in the plot, complaining that Mariana had not adequately compensated him. The rumors that Mariana planned to replace him with a Jesuit and permanently exclude the Dominicans from being confessors to the king were also a motivation. While Carlos II may have been easily manipulated by these two older authority figures, his willingness and ability to keep the plots from his mother show his growing independence.[57]

While Manzano and Montenegro plotted to shape Carlos II's political regime and diminish his mother's power, Mariana was resolving an external crisis that played a key role in the events that eventually led to her exile: the revolt of Messina in Sicily in spring 1674. The revolt was caused by deep and

decades-long socioeconomic conflict between the great barons engaged
in large-scale agricultural production and the merchant urban elite who
worked in the silk industry, but it was triggered by an economic crisis in 1671
and 1672. Internal disorders culminated when a group of men denounced
the ineffective government and began mutinying. The revolt proper started
on July 7, 1674. Mariana was unable to quickly quell the situation because
the war with France had tied up military resources on the continent. She
sent men and galleys and devised a solid strategy to deal with the situation, which she sent to the governors of Sicily. But the rebellion became
another theater of war when Louis XIV began supporting the rebels. Lira
soon brought the Dutch into the conflict, thus extending the war against
France into the Mediterranean and the Catalonian frontier. "We find our-
selves in open war all over," the Prince of Astillano wrote from Catalonia.[58]

This is when Mariana made a strategic mistake: she appointed Don Juan
to suppress the revolt in Messina. This time, though, unlike the appointment of Don Juan as governor of the Low Countries and general of the army
of Flanders, she really was trying to keep him out of Madrid. The king's
fourteenth birthday was just months away, and anything could happen once
the date arrived. Mariana named Don Juan vicar-general of the king in Italy
on April 1, 1675, and he accepted with gratitude. Mariana and he worked
together on the details of the mission: he and the celebrated Dutch admiral,
Michiel de Ruyter, were to coordinate a joint enterprise against the rebels
and France. But Don Juan never arrived in Italy, leaving Ruyter to undertake the campaign himself, initially successfully. Unbeknownst to Mariana,
Carlos II had countermanded her orders.[59]

The letters of the Aragón brothers and other observers reveal how
easily the king's teacher and confessor manipulated Carlos II. The young
king wrote to Cardinal Aragón on October 11, announcing his upcoming
emancipation. The king asked Aragón to come to Madrid, prepared to take
permanent residency in the city, in order to assist him in the government
of the monarchy. Carlos insinuated that he intended to name Aragón his
valido: "It would please me very much to see you at court before November 6, with your household, as I trust of your person as I take over the government of my kingdoms." Aragón responded warmly but acted cautiously.
His correspondence indicates that serious health problems, even though
he was relatively young, prevented his journey, but the astute cardinal was
not an impulsive man. Seeing how easily Ramos del Manzano and Álvarez

de Montenegro manipulated Carlos, Aragón expressed his reservations regarding the king's reliability to stand his ground if confronted by his mother. Although unaware that Carlos II had written to Don Juan at the same time he wrote to Aragón, Aragón was, of course, right. Carlos II had ordered Don Juan to arrive at court *on* the very day of Carlos II's birthday to become principal advisor. "On the sixth [of November], I come into the government of my states," Carlos II wrote to Don Juan on October 30, 1675. "I need your services to assist me in my duties because *I plan to say farewell to my mother*" (emphasis mine).[60]

The plotters served the king badly: rather than helping him claim a measure of autonomy, they encouraged him to go behind Mariana's back. Their handling of the situation provoked a confrontation between mother and son that had dire political consequences for the entire court. Cardinal Aragón did not know that the king had recalled Don Juan to court. Don Juan naïvely believe that Carlos II would be able to stand up to his mother. Mariana continued negotiating with Don Juan about his mission to Messina, not knowing that Carlos II was issuing orders contradicting hers. This all led to the convoluted events of November 6, starting Carlos II's rule off on a shaky foundation and undermining Mariana's transition as well.

Mariana had done all she could to solidify her position and had tools to carve a place in her son's regime. Their personal relationship meant she had influence on the king. We can see their closeness from later events and extant correspondence. The documents make clear that even as the convoluted events were launched, Mariana had considerable prestige from her accomplishments as governor. She had substantial dynastic and political capital as the wife of one king and the mother of another and commanded a solid network of patronage. Further, she had already shaped her son's regime—her legacy resounded in the composition of councils of government, institutions, and the king's household—and she could expect to play an active role in the government as her son's curator. She had anticipated the difficult transition and done everything she could to retain influence in the new regime. She had successfully navigated extremely complex matters of war and diplomacy. Now she had to negotiate her new position in her son's regime; this turned out to be her most difficult task and her only failure.

CHAPTER 6

The Politics of Motherhood, November 6, 1675, to 1677

After much anticipation, Carlos II's birthday and legal emancipation finally arrived on November 6, 1675. The city was bubbling with excitement, but unbeknownst to Madrid's inhabitants, the palace was in the midst of a mini-revolution. A plot to install Don Juan at court as Mariana's replacement had been set in motion. Following the king's instructions, Don Juan entered Madrid early that morning in a very public and ceremonial procession toward the Alcázar. He met with the king privately and then left for the palace of the Buen Retiro, having attempted to pay his respects to Mariana, who demurred, claiming a migraine. Carlos II attended the planned religious services along with the entire court except for Mariana, who was conspicuously absent. He went to see his mother afterward and remained for two hours in her chambers. Witnesses who saw the king coming out of his mother's quarters reported the change in Carlos's demeanor as well as "clear signs that he had been crying a lot." Back in his chambers, he was admonished by the Duke of Alburquerque and the Duke of Medinaceli, his *mayordomo mayor* and *summiller de corps*, respectively, about the necessity to act in matters of state with his mother's knowledge and consent. By the afternoon, the king's plans had been completely reversed. Medinaceli went to the Buen Retiro armed with a royal decree in the king's hand that ordered Don Juan to leave the court immediately and travel to Sicily. Helping Spain put down the revolt in Messina was, the king wrote, the best service Don Juan could provide to his royal person.[1]

It is hard to believe that Don Juan showed up at court naïvely believing that Mariana would accept her son's decision without a fight or that the king would be able to stand up to his mother. Mariana's intervention was conclusive, but the swiftness of her victory surprised everyone, especially Don Juan, who left Madrid the next day, having been refused a second audience with the king. He stopped on his way to write a letter in which he dared the king to "seek liberty from the yoke of those who control him." The manifesto did not have the same effect as those he had deployed against Nithard, at least not immediately. But the logic of the king gaining his "liberty" eventually had an effect. Mariana had easily aborted this coup, but at what cost? Carlos II's inability to stand up to her inaugurated a political crisis that exploded at the end of 1676.[2]

Mariana dismissed, exiled, and replaced those involved in the coup attempt, tightening her control over the king to avoid another attempt. Mariana named Valenzuela ambassador extraordinary in Venice; he had not been the immediate cause of the coup, but Castel Rodrigo suggested to the queen that his temporary absence would pacify critics and help calm the court. Valenzuela left but only made it to Granada; he was back at court by March. Mariana needed him, as competition for the king's attention created frenetic activity at court; entertainments increased at the same rate as conspiracies against Mariana, who was deemed directly responsible for Valenzuela's growing centrality at court. Mariana's power over the king became the main source of discontent, provoking reactions.

A year after Carlos's emancipation, a *Confederación* (a coalition of twenty-three nobles) demanded the king's permanent separation from his mother, Valenzuela's dismissal, and the installation of Don Juan as the king's main advisor. This time, Don Juan was better prepared. He gathered a force of ten thousand men and started his march on Madrid in early January 1677. Since his large force seemed to threaten a civil war, even the queen's supporters were counseling Carlos II to distance himself from her. With advice from some of his closest supporters, men who had once been on Mariana's side, on January 14, the king installed himself in the palace of the Buen Retiro, on the outskirts of the city, where Don Juan soon joined him. A few weeks later, he ordered his mother to "retire," and after weeks of negotiations, the city of Toledo was chosen for her new residence. Although the diplomatic correspondence presented Mariana's retirement as self-elected, she had no choice in the matter and was, for all practical purposes, exiled.[3]

The conspiracies during 1676 were ostensibly intended to remove Valenzuela, but although that was important, the real reason was the king's lack of autonomy, which was blamed on Mariana. Motherhood, therefore, was identified as the source of the political upheaval at court. A careful reading of texts from this period—gazettes, letters, Council of State deliberations, and memoranda—reveals that Mariana's influence over her son was a major problem, but it is equally clear that no one found it surprising. The Spanish ruling elite, particularly the men, understood Carlos's difficulties in limiting his mother's authority. But while his "reverential fear" of his mother had been acceptable when he was a minor, after his legal emancipation, it was not. The court was experiencing a crisis of kingship—either Carlos continued to respect and obey his mother or he assumed his responsibilities as king—and it seemed to have only one solution: separating the king from his mother.[4]

So long as Mariana was nearby, Carlos II was unlikely to be able to limit her authority. Mariana's ability to propel Valenzuela's political and social ascent, her unilateral decisions about the king's marriage, and her tight control of the court and the government confirmed the general consensus: the king would not be *king* until Mariana's power diminished. His fourteenth birthday was a milestone, but the separation from his mother loomed larger still. All this meant that Mariana could not prevent her exile, despite her successful regency and many supporters.

MOTHER AND SON, QUEEN AND KING

The transition from royal minority to royal emancipation was always pivotal for a regent; the skill with which she surrendered power could define court politics for years to come. The personal and political relationship between mother and son—also queen and king—had changed: the king was supposed to assume personal and political authority over his subjects, which included his mother. The mother had to transition gracefully from ruler to subject, even as she continued, ideally, to exercise influence. The process, of course, was shaped by the specific political and cultural traditions of the court. The French monarchy, for example, held special ceremonies at the end of royal minorities to mark the beginning of the king's reign as an adult. These confirmed, however, the queen mother's residual power and, in some cases, affirmed her right to continue participating in Council of State meetings. While the Spanish monarchy did not have such rituals, Mariana was not without protection. She was curator of the king, and Philip IV's testament required that Carlos II rely on his mother and the Junta de Gobierno when he came to power. Nevertheless, the conditions of the curatorship were vague, as was the extent of the role Mariana should exercise.[5]

On November 4, two days before Carlos II's birthday, Mariana, in conjunction with some members of the Junta de Gobierno, proposed that Carlos voluntarily extend his minority for two more years. The king refused to sign the document; because it is known only through references in other contemporary sources, it is not clear on what basis Mariana made the request. Mariana respected Carlos II's refusal and relinquished her duties on November 6. Nevertheless, the request proved deeply controversial. An anonymous *arbitrista* pointed out how unprecedented and damaging it would have been "for a king of Castile to declare himself incapable of governing after reaching the age of emancipation." Thankfully, he noted, the king, likely "guided by God's light," refused to accept this outrageous proposition. It was obviously *not* Mariana's intention to declare the king incapacitated as the critic suggested. But the assertions reveal how unwise the request was; not only did she compromise Carlos II's position as king, but she opened herself up to criticism.[6]

Mariana's behavior in the aftermath of the coup greatly contributed to the perception of a king dominated by his mother, heightening discontent rather than calming it. Mariana exiled the two men at the center of the plot—the king's teacher, Ramos del Manzano, and his confessor, Álvarez de Montenegro—so quickly that neither had time to bid farewell to the monarch. The nobles involved, especially the Counts of Medellín and Monterrey, were denied access to the palace. Her rapid response actually made things worse—it would have been far better to have had Carlos, who was actually in charge of the government, dismiss the men. It is significant that for a while at least, Carlos refused to confess to any other priest than Montenegro.[7]

In treating her son as a child rather than an emancipated king, Mariana made her situation untenable. Carlos expected to exercise his position and show a modicum of independence from his mother. Using Medinaceli as a go-between, he sent Monterrey a note telling him to remain in Madrid, knowing perfectly well that he was thereby contravening his mother's order. Mariana found out and reprimanded Medinaceli for delivering the king's message; Medinaceli pointed out that he could hardly disobey the king. Medinaceli's situation illustrates that the court's difficulties went deeper than factional struggles or competition for patronage. Medinaceli had received an appointment to the Council of State for his service in neutralizing the plot of November 6. Nevertheless, Mariana's orders affected the principle regulating the relationship between the king and his subjects. Not only had she forced the king to act behind her back, but she had reprimanded a high officer of the court for following the king's orders. Medinaceli was reportedly so upset (*destemplado*) by the exchange that he "spent the rest of the day in bed."[8]

Mariana's actions were a major political and strategic miscalculation. So great was the frustration with the king's apparent powerlessness that some even considered kidnapping him to free him from his mother's influence. Fortunately, Cardinal Aragón saw that the scheme was abandoned. It would have been equally disrupting to kidnap the king in this manner. Aragón, whose brother was one of the main conspirators, had been well informed about everything, but he acted very cautiously and prudently. Aragón's dedication and common sense, in combination with his ecclesiastical position, made him a figure on whom all three—Carlos, Mariana, and Don Juan—could rely. But he could not stop the floodgates of change. Signs of Mariana's weakening position began emerging from the first days of Carlos II's rule. While just private criticisms at first, by late 1676 they were an outcry.[9]

The official transition of power went forward as Philip IV's testament required, with Mariana ordering the Council of State to address all documents to Carlos II and announcing the emancipation to foreign dignitaries. But Carlos appeared unable to fill the role his mother had played for so long. On November 28, the Count of Villaumbrosa, the president of the Council of Castile and a central figure in Mariana's government, consulted with the queen privately and expressed concerns about the king's reticence to participate in matters of state. He begged the queen to attend the meetings he now held with the king in order to "support [him] with Your Majesty's many years of experience." Additional consultations occurred on December 8, 11, and 13 as Villaumbrosa tried to accelerate the transition so the government could function. On December 13, 1675, Carlos announced he would rely on the Junta de Gobierno to govern, and a system was worked out whereby

Mariana met with Villaumbrosa after he met with the king. She remained, therefore, the de facto governor, but without the de jure protections she had previously had.[10]

The court was experiencing a power vacuum. Although Mariana had established a way to work with Villaumbrosa, she was a shadow ruler. The uncertainty does not show in the Council of State deliberations, which were handled by a secretary who took orders from Mariana. But it explains why the Aragón brothers' correspondence talks about several figures rumored to have achieved the position of the king's *valido*. From December 1675 to November 1676, Medinaceli, Villaumbrosa, Mejorada, Cardinal Aragón, and both the admiral and constable of Castile, were identified as having taken control of the government. Mariana, once the glue that held it together, was now one of many figures competing for power. The current state of affairs "made family members run away from each other," as one of the letters from this dangerous period put it. To make matters more difficult, Carlos was a restless adolescent who wanted hunting expeditions, games, and diversions. The entire court was caught up in fulfilling the whims of a fourteen-year-old boy who did not have enough political backbone to either take the government personally or support one of the candidates, perhaps even his mother, to share the job with him.[11]

What was the legal situation? The testament said, "Once [the king] reaches his fourteenth birthday, [he] will begin governing completely, utilizing the advice and assistance of his mother and the majority opinion of the Junta de Gobierno." Based on a contextual analysis of two royal inventories—usually conducted at the beginning and the end of guardianships—as well as Mariana's postregency portraits, Mercedes Llorente has suggested that Carlos II remained under the curatorship of his mother until his twenty-fifth birthday. In theory, the curatorship would have given her a legal basis to take an official political role in her son's regime, but it was certainly unclear what that role was. One way or another, Mariana's juridical status changed dramatically after Carlos II's fourteenth birthday, when her governorship and tutorship ended. What then would it mean for Carlos to follow his father's testamentary mandate that he should "govern completely, but with the advice and assistance of his mother"?[12]

I would like to suggest that while legal definitions of guardianship are important, so too are cultural norms. In order to understand the expectations of Carlos II's subjects, particularly the male members of his court, we must look at the male life cycle in early modern Spain. There were other markers of adulthood besides legally coming of age, and they were just as important in Carlos's ability to truly rule. In many early modern societies, including Venice and Florence, men went through an extended period of youth based on marriage practices and economic strategies, which prevented men from fully achieving adulthood until their midthirties and in some cases longer. In Spain too, males could come of age at a variety of times: at twenty-five; when they married; or, if their fathers died, at fourteen. These variations explain why there were two types of legal guardians: tutors were guardians for boys fourteen and younger (twelve for girls), while curators were guardians of adolescents from fourteen to twenty-five. Young people under a curator's care, according to Grace E. Coolidge, enjoyed a measure of independence but not necessarily total autonomy. They could reject the appointment of a curator, have a say in the appointment, or nominate their own candidates. Curatorship was a transitional period that illustrated the ambivalent position of a male heir, who could inherit and even choose his own guardian yet still be under the partial supervision of another adult. While noble or royal men were pushed into their positions at a young age if their fathers—or mothers, if they had inherited through the female line—died, this did not automatically mean adulthood.[13]

"BECOMING A MAN, JUST LIKE HIS FATHER"

Observations made about Carlos II by people close to him reveal that seventeenth-century Spaniards were well aware that their king was a young man and that even after his legal emancipation, he still had much growing up to do. "The king's height is in proportion to his age, his body slim, and his constitution robust and agile," reported a contemporary. "The king is enjoying himself [hunting] very much; soon we should see him very grown up, since the countryside suits him a lot, just like his father," noted one court officer to another privately. At the time of these comments, Carlos II was almost thirteen and a half, very close to the age of legal emancipation. The nuns at the Descalzas Reales reported that Carlos was becoming a "man" and also noted that "he looked just like his father." He was then fifteen and a half years old and emancipated. The comments reveal the interest in Carlos II's maturation process and his difficult situation; everyone understood that he was still a growing young man, but he was also the king and under pressure to act as an adult. Mariana offered no help, since her continued infantilization of him was so emasculating.[14]

The plans for Carlos II's marriage reveal these dynamics at work. Ferdinand Bonaventure I, Count of Harrach, arrived in Madrid in late October 1673, replacing Pötting, who was leaving after ten years as ambassador. Less than a year later, Harrach initiated marriage negotiations on behalf of Emperor Leopold I, proposing his daughter, the Archduchess Maria Antonia of Austria (b. 1669), then almost six, as Carlos II's future bride; the king was twelve years old. Maria Antonia was the only surviving daughter of the Infanta Margarita and thus Mariana's granddaughter. Mariana received the proposal politely and sent it to the Council of State for deliberation, but did not respond immediately to her brother's proposition. At this point, it was in her best interest to not offend Leopold, who was her main military and diplomatic partner. From the very beginning, Mariana's approach to the marriage proposal was not based entirely on dynastic or affective ties: she considered it as part of her foreign policy. In 1674, Mariana and Leopold were concluding numerous diplomatic and military alliances in the fight against France.[15]

The progress of the war by 1676 was not very hopeful. Not only had the war extended into new areas in the Mediterranean, Catalonia, the Low Countries, and Central Europe, but Admiral De Ruyter, the leader of the Dutch Navy, had been fatally injured in Messina in April. It was a major loss for the Spanish and Dutch forces, but not an isolated one. Spain was facing difficulties on the Catalonian frontiers as well. For Mariana, now the union of her son and the emperor's daughter was the most efficient way to cement the dynastic bloc at a very difficult juncture in the war. The marriage would send a clear message to Louis XIV and the rest of Europe that the Spanish and Austrian Habsburgs were firmly and jointly committed to the war. From the vantage point of international politics, it was a welcome idea.[16]

Yet the marriage proved controversial from the very beginning, largely because of the archduchess's age. The main problem was not the age difference—Maria Antonia was seven years younger than Carlos II, but Mariana had been thirty years younger than Philip IV—but the fact that the archduchess would not be able to bear children for many years. The future of the succession was at stake. In 1674, when the marriage was first proposed, doctors concluded that the consummation of any marriage would have to be delayed for at least two or three years, until the king reached puberty. Cardinal Aragón urged Mariana to leave the decision up to Carlos II when he was old enough. Mariana followed his advice at first but changed her mind in September 1676, probably because of the war and the disorder at home, already out in the open. When Mariana confirmed the marriage, the councilors of state were not pleased.[17]

Spanish law may have allowed twelve-year-old girls to marry, but Spaniards did not expect women to bear children before they were fifteen or sixteen years old. The issue of reproductive age was extensively and explicitly debated in the Council of State before the confirmation of the marriage. Councilors did not want their king to have to wait until his twenties to begin married life—but that was when Maria Antonia would be old enough to bear children. On June 4, 1676, the Council of State discussed all the princesses of Europe who might be suitable. Maria Antonia's position in the succession made her incredibly valuable, but she was so young. At the same time, if Carlos did not marry her, she might marry into France. The councilors' solution was to keep the engagement in the air, hoping the archduchess would move to Spain and be raised in the king's court under Mariana's tutorship. That would not address the problem of Carlos's sex life and procreation, but having a potential successor in Madrid would have been a very suitable alternative. Instead, Carlos II announced the engagement in September 1676 with official letters to all princes of Europe; the official announcement closed the door to a more discrete solution as members of the Council of State wanted. At this point, the court began descending into disorder. The marriage capitulations were drafted and signed by October, even though the archduchess was only eight years old. The Marquis of Balbases, the Spanish ambassador in Vienna, sent news that the proxy ceremony had been scheduled for December of that year.[18]

The timing of the *Confederación* of nobles demanding that the king be separated from Mariana suggests that the marriage was a key issue. Marriage was a major milestone in an early modern male's life, particularly if he had a royal or aristocratic line to ensure. The consummation of the marriage marked the crossing of the boundary between childhood and adulthood. The significance of Mariana's decision to confirm Carlos II's marriage to a child cannot be underestimated. With the stroke of a pen, she extended

Carlos II's childhood for several years; it was one of her greatest errors in this period. Once Carlos was deemed physically mature enough for married life, it was unthinkable to postpone his marriage to an adult bride longer than necessary.[19]

Carlos had issued the orders, but everyone knew Mariana had made the decision. Carlos's education had stressed obedience to fathers and mothers. In the educational treatise *Nudrición Real* that Mariana commissioned in 1671, Pedro González de Salcedo placed "reverence to parents" second only to "fear of God" and above "love of subjects" in the hierarchy of moral concepts to be inculcated in the young king. An entire chapter explained how "royal parents should teach their children the natural dictum of loving and fearing them." Children should venerate their parents "as if they were gods on earth"; violating this precept was a "horrendous crime" that would incur "divine indignation" from the heavenly court and "loathing and contempt" from the earthly one. Salcedo often referred to Mariana as "the Supreme Royal Maternity." Not only in his choice of bride, an area in which royal mothers were particularly influential, but in everything else, Carlos was supposed to abide by his mother's wishes.[20]

Notions about the power of motherhood on a youngster played a role in the ministers' expectations as well. When describing the two-hour meeting in which Mariana convinced Carlos II to ask Don Juan to leave Madrid, a gazetteer explained that Mariana "triumphed with tears and persuasions over the young king, barely fourteen years of age." In a private memorandum, Villaumbrosa wrote persuasively to Carlos, "Because Your Majesty is under the influence of the *reverential fear* of your mother, it is clear that Your Majesty is overwhelmed and cannot govern by himself" (emphasis mine). Thus one of the moral precepts basic to a king's education denied the king the proper exercise of his office. How could Carlos II maintain the proper reverential fear of his mother and emancipate himself from her power? Those closest to him understood his predicament. Shortly after he took power, Don Juan commissioned a text that addressed the situation. It recorded a conversation between him, Carlos II, and a Franciscan friar: "The true relation of a colloquy that for the space of one hour took place between Don Carlos II, of sixteen years of age, . . . Don Juan of Austria, of forty-eight years of age, and a friar and theologian, of sixty-seven years of age . . . in the royal palace on 4 April 1677." If the date is correct, Carlos was fifteen years old, but he had entered his sixteenth year of life. Written by the friar, who spoke with the compounded moral authority of age and religion, the text captures Carlos II's dilemma.[21]

The author praised Carlos's potential but also indicated that the king was still too young: "Sir, I cannot ignore my duty to inform you that even though your royal talent is in conformity with your sovereign greatness, you have no experience; Your Majesty is still a child." Yet Carlos's recent decision to separate from his mother demonstrated that the king was exhibiting clear signs of maturity:

> It is true what God said, that in getting married, the man leaves his father and mother to be with his wife for the rest of his life. Your Majesty is now married to the Monarchy. How could one otherwise explain the impetus and strength Your Majesty received to wean yourself from your mother's breast [*destetarse*], and separate from your Saintly Mother, the Queen, who gave you life, bore you, nourished you, and educated you, so that Your Majesty is better able to assist, govern, and defend your wife, the monarchy[?].[22]

Mother and monarchy emerge as two female figures competing for Carlos II's love. The king appears torn between the hold each has on him: one demanded his submission, and the other would have him dominate. The language reveals the powerful cultural, social, and political images of motherhood in general, especially queen mothers, current in Spain. It would not be easy for Carlos to separate himself from his "saintly mother, who gave you life, bore you, nourished you, and educated you."[23]

The language used by the friar in his *relación* conforms to cultural values that emphasized respect and reverence for mothers but strongly suggests that Carlos II's separation from his mother was necessary for him to become a husband to his "wife," the Spanish monarchy. In this context, marriage embodies social and political concepts: as a benchmark used to determine legal emancipation, it solidified the king's position as an adult male. In addition, the fact that he was "married" to the monarchy described an essential aspect of Spain's political culture, in which the submission of the wife to the husband paralleled that of subject to ruler. The husband's duty to the wife was like the ruler's obligation to "assist, govern, and defend" his subjects. This grave responsibility was powerful enough to help Carlos II take the huge step of separating from his mother; as the friar suggests, it took the entire strength of the monarchy to give the young king the "impetus" to *destetarse*.[24]

A son's ability to "wean himself from his mother's breast," or *destetarse*, was crucial to the assertion of maturity and masculinity, both essential qualities in a ruler. A popular seventeenth-century dictionary, *Tesoro de la Lengua Española o Castellana* (Treasure of the Spanish or Castilian language) referred to a proverb in its definition of a *niño* (male child): "There are youths that are such mama's boys that although they are old enough, they do not know how to free themselves from their mother's lap; these turn out to be either great fools or vicious rogues." "Mama's boys" were scorned and seen as categorically flawed. And for Carlos II, the stakes were especially high. As soon as Mariana forced him to reverse a decision he had made publicly just hours earlier, the court descended into a crisis of kingship and masculinity. Attaining his majority, possessing his own royal household, and signing government papers were not enough to make Carlos II king. Coming of age required him to change his relationship with his mother. In light of his failure to do this peacefully, the conditions were ripe to do it forcefully: it would be necessary to send in an army, carry out a politico-military coup, and exile a queen mother to wean Carlos from his mother's breast, all quintessentially masculine actions.[25]

MOTHER VERSUS MONARCHY

In a missive he wrote to Cardinal Aragón as the conspiracies against Mariana escalated during 1676, the Duke of Alba, one of the leading rebels, identified the crux of the problem: "As long as the queen mother continues to be close to the king, we will not obey in anything, because it will not be the king who orders us, but his mother." This was not an isolated comment. "It was not Valenzuela" who was the problem, Pedro of Aragón affirmed in August 1676, but the queen's influence over the king, and unless "we liberate him," nothing would change. By then, the court had descended to near chaos with open plots. By the summer of 1676, Mariana was trying to give Valenzuela a position in the two royal households; the whole court recognized her desire to make him *valido* in her son's regime.[26]

The problem of how matters of state were handled had not been fully resolved. Mariana attempted to find a mechanism to create a temporary form of government until Carlos became more confident. In July 1676, she proposed forming a triumvirate of Valenzuela, Medinaceli, and Cardinal Aragón that would be called a Junta de Gobierno. Although Mariana's role was unclear, Valenzuela's membership would let her participate in policy making, and this explains why she fought for his place in Carlos II's regime. The other two members lent the group legitimacy. Medinaceli was a representative of the political elite and Cardinal Aragón of the ecclesiastic one; they both had highly prestigious lineages. Medinaceli seemed to have been amenable, but Aragón refused to share the political spotlight with Valenzuela, and the scheme was dropped.[27]

Although Valenzuela had control of court entertainments and activities, he had not yet penetrated any governing institutions. After the three-member junta scheme evaporated, rumors started that he was to be appointed to the Council of State. This exacerbated an already unstable situation. This appointment did not materialize, likely because of the opposition. But fate intervened: during a hunting expedition in El Escorial, Carlos II accidentally shot Valenzuela. The injury was not life threatening, but the king felt terrible, and he elevated Valenzuela to a grandeeship on the spot. This was the highest social recognition the king could grant to his nobles, one that was highly coveted and not easily obtained. Moreover, Carlos invited Valenzuela and his family to move into the palace, giving them the rooms that had belonged to Prince Baltasar Carlos. The nobility, particularly the grandees, were furious. The situation was aggravated by rumors that he had been named prime minister—the first time that title was used. I have not been able to confirm Valenzuela's appointment in his personal papers. His testament, which lists all the offices he received from Mariana and the grandeeship from Carlos II—does not mention being named prime minister. Nevertheless, Valenzuela's elevation to a grandeeship and his residence in the palace signaled him as the most powerful individual at court. An inevitable backlash followed, with many grandees refusing to attend court events. Since Mariana was held responsible for Valenzuela's elevation, they were both seen as liabilities.[28]

It was at this moment that twenty-three members of the upper nobility formed a *Confederación* to demand Valenzuela's resignation and his replacement by Don Juan and Carlos II's permanent separation from Mariana. The text written by the *Confederación* bluntly identifies the king's mother as the "root of all troubles." Her "bad influence" on the king "produced all the malaise, loss, ruin, and disorder that we have experienced of late and, particularly, the execrable elevation [of Valenzuela]." The best service they could render to the king was to "separate the mother completely and permanently from the son." The list of the nobles, most of them grandees, was sizeable, but with an approximate number of seventy-two, they were not in the majority. And those who did not sign—Medinaceli, the admiral of Castile, the constable of Castile, the Duke of Alburquerque, and many other members of the upper aristocracy—were as important as the ones that did, indicating that Mariana still had substantial support from the ruling elite. But the crisis went deeper than simple factionality. Mariana's perceived control over her son endangered the body politic, and to preserve it, she would have to go.[29]

Mariana's refusal to surrender power led to a political crisis, with Mariana opposed to the grandees who wanted the king liberated from his mother. Once the rebellious nobles presented their demands to the king, events unfolded quickly. Mariana and Carlos ensured the safe removal of Valenzuela to El Escorial, where the king personally asked the friars to take him under their protection. Cardinal Aragón recommended that Mariana and Carlos immediately summon Don Juan to court and offer him a place in the government. This time, the king wrote to his half brother with Mariana's consent, and she sent a note of acknowledgment and approval as well. The two missives went out on December 27, 1676, and gave the impression that authority still rested in royal hands. Don Juan pledged his service to the king and the monarchy in a note dated January 1, 1677. All this civility, however, could not disguise the fact that still nothing had been said about Carlos II's separation from Mariana.[30]

The nobles of the *Confederación* resolved to "swear obedience [to the king] before anything else," language that made it clear that their opposition was directed at the king's mother and Valenzuela, not the king himself; nor was it an act of rebellion against royal authority. Yet if the events of November 6, 1675, had taught Don Juan and his supporters a lesson, it was that they needed an army to combat Mariana. On January 1, Don Juan started marching on Madrid with a sizeable force that grew as others joined him on the way; eventually he commanded approximately ten thousand men. But Mariana had also learned from experience: her armed guard was commanded by a loyal supporter, the lieutenant coronel, the Count of Aguilar.

With more than three thousand men, augmented by the construction work-ers' guild (*albañiles*), which Valenzuela had put at Mariana's disposal, it was still smaller than Don Juan's forces.[31]

During the dangerous weeks of early January, Carlos II discussed his options with Medinaceli and Villaumbrosa. Villaumbrosa put his plans into a memorandum that served as a blueprint for Carlos's subsequent actions, offering Carlos a solution to his dilemma. Villaumbrosa acknowledged that no counsel was "devoid of danger and great inconveniences" and urged the king to act with moderation. "Histories of kings," he wrote, "show that those with the most courage and wisdom in the art of governing are those who have complied with the ministry of kingship and have been able to yield to the times and to reason, have tolerated the most, and have not let human affection dominate." Villaumbrosa urged the king to avoid the use of force at all costs. To do otherwise would create "a battle between loyalists, between relatives, and between subjects of the king." Villaumbrosa pro-posed several strategies. First, the king should not punish the nobles who had signed the *Confederación* but instead proclaim his appreciation of them as representatives of the monarchy's most illustrious houses. Carlos should also accept their desire to see Don Juan installed as his chief minister. He should remove Valenzuela from El Escorial, where the fallen minister was still hiding, and revoke the royal grants given to him, particularly the gran-deeship, the most contentious of the many privileges he had accumulated during his spectacular rise to power.[32]

Villaumbrosa then addressed the crux of Carlos II's dilemma: his mother. Don Juan's major goal was, according to Villaumbrosa, quite simple: to separate the king from his mother and demand she relinquish the reins of government. "It is understood," Villaumbrosa continued, "that so long as the queen is in the government, Valenzuela will continue play-ing the part he has played thus far; [and] because Your Majesty is under the influence of the reverential fear of your mother, it is clear that Your Majesty is disempowered [*violentado*] and unable to govern by Yourself." Villaumbrosa expressed the growing political consensus: Mariana's power as mother could not coexist with the full and free exercise of kingship. The fact that these words came from a man who had been Mariana's right hand, a trusted collaborator, reveals the depth of the crisis, as even Mariana's sup-porters realized that the time had come for her to relinquish power.[33]

The most courageous kings, Villaumbrosa wrote, were those who did not "let human affection prevent them from complying with the ministry of kingship." By "human affection," Villaumbrosa evidently meant the love and "reverential fear" Carlos had for his mother. His ministers and subjects expected Carlos to put his obligations as king above those of a son even as they understood how difficult this was. In the end, Carlos showed political maturity: a gazetteer commented that thanks to the counsels of Villaumbrosa and Cardinal Aragón, Carlos II acted more "obedient to necessity than to the mother." Villaumbrosa's efforts did him little good, however; when Don Juan became Carlos's chief minister, he exiled Villaumbrosa, whose ties to Mariana were widely known. However, Don Juan changed his mind about Villaumbrosa, probably after being given evidence of his role in facilitating the separation of the king from his mother, and reinstated him later that year. Although he was one of the architects of Mariana's exile, Villaumbrosa saw this not as an act against Mariana but as a solution to the monarchy's problem. He strove to resolve the crisis while protecting the queen's decorum as she transitioned to a new role.[34]

Villaumbrosa's plan allowed the king to separate himself from his mother without entirely violating his filial obligations: "If the queen has resolved to leave the government, as I understand it," he wrote, "Your Majesty should publish it with royal decrees sent to the councils, with the most affectionate words and *with the esteem appropriate to that of a son for his mother*" (emphasis mine). Next, the king should move to the palace of the Buen Retiro, letting the queen stay in the Alcázar and move out at her leisure. In Villaumbrosa's scheme, the separation of mother and son would be peaceful and harmonious. While Carlos II, assisted by Don Juan, assumed the government of the monarchy, "the queen would be able to live in the quiet and peacefulness of her state, taking a rest from the amount of work and difficulties that she suffered while at the head of the government, *venerated and assisted by your majesty with all the appropriate decency, convenience, and affection*" (emphasis mine).[35]

Villaumbrosa's suggestion was based on long-standing traditions that encouraged women to observe a secluded life after being widowed. The Habsburg dynasty also subscribed to the idea of retirement, an example set by Emperor Charles V when he abdicated in 1556. But at times, these cultural expectations were contrary to the realities of early modern life, and Spanish widows continued to play active roles in the economic, social, and cultural lives of their communities. Nonetheless, these traditions gave Villaumbrosa a way to mask Mariana's exile as retirement, paving the way for her to exit with dignity. Mariana, however, had no intention of following this script.[36]

Once the nobles had given their king this ultimatum, tensions between Carlos and his mother grew exponentially. Mariana and Carlos left a limited record of their relationship; their only correspondence is from their period of separation. But indirect evidence suggests that they had a strong emotional bond that emerged after they were separated. Mariana's love of Carlos had the potential of bringing her concrete political advantages, but there is no reason to believe she did not sincerely feel affection for him. At this point, however, political circumstances put Mariana and Carlos on opposite sides.

Would Carlos defend his mother, even if it meant driving the monarchy toward civil war? Very little documentation survives that elucidates what the king was thinking, but a letter to Medinaceli gives a sense of his predicament: "My mother said that I should be aware that she wanted to get out of this story [*cuento*]," Carlos wrote, "but I can see that she did not really want to do so." "She told me that if I thought it was appropriate to force her out, then I should do what I thought best," he said. "I told her . . . that I was going to give her an answer tomorrow; so I order you to see what we can do about all of this, so that we can get out of this mess [*enredo*] as soon as possible." Mariana evidently expected her son to protect her interests, but on January 14, Carlos decided to follow Villaumbrosa's plan.[37]

For the modern observer, the way Carlos and his closest companions proceeded seems almost farcical. Carlos II and Mariana attended a play in honor of Archduchess Maria Antonia—who was still in Vienna in her father's court—and later dined together. Then Carlos left for his chambers, escorted by Medinaceli, his *summiller de corps*, as etiquette required. At about ten, after everyone had retired for the night, Carlos II arose and dressed again, helped by Medinaceli. "With great demonstration of cleverness," reported a gazetteer, the king and his companions locked up the servants so that they would not report the king's flight. Carlos and Medinaceli went through the palace, crossed the gardens, and finally reached the entrance, where the royal carriage was waiting to take them to the palace of the Buen Retiro. The Prince of Astillano, mayor of the palace, had been warned just two hours earlier that the king's arrival was imminent. Only four nobles (Medinaceli, the Count of Talara, Cardinal Aragón, and the Prince of Astillano), two valets, and a servant attended Carlos, a minimal number compared to the dozens of men who usually attended to the king's every need. The monarch of Europe's largest empire surreptitiously fled his own palace to avoid his mother's wrath, accompanied by four members of the ruling elite who seemed as nervous, if not more so, about confronting the queen as he did. Perhaps more than any other event, this desperate plan illustrates the power of motherhood.[38]

A CHANGE OF REGIME

The next day, Villaumbrosa broke the news to the queen, with her confessor on hand to provide consolation. We can see her initial reaction from a short letter she wrote to her cousin, Sor Mariana de la Cruz, a resident of the Descalzas Reales and the illegitimate daughter of the Cardinal-Infante Ferdinand of Austria: "I assure you that this blow has pierced my heart and that it will be necessary to believe that God's assistance will help me find resignation in his Divine Will, as I desire to do with all of my ability." Reporting "great sadness," she wondered why "God has me here facing so much work" and requested spiritual support in the form of prayers from the nuns "so that I can tolerate this blow." She expected to visit the nuns as soon as possible to seek consolation, "something that I need to do very much so, I assure you." Portraying herself as more sorrowful than angry, in this letter, Mariana did not allocate blame as she did later. Her mild reaction and hurt tone may also be the result of not knowing the extent of Carlos's participation in the events. Judging by her subsequent letters and actions, she quickly recovered her composure.[39]

Widespread approval greeted Carlos II's decision to separate from his mother; the king seemed to enjoy both the attention and his newfound freedom. Joyful demonstrations were common inside the palace and in public ceremonies. The nobility lavished gifts on the young king, including tapestries and jewels valued at three hundred thousand ducats from Pedro of Aragón; an outfit adorned with diamond buttons and embroidered with emeralds and rubies sent by the Duchess of Bejar; and the twenty-five horses with exquisite hangings that the Duke of Osuna offered the young

king. A chronicle described Carlos as "rejoicing in the sweetness of reigning," calling his face "a house of pleasure" for those witnessing it, an "Aranjuez in its delights."[40]

As soon as Carlos II left the Alcázar, preparations for Don Juan's arrival
began. As Villaumbrosa had suggested, the king sent Cardinal Aragón as
an intermediary; they met privately on January 19. Cardinal Aragón negotiated the terms of agreement with Don Juan: Carlos II would dismiss
Mariana's royal guard from the city, and in return Don Juan would enter
Madrid without his armed force. In the following days, Don Juan received
unequivocal evidence of the king's firm support. On January 21, Carlos II
issued a public statement announcing that he had separated from the
queen "in consideration of my royal service and to provide consolation to
my kingdom and my subjects." He said that the queen would remain in the
Alcázar with all "the decency appropriate to her royal person." Having lost
her son and army, Mariana no longer controlled the state and the court.
However, the regime could not fully change until Mariana actually left the
court. So many layers of tradition legitimated her political authority that
her mere presence in Madrid would make it impossible for Don Juan to
consolidate his power.[41]

Once Don Juan saw that the king was safely isolated from his mother,
he entered Madrid with a small following on January 23. By the end of January, Carlos II and Don Juan were residing at the palace of the Buen Retiro
while the queen was still in the Alcázar. She had not lost all support, but
her position had been weakened considerably. At this point, Don Juan and
his supporters mediated between mother and son in order to safeguard the
king's political prerogatives. Fearing her influence on him, they worked to
keep Mariana away from Carlos II, even suspending the procession of San
Blas, scheduled for February 3 and customarily attended by Mariana and
Carlos, to prevent an encounter between the two.[42]

Don Juan also worked to eliminate Mariana's supporters from court,
which was no easy task. On January 24, he removed the admiral of Castile from office and exiled him to his estate in Rioseco. Since Valenzuela's
flight, the admiral had been the acting first master of the horse and thus had
significant authority over an important section of the queen's household;
Don Juan threatened severe punishments to those who remained loyal to
the admiral. The Count of Aguilar, lieutenant coronel of the royal guard,
accused of having participated in a 1675 conspiracy to assassinate Don Juan,

also lost his offices and went into exile. Other key figures, including the vice-chancellor of Aragon, the Marquis of Mejorada, and the fool Alvarado, a favorite of Mariana, were banished as well. Alvarado's substantial wealth and property—valued at more than two hundred thousand ducats—were seized. Don Juan reinstated those who had been disciplined for supporting his earlier bid for power, including the two main plotters, Father Montenegro and Ramos del Manzano.[43]

Valenzuela bore the brunt of Don Juan's revenge. Before Carlos II could send his mother's protégé to another location, the Duke of Medina Sidonia and the heir to the Duke of Alba, Antonio de Toledo, captured Valenzuela at El Escorial on January 22. This violation of ecclesiastical jurisdiction immediately provoked a diplomatic conflict with the pope, who excommunicated the two miscreants and demanded Valenzuela's release. Political expediency, however, overshadowed diplomatic concerns, and Valenzuela was taken in chains to Consuegra on January 26, his right to trial notwithstanding. His wife was forced to enter the Convent of Santa Ursula in Toledo: pregnant and with small children, she left Madrid with just what she had on. These illegal procedures could only be implemented with the king's signature, as Villaumbrosa informed Carlos and Don Juan. On January 27, Carlos II issued an amnesty to all those who had supported Don Juan. He invalidated the royal grants given to Valenzuela, including the grandeeship, arguing that the elevation was "not from his own volition and freedom." This statement clearly indicted Mariana for having manipulated her son.[44]

Mariana, who later referred to all the events leading to her exile as "demonstrations" disrespectful of her royal status, remained serene but defiant. When rumors circulated that she would have to move to the city of Alcalá, a gazette reported that her ladies began to lament and cry, while the queen "continued reading," as if nothing had been said. Rumors of conspiracies against Don Juan's life were rampant, virtually all associated with Mariana and her supporters. One gazette, for instance, reported that the queen had fomented the plots against him. Another suggested that she planned to personally assassinate Don Juan by hiding a pistol in her sleeve and firing it when he kissed her hand. Allegedly warned by one of Mariana's ladies, Don Juan excused himself from the audience that was to take place on January 24. The episode sounds farfetched, but it appeared in several manuscripts. Don Juan took the rumors seriously; he believed that as long as the queen remained in Madrid, his life was in peril, and he spent large sums on a personal guard. But he had the king's support, which was decisive.[45]

A SELF-ELECTED RETIREMENT

The court's instability was exacerbated by Mariana's presence, but it had not yet been determined where she would go. Her place of residence presented "great difficulties" because "the one condemned to exile was to be the mother and the judge her son." After Mariana deemed several locations unacceptable, the Alcázar of Toledo was agreed on. Carlos II and Don Juan tried to make it look as if Mariana was taking the initiative regarding her future. Carlos II wrote to the Toledan officials on February 14, telling them that his mother had decided to move there. He made the decision public the same day. The royal decree required Mariana to "retire," as was supposedly stipulated in his father's testament, and gave her fewer than two weeks to prepare her household. She only received a potential list of household members who were to follow her to Toledo on February 25. Mariana maintained her stoic demeanor and sent a courteous letter to the Toledo officials. But despite her facade of politeness and courtesy, these humiliating procedures trampled on her freedom and the prerogatives granted to her by Philip IV.[46]

Mariana was especially pained by Carlos II's lack of tact, and she reproached him in a letter written on February 18:

> My son: I'm not sure why it is considered charity to do to a grief-stricken woman what is being done to me, without attending to the quality of my person and other circumstances, which should not escape your attention. Even though you tell me that the testament of the king, my lord and husband and your father (who enjoys a better crown now), ordered that I retire to Toledo, that is not the case. And if he had ordered such a thing . . . he would have never agreed that [my departure] would be so sudden and under the threat of such violence, basically putting me in the same position as that of a prisoner, a posture utterly indecorous and even insulting to my person. It would have been appropriate to give me enough time to put together my family, as befits a woman like myself. It is that hypocrite who causes all of these problems, and he is nothing short of

manipulating and deceiving you with his lies, as time will show you, for your detriment and that of my feelings, since I love you more than he does. I, the Queen.[47]

The queen's anger and outrage are palpable, in part because Don Juan— "that hypocrite"—had blatantly distorted the king's testament. Philip IV had given Mariana the option of retiring if she so desired, but he never mandated it. In fact, Mariana had the right to choose any place as her permanent residence. Philip IV's testament had granted her the enormous sum of three hundred thousand *ducados* annually for the rest of her widowhood and sovereignty over whatever city she chose as her residence. Mariana's letter reveals her sense of herself as a member of a powerful dynasty and, moreover, as one with a special position within it. Even her signature, "I, the Queen," was in the style of formal official correspondence.[48]

At this point, however, Mariana had run out of options. Political expediency dictated that she leave court as soon as possible. Once her departure was scheduled for March 2, her communication with her son was largely broken off. In the last letter before her departure, Mariana seems to have accepted her personal and political losses: "Son of my life: on the occasion of my departure and because of my affection, I cannot leave without telling you with how much pain and despair I leave without seeing you; and I assure you that even though I do not have this relief, I will never lose the obligations that I have as mother, because of the great love that I have for you."

She requested that the members of her household that stayed in Madrid—or her family, as they were called in household papers—be cared for and treated fairly. She asked that Carlos write her often. After blessing him, she signed the letter "Your mother who loves you best," which became her customary signature in letters to Carlos. There is a significant change of tone and perhaps attitude here. The accusations and defiance are gone; only resignation remains. The language of a mother's love begins to dominate, a language she would master in subsequent correspondence and that may have helped in her later rehabilitation and return to Madrid.[49]

Mariana's tone of resignation was echoed in her actions, which gradually began to turn public opinion to her side. A gazette reported that the queen, "denied of the consolation [of seeing her son], went down to enter the carriage, full of majesty, serenity, and equanimity; her dignity increased

by the venerable veils that she wore." Even before she left Madrid, a change
was brewing: Mariana was starting to be seen not as the dominant figure
who denied the king his rightful position but as a devoted mother who, in
her widowhood and solitude, was robbed of the consolation of her son's
presence. Don Juan felt the shift too. His denial of Mariana's wish to see her
son before her departure was seen with disapproval. It was "not possible,"
the author opined, that the king would not want to see her, given his age
and affection; "only violence could have impeded such a thing."⁵⁰

As news of the events in Madrid circulated in foreign courts, Carlos II
and Don Juan were criticized. In France, the queen, Mariana's cousin and
stepdaughter, complained to Sor Mariana de la Cruz, the same relative in
the Descalzas Reales with whom Mariana corresponded frequently, about
Carlos's behavior. "I cannot approve that they have forced the queen to
leave Madrid," Maria Theresa wrote, "and more so that her son did not go
to bid farewell to his mother." She repeated this outrage in other letters: "I
cannot stand what they are doing with the queen mother." "After all," she
protested, "[Mariana] is his mother and his father's wife, and even if this was
not enough, she is also a great princess." Maria Theresa told Sor Mariana
that her "relative" strongly disapproved of Carlos's behavior; this relative,
she clarified in a later letter, was none other than Louis XIV. Her husband,
Maria Theresa affirmed, had always been "an obedient and good son of his
mother." That mother, of course, was another Habsburg matriarch, Anne
of Austria, who had been queen regent during her son's minority. Although
deeply ironic considering that Louis XIV had been Spain's major threat,
he was hailed as an example the young Carlos should emulate. Emperor
Leopold I also protested directly to the king, asking his nephew to preserve
Mariana's "decorum." Like Louis XIV, he also had a mother who had been
respected and valued. But while Carlos was faulted, it was Don Juan who
eventually paid a high political price for meddling with the king's mother,
the former king's widow, and a "great princess."⁵¹

THE HAND WITHOUT THE SCEPTER

Getting Mariana settled in her "retirement" was not simple. Don Juan and
Carlos II had to find an appropriate residence, organize a royal household
to accompany her, and design appropriate rituals of entry into the city. They
had to preserve the queen mother's "decorum" while trying to eliminate

all vestiges of her political authority. They needed Mariana to cooperate in the fiction of a self-elected retirement, and she complied to an extent but continued to defend her royal status in every possible way. Both sides were forced to negotiate and compromise.

Mariana fought to retain as many symbols of royal authority as possible, demanding, for instance, to live in a royal palace. She refused to move to a private palace, affirming that she was not a "subject of the king." She declined the offer to reside even temporarily in the archbishop's palace in Toledo, purportedly saying that she was not a "housekeeper of a priest" (*ama de cura*). The "Diario de noticias" reported that Mariana had considered her brother's suggestion that she retire permanently to the Descalzas Reales but had rejected the idea, although residing in the convent was a tradition among Habsburg widows. In the end, all agreed that Mariana would move to the royal palace in Aranjuez until the royal residence in Toledo was renovated.[52]

There were no previous models in the history of Habsburg Spain of a royal widow maintaining what amounted to a sort of alternative court. The process of establishing Mariana's household required a good deal of compromise on both sides. A week after Carlos's decree of expulsion, Mariana was handed a list of potential members of her royal household. It included almost two hundred attendants and servants, with the members of her private chamber and her guards making an additional hundred. The final number included ninety-eight attendants, including the ladies of Mariana's chamber, thirty guards, and others hired locally for various tasks. Although custom held that only the reigning sovereign had German and Spanish guards, Mariana was allocated some. Whenever she left her palace in Toledo, at least twenty-four guardsmen attended her, but of course two guard units were a far cry from Mariana's personal army, now serving on the Aragonese front.[53]

Mariana's entry into Toledo on April 1, 1677, involved tremendous pomp and ceremony, with the celebrations deploying symbols associated with the Habsburgs and ruling monarchs. Escorted by her one-hundred-person entourage, she entered the city through the Puerta de Bisagra, built in 1556 and prominently displaying the coat of arms of Emperor Charles V, Mariana's great-great-grandfather. As she sat under this arch, she was treated to a simulacrum of battle enacted by more than three hundred men representing harquebusiers and pikemen. The spectacle, punctuated by the continuous explosion of gunpowder and the sound of trumpets, was set amid the elaborate decorations designed specifically for the occasion. The city also unveiled a military tent that had been used by Emperor Charles V himself, displayed for the first time in more than a century. After attending a religious service in Toledo's imposing cathedral, Mariana was honored with masques, luminaries, fireworks, processions, equestrian shows, civic rituals, and dances. The procession culminated in the Alcázar amid "the tolling of the bells that could be heard all over the city." The entire ritual highlighted Mariana's position as ruler.[54]

Nevertheless, the festivities celebrated the past. They were a commemoration, not the start of something new. This backward-looking orientation was also used to explain Mariana's retirement. As a text published a few months after the event put it, Mariana was following the model of other great rulers, including Charles V, who had retired from public view and left the seat of government "in order to not let the hand be seen without the scepter in the same place where the scepter was seen in the hand."[55]

SETTLING INTO RETIREMENT

Everyone at court in Madrid recognized that Mariana, even safely in Toledo, still had an important position in the political and dynastic hierarchies; the most threatened by her power and position were those closest to Don Juan. During the first several months of her exile, therefore, their main goal was to keep her as far from her son as possible. Mariana received private letters, or *cartas particulares*, which kept her well informed about Carlos. Her letters to Carlos II from the early part of her exile do not survive, but manuscripts and gazettes frequently mention them. But as she confided to Cardinal Aragón, she received only intermittent responses or none at all. The early months of her exile, therefore, were difficult for the queen, who had a hard time adapting to being away from Carlos and the court where she had lived for more than twenty-seven years. In one of his letters about the queen's sadness, Aragón noted that she "loved her son excessively [*desatinadamente*] without thinking about anything else."[56]

Mariana complained about suffering from recurrent migraines (*jaquecas*), a lifetime ailment that seems to have worsened during this period. On her way to Toledo, Mariana wrote to Sor Mariana, thanking her for her letters, the food basket the nuns had sent, and their prayers, "which I have never needed more than I do at this moment." She was, she said, trying "to accept God's will at all times." Composed a little more than two weeks after her departure from Madrid, the short missive reveals how much the recent events had affected her. Her lifelong friendships with the religious women were critical in this moment of isolation; they encouraged her and gave her news about Carlos and events in Madrid. And since Maria Theresa also corresponded with the nuns, her communication network was thus extended to her relatives in foreign courts. Mariana's friendship with Maria Theresa was regulated by their official positions as queens of rival monarchies, and it was thus very unlikely that they could talk about these intimate matters directly. As a matter of decorum, it is also very unlikely that Mariana would have discussed her situation with Leopold. Mariana's extant correspondence and her testament indicate stronger affective ties with the nuns in the Descalzas, with whom she could be more frank and open about her predicament, than with relatives who were also rulers.[57]

Mariana's difficulties were to a great extent the result of specific strategies followed by Don Juan, who wished to erase the queen mother's presence from the court's political networks, from private spaces, and from the king's mind. The exile of Mariana's supporters, which began even before the queen left the court, continued throughout the entire period of Don Juan's tenure in office. Don Juan worked to lessen Mariana's presence in the Descalzas Reales as well. The nuns had always supported the queen, and Carlos II visited frequently. Don Juan rescheduled the traditional royal vacation to Aranjuez because it was too close to Toledo, planning instead a trip to Aragon so that Carlos could swear the *fueros*. This ceremony was of critical political importance to the Crown of Aragon; in it, the king confirmed the rights and privileges of his Aragonese subjects in front of the Cortes, or parliaments. Don Juan's motives fit his political aims, but it is also undeniable that the trip offered him a chance to keep the king as far from his mother as possible. The journey to Aragon began on April 21, relatively soon after Mariana left Madrid, and ended on June 12. Harrach requested on behalf of the queen that she be allowed to see her son before his departure. Mariana found the request humiliating but agreed to it. In any case, it was denied.[58]

Erasing Mariana's symbolic presence from the court was another of Don Juan's projects, starting with the removal of the equestrian statue of Philip IV from the principal door of the Alcázar, which served as a powerful visual reminder of Mariana's right to play a more active role in her son's government. Don Juan wanted the statue gone before Carlos's expected return from Aragon on June 12. He was able to meet this dead-line—but with great difficulty, since the work took longer than expected. It became the talk of the city, giving plenty of ammunition to satirists, who mocked Don Juan with a riddle:

> For what purpose did Don Juan come to Madrid?
> To lower the horse and to raise the price of bread.
>
> [A que vino el Señor Don Juan?
> A bajar el caballo y subir el pan.]

Don Juan saw every attack and problem as connected to Mariana's resid-ual authority. Perhaps this was why he operated via a regime of exiles and retaliations that not only was ineffective but contributed to opposition and facilitated Mariana's rehabilitation.[59]

Removing the horse was not enough; soon after Carlos's return from Aragon, a diplomatic event brought Mariana back into his life and that of the monarchy. On June 17, the imperial ambassador presented to Carlos the ratified capitulations of the marriage contract of the emperor's daughter, Archduchess Maria Antonia, and requested on behalf of Leo-pold that the king follow suit. The marriage was supposed to have taken place in December 1676 but was suspended given the events in Madrid. Harrach was Leopold's ambassador, but his connections to Mariana went beyond mere diplomatic connections with the queen's family in Vienna: the Countess of Harrach, his wife, maintained a lifelong correspondence with Mariana and had known the queen since they were very young. Harrach defended the queen as much as he could, writing a scathing attack on Don Juan in January 1677, a manifesto that, copied in manuscript form, widely circulated in Madrid. Mariana's correspondence with the ambassador after she left the court indicates that the queen was behind this sudden move on Leopold's part. The request for the ratification was Harrach's—and Leopold's—calculated political blow to the new regime and an attempt to aid Mariana's cause. As such, it provoked strong criticism in the Council of State.[60]

Carlos II's marriage to Maria Antonia would have had significant politi-cal consequences for Mariana. Since the little archduchess was only eight,

Mariana would have had a strong claim to guardianship, so as a matter of protocol, the marriage would likely have required Mariana's presence at court. Harrach's public announcement was clearly intended to force Carlos and his ministers to agree to the marriage, but the ministers opposed it because of the bride's age, while Don Juan opposed it because it could bring Mariana back to court. But officially breaking the engagement was untenable, since Spain and the Holy Roman Empire were in the middle of a war against France. It had taken Mariana and her diplomats years to gain Leopold I's support against Louis XIV; Carlos and his ministers, Don Juan included, could not jeopardize the alliance, especially when, as part of the marriage negotiations, Mariana had just further publicized it by notifying all European rulers of the upcoming nuptials. Moreover, there was another threat to the alliance, as rumors had reached Leopold's court that Don Juan was considering ceding the Low Countries to France.[61]

After a decade of unrelenting work, Mariana's legacy seemed to be in danger, but the Council of State would not accept the loss of the Habsburg alliance and had no intention of giving up the Spanish Netherlands. Its members concluded that seeking peace with France and cementing it with the king's marriage to Louis XIV's niece, Marie Louise of Orleans, just a year younger than Carlos, was the ideal solution. But it was impossible to either seek the marriage or break the engagement to the archduchess while fighting the war. Carlos informed Leopold that he could not confirm the marriage, but he promised not to make any official announcement unless it was mutually agreed on. The Council of State identified Mariana as the ideal intermediary in this delicate situation and suggested that Carlos ask his mother for help. All this put Mariana in a quandary. She had clearly wanted Carlos's marriage to the archduchess. Would she persist in her original goal or help her son extricate himself from an engagement she had negotiated in the first place? Cardinal Aragón was convinced that Mariana's "tender love" for her son would prevail and that she would help him solve this diplomatic predicament. These questions were not resolved until 1679, but in the short term, they opened a positive line of communication and put Mariana in the fortunate situation of being able to help Carlos. Carlos was also pressured by Leopold to treat his mother with proper respect. It is unclear how much Leopold's request weighed on the king, but Mariana's situation began to improve. Maria Theresa wrote to the Descalzas Reales in August, expressing her happiness at knowing that "the queen was settling into her retirement."[62]

Outside the Council of State, Mariana also began to make some gains. Her absence began to cast a shadow on Don Juan's ministry. A gazette reported that Don Juan's preoccupation with the king's love for his mother had accelerated Don Juan's aging. Another noted that he was "more pre-occupied with conserving the king than the kingdom." Thus he "continues to monitor the letters that go back and forth to Toledo" between Carlos and his mother. This is the one indication we have that communication between mother and son had resumed outside of the exchanges that took place over the king's marriage with Mariana and Leopold, as only the letters that Carlos wrote to Mariana after 1678 have been preserved. The political discourse had shifted so much that Don Juan was shown trying to be a substitute mother: a gazetteer noted that Don Juan "began to comb and to cut the king's hair, as if a comb or anything else could be more caring, affectionate, or natural than the love of his mother." Motherhood was still being used as a political tool, but now against Don Juan, not Mariana.[63]

Mariana took active measures to remain in her son's mind. For his six-teenth birthday, the first time she was not there to celebrate with him, she sent several presents, including a portrait of herself in a splendid frame decorated with eight large diamonds. The significance of this gift cannot be underestimated, considering the affective and symbolic function of royal portraits in early modern courts, almost taking the place of the person they represented. By 1678, Mariana had an active communication network in place that linked her to her son and the court. In the next two years, she suc-cessfully marshaled her political, dynastic, and affective capital and staged her comeback.[64]

CHAPTER 7

Reconciliation, Vindication, Triumph, 1678–1679

Mariana's exile was certainly the low point of her political life, but it was also beneficial for her son, for Spain, and even for her. The separation provided a healthy distance between the mother and son that allowed them to adapt to their new political roles. The process took place in stages, however. It helped that the queen's ties to Carlos and Madrid were never completely severed and that as early as 1677, Carlos, Don Juan, and the Spanish ministers realized they had to rely on Mariana to resolve the question of the king's marriage. But even with this ongoing communication and their mutual affection, there was real tension between the two. Gradually Carlos found ways to limit his mother's authority over him, and Mariana learned to defer to her son. Given their relationship, this was not a private process but one mediated by members of the court.

Mariana's absence from Madrid benefitted her in another fundamental way: her regency looked much better now that people could compare it to life under Don Juan. His position has been the subject of debate; some scholars equate him with a prime minister/*valido*, even though he did not have the title. But because he took power with the threat of force, he has also been called a protodictator. And even though he took power with the backing of multiple important court figures, his behavior suggests that he never felt fully secure in his authority. He kept a tight rein on the young king, and in his quest to consolidate power, he implemented a harsh policy of exiles and dismissals that alienated many. His management of royal patronage also drove people into opposition, even some who had initially supported him. Gradually at first, then more openly, the "malcontents," as they were called in manuscripts and letters, became more vocal and numerous. They rallied behind Mariana, who became the center of the opposition to Don Juan, and as early as 1679, Mariana and Don Juan found themselves in a situation like that of early 1677, but with their roles reversed.[1]

Mariana's intercession with the emperor to help the king pursue a marriage alliance with France strengthened the case for her return. By the time Carlos's marriage to the French princess, Marie Louise of Orleans, was confirmed in the summer of 1679, a regime change was imminent, with the clarification of the political relationship between mother and son the only missing piece. Mariana could not be seen as a threat to the king as she had been in his first year of rule: Carlos deftly eliminated this last obstacle to his mother's return by setting specific conditions, which she gladly and graciously accepted. This chapter follows the process of reconciliation that led to Mariana's triumphal return on September 27, 1679.

COMMUNICATION NETWORKS

The correspondence between Mariana and Carlos is the most important first-person account of what transpired between them. Although Carlos wrote often to Mariana, only fifty-eight letters, from April 8, 1678, to September 20, 1679, are extant. The handwritten originals did not survive; we have the drafts, written with a secretary's help, which feature corrections, crossed-out passages, and comments added or removed. The letters reveal Carlos's personality and insecurities, as well as the reverence in which he held his mother. While only ten of Mariana's letters from her exile survive, her voice can be heard clearly in Carlos's letters as he reacts to his mother's comments. All ten of Mariana's letters are undisputed holographs—that is, written in her own hand without the assistance of a secretary. For the Habsburgs, writing letters in their own hand was significant, which is confirmed by archival evidence of the special treatment recipients gave such letters. In this case, Mariana's writing in her own hand indicated her interest in cultivating affective ties with her son. Written in a steady hand, her letters reveal her confidence and clarity.[2]

The extant letters date from April 1678, but we can deduce from the gazettes and the deliberations about the king's marriage that regular contact between the two began in the fall of 1677. This contact was part of a larger communication network: weekly (often daily) oral messages, letters, gifts, portraits, and documents traveled between Toledo and Madrid, carried by a range of people, from the top political officers in each royal households to lower-ranked administrative officials. Only when read within the context of this larger exchange does the correspondence make sense.

A division of labor in how information was transmitted highlights the multiple aspects of Mariana's and Carlos's relationship and how they were mediated by others. Mariana's beloved court dwarf, Nicolás Pertusato, who also served in Carlos II's chamber, for example, brought news of Carlos's activities to Mariana and updated him on her health and well-being. The Duke of Medinaceli carried intimate and personal information, reporting to mother and son about each other's health and assuming the role of intermediary when they quarreled. The Marquis of Mancera, Mariana's *mayordomo mayor*, served as the queen's special envoy, carrying her personal letters and messages to Carlos. The king's secretary, Jerónimo de Eguía, and Isidro de Angulo, the queen's, brought political and administrative documents. Other court officers were dispatched when needed. The nuns at the Descalzas Reales formed another link; they kept the queen abreast of events in Madrid, informed her about Carlos's health, and told relatives at foreign courts about Mariana's state of mind.[3]

To make sure that communication between Madrid and Toledo was speedy and ongoing, Mariana designated funds for a young officer (*mozo*) to sleep in the palace, ready for "any kind of errand that may be needed to be run in the middle of the night." Carlos chose couriers according to the urgency of the situation: "I send you this news via courier, which will be faster than Leiba, and for this reason I do not respond to your letter," he wrote on August 20, 1678. A letter Carlos wrote Mariana on April 14, 1678, gives a sense of their many modes of communication. He explained that he had not responded fully to her letters when he had written the previous day because he needed to attend a special Mass celebrating the end of the revolt in Messina. The busy Carlos also relied on others to keep his mother informed: "Porras will tell you how thankful I am for your gift." He then mentioned that his secretary had already forwarded the queen's secretary "copies of the letters that I sent to my uncle [the emperor]," letters that dealt with his marriage. He also commented casually that Nicolás (Pertusato) gave him "frequent news" about her. His mention of all these people in a single letter highlights the dynamic and frequent exchange of information between mother and son.[4]

Their frequent communication indicated a change in the political climate at court. The most important shift to note, albeit one that was taking place behind the scenes, was the growing importance of the Duke of Medinaceli. Medinaceli's tenure as prime minister began in February 1680 (he served until 1685). While his ministry has been studied as part of the revisionist histories of Carlos II's reign, it has been assumed that his rise to power took place after Don Juan's death in September 1679. Among Medinaceli's papers, however, I have found a holographic note by Carlos II offering him the position of prime minister dated February 1678—two years earlier than when he actually rose to the office. This important piece of evidence indicates that a change of regime began to emerge as a possibility in the middle of Don Juan's ministry. As I discuss in the rest of the chapter, Medinaceli's rise has to be seen in the context of Mariana's exile and her renegotiation of her political relationship with the king and his court. It should be remembered that Mariana had appointed Medinaceli as *summiller de corps* of the king's household, the highest court office, and had rewarded him again with a position in the Council of State for his intervention on her behalf in the November 6, 1675, plot. Medinaceli was the one who helped Carlos move out of the palace, thus aiding in Don Juan's bid for power and precipitating Mariana's exile. He was able to maintain his position when Don Juan rose to power. Yet, by the same token, Medinaceli was an early figure in facilitating communication between Mariana and Carlos, and indeed, tracking the appearance of names in the correspondence reveals the shifting political loyalties at court as well as the outlines of the regime that would follow.[5]

LIMITING MATERNAL AUTHORITY

A changed political climate and regular communication did not mean that the rift between Mariana and Carlos had been mended; indeed, their power struggle was still palpable in 1678. Mariana let her son know she was still offended by her treatment and that she resented her exile, her exclusion from his life, and having to accept a politically subordinate role. Carlos limited his mother's attempts to control him, relying on his position and, to some degree, on Don Juan to keep Mariana in check. So poor was the relationship between his mother and his half brother that Carlos eventually had to take sides. Yet by working through these conflicts, Carlos and Mariana shaped new political and personal roles.

One of the few exchanges that can be reconstructed in its entirety illustrates the processes of negotiation and reconciliation. The letter Mariana wrote Carlos on June 10, 1678, began sweetly enough: "Son of my life, I was delighted with the news from Medinaceli that you are well and that even though you may have been tired by yesterday's functions, the cloudy day perhaps gave you respite during the procession." She reported having visited the archbishop's palace to see a beautiful Virgin housed there and told Carlos that she had just suffered a "quite severe" migraine, which she thought she "must have gotten . . . in the middle of the night, since during the day, the weather was rather cool and not hot at all." Then she abruptly began reproaching him: "I cannot help but always remind you of that subject, which in not responding to it, the only thing you can expect is that I will keep repeating it. Because you do not give me a response, I have no choice but to keep asking." The subject of this rather brusque request was Valenzuela, who was about to leave for the Philippines to serve ten years of exile. She ended by requesting that Carlos allow Dr. Astorga, her personal physician, to return to Madrid and then closed the letter with the formulaic good-byes and her characteristic "Your mother who loves you most" (*Tu Madre que más te quiere*).[6]

The distance from Toledo to Madrid was approximately fifty miles, which was easily covered in less than a day on horseback, allowing Carlos to respond the next day. Carlos began by offering affection and respect. He commented on his activities, his enjoyment of the countryside, and the Corpus Christi celebrations, including the famous *autos sacramentales*, or liturgical dramas, created especially for the occasion. He assured her that her petition for a man named Moles was "very present" in his thoughts. But he did not mince words on the most important part of Mariana's previous letter: "I resent that you imagine that I do not read your letters and that you surmise such a thing because I did not respond to the secret business, about which I have already clearly told you that it would be impossible to change what has been already resolved." He repeated that he was not willing to do her bidding on that matter and ended his letter rather abruptly, without his usual affectionate lines before his signature and the date.[7]

When she responded several days later, Mariana was more subdued. She told him of her happiness at learning of his good health and receiving his letters, "since I have no other relief from the moment that I separated from you than having them." Her motherly concerns included a warning about the importance of protecting his fair skin from the sun, and she hoped that "he would not tire himself too much during the frequent processions in which he took part." Only then did she address his sharp response to her original request:

> My son, what you respond about that matter that I have requested of you so many times, I have plenty of reasons to insist that these public demonstrations conducted [against me] were done so in utter disregard for my decorum, to which you should attend to very much; but I see that it is futile to insist because you are so set [empeñado]. Someday, I am sure, you will recognize the reasons that led me to confer the royal grants to him. Now, I ask you to ensure that his poor wife be left alone and given something to survive, since she has had enough with her own misfortunes, and as a defenseless woman, it seems more appropriate to exercise moderation with her.[8]

The exchange was political, but it also touched their personal relationship. In insisting to Carlos that she had had good reason to have given Valenzuela such a prominent position, Mariana both justified her actions and advocated for her protégé and his wife. Her imperious tone indicates a strong sense of self and confidence in her judgment. Mariana also implicitly reproached Carlos for not understanding what she had gone through, as indicated by her hope that one day he would better understand "her reasons." Her request to help Moles was also a reference, albeit indirectly, to Valenzuela's situation, as Moles was imprisoned because he was Valenzuela's confidant. Mariana's intercession for him was thus an additional statement that her previous decisions had been fully justified.

But even within this exchange, we can see Mariana's immediate adaptation, as she opted to use persuasion rather than pressure. For example, she defended Valenzuela's wife by appealing to Carlos's sense of chivalry, arguing she was a "defenseless woman" who should be left in peace. Mariana's defense of Valenzuela can be seen as a sign of loyalty—a consistent attribute—but the exchange also illustrates Mariana's concern about her image, seeing the public demonstrations against Valenzuela and his wife first and foremost as a personal affront.

Carlos navigated the situation with firmness and tact. In his response, written four days later, he started with a few polite remarks regarding their health and the weather and then assured her, "No harm has been done to the woman you name, either in word or deed." He made no mention of Valenzuela or Mariana's protestations regarding her decorum, but he agreed to her request on behalf of her physician. This was not a small matter: Mariana's intercession here was also tied to her "decorum," as she justified her request on the basis that the man "should not be losing" the comforts he enjoyed in Madrid "for serving me loyally." This rationale—that people should not suffer for having been loyal to her—lay behind many of her requests for favors for people in her household and is one of her most frequent topics.[9]

Although the queen could no longer fulfill the needs of her former clients with the stroke of a pen, she felt entitled to demand that her son meet them. She bombarded him with petitions on behalf of people formerly or currently in her service. Carlos conceded some of these: the daughter of Mariana's secretary, for example, received a pair of shoes "because you asked." But just as often, he delayed or refused. Mariana, for example, campaigned to obtain a grandeeship for the Marquis of Mancera, her newly appointed *mayordomo mayor*. He had taken his post in Mariana's household when her political fortunes were at an especially low ebb, and she wanted to reward him and make a display of royal patronage. It is not clear when she first asked Carlos for this, but it was a frequent topic from 1678 onward. Alleging a new restraint in the distribution of royal patronage and evidently influenced by Don Juan, Carlos refused, telling Mariana that such royal grants "have to be closely regulated and must be made to those subjects whose contributions are lengthy, important, and of great and relevant service." Mancera had been viceroy of New Spain (Mexico) and had long served the Crown, but it is debatable whether his resume was sufficient for such an important elevation. Regarding the *encomienda* (a tribute of labor) the queen requested for her lady-in-waiting, "La Manrique," Carlos refused on the grounds that it was reserved for military service and would unduly strain the royal budget.[10]

Mariana's inability to reward her followers, or have them rewarded, caused a great deal of tension between her and Carlos. When Mariana wanted to grant a favor to Valenzuela's wife, Maria of Ucedo, it was

Mancera who carried out her wish. This was a clear affront to the king, even if Mariana was justified in wanting to protect Ucedo, and Carlos rebuked Mancera for obeying Mariana. Tensions repeatedly flared over similar situations as mother and son struggled over who held ultimate authority.[11]

Mariana continued to insist that Carlos make good on her requests for royal grants, which took the form of financial, political, or social awards. Feeling pressured by his mother's demands, Carlos asked his confessor for a written consultation on the subject, which he then sent to Mariana. From Carlos's letter, we learn that she objected to the confessor's argument that the king should make such grants solely based on "his conscience, faith, and as a recognition of the personal merits of the interested parties." Perhaps expecting this reaction, Carlos had noted, "It is not my intention to deny all royal grants to the ladies of the court." In October, Carlos informed his mother that he was inclined to favor Mancera and promised to keep "La Manrique" in mind, but still did not give in. He did grant most of the (quite numerous) smaller requests. What is evident in these tense exchanges is that Carlos could now hold his own with his mother. Nevertheless, she did have one high card: she was the king's mother.[12]

"TU MADRE QUE MÁS TE QUIERE"

In all communications with her son, Mariana emphasized maternal affection and authority. She could be demanding and stern, but she always began and ended her letters with expressions of her love. This language may not seem unusual in correspondence between mothers and sons, but in this case the mother was a queen, former regent of the monarchy, and the son was the ruling sovereign. Love was used in political discourse to describe the relationship between ruler and subjects. Motherly love in particular was utilized by French political theorists as the main justification for a queen mother's claim to the regency: a loving mother would look out for her son's interests and, concomitantly, those of the monarchy. She would rule selflessly instead of seeking power for herself. The same theorists believed that male regents were more likely to usurp political power, because they loved power more than they did the monarch.[13]

Motherhood in early modern Spain was not the only sanction for Mariana's regency, which was based on legal, dynastic, and political traditions.

Nevertheless, it was a powerful construct in the political culture of Habsburg Spain. Parental influence—of mothers as much as fathers—on their children was a pervasive value among the aristocracy and royalty. As we have seen, motherhood was the main reason for the crisis of the monarchy and Mariana's exile, and it continued to have strong political implications. Mariana's expressions of maternal affection cannot be taken transparently, but it would also be wrong to consider them merely Machiavellian calculations. Love and political gain were not mutually exclusive within the complex system of cultural values—dynastic, social, political, and even religious—that operated in Mariana and Carlos's relationship.

In her missives, Mariana demonstrated interest in Carlos's daily life, the details of which he often, if at times reluctantly, reported to her. She always responded positively to his activities, whether his improvement in horsemanship or his attendance at plays, his hunting or his participation in celebrations and public functions. She filled her letters to him with praise and encouragement. She also worried about his health—a common topic in the early modern period, but one that allowed her to express motherly love. When she praised his prudence in sheltering himself from the sun during his hunting trips, for example, she said, "Your health is what matters the most." But praise alternated with reprimands: his failure to write is a constant theme, as according to her, his letters were her only consolation. She wrote often; Carlos usually mentioned having received two or three missives from his mother for every one that he wrote. That he was a dilatory correspondent was perhaps not surprising for an adolescent boy.[14]

Mariana's often effusive expressions of affection put great pressure on Carlos, which may explain why he responded less frequently and vacillated between trying to appease his dominating mother and assert his own independence. The letters themselves testify to his insecurity; sections are often crossed out and written over as the young king struggled to find the right words to convey filial affection without appearing childish. For example, on one occasion, he told his mother how advanced he was in his riding exercises, only to cross out the remark and substitute a more impersonal note about his health. Apparently feeling the need to assure his mother that his affection for her had not waned, he apologized for not writing more often but explained, "[It is] because of the impediments that I have and since I also know that Medinaceli keeps you well informed about my health."

Still, the language he chose was perhaps not exactly what Mariana wished to hear, as he stressed on May 19, 1678, "My affection [*cariño*] . . . to you is in line to my obligations." His next letter must have pleased her more, as he assured her of "his continued affection" and said that not writing was not "because of a lack of feeling." No political news or queries about health or felicitations on birthdays and name days passed without expressions of love. The day before Mariana's name day, for instance, Carlos wrote, "The joy with which I celebrate the day tomorrow and the wish that you have a wonderful day, oblige me to send Leiba with this letter so that he can bring me news about you, which I await with impatience. I hope that what he gives you will be to your liking, which is a sign of my affection, which will always be equal to my obligations and how much I owe you."[15]

Although these expressions may sound formulaic, the very act of stating them had political implications. What Carlos implied in recognizing his "obligations and how much I owe you" was that Mariana had performed a great service on his behalf as governor of the monarchy. But Carlos was also threading a delicate balance, worried that his mother would interpret his comments as an overture for her return, something for which he was not yet ready. Perhaps this was why in September 1678 Carlos thanked Mariana for her demonstrations of affection on having seen his portrait but then crossed those thanks out.[16]

In her letters, Mariana did not use her name or the official "I, the Queen" but signed all her letters "Your mother who loves you most," a statement with multiple meanings. Mariana first used it on January 18, 1677, the day after Carlos had signed the decree exiling her. In that bitter letter, she employed the expression to distinguish herself from Don Juan, "that hypocrite," who had deceived and manipulated Carlos: "Time will show you . . . that I love you more than he does," she wrote. The fact that Mariana then adopted a version of this as her signature in her correspondence shows how swiftly she began delivering her message to Carlos. By "who loves you most," Mariana meant that she loved him more than Don Juan did or could. She, not his half brother, had his best interests at heart. The phrase implied that she was entitled to participate in the political life of her son and the monarchy and asserted her superiority to the usurper. This motherly love was powerful, as Mariana was about to prove to Carlos and the ministers of the court in the most effective way she could: the diplomatic realm.[17]

MATERNAL DIPLOMACY

On January 5, 1679, Carlos II notified his mother that he intended to ratify the terms of the Peace of Nijmegen, ending the war Mariana had started in 1673. The war's end also opened the door to resuming talks about the critical issue of the king's marriage. As early as August 2, 1677, Carlos II and his ministers had set their sights on Marie Louise of Orleans, Louis XIV's niece. Not only could she help secure the succession as an adult bride, but a Franco-Spanish marriage was considered essential for a lasting peace. Carlos had told Leopold in the fall of 1677 that he could not confirm the marriage to the little archduchess, explaining that he had to consider his subjects' central concern—securing the succession. His ministers, he said, had unanimously demanded that he marry a woman nearer his age. Carlos and Leopold reached an accord by the end of 1677, with Carlos promising to postpone any final decision until they reached a "common agreement." Mariana, as discussed earlier, had been part of these exchanges and was expected to arbitrate.[18]

Carlos summoned the Council of State on January 7, 1679, to reopen discussions about his marriage. This was a mere formality: the councilors simply confirmed that Marie Louise was the preferred candidate. The real issue was how to get the king out of the engagement to the Austrian archduchess. Mariana immediately emerged as the only person who could extricate the monarchy from its delicate predicament. Medinaceli opined that the queen would be able to make "the Emperor understand that ultimately she [Mariana] was the only one who has the right to force your majesty to alter what has been already decided." Medinaceli's point that she was "the only one" indicates Mariana's position as mother of the king.[19]

Yet would Mariana agree to help Carlos dissolve the engagement, since she had negotiated the original agreement? Further, Maria Antonia was her granddaughter; would Mariana be willing to give up the chance to live in close proximity to her daughter's only surviving descendant? Supporting the French match would require a tremendous sacrifice on Mariana's part. Medinaceli reassured Carlos, "The great love the Queen, our lady, has toward Your Majesty and that which she has always shown for this monarchy will always prevail in her judgment." These words, expressed in the monarchy's highest political council by a leading member of the ruling elite, marked the beginning of a turn toward Mariana's political vindication. Aside from what it says about Mariana, Medinaceli's speech can also be seen as a calculated move to win the queen's favor in anticipation of a regime change. Given that he had already been offered the position of prime minister, he may well have viewed the queen as an important figure in the regime that was forming. If so, he was right.[20]

Once the decision to break the king's engagement and negotiate a new one was made, events unfolded quickly. Carlos took an active role in the debates on his marriage within the Council of State, answering his councilors in his own hand. On January 17, he announced his decision to marry Marie Louise but requested that his councilors keep it secret until the emperor was informed. All the letters to Vienna and Toledo were written by the king's own hand, but the Council of State was involved: Carlos submitted his letters to Mariana and Leopold I to his councilors *before* sending them out, and his councilors approved them, praising the young sovereign for his tact.[21]

Carlos worded his letter to Leopold very carefully. He cited the age difference and expressed his regret at rejecting Maria Antonia, given their strong familial ties. He informed his uncle that he had chosen Marie Louise of Orleans for her personal qualities, not out of political considerations. To emphasize that this was a family affair rather than a diplomatic matter, Carlos informed Leopold that he had forgone using the offices of his ambassador. This was only a ploy, as the ambassador received ciphered copies of Carlos's letters and was instructed to feign ignorance. Instead, Carlos would rely fully on his mother—as he told Leopold, he was convinced that "her prudence would prevail over her personal inclinations." His mother's prudence was thus established as an example for Leopold to follow.[22]

Carlos's letter to his mother was a model of tact as well. He told Mariana that he had rejected the idea of marrying Maria Antonia only with great difficulty, but the "unanimous counsels" (*uniformes consejos*) of his ministers left him no choice. He had to choose between reasons of state and personal preference, and the necessity of marrying a bride who could give him and his subjects an heir without delay trumped his ability to follow "his own wishes" as well as "his inclination and affection." Here, Carlos showed he was able to cast his decision in words his mother could understand and approve. He ended by telling her that he was only waiting for her letter to send his to Vienna:

I trust that with your affection, you will express in it to my uncle whatever I may not have gotten right regarding the mortification and tenderness of my decision and how secure he should always feel of my friendship and the unity of our house. All of this, I trust to your great prudence, and I am certain that all the continuous and fervent prayers offered will result in the best resolution of this business and whatever will be best for our house.[23]

We do not have Mariana's responses to either Carlos or Leopold, but later correspondence confirms that Mariana fully endorsed her son's decision.

Her intervention was needed because the emperor did not take the news well. He was unconvinced by the age argument, pointing out that he had waited until he was twenty-six to marry Margarita. Surely Carlos could likewise wait to marry Maria Antonia, who was only ten years old at that moment. But if Leopold was unhappy about the broken engagement, he was more upset with Carlos's choice of a French bride. He urged Carlos to consider the daughters of the Duke of Neuburg and the Duke of Bavaria instead. They were of appropriate age and related to German princes who were important allies—that is, they were not French. Although Leopold expressed his concerns to his nephew in a reasonable tone, his ministers were furious. A wave of anti-Spanish sentiment spread in the imperial court, which caused great concern in Madrid. The Spanish ambassador was harshly reprimanded for his inability to calm the waters in the imperial court—this after he was told to keep quiet about the entire situation. Carlos politely responded that he had already considered the two princesses in question and had rejected one because of her age and the other because of her fragile health. These were excuses. The Bavarian candidate, Marie Anne, married Louis XIV's son at the end of the year, and the second candidate, Marie Sophie, became queen of Portugal.[24]

Carlos sent Mariana copies of the Council of State deliberations and his letters to Leopold to help her craft her letters to Vienna. Leopold also relied on Mariana's mediation, "not doubting" wrote the emperor, "that she will always agree to do what is best for the prosperity of our house." Mariana's letters to Leopold have not survived, but Carlos's letters confirm how successful her efforts were and how grateful he was to her: on April 2, he wrote, "I recognize how much I owe you and the pains to which you too look out for my interests." Two weeks later, Carlos told her, "How grateful I am for your finesse, and I assure you that I will always respond with the trust and attention that is appropriate to it." On May 4, he wrote, "I am very certain that it was mainly due to you the way that my uncle has taken this business and that he finally recognizes how necessary and convenient it is that I marry at once." Fewer than four months had passed since Carlos asked his mother for help, and Mariana had delivered. Carlos had surely done his part in smoothing the situation, but he recognized his mother's role in freeing him to pursue Marie Louise's hand in marriage.[25]

Mariana agreed to support her son's marriage to the French candidate, offering to write to Paris as soon as she knew about Carlos's choice. Initially, Carlos declined her offer, but after he had formally broken his engagement with the archduchess, he asked Mariana to write to the queen of France. The Marquis of Balbases was already on his way to Paris, and Carlos wanted his mother to help ensure the mission's success. Despite his lingering suspicions about Mariana's true feelings, she handled the situation gracefully. Carlos praised her prudence, agreeing with his mother that it was better to "dissimulate any hint of mortification." Even with Mariana's familial ties to the archduchess, it was important that she be seen as supporting her son's marriage.[26]

Mariana's true feelings cannot be known, but she made a wise political decision. While her actions at this crucial moment helped her own cause, she may also have supported the Franco-Spanish match because of her ties to the queen of France, if not the king, Mariana's bête noire. Queen Maria Theresa had strongly supported Mariana during her exile, and the two were cousins who became stepdaughter and mother after Mariana married Maria Theresa's father. Only three years apart in age, they had been inseparable companions for nearly ten years in Madrid. The French ambassador described the ties between them as a "liaison of queen mothers." But just as it seemed that a reconciliation with Carlos, and perhaps even a return to Madrid, was a real possibility, a serious setback occurred.[27]

THE MANCERA INCIDENT

Two years into exile, Mariana's prospects had improved so much that even relations with Don Juan had become more cordial. In November 1678,

Mariana requested financial assistance for the Countess of Trautson, the wife of the new imperial ambassador to Madrid, who wished to return to her German lands after her husband's death. Carlos told Mariana on December 1678 that Don Juan "was prepared to obey you." These improvements emboldened the queen, and only weeks after Carlos II requested her intercession with the emperor about the marriage, she tried to force a reconciliation. The Marquis of Mancera, her *mayordomo mayor*, went to see Carlos at Aranjuez. Mancera arrived with a letter and instructions from the queen to convey to the king her "ardent and affectionate motherly desires to see him and hug him even if for only an hour." This would have been easy to accomplish, as Aranjuez was only about twenty-seven miles from Toledo. Mancera said that the queen had given him permission to discuss her desire to see Carlos with Don Juan if necessary; according to Mancera, Don Juan accepted the letter but refused him access to the king. After waiting for hours, Mancera left without having been able to personally deliver the queen's message to her son.[28]

Mancera felt utterly humiliated by Don Juan's behavior and sent a letter protesting the incident to the king's secretary, Jerónimo de Eguía. It was later copied and distributed widely among members of the elite, becoming one of the earliest manifestos against Don Juan's regime. Copies can be found in various repositories, but its distribution can best be gauged by its mentions in the gazettes. Mancera had a list of grievances dating from when he became Mariana's *mayordomo mayor* in Toledo. He felt "aggrieved and slighted" when a promised appointment to the Council of State went instead to the Marquis of Cerralbo, a member of Don Juan's household. He could not understand how a *caballerizo mayor* in Don Juan's household could be placed above the queen's *mayordomo mayor*, a position with "more antiquity" that was also "higher in the hierarchy of royal household posts." He complained about not being allowed to execute the queen's orders—the time, already mentioned, when the king disciplined him for carrying out Mariana's decree on behalf of Valenzuela's wife, as well as a time when an administrative decision he made was reversed without his knowledge. Such behavior was not simply an insult to him but an insult to the queen herself. Don Juan's measures were "opposed to *natural maternal and filial affection*" and as such "detrimental to these kingdoms and the entire Christian Republic" (emphasis mine). Mancera was not just talking; he resigned his post.[29]

Although the letter/manifesto was written in February, Carlos did not talk to or confront his mother about it. He simply ordered Mancera to return to his estates, which amounted to banishment. Mancera moved to his estates, after which the incident seemed to die. Carlos said later that he ignored it to avoid a scandal. More likely, he did not want to antagonize Mariana at the very moment that the queen was helping him move his marriage forward. Mariana also maintained cordial communications with her son, asking him to pardon Mancera. On May 6, Carlos politely but firmly refused, informing her that he had told Mancera to remain in Ilescas until further notice.[30]

After the May 6 letter, Mariana once again tried to force a face-to-face reunion. This provoked the longest, and perhaps the harshest, letter from Carlos on record and brought the Mancera incident to the surface without a pretense of civility. The tone and style of the letter differ from his others, suggesting that the king was not acting alone. Carlos defended Don Juan by refuting the accusations against him one by one and insisting that Mancera had twisted what had actually happened. He also accused his mother of fomenting political disorder, noting that Mancera had written a paper against the government and distributed it to the court and outside Spain. If Mariana supported her *mayordomo mayor* after his dissemination of a pamphlet so full of "falsehoods and seditious statements," she was effectively trying "to diminish my authority and disturb my government." Carlos was also very upset that she would give credence to the "false and malicious reports that come to your ears." These strong accusations put Mariana in a delicate position: if she defended Mancera, Carlos could take it as a direct challenge to his authority. If she did not, Don Juan won by default. Carlos stopped Mariana in her tracks, significantly setting back her efforts for reconciliation.[31]

From Carlos's letter, it is possible to deduce that Mariana confronted her son and insisted that their reunion was inevitable: she intended "to go to the end of the world" to find him. The king responded, "In any time, case, or circumstance you should never even think of moving from where you are to find me, ~~without my express wish~~" (strikethrough in original). Leaving no doubt where he stood, Carlos told his mother that he would not compromise his royal authority for her sake. God, he said, had placed him in his position, and he would never fail to fulfill the obligations he bore as king. Carlos would consent to see her "only when I judge it convenient."

She should not, however, consider this refusal an indication that his filial love had been diminished.[32]

Whether in collusion with Don Juan or not, Carlos took his side. "If what you insinuate about influences," Carlos wrote to his mother, "you said because of Don Juan, you have no reason to believe it." Don Juan "has no intention other than to serve me." Carlos added, "Had you not doubted that, perhaps things would not be now ~~in the Monarchy~~ as you say they are" (strikethrough in original). He also assured his mother, "I am working diligently and doing everything in my power to improve the current situation." He was punishing Mancera not for obeying her, Carlos told his mother, but for *not* obeying her, since in the end, "you and I should believe [Don Juan] more than Mancera." He made some effort to appease Mariana by approving the grant she had requested for "La Manrique" more than nine months ago. He told Mariana that Mancera would be replaced by the Marquis of Mondejar and said that his orders to fire and banish Mancera "could not be revoked." Mariana had no choice but to accept his decision.[33]

Mariana did not give up easily, although she shifted back to a more conciliatory tone. She tactfully asked her son not to publish the appointment of the new *mayordomo mayor* yet. Carlos agreed. She continued to defend Mancera and evidently sought to obtain his return to court and her service, although she avoided her previous confrontational tone. Continuing to accuse Mancera of seditious acts, Carlos firmly rejected his mother's pleas, and even without a resolution, tensions subsided. On May 15, Carlos stated that he would like to pardon Mancera simply because she was asking him to do so but that he could not, as he had to protect his own authority. On May 19, Carlos curtly refused to discuss the issue further: "Regarding Mancera, I repeat that it is inconvenient for me and for you that he return to your service." Mariana did not bring up the subject again until her return to court had been decided.[34]

In the Mancera incident, Carlos was forced to mediate between Mariana and Don Juan. Carlos took some pains to justify Don Juan's actions to Mariana, and ultimately the conflict gave Mariana and Carlos the opportunity to redefine their roles vis-á-vis the other. Even if Don Juan had been behind the accusations that Mariana and Mancera were fomenting political disorder, the situation allowed Carlos to delineate and circumscribe Mariana's future role. When the final reconciliation occurred, it was on Carlos's terms, not Mariana's.

The Mancera incident also allows us to evaluate the state of Don Juan's regime. Mancera's overt challenge to Don Juan, as disastrous as it was for Mancera and Mariana, had wider resonance. Don Juan had become the king's principal advisor, not as a *valido* who had the ruler's support, but by imposing his presence. Yet he did not act unilaterally and had received decisive support from the grandees of the *Confederación*. Even with this "legitimacy," however, Don Juan faced challenges in consolidating his position: from the first—as the early gazettes and manuscripts circulating in Madrid showed—he was never secure. The initial threats came from the presence of the queen and her supporters at all levels of the court. This explains why throughout his two and a half years of rule, Don Juan dedicated significant effort to counteracting plots and replacing Mariana's patronage networks. Although, as scholars have shown, Don Juan adopted sound domestic policies, he was unable to consolidate his position. Discontent with his regime was out in the open by 1679.[35]

Although a gazetteer described Mancera's language as "insolent and harsh," Mancera was not alone. By 1679, the voices of those Don Juan had exiled and the "malcontents" in Madrid had gotten louder. The Count of Medellín, who had vocally supported Don Juan at the time of the *Confederación*, died in early 1679, reportedly "in opposition and discontent." Medinaceli had been granted the presidency of Italy (an important post), but to receive it, he had to give up the title of general of the Andalusian coasts, which Mariana had granted to his father early in her regency and then conferred on him. "The duke did not understand," the gazette reported, "why it was considered a prize to gain a post in his person and lose one for his house." The announcement of the future queen's royal household in the summer of 1679 increased the discontent. The number of political papers against Don Juan's government—many by Jesuits, who had always supported Mariana—multiplied exponentially. In short, the Mancera incident provoked a tense situation between mother and son but also marked the beginning of the end of Mariana's ordeal.[36]

"MY RESTITUTION IN ALL AND WITH ALL"

Opposition to Don Juan quickly became support for the queen's return. The Marquis of Villars, the French ambassador to Madrid (who arrived in late

June 1679), noted in his memoirs that a mistrustful Don Juan was becoming increasingly isolated, while the party of the queen swelled. This is confirmed by other manuscript accounts and gazettes describing the climate of the court. Carlos, however, was not going to be pushed around the way he had been the day of his fourteenth birthday. He confronted his mother by saying, "The voices against my government are said to be coming from your palace [in Toledo]"; he then urged her to discourage open criticisms and gossip and threatened severe punishment to those engaged in "seditious" acts. This was the last confrontation recorded in Mariana and Carlos's personal correspondence. Thereafter, Mariana took a very different approach, understanding that to win a permanent place in her son's life and regime, she would have to demonstrate her willingness to abide by his wishes.[37]

Indeed, her compliance and self-effacement reveal her political skills more than her natural inclinations. While the malcontents increased, a gazette reported that the queen looked at the "shipwreck of the court, from the balcony of tranquility." She refused to foment activities that "could divide and disturb the king's service, something that was also observed in the constancy and loyalty of the exiled ones." Another gazetteer compared her attitude to the true mother who was revealed when Solomon threatened the life of her child. Mariana's restraint was the act of abnegation that preserved Carlos's authority, but it was genius too, because it led others to call for her return. And they did, rallying behind Mariana as they previously had behind Don Juan. Once again, the ruling elite were the ultimate arbiters of court politics, even though the king was now older and confident enough to put himself at the head of his ministers and grandees. The situation was unclear. Carlos had not set a date to see his mother; his marriage was still being negotiated with the French court; and Don Juan, despite his growing problems, still controlled the government.[38]

The confirmation and subsequent announcement of the king's marriage on July 13, 1679, opened the floodgates of reconciliation. Carlos wrote to his mother immediately: "I did not want to delay giving you such good news because I know the great affection that you have for me." The next day, Mariana sent him several letters discussing the jewel being made for Marie Louise and a new portrait of the king; Carlos had asked Mariana to approve them before they were sent to Paris and requested that Mariana handle the official correspondence with the French royals as protocol required. Just days later, the king mentioned that Balbases was bringing her a copy of a letter he had received from the queen of France. One should not regard these demonstrations of respect toward the queen mother as trivial or merely window dressing. On the contrary, they highlight Mariana's centrality in an event of critical importance to the future of the monarchy and foreshadow her reinstatement.[39]

Having been drawn into the center of this major dynastic event, which coincided with the renewal of diplomatic relations between the two monarchies, Mariana, even in exile, easily upstaged Don Juan. Don Juan's illegitimate birth presented obstacles for his full participation in the elaborate events surrounding the king's marriage. Don Juan expected the French ambassador to Madrid, the Marquis of Villars, to award him the same privileges the papal nuncio enjoyed—the same privileges Don Juan had been accorded in the Spanish protocol. Louis XIV instructed Villars to reject the request and threatened to change the protocol for the Spanish ambassadors at the French court if Spain protested. Wanting to preserve the Spanish diplomatic corps's privileges with the French, Carlos asked the Council of State for etiquette guidelines for Don Juan to follow. The council recommended that Don Juan refrain from contact with the French royal family until Balbases confirmed that Spanish privileges would not be jeopardized. Don Juan could write to his half-sister, Queen Maria Theresa, privately but not as part of the official correspondence. The limitations on Don Juan undermined his position, and the once powerful chief minister appeared ever more dispensable. For the first time, French diplomacy worked to Mariana's advantage.[40]

Queen Maria Theresa surely helped Mariana by referring to her as "my mother," which Mariana became when she married Philip IV, even though she was only a few years older than Maria Theresa. Forms of address among rulers of different monarchies were carefully gauged, strictly observed, and modified, if necessary, to reflect shifting political and dynastic connections. Marie Louise of Orleans, for example, once Maria Theresa's niece, became her "sister" upon her marriage to Carlos. These blood and marital ties greatly enhanced Mariana's authority. Philippe I, Duke of Orleans, the father of the bride and the younger brother of Louis XIV, assured Mariana that he had instructed his daughter to "show Your Majesty the respect and affection that she should give to a Mother and to a Queen like you, in whom such great circumstances come together." The circumstances he was alluding to were Mariana's birth and marriage, which had made her the daughter, sister, and mother of several ruling monarchs and their consorts, as well as governor of the monarchy on behalf of Carlos. Louis XIV instructed his ambassador to visit the queen mother in Toledo as soon as he arrived in Spain, even if the visit risked being perceived as political interference, and Villars's very public presence in Toledo was a strong statement that provoked considerable comment at the Spanish court.[41]

By August, the court and the monarchy again found themselves at a crossroad. Support for Don Juan was waning rapidly, while the queen mother's prestige grew. The "exiled ones" (*desterrados*)—important men who had swelled the ranks of Don Juan's enemies—asked the king to pardon them, with the king's confessor, Fray Francisco Reluz, acting as intermediary. The confessor also played a key role in the final reconciliation between the king and his mother, paving the way for a reunion after more than two years. By now, the topic of when the king would reunite with his mother was being discussed in the open. A gazetteer reported that Father Reluz advised the king that he could not continue "without great regret to be separated from direct communication with his mother, to whom he owed *filial reverence*" (emphasis mine). Once again, Carlos's filial obligation to his mother took center stage in the political discourse, although very differently than it had when Mariana faced the nobles' *Confederación*. A gazette reported that Don Juan was utterly offended by the confessor's advice to Carlos; the anonymous author was convinced that Reluz would soon be thrown in jail.[42]

In fact, Mariana's return was being carefully negotiated behind closed doors, as the reconciliation between mother and son was a deeply symbolic political event that required elaborate preparations. There was no doubt that Mariana had exercised too much control over the king, and during the weeks preceding her return, specific precautions were taken to set the boundaries of her political role upon her return.

THE QUEEN ACCEPTS CARLOS'S "PRUDENT SAFEGUARDS"

Mariana and Carlos II's reconciliation was far more than a family matter. It was a crucial political event and an implicit overturning of the

Confederación. Carlos clearly understood the stakes, insisting that Mariana accept a number of "prudent safeguards" before she could be reinstated. He asked his confessor whether he would violate his obligations as king if he reunited with his mother. "Government considerations had kept them apart," he wrote, but the queen's repeated and fervent requests had willed him into granting her the "consolation" of his presence. "My own consolation would not be small," Carlos added. Reluz assured the king that a reunion with his mother was not just acceptable but highly desirable. Carlos then sought the help of the archbishop of Toledo. The successor to Cardinal Aragón, who died in 1677, was Cardinal Luis Fernández Portocarrero, who went on to play a major role in the king's reign. He became the mediator between mother and son and negotiated the "prudent safeguards" for Mariana's return. That two such highly placed and influential religious figures were involved in the final stages of the reconciliation process emphasizes the event's significance.[43]

In his instructions to the cardinal, Carlos did not articulate what the "safeguards" were—they were to be discussed orally—but he did not mince words when he explained their purpose. Carlos wanted to be reunited with his mother "to comply with my obligations as son, *without abandoning those of my conscience and dignity [as king]*, the limits of which I cannot exceed, nor could I ever imagine that Her Majesty would propose or condone such a thing" (emphasis mine). Don Juan's growing unpopularity was not by itself sufficient to secure Mariana's restitution. Before bringing his mother back to court, Carlos had to be reassured that she would not intervene in government matters as if she was still the governor of the monarchy. Carlos also requested secrecy from his mother, "since it is important not to publish the reunion before it is appropriate [to do so]." This additional safeguard was put in place to avoid a disorderly and scandalous change of regime. Portocarrero met with the queen sometime between August 13 and 15 and reported to Carlos that Mariana did not object to Carlos's conditions—we can presume the conditions of her return and the request for discretion while these negotiations were under way. "Her Majesty expressed her delight . . . at the prospect of seeing Your Majesty," Portocarrero wrote. "This was clearly her principal desire." Once she accepted the terms, only two questions remained: when she would return to the court and how the king would deal with Don Juan.[44]

More than a month elapsed as arrangements were made. Mother and son continued to communicate frequently, but not many letters survive from August 13, when Carlos first proposed the reunion, to September 21, their actual encounter. On August 17, Carlos sent a brief note thanking Mariana for agreeing to the "prudent safeguards." He also informed her that the Duchess of Terranova, the *camarera mayor* of the new queen's household, would stop in Toledo, another sign that the French marriage had helped connect mother and son.[45]

Just as the king's separation from his mother in the early weeks of 1677 had to be carefully planned, so too did his separation from his half brother. Don Juan fell ill on August 24 but seemed likely to recover. Still, it meant a delay, as the king may not have wanted to dismiss Don Juan while he was bedridden. During the first weeks of September, however, Carlos pardoned Mancera and the "exiled ones." Mariana thanked him in her missive of September 13, telling him that she had not written to Don Juan, as she knew he was "indisposed" and did not want "to disturb him" (*embarazarle*). She said she would write when he was better, adding, "I am satisfied and appreciate his part in pardoning Mancera." The fiction of cooperation, which resembled the way Mariana had been forced to cooperate in her own exile, continued. Even on his sickbed, Don Juan must have known that his tenure was about to end.

Mariana continued to pressure Carlos. That same day, she wrote a second letter, using the assuaging language of motherly love, which had by now completely replaced the voice of maternal authority. "My son, I expect from you and because of your affection that you will make sure that I will be able to see you as soon as possible," she told him. He should not forget that she expected "the consolation [of his presence], which has been taken from me for so long." Her longing was no longer threatening: "I know you will try to console me in all that I desire; my maternal love and affection have always been present in all occasions, and I trust in God you will recognize this more and more every day, not doubting that you will believe it so." The shift in tone perhaps also indicates her awareness that the end of her ordeal was near.[46]

Don Juan died four days after this letter was written, on September 17. Carlos informed his mother the following day in a very succinct note, reproduced here in its entirety: "My Lady and Mother, I could not write to you yesterday due to the death of Don Juan. God took him at 12. I am only writing this note [now] and later will respond to your letters." The timing of his death was certainly suspicious. I have not found rumors of foul play, although Maura identified one Italian author's report of poisoning. The nature of Don Juan's illness was not clear when he died; it was not uncommon to conduct a postmortem diagnosis, and this attributed the cause of death to bladder and liver problems.[47]

Mariana interpreted Don Juan's death as divine intervention. In writing Carlos after she heard, she repeated how much her exile had wounded her but also voiced her expectations of better things to come:

> Son of my life. I did not want to delay responding to your letter that you sent me, which I received a little while ago with the post and where you tell me about Don Juan's death. God may keep him in heaven; nothing better could be wished for him. Tell me if you are planning any public demonstrations for his death so that I can do the same, since I don't want to err on anything. I am in good health, thank the Lord, and the weather has been cooler lately[.] My son, with the affection that I have for you as mother, I feel the urge to tell you that since God has allowed the death of Don Juan and you can begin to understand everything for yourself, I completely trust that you will recognize the extent to which [his] bad counsels and intentions made me suffer so intensely after I was separated from you[.] I have great confidence that you will allow *my restitution in all and with all*. I put myself in your hands so that you can dispose of my return according to your greatest pleasure and service, which will be mine always, as you would admit, has always been, now that you have complete understanding and knowledge of everything. God will assist you with clarity to get everything right. Your mother who loves you most.[48] (emphasis mine)

The letter underscores Mariana's willingness to completely defer to her son and her awareness that her return depended not on Don Juan's elimination but on her son's wishes. Only from the king, her son, could she expect "restitution in all and with all."[49]

Mariana did not have much longer to wait. Carlos, who had not visited Don Juan in the weeks he was ill, ordered the body moved to the palace of El Escorial—it had a separate site designated for junior members of the dynasty, including illegitimate children—without seeing it. A gazette reported that as Don Juan's funeral cortege left Madrid, Carlos left too, but to Toledo, accompanied by the "exiled ones." The king's intentions were an open secret at court, with the Duchess of Bejar, for example, congratulating Mariana on her imminent reunion three days before it took place. On September 20, Carlos wrote to his mother, "I will arrive in that city tomorrow at 11, God willing." Knowing the queen's eagerness, he added, "You do not have to leave your house, only wait for me there." He assured her, "[The] joy of seeing each other so soon would be no less for me than for you."[50]

Mariana described her happiness at the prospect of seeing her son as strong enough to erase the painful events of the last years: "I do not know how to begin this letter of joy with the prospect of having the consolation of seeing you so soon. . . . I don't remember anything of what had occurred [then], and I only have the great consolation that I will see you so soon." An additional source of comfort was the fact that Carlos did not prohibit her from making the news public. This time it was finally going to happen.[51]

KING AND GOOD SON AT LAST

On September 21, Mariana got what she had fought so long and hard to obtain. As promised, Carlos came to Toledo and spent many hours with her, returning to Aranjuez in the evening. As soon as he left, Mariana went to her desk to write him: "I never had a better day in my life," she said, and her feelings of gratitude were equally overwhelming. "I do not know how I will pay you in my entire life so many attentions as I owe you, and you can be sure that I will ever be grateful to you. I have no doubt that God will reward you for this very beautiful action that you have taken." Yet even as she expressed her joy and gratitude to her son, she was also thinking about her political restitution, telling Carlos, "Let me know when and how you would like to arrange for my return." He should make all the decisions, because "I only want to do everything to your liking." It had taken two and a half years of exile for Mariana to accept a new place at court and in her son's life. Her willingness to modify her behaviors allowed her to carve a political role different from that which she had had as queen consort and queen governor and tutor.[52]

Mariana left Toledo on September 27. Retracing her difficult and painful journey into exile, she spent the night at Aranjuez, continuing on to Madrid the following day. She entered the city to acclaim from both those who had been her supporters and those who had stood with Don Juan. A gazetteer reported, "The queen made her entry received by the hearts of everyone with such acclamations and general applause that it is hard to comprehend or explain." The Venetian ambassador described Mariana's return to court as "a triumph and a very rare lesson in Divine Justice."[53]

The mending of Carlos and Mariana's relationship had profound political implications; indeed, it was ultimately no less important in the history of Spain and European diplomacy than her formal regency had been. To a large extent, Carlos defined his identity as an adult male by having asserted political and personal independence from his mother, and this new persona in turn transformed the practice and perception of kingship. Mariana's restitution thus marked the end of the process that began the day of Carlos's fourteenth birthday. When Carlos saw his mother again in September 1679, he was very close to his eighteenth birthday, about to get married, and well aware that his obligations as king superseded those of a son (fig. 9).

Mariana's return was also a validation that "filial reverence" to mothers was expected of sons, even kings. The necessity of Carlos respecting this value was embedded in the language used by his confessor, the gazettes, and Habsburg correspondence. "Filial reverence" was a through line in the political discourse facilitating Mariana's triumphal return to court, just as it had been in the months leading to her exile. When Queen Maria Theresa wrote to congratulate her younger brother, she did not miss the opportunity to underscore this concept. Although the occasion of her letter was his marriage, she congratulated Carlos on his decision to "restore the Queen, My Lady and My Mother to his presence." She expressed her joy because of the "love I have for my mother," going on to assure him, "[Mariana] is extremely happy [contentíssima]." "But this does not really surprise me," she added, "especially seeing what a good son Your Majesty has shown yourself to be on this occasion." With those last few words, Maria Theresa subtly chastised Carlos for the occasions on which he had not been a good son. As Mancera had eloquently written in his controversial paper, Habsburg motherhood

FIGURE 9 Juan Carreño de Miranda, *Carlos II in Armor*, 1681. Oil on canvas. Museo del Prado, Madrid, inv. P007101. Photo © Museo Nacional del Prado / Art Resource, New York.

was the pillar of everything right in "the entire Christian republic." At that time, Carlos and Don Juan had violated the principle. Now, finally, Carlos—like other Habsburg males—had achieved the maturity necessary to fulfill his obligations as a son without compromising his obligations as king.[54]

Conclusion

Mariana's Historical Legacy

In the months following Mariana's return, the court underwent a transformation. Marie Louise, now Queen María Luisa, arrived in late November 1679, taking the space in the Madrid Alcázar that Mariana had occupied for twenty-seven years—sixteen as queen consort and eleven as regent. Carlos officially named the Duke of Medinaceli prime minister in February 1680, fulfilling the promise made during Mariana's exile. Flanked by his beautiful French bride and a political advisor he had chosen, Carlos was now firmly at the court's center. The court had two queens—a reigning queen, or *reina reinante*, and a queen mother, or *reina madre* (as they were referred to in order to avoid confusion)—with a clear hierarchy between them. Mariana started a new—and last—stage of her long political trajectory. Figure 10 depicts Mariana as she looked for the last sixteen years of her life, still wearing widow's weeds but no longer shown with the accouterments of reign—the desk, papers, and inkwell.[1]

Mariana ceded the center but did not retreat to the background completely; instead she found the right space—literally and symbolically—in her son's court. Breaking with tradition, she did not make the Convent of the Descalzas Reales her permanent residence, as Habsburg widows had always done. Instead, Mariana moved into a private palace three hundred meters from the royal palace and connected to it via a passageway. It was the most important nonroyal structure in the city and had been built and occupied by former *validos*, including the Duke of Uceda, who built it in

FIGURE 10 Juan Carreño de Miranda, *Queen Mariana of Austria*, ca. 1677–79. Oil on canvas. Graf Harrach'sche Familiensammlung, Schloss Rohrau, Austria. Photo: Graf Harrach'sche Familiensammlung.

1619, and Don Luis de Haro, who lived there from 1644 to 1661. Carlos designated the palace as Mariana's residence at the last minute, and a small army of workers—about 130—began repairs at breakneck speed in late September 1679, within days of Mariana's arrival. She moved in with a full royal household of several hundred attendants on November 26 and stayed until her death. From the palace, she was drawn back into the very center of European politics.[2]

The fact that neither of Carlos's two wives—when María Luisa died in 1689, he married Mariana of Neuburg—had had children kept Mariana active and influential in dynastic politics. Securing the succession of the Habsburgs in Spain had been Mariana's driving force, and it remained so to the end. Maria Antonia, the king's ex-fiancée, was his heiress, and her 1685 marriage to Elector Maximilian II Emanuel of Bavaria gave the Bavarians a privileged place in the succession over, in Mariana's view, the Austrian Habsburgs. Mariana's dynastic loyalty was to Margarita's descendants—that is, Maria Antonia and her Bavarian family—which put her at odds with her brother, who wanted his son rather than his daughter to succeed to the Crown. When Maria Antonia died in 1692 shortly after giving birth to a son, Joseph Ferdinand of Bavaria, that son became Mariana's preferred candidate. That preference had a tremendous impact on the politics of the court, as it became increasingly clear that Carlos's direct line would die out. Mariana's palace became a hub of activity, a center where diplomats from the Holy Roman Empire, France, Savoy, and Bavaria engaged in a brutal diplomatic battle over the future of the Spanish Crown.[3]

As the ruling monarch of Spain, Carlos II had the right to name his successor in his testament. His choices were descendants of his female relatives—his older sisters, Maria Theresa of Austria and Margarita of Austria, or of his female ancestors, Maria of Austria and Catalina Micaela of Austria. The relatives he chose could be deceased, as Spanish law allowed their rights to be passed on to their descendants. The women's marriages into powerful states—France, the Holy Roman Empire, the Electorate of Bavaria, and the Duchy of Savoy—threatened the continent with a pan-European war. Aside from the complex familial ties that made the selection a very complicated legal and dynastic matter, there were major geopolitical consequences. Mariana's intervention in the politics of her dynasty once again had international reach: the final decision had the potential to alter the political boundaries of the continent and bring major shifts in overseas colonies and trading routes. Her support for the Bavarian elector was essential in Carlos II's decision to name Mariana's great-grandson, Joseph Ferdinand of Bavaria, as his heir in both his first and second testaments. Although the Bavarian prince died before he could succeed, during Mariana's lifetime, his position was unassailable. When Mariana succumbed on May 16, 1696, to breast cancer, Maximilian II, Maria Antonia's widower and the boy's father, lamented the queen's death "as a great loss for our [the Bavarian] cause."[4]

Eulogies praising the queen dowager came from all over the Spanish Empire, and reports of miracles attributed to her quickly began to circulate. These miracles and her body's reported "incorruptibility" three years after her death led to a beatification proceeding in the last years of Carlos's reign. Mariana's path to sainthood, however, came to an abrupt end when the new dynasty, the Bourbons, took power. Both the beatification proceedings in 1698 and its abandonment in 1702 were as politically motivated as everything else in her life had been.[5]

Mariana's legacy was soon forgotten, in part because the Bourbons rewrote the history of Carlos II's reign to enhance their position. Indeed, some of the most persistent misunderstandings about the king, reinforced by the historiography of the Enlightenment, can be traced to the Bourbons. But the greatest damage to his historical reputation came in the nineteenth century, when the narrative of an incompetent, fragile, and sickly ruler was fully developed. Mariana's story was so entangled with her son's reign that these ideas also shaped discussions of her regency. And when reinforced by nineteenth-century notions about women's lack of political interest or skill, they reduced her political significance to virtually nothing.[6]

Thankfully, much has changed. Carlos II's reign has been shown to have been a period of fiscal, demographic, and economic renewal, and though improvement was not consistent across all territories, this recuperative view has replaced the paradigm of decline. And since it has become clear that the seeds of the Bourbon eighteenth-century reforms were planted during the reign of the last Habsburg, these findings cast new light on Bourbon history as well. But the revisionist histories have focused almost exclusively on the last decades of Carlos's reign, 1680–1700. In some ways, this is understandable, for it marked the beginning of his reign as an adult, it was more stable, and it had the greatest financial, demographic, and fiscal improvements. But it leaves out Mariana's legacy.[7]

In fact, Mariana's regency and exile were critical periods in the history of Spain and of Carlos II's kingship. When Mariana took power, the monarchy, facing the imminent loss of Portugal and severe financial difficulties, was in disarray. Under her leadership, Spain's military capacity grew substantially. By 1668, the army of Flanders—with which Mariana faced France—grew from 10 to more than 60,000 men. Christopher Storrs calculates that Carlos II's armies in 1674 and 1675 totaled approximately 100,000 men. Though the numbers were smaller than they had been at the peak of Philip IV's reign—about 170,000 in 1635—the headcount must be seen in the context of diplomatic gains that substantially increased Spain's military capacity. France, which had Europe's largest armies and posed the greatest threat to Spain, had in place a number of diplomatic alliances that greatly exacerbated Spain's difficulties when Mariana came to power in 1665. By 1673, the two monarchies reversed roles. The first offensive military coalition against France, the Quadruple Alliance of 1673, was also part of a cluster of defensive leagues Mariana negotiated with Emperor Leopold I, German princes, and Scandinavian powers. Mariana built a web of coalitions around France resembling, and perhaps even surpassing, those France had woven around the Habsburgs.[8]

The loss of Portugal notwithstanding, under Mariana, Spain was the largest conglomerate on the continent, with overseas possessions that dwarfed other powers with imperial aspirations. Her legacy, however, was a matter of not simply preserving the empire but forging a new path. This can be seen in the way she put Anglo-Spanish relations on the collaborative course that was crucial to her creation of the first Triple Alliance (1668), her extrication of the monarchy from the dangerous juncture of 1665–68, and her ability to build an extraordinary legacy of diplomatic accomplishments. This new Anglo-Spanish collaboration had other consequences: it opened Spanish markets in Europe for English merchants and achieved the recognition of Britain's possessions in the New World. Although these issues deserve further investigation, they should not be dismissed as losses for Spain. At the very least, this new stage of collaboration brought Spain stability and gained critical alliances. Under Mariana, Spain's collaboration with the Dutch was also critically significant, as it helped her build that first offensive coalition against France. Spain's dual collaboration with the restoration government of Charles II and the Dutch and its effect on Spain's overseas possessions should be reconsidered—and no longer studied in terms of rivalry—because it is fair to say that the Treaty of Madrid (1670) and the Peace of Westminster between England and the Dutch (1674) put the long, tangled history of the three empires on a new course. These shifts—largely the result of Mariana's unrelenting efforts—had a long-lasting, if not yet fully understood, impact.

Another part of Mariana's legacy is the men she promoted. The many effective ministers and diplomats she appointed speak not only of her ability to identify talent and inspire loyalty but to the decline paradigm's inadequacy, as her appointments do not represent the intellectual stagnation and inability to adapt that are considered evidence of declining empires. It is unfortunate that historians' neglect of this period has kept the men who were instrumental in the regency—and beyond—in obscurity. The Marquis of Aytona, the Count of Peñaranda, the Marquis of Castel Rodrigo, and the Marquis de la Fuente—not to mention diplomats like Esteban Gamarra, the Count of Molina, the Marquis of Fresno, or the Marquis of Balbases—have remained marginal because of too narrow a focus on court politics. Relatedly, this focus, which gave too much or the wrong kind of importance to Nithard, Valenzuela, and Don Juan, served to diminish Mariana's agency. The roles of all these men are ripe for reconsideration, starting from the recognition that the most important figure in each of their trajectories was the queen.

Mariana's role in changing the course of Spanish history is more evident in the early years, when the permanent loss of the Spanish Netherlands was imminent. She had the foresight to see that keeping Portugal at all costs—a move supported by the majority of her councilors, including her confessor—was wrong and that giving it its independence was the only way to resolve the monarchy's predicament and recuperate its footing. The rest of her governorship—aside from the temporary setback of the coup of 1668–69—built on this initial, herculean effort. The War of Devolution was short, but the terms of its settlement reverberated to the end of the century. Mariana denied Louis XIV his dream of claiming the Spanish Netherlands and created the conditions for Carlos II's continued control. Further, the upholding of the principle that Maria Theresa's renunciation was legal was a decisive victory for both Spain and Mariana.

Mariana's story resonates today not as an exception but as part of a growing body of scholarship that has studied queens in order to chart a new understanding of the political history of monarchies and European diplomacy and warfare. These women's long absence from history reveals more about the eras their histories were written in than it does about those in which they lived; recall, for instance, that Mariana belonged to a dynasty (the Habsburgs) and ruled in a monarchy (Spain) that respected, valued, and empowered women. When we put these women in their rightful place at the center of history, we can better see not just them but the rich complexity of the kingdoms and eras in which they lived.

NOTES

Introduction

1. Eulogy BNE VE 119–16. For miracles, see Baviera and Maura, *Documentos inéditos*, 550–51; and Gómez Vozmediano, "En olor a santidad," 567–73. Colonization of the Mariana Islands began in 1668 and concluded in 1695; see Ibañez, *Islas Marianas*, 30–31.

2. For Spain's political configuration, see Elliott, *Revolt*, 2–11; and Elliott, "Composite Monarchies," 53–54, 64–65.

3. For the cost of war in the sixteenth century, see Tracy, *Charles V*, 5–15, and part 2, 109–228; and Parker, *Grand Strategy*, 41, 82, 133, 136, 155, and 165.

4. For the 1640 crisis and ministry of Olivares, see Elliott, *Revolt*, 420–522; and Elliott, *Olivares*, 553–622.

5. Hume, *Queens*, ix, 361, 401; Kamen, *Spain*, 329; Tomás y Valiente, *Validos*, 19; Domínguez Ortíz, "Introducción," xxxiii; and Lynch, *Spain*, 258.

6. Maura, *Carlos II*, 1:210, 237. For a lucid discussion of Maura's influence on the historiography of Mariana, see Oliván Santaliestra, *Mariana*, 85–89.

7. The literature on the Spanish decline is enormous. Worth mentioning are the series of articles in the scholarly journal *Past and Present*: Elliott, "Self-Perception," followed by his studies on Olivares and the Revolt of Catalan; Kamen (1978), "The Decline," and Israel's response (1981); and Hillgarth, "Spanish Historiography." For a lucid overview of the role of Spanish decline in U.S. historiography, see Kagan, "Prescott's Paradigm." For the context from the Spanish point of view, see Elliott, *History*, particularly chapter 4, pp. 114–35. For the historical evolution of the historiography of decline, see Rawlings, *Debate*.

8. On negative views of Carlos II, see Contreras, *Carlos II*; Langdon-Davies, *The King*; Pfandl, *Karl II*; and Lynch, *Spain*, 258. On revisionist histories of the reign, see Kamen, *Spain*;

Sanz Ayán, *Banqueros*; Ribot García, "Centenario," and *Orígenes*, 17–23. On the economy, see Yun Casalilla, "De centro a la periferia"; and on military and imperial considerations, see Storrs, *Resilience*. Scholars are slowly crafting a very different picture of Carlos II. On his childhood, see Mitchell, "Growing Up," 189–206. On the king's education, musicianship, and frequent hunting expeditions, see Ribot García, "El rey," 12–52. On Carlos II's art patronage, see Bassegoda, "El Escorial," 35–47. On the reforms, see Peña Izquierdo, *Austrias a Borbones*. On fiscal reforms, see Sánchez Belén, *Política fiscal*. On science, see Aranda, "Spanish Science," particularly chapter 2, pp. 45–86.

9. Campbell, "Women," 109–24; López Cordón, "Mujer," 49–66; López Cordón, "Las mujeres," 108–39; Goodman, "Conspicuous," 163–84; Oliván Santaliestra, "Mariana de Austria," and "Pinceladas políticas," 113–32; and Llorente, "Imagen," 211–38, and "Mariana of Austria's Portraits," 197–222.

10. On the reforms, see Peña Izquierdo, *Austrias a Borbones*. On fiscal reforms, see Sánchez Belén, *Política fiscal*; and on science, see Aranda, "Spanish Science," particularly chapter 2, pp. 45–86. On the most recent synthesis of the revisionist work, see the edited volume by Saavedra Vázquez, *La decadencia*.

11. Coolidge, *Guardianship*; Hoffman, *Raised to Rule*. On queens, see Earenfight, "Partners in Politics," xiii–xxviii; Earenfight, "Absent Kings," 33–51; Earenfight, *Other Body*; Earenfight, *Queenship*; and Liss, *Isabel*. On aristocratic women, see Nader, *Mendoza Family*. On peasants, see Poska, *Women and Authority*. On merchant classes, see Cook, "Women." On widows, see Fink De Backer, *Widowhood*; and on medieval traditions, see Dillard, *Daughters*.

12. Barrio Gozalo, *Roma*; Yetano Laguna, "Relaciones entre España y Francia"; and Fernández Nadal, *La embajada de Londres*.

13. On favoritism as a European-wide phenomenon in the seventeenth century, see Elliott and Brockliss, *World of the Favourite*; and Feros, "Images of Evil." For the Spanish case, see Elliott, *Olivares*; Feros, *Kingship*; Tomás y Valiente, *Validos*; and Escudero, *Validos*.

14. See Elliott, *Olivares*; Feros, *Kingship*; Thompson, "Institutional Background"; Boyden, *Courtier and the King*; Tomás y Valiente, *Validos*; and Escudero, *Validos*.

15. Storrs, "Army of Lombardy," 371–97.

16. On the usefulness of queens in understanding larger historical issues, see Patrouch, "Dynastic, Imperial, International," 217–19; Calvi, "Introduction," 1–15; Calvi, "Women Rulers"; Akkerman and Houben, *Politics of Female Households*; and Earenfight, *Other Body*. On proprietary queens, see Levin, *Heart*; Liss, *Isabel*; and Weissberger, *Queen Isabel*. On queen consorts, see Orr, *Queenship*; and Earenfight, "Partners in Politics," xiii–xxviii.

17. Crawford, *Perilous Performances*, 3, 19–21; and Cosandey, "Puissance maternelle," pars. 2–4.

18. Charles V inherited four different dynastic lines, largely from his female relatives, including his mother, Queen Juana of Castile and Aragon, and his two grandmothers, Isabel of Castile and Mary of Burgundy. Regents—or governors, as they were called in Spain—included Charles V's consort, Empress Isabel of Avis, and his two daughters, Empress Maria of Austria and Princess Juana of Austria. Women ruled the Netherlands as governor regents uninterruptedly from 1507 to 1567. Isabel Clara Eugenia, Philip II's oldest daughter, became the sovereign ruler from 1598 to 1621 and then regent from 1621 to 1633. On Habsburg matrimonial strategy, see Patrouch, "Bella gerant alii"; and Fichtner, "Dynastic Marriage." On Iberian traditions, see Earenfight, "Partners in Politics," xiii–xxviii; and Dillard, *Daughters*, 1–12.

19. My thinking in this paragraph has been shaped by Bertelli, *King's Body*, chapter 3, particularly p. 61; and Earenfight, *Other Body*, 1–18.

20. On the rituals upon the king's majority, see Cosandey, "Puissance maternelle," 10; and Crawford, *Perilous Performances*, 54 (for Charles IX). On Spanish curatorship, see Coolidge, *Guardianship*, 22. On Mariana's

curatorship, see Llorente, "Mariana of Austria's Portraits," 216.

21. BNE ms. 9399, fol. 85r.

Chapter 1

1. Marriage capitulations of Maria and Ferdinand, AGS PTR leg. 57, doc. 153; and Hengerer, *Ferdinand III*, 125.

2. On Habsburg matrimonial strategy, see Patrouch, "Bella gerant alii," 25–36; Fichtner, "Dynastic Marriage," 246–47; and Palos and Sánchez, *Early Modern Dynastic Marriages*, 1–18.

3. On Habsburg children wearing amulets while nursing, see Cortés Echánove, *Nacimiento*, 33–35. On lifestyle at the court of Vienna, see Hengerer, *Ferdinand III*, 138, 545; Höbelt, *Ferdinand III*, 103; and Keller, *Hofdamen*. On the education of Habsburg children, see Hoffman, *Raised to Rule* (on the Spanish court), 25–79; Patrouch, *Queen's Apprentice*; and Weiss, *Kindheit* (on the imperial court). For an iconographical analysis of this portrait, see Oliván Santaliestra, "Mariana de Austria," 38–40.

4. On Maria's political influence, see Tercero Casado, "Spanish Party," 39–53. On the emperor's regard for his wife and the influence of Empress Eleonora, see Hengerer, *Ferdinand III*, 128, 130–31, 138. On the influence and power the empresses exercised through their households, see Keller, *Hofdamen*; and Ingrao and Thomas, "Empress-Consort."

5. On the women in the imperial court of Vienna, see Keller, *Hofdamen*, particularly 52, 67–68; and Keller, "Ladies-in-Waiting," 77–99. On Empress Maria of Austria (1527–1603), see Marek, "Las damas." On the dissemination of Spanish-Burgundian traditions, see Oliván Santaliestra, "Modelo borgoñón." On the godmothering of an eleven-year-old child, see Mariana's letter to Ferdinand III, December 18, 1646, Riksarkiv, Extranea 195 XVI Tyskland. Arkivfragment Kejsar Ferdinand III, 1641–47. I thank Renate Schreiber for providing me with the letters Mariana wrote as a child to her father between 1641 and 1647; Hoffman, *Raised to Rule*, 217.

6. Hengerer, *Ferdinand III*, 138, 545; Höbelt, *Ferdinand III*, 103; and Weiss, *Kindheit*, 102–3, 108.

7. On Trautson, see Keller, *Hofdamen*, 67–68. On Leopold's upbringing, see Spielman, *Leopold I*, 33–34; and Weiss, *Kindheit*, 10. On Mariana's language skills deducted from her childhood letters, see Riksarkiv, Extranea 195 XVI Tyskland. Arkivfragment Kejsar Ferdinand III, 1641–47. Her letters in Spanish will be discussed in chapter 7; AHN E. leg. 2729. On Nithard, see Lozano Navarro, *La compañía*, 298–99; and BNE ms. 8344.

8. Coreth, *Pietas Austriaca*, 52; Mariana to Ferdinand III, October 8, 1647, Riksarkiv, Extranea 195 XVI Tyskland. Arkivfragment Kejsar Ferdinand III, 1641–47; Patrouch, *Queen's Apprentice*, 348; and Hengerer, *Ferdinand III*, 130–31.

9. Ferdinand I created the Styrian cadet line for his third son, Archduke Karl. For a concise overview of these events, see Parker, *Thirty Years War*, 1–61; Sánchez, "A House Divided," 887–89; and Helfferich, *Thirty Years War*, ix–x.

10. Allen, *Pax Hispanica*, vii–xi; Elliott, *Olivares*, 65–75; Parker, *Thirty Years War*, 38–45; and Helfferich, *Thirty Years War*, 1–14.

11. On Maria's engagement to the Prince of Wales and eventual marriage to Ferdinand III, see Elliott, *Olivares*, 218; Hengerer, *Ferdinand III*, 130; Hoffman, *Raised to Rule*, 127–37; and Redworth, *Prince and the Infanta*. On the political and diplomatic background to 1634, see Tercero Casado, "Spanish Party," 54–67. On shifts after 1635, see Helfferich, *Iron Princess*, 4; and Richelieu cited in Sonnino, *Mazarin's Quest*, 16.

12. On the "Union of Arms" and constitutional problems in Catalonia, see Elliott, *Revolt*, particularly xi, 202, 536–40; for Olivares's policies and declaration of war, see Elliott, *Olivares*, 486.

13. On the beginning of the revolt and expenditures of war, see Elliott, *Revolt*, 469–73, 517; on Portugal's rebellion, see Valladares, *Rebelión de Portugal*; on Medina Sidonia's attempt, see Salas Almela, *Conspiracy*. On Westphalian negotiations at this juncture, see Helfferich, *Iron Princess*, 161. On Maria's role during the negotiations, see Tercero Casado, "Spanish Party." On the emperor's reaction to Maria's death (he went into seclusion), see Hengerer, *Ferdinand III*, 247–48; on Philip IV's grief, see his letter to

Sor María of Ágreda of June 17, 1646, in Seco Serrano, *Espistolario*, 64.

14. Philip IV to Sor María, July 11 and 29, 1646; Baltasar Carlos to Sor María July 20, 1646, in Seco Serrano, *Espistolario*, 64, 68–69; and Council of State deliberation, July 4, 1646, AHN E. leg. 2653, exp. 1. Mariana began to preside over all the women employed in the royal household of her mother; see Keller, *Hofdamen*, 160–61.

15. Valladares, *Rebelión de Portugal*, 97; and Sor María to Philip IV, November 17, 1646, in Seco Serrano, *Espistolario*, 87. The emperor's letter is mentioned in the Council of Castile deliberation of January 10, 1647 (AHN E. 2653, exp. 1) and by Philip IV to María of Ágreda, January 9, 1647 (Seco Serrano, *Espistolario*, 89). On the aftermath of Maria's death, see Hengerer, *Ferdinand III*, 250; and Mariana to Emperor Ferdinand III, September 28, 1647, Riksarkiv, Extranea 195 XVI Tyskland. Arkivfragment Kejsar Ferdinand III, 1641–47.

16. On the frequency of uncle-niece and first cousin marriages among the Spanish aristocracy, see Coolidge, "Families," 22, 106. On the large age gap between spouses among Italian aristocracy, see Klapisch-Zuber, *Women, Family and Ritual*, 19–20; Ruggiero, *Boundaries*, 13–14; and Kent, "Women in Renaissance Florence," 28. For the paper against her candidacy, see RAH K9 fols. 53r–66v; an analysis of the text appears in Oliván Santaliestra, "Mariana de Austria," 44. On marriage capitulations, see AGS PTR leg. 56, doc. 52.

17. Philip IV to the countess of Paredes, May 5 and June 9, 1648: "Mi sobrina ... de quien Lumiares me envía muy buenas nuebas y dice que está muger en todo, con que no se puede dudar lo que escrivieron las mugeres"; and Vilela Gallego, *Felipe IV*, 29–31, 33–35. On the play celebrating Mariana's fourteenth birthday, see Cobo Delgado, "Nuevo Olimpo," 31–32.

18. On the ongoing Westphalian negotiations, see Philip IV to Sor María, February 15, 1646, in Seco Serrano, *Espistolario*, 51; Tercero Casado, "Jornada," 646–49, 653; Council of State deliberations, December 1648, AHN E. legs. 2779 and 2653, exp. 1; and Treaty of Westphalia, Article III, the Avalon Project, http://avalon.law.yale.edu/17th_century/

westphal.asp (accessed July 5, 2015). On Mariana's journey, see Zapata Fernández de la Hoz, "Travesía," 346.

19. Zapata Fernández de la Hoz, "Travesía," 350–51; Tercero Casado, "Jornada," 658–60; and Keller, Hofdamen, 69, 160–61.

20. Zapata Fernández de la Hoz, "Travesía," 353–55; and Tercero Casado, "Jornada," 658–60. On Mariana's entry in Milan, see Zaggia, "Lombardy," 207. Horse ballets reached their height in France in the seventeenth century under the Italian-born queen Marie de Medici; see Mariana to Carlos, October 28, 1679, AHN E. leg. 2729.

21. Philip IV to Paredes, December 7, 1649; Vilela Gallego, Felipe IV, 65–67. On Mariana's royal entry in Madrid, see Zapata Fernández de la Hoz, "Nuevo mundo," 2:1249–65.

22. On the dissemination of Burgundian-Spanish etiquette traditions outside Madrid, see Oliván Santaliestra, "Modelo borgoñón." On the Spanish court, see Elliott, "Court," 145. On consorts' households, see Sánchez, Empress, the Queen and the Nun, 43–45; Hoffman, Raised to Rule, 29–46 (Madrid); and Keller, "Ladies-in-Waiting," 77–99 (Vienna).

23. Mariana's activities during her consortship are detailed in the diaries of the Marquis of Osera (1657–59) and Dutch ambassador Huygens (1660–61): Martínez Hernández, Escribir, 149, 212, 271, 306, 803–4, 963, 1060; and Ebben, Un holandés, 176–77, 188–90, 193–94, 200 (I thank Bernardo J. García García for providing me with this reference). Also see Venetian ambassadors' reports from 1649 to 1665: Basadonna (1649–53), Quirini (1653–56), Zane (1655–59), and Zorzi (1660–67), in Barozzi and Berchet, Relazioni, 203–353. The quote is from Malcolm, "Spanish Queens," 175–76. Also see Elliott, "Philip IV," 175; and Brown and Elliott, Palace for a King, 229.

24. Brown and Elliott, Palace for a King, 229; Martínez Hernández, Escribir, 212; and Malcolm, "Spanish Queens," 177.

25. Oliván Santaliestra, "Mariana de Austria," 50; and Malcolm, "Spanish Queens," 177.

26. On queens' royal households in the Spanish court, see Sánchez, Empress, the Queen and the Nun, 11–60; Labrador Arroyo, "From Castile to Burgundy," 119–48; and Hoffman, Raised to Rule, 25–53. On Mariana's affinity

with the future countess of Harrach, see Ebben, Un holandés, 188 (Huygens's entry for December 25, 1660). On Leonor de Velasco y la Cueva, Condesa de Siruela, see DBE Tomo 49:542–44; Oliván Santaliestra, "La dama," 2:1301–56; and Sor Clara to Mariana, January 11, 1647, from the Descalzas Reales, Madrid, Riksarkiv, Extranea 195 XVI Tyskland. Arkivfragment Kejsar Ferdinand III, 1641–47. On Mariana and Maria Theresa's friendship, see Philip IV to the Countess of Paredes, in Vilela Gallego, Felipe IV, 57–60. For evidence of Mariana's lifelong friendship with the nuns in her testament, see AHNSN Frías, caja 62, doc. 165 (copy) and letters to Carlos, AHN E. leg. 2729. On Mariana's affinity with Magdalena de Moncada, see DBE Tomo 35:528; Malcolm, "Práctica informal," 38–48; and Martínez Hernández, Escribir, 149.

27. Philip IV to the Countess of Paredes, October 18, 1649, San Lorenzo, El Escorial, in Vilela Gallego, Felipe IV, 57–60; Philip IV cited in Malcolm, "Spanish Queens," 174; Osera's diary entry for December 28, 1658, in Martínez Hernández, Escribir, 862; and Barozzi and Berchet, Relazioni, 238.

28. Philip IV to the Countess of Paredes, May 24, August 16, and December 13, 1650, and March 11 and 26, 1651, in Vilela Gallego, Felipe IV, 81–83, 85–87, 93–95, 105–7, 113–15. On wet nurses, see Cortés Echánove, Nacimiento, 71.

29. Philip IV to the Countess of Paredes, July 25, and August 8, 1651, in Vilela Gallego, Felipe IV, 129–31.

30. Wunder, "Women's Fashions," 161–66; Oliván Santaliestra, "Representational Strategies," 218–19, 226; and Ebben, Un holandés, 176 (December 17, 1660).

31. On Portuguese and French matches, see Valladares, Rebelión de Portugal, 105–10; and Stradling, Philip IV, 294. On imperial matches, see Martínez López, "La Infanta"; and Paz y Meliá, Avisos, 43, 57.

32. For rumors about the swearing-in ceremony, see Martínez López, "La Infanta," 92–93; and Paz y Meliá, Avisos, 43, 57. On Mariana's pregnancies, see Cortés Echánove, Nacimiento, 69–93.

33. Usunáriz Garayoa, España y sus tratados, 335–36, 338.

34. Ibid., 335–38.

35. Spielman, *Leopold I*, 30–31; Mazarin quoted in Usunáriz Garayoa, *España y sus tratados*, 339; and Martínez López, "La Infanta," 94–98.

36. On the reception of news of the birth in Madrid, see Barrionuevo, *Avisos*, 120–21. On the Imperial Diet of 1657, see Spielman, *Leopold I*, 31. On the impact of Felipe Próspero's birth on diplomatic negotiations, see Usunáriz Garayoa, *España y sus tratados*, 339–42; and Valladares, *Rebelión de Portugal*, 167.

37. Valladares, *Rebelión de Portugal*, 166–67.

38. On reinterpretations of the treaty, see Serra, "Treaty of the Pyrenees," 81; Valladares, "Tratado de Paz," 137; and Usunáriz Garayoa, *España y sus tratados*, 341. For the text of the treaty, see Usunáriz Garayoa, *España y sus tratados*, 349–95. Today, the small town of Llívia (population 1,500) is in Catalonia, within the geographic confines of the Department of the Pyrénées-Orientales, in southern France.

39. Zanger, *Scenes from the Marriage*. On legal strategies of French state-building, see Sahlins, *Boundaries*, 16, 32–33. On precedents for Maria Theresa's marriage, see McGowan, ed., *Dynastic Marriages*. On Philip IV's shifting attention to Portugal, see Valladares, *Rebelión de Portugal*, 165.

40. Cortés Echánove, *Nacimiento*, 71; and APR Hist. caja 94, exp. 190.

41. Valladares, *Rebelión de Portugal*, 182, 187, 189–90.

42. Belcher, "Spain and the Anglo-Portuguese Alliance," 67–88; and Valladares, *Rebelión de Portugal*, 187.

43. Villa-Urrutia, *Relaciones entre España y Austria*, 67, 70. Mariana to Leopold I, n.d., minuta de carta, AHN E. leg. 2661, exp. 208; and Council of State deliberation, January 1663, AHN E. leg. 2799.

44. Council of State deliberations of February 21, 1663; January 18 and July 8, 1664; and March 26, 1665; marriage capitulations (copy); circular letter announcing the marriage by Philip IV (copies), AHN E. leg. 2799; report by Diego de Prado, Vienna, February 21, 1665, AGS E. leg. 2378; and Martínez López, "La Infanta," 93–94.

45. Valladares, *Rebelión de Portugal*, 189–91; Council of State deliberations, March 26 and

August 28 and 30, 1665, AHN E. leg. 2799; and Pötting to Philip IV, August 22, 1665, AGS E. leg. 2799.

46. Mariana to the Council of State, August 29, 1665, AGS E. leg. 2683.

47. The reconstruction of these events is based mainly on the diary of Cristóbal Crespí de Valdaura (1599–1670), vice-chancellor of the Council of Aragon, BNE ms. 5742, fols. 359v–362r. They coincide with the shorter account of the imperial ambassador, Pötting, *Diario*, 1:135–36.

48. The discourse's text is from BNE ms. 5742, fol. 361r. For the name of the person who spoke for the king, see Maura, *Carlos II*, 1:112.

49. The events are described in BNE ms. 5742, fols. 360v–361r.

50. BNE ms. 5742, fol. 362r; Maura, *Carlos II*, 1:113. Crespí did not mention this episode.

51. Varela, *La muerte del rey*, 17–18, 79.

52. BNE ms. 5742, fols. 362v–363r.

53. For Mariana's royal decree, see September 17, 1665, AGS E. leg. 4128. On the breaking of the seals and the swearing-in ceremony, see BNE ms. 5742, fols. 363r–364r; and Council of Aragon, minutes, September 17, 1665, AHN Consejos leg. 7259. On the transfer of the keys, see ADM Hist. leg. 68, ramo 22.

54. On the proclamation of Carlos II, see RAH ms. 9/3746 fols. 156r–157v; for Philip IV's burial, see BNE ms. 5742 fols. 364v, 366r. On the heart kept in the Franciscan convent of San Gil, the body in El Escorial, see Varela, *La muerte del rey*, 17–18, 79; and Orso, *Art and Death*, 81. The archbishop of Embrun is quoted in Maura, *Carlos II*, 1:115.

55. Jordan Gschwend, "Retratos de Juana," 42–65; and Cruz, "Juana of Austria," 103. On Isabel's political partnership with Emperor Charles V, see Tracy, *Charles V*, 11.

56. Habsburg governors such as Margaret of Austria (1480–1530), Mary of Hungary (1505–1558), and Margaret of Parma (1522–1586) ruled the Netherlands almost uninterruptedly from 1507 to 1567. These were not isolated instances. On guardianships exercised by aristocratic women, see Coolidge, *Guardianship*, 22.

57. Van Wyhe, "Monastic Habit," 258–60.

58. For the idea of retirement among widows, see Vives, *Education of a Christian*

Woman, 299–325. On widows' role in the civic life of their communities, see Fink De Backer, *Widowhood*, 6, 9–10, and part 2, pp. 111–219.

59. On Mariana's demeanor her first day as regent, see BNE ms. 5742, fol. 364r. On rulership and self-fashioning, see Burke, *Fabrication of Louis XIV*. For French queen regents, see Crawford, *Perilous Performances*. On Spanish kingship, see Elliott, "Philip IV," 169–89. On Mariana as regent, see Llorente, "Imagen"; and Llorente, "Mariana of Austria's Portraits."

Chapter 2

1. Habsburg traditions of corulership with women are abundantly documented. See, for example, Cruz, "Juana of Austria"; Jordan Gschwend, "Retratos de Juana" and "Mujeres mecenas"; Sánchez, "Sword and Wimple"; Raviola, "Three Lives"; and Cruz and Stampino, *Habsburg Women*. On Iberian political traditions, see Earenfight, "Partners in Politics," xiii; and Earenfight, "Absent Kings," 33–51. On aristocratic families choosing women as guardians, see Coolidge, *Guardianship*, 42.

2. On the Spanish Habsburg court, see Elliott, *Spain and Its World*, 142–61; Rodríguez-Salgado, "Court of Philip II," 205–44; Martínez Millán, "La corte," 17–61; Hortal Muñoz and Labrador Arroyo, *Casa de Borgoña*; and Redworth and Checa, "Courts of Spanish Habsburgs," 43–65. As a gendered space and one that extended outside the palace, see Sánchez, *Empress, the Queen and the Nun*, 11–35; and Martínez Millán and Marçal Lourenço, *Relaciones discretas*, which has three volumes dedicated to the queen's household. Labrador Arroyo, "From Castile to Burgundy," 119–48, gives an overview of the evolution of the queen's household under the Habsburgs. The Spanish nobility, which included nontitled gentry, or *hidalgos*, comprised about 10 percent of the population. This was significantly higher than the rest of Europe. The grandees, or *grandes*, had a special place in court ceremonies by virtue of their social status. All nobles—including the grandees—were invested in the power of the monarchy, which intensified their competition and drove the court's political dynamics. On the Spanish

nobility and its relationship with rulers, see Liss, *Isabel*, chapters 5 and 6; Nader, *Mendoza Family*; Elliott, *Imperial Spain*, 15–16, 114–16, 259–62, 313–15, 348–49, 363–65; and Dewald, *European Nobility*, 23–25.

3. Information about Mariana's tutorship, curatorship, and governorship appears in Philip IV, *Testamento*, clauses 21 and 35, pp. 40–43, 51–53. The distinction between the tutorship and the curatorship is discussed in Coolidge, *Guardianship*, 21.

4. Philip IV, *Testamento*, clause 36, pp. 52–53. The formation of Carlos's royal household appears in APR RCII, caja 92, exp. 3. On the significance of the royal households as the foundation of the court system, see Asch, "Court and Household," 9; Rodríguez-Salgado, "Court of Philip II," 205–44; and Martínez Millán, "La corte," 17–61.

5. On the Spanish system of ruling by *consulta*, see Elliott, *Imperial Spain*, 176–77. On Spanish kingship, see Elliott, "Philip IV," 169–89; and Ruiz, "Unsacred Monarchy," 109–44. On paper, see Elliott, "Self-Perception," 42; the numbers on the Council of State are my estimates.

6. Philip IV, *Testamento*, 40–43, 51–53; and Philip IV cited in Mitchell, "Habsburg Mother-hood," 178. Queen mothers in France had tutorship rights and various levels of authority over administration of the state. France offers an ideal comparison because it had several female regencies in the sixteenth and seventeenth centuries. Lightman, "Sons and Mothers," 26–31.

7. Sevilla González, "La Junta de Gobierno," 601–2.

8. Philip IV, *Testamento*, clauses 9 and 64, pp. 13–15, 74–75; arrangements for members of the chapel and other sections of the king's household are detailed in the Aytona papers, ADM Hist. leg. 68, ramo 22.

9. I calculated the numbers by averaging José Jurado Sánchez's figures. He counts 1,270 members of the king's household in 1622; 1,400 in 1699; and 500 in the queen's household in 1667. These numbers are not far from the 1,700 total that Elliott gives for the combined households in 1623; 1,800 members seems an accurate figure. Jurado Sánchez, *Economía de la corte*, 26, 34; Elliott, "Court,"

144–45. On the system of paying servants with emoluments and gajes, see Simón Palmer, *Cocina de palacio*, 79; and Nuñez de Castro, *Solo Madrid es corte*. On the number of dishes, see "La Bianda del Rey y la Reyna," APR Adm. leg. 928.

10. "Reforms of 1666," in APR Adm. leg. 928. For Aytona's recommendations, see October 16, 1665, ADM Hist. leg. 68, ramo 22. On Medina de las Torres, see Stradling, "Spanish Statesman," 1–31; On Montalto, see APR Personal, caja 696, exp. 7; and Pilo Gallisai, "Todos los hombres," 257–75. On Aytona, see Mesa Gallego, "Itinerario biográfico," 41–77.

11. Aytona to Mariana, October 16, 1665, ADM Hist. leg. 68, ramo 22.

12. Reforms from 1665 to 1675 and Medina de las Torres's report in APR Adm. leg. 5647 and 928. On the 1620s reforms, see Elliott, *Olivares*, 114, 150. For the later reforms (1647–51), see Labrador Arroyo, "Formación de las etiquetas generales," 99–128.

13. Aytona to Mariana, October 16, 1665, ADM Hist. leg. 68, ramo 22.

14. On the *camarera mayor*'s ceremonial prerogatives, see Medina de las Torres, vote, Council of State deliberation, August 2, 1667, AHN E. leg. 674 exp. 18; and Mariana's decree, September 22, 1665, AGS E. leg. 4128.

15. On the *aya*'s function and prerogatives, see Medina de las Torres, opinion recorded in Council of State deliberation, August 2, 1667, AHN E. leg. 674 exp. 18.

16. Starkey, "Court, Council, and Nobility," 175–203; Boyden, *Courtier and the King*, 93–115; and Elliott, *Olivares*, 136.

17. On Baldueza, see AHNSN Osuna, caja 127, exp. 44; APR Personal, caja 1099, exp. 29; Elvira Ponce de León y Álvarez de Toledo, Marquesa de Villanueva de la Baldueza (d. 1691), DBE Tomo 41:957–59. On Los Velez, APR Personal, caja 1084, exp. 11; and Maria Engracia de Toledo Portugal y Pimentel, Marquesa de los Velez, DBE Tomo 47:1036–38. On Velez during the regency, see Sánchez Ramos, "Poder de una mujer," 32. On the roles of these women during Mariana's regency, see Oliván Santalliestra, "La dama," 2:1301–56.

18. Mariana to Montalto, January 24 and August 19, 1666, APR RCII, caja 83, exp. 1; and

Montalto to Mariana, August 19, 1666, APR Adm. leg. 698.

19. On the practice of *galanteos*, see López Álvarez, *Poder, lujo y conflicto*, 486–88.

20. Montalto to Mariana, August 19, 1666, APR Adm. leg. 698.

21. Mariana to Montalto, n.d., APR Adm. leg. 698.

22. Cardinal Chigi to Mariana, March 7, 1667, received in late March, AGS E. Roma leg. 3131; BNE ms. 8360, fols. 70r–79r; and Pilo Gallisai, "Todos los hombres," 261. Montalto was a widower and not a priest, but noblemen of his stature could be and were promoted to the position of cardinal. These were not ecclesiastical appointments: a lay cardinal was an elector of the pope and thus prince of the church. The Duke of Lerma, for example, became a cardinal in 1618, also in widowhood; the Cardinal-Infante Fernando was also a lay cardinal.

23. Mariana to Aytona, November 20, 1668, ADM Hist. leg. 69.

24. On previous dukes of Alba serving as *mayordomos mayores*, see Boyden, *Courtier and the King*, 110; and Elliott, *Olivares*, 396.

25. APR RCII, caja 117, exp. 2.

26. Philip IV, *Testamento*, clauses 22 and 23, pp. 42–47.

27. Maura, *Carlos II*, 1:119; Tomás y Valiente, *Validos*, 18–19; and Domínguez Ortíz, "Introducción," xxxiii.

28. Philip IV, *Testamento*, 40–43, 51–53; Sevilla González, "La Junta de Gobierno," 601–2.

29. Minutes of the Council of Aragon, September 17, 1665, AHN Consejos, leg. 7179; Crespí's diary, entry of September 17, 1665, BNE ms. 5742, fols. 362v–363r; and the report in Vienna, Haus-, Hof-, und Staatsarchiv, Vienna, Spanien Varia, Karton 18, Fasz. 18; I thank Rocío Martínez for providing me with a copy of this document. For the phrase "Vuestra Magestad mandará lo que fuere servida," see Council of State deliberations found in AGS or AHN.

30. Baltar Rodríguez, *Juntas de Gobierno*; and Barrios, *Consejo de estado*, 145.

31. Hermosa Espeso, "Testamento de Felipe IV," 108.

32. Franganillo, "La reina Isabel," 446–58.

33. On the importance of dying well, including having a testament, see Eire, *From Madrid to Purgatory*, 24–66.

34. Partida II, Título XV, Ley III, cited in Hermosa Espeso, "Testamento de Felipe IV," 103, 109. The principles of self-government allowed the Catalans to establish a republic, which nevertheless lasted only a week. They also claim their right to self-government to place themselves under the protection of the Louis XIII of France; see Elliott, *Revolt*, 487–522.

35. The principle of obeying but not complying is found in Elliott, *Empires*, 131.

36. For Castrillo's biographical profile, see Maura, *Carlos II*, 1:146–49. He rose to power under Olivares; see Elliott, *Olivares*, 440.

37. For Peñaranda's biographical profile, see Maura, *Carlos II*, 1:150–55.

38. On Crespí, see ibid., 1:155–56, and BNE ms. 5742. On Aragon, see Estenaga y Echevarría, *Cardenal Aragón*; and Molas Ribalta, "Duquesa de Cardona," 133–43.

39. On Aytona, see Maura, *Carlos II*, 1:157–61. On his sister and Mariana's friendship, see Martínez Hernández, *Escribir*, 149.

40. Aytona to Mariana, February 2, 1666, ADM Hist. leg. 70.

41. On the Junta de Inglaterra, see AHN E. leg. 2797, exp. 24. On prohibition against foreigners, see Philip IV, *Testamento*, clause 33, p. 51. Complying cities included Burgos, Toledo, León, Valladolid, Seville, Jaén, Cuenca, Toro, Soria, Zamora, and Segovia. Nithard does not mention the three cities who refused him citizenship or on what basis. BNE ms. 8344, fols. 159v–168r; and meeting of the Junta de Gobierno, March 27, 1666, BNE ms. 8344, fol. 170r. The thirty-six-point disquisition commissioned by the Dominican order protesting Nithard's appointment was titled "Dudas políticas" (Political doubts); several copies survived (AHNSN Osuna, caja 571, doc. 145). According to the imperial ambassador, it circulated widely in Madrid and foreign courts; see Pötting, *Diario*, 1:264.

42. On Medina de las Torres's paper, see Oliván Santaliestra, "'Discurso jurídico,'" 7–34; Hermosa Espeso, "Testamento de Felipe IV," 103; and a copy in Nithard's memoirs, BNE ms. 8344.

43. Barrios, *Consejo de estado*, 150. On the *cédula* of 1612—revoked in 1618 at the same time of Lerma's dismissal—see Tomás y Valiente, *Validos*, 80–81, and appendixes 1 and 2, 157–58; on the Council of State and Olivares, see Elliott, *Olivares*, 131–68; and on Luis de Haro and the Council of State, see Tomás y Valiente, *Validos*, 98–100.

44. Mariana's royal decrees of September 17, 1665, and September 23, 1665, AGS E. leg. 4128. On the appointments of seven councilors, see Pötting, *Diario*, 1:171; Maura, *Carlos II*, 1:241; Cordero Torres, *Consejo de estado*, 52; Barrios, *Consejo de estado*, 150–52; Danvila y Collado, *Poder civil en España*, 2:214; Escudero, "Consultas," 109–12; and Escudero, *Los secretarios*, 4:983–87.

45. Escudero, *Los secretarios*, 1:343–44.

46. Estela, "Mecenazgo de los Marqueses de Mejorada," 472–74; Escudero, *Los secretarios*, 1:270–72; AHN E. leg. 2797.

Chapter 3

1. The warning from France came via the Spanish ambassador in Paris, Gaspar de Teves y Tello de Guzmán (1608–1673), 1st Marquis de la Fuente. De la Fuente to Philip IV, August 23, 1665, AHN E. libro 129, núm. 199. See de la Fuente's biographical profile in Yetano Laguna, "Relaciones entre España y Francia," 55–80.

2. On the army of Flanders in 1665, see Hayley, *English Diplomat*, 29; Lonchay, *Correspondance*, 4:810; Sánchez Belén, "Relaciones internacionales," 148; and Aytona's memorandum to Mariana, February 2, 1666, ADM Hist. leg. 70. On the dismantling of the army of Flanders after the Pyrenees treaty, see Parker, *Army of Flanders*, 190. For marriage negotiations and the disputes over the *infanta*'s departure, see the Council of State deliberations during 1664 and 1665, AHN E. leg. 2799.

3. For the course of the war in summer 1665, see Valladares, *Rebelión de Portugal*, 189–91. The Council of State papers are held in several collections, mostly in the Archivo de Simancas, Valladolid, and the Archivo Histórico Nacional, Madrid.

4. The collections informing this chapter are mainly from the Archivo de Simancas.

Particularly important for the period 1665–68 are Estado Inglaterra and Estado Negociaciones en La Haya. I have relied on the Aytona Papers from the Archivo Ducal Medinaceli as well as additional documents from the Archivo Histórico Nacional, Madrid.

5. Carlos is named in clause 10, and lines of succession favoring the Austrian Habsburgs are in 12 and 13; see Philip IV, *Testamento*, 15–23. For an excellent analysis of the lines of succession, see Sevilla Gonzáles, "La Junta de Gobierno," 596–600.

6. Catalina Micaela's descendants are named in clause 14, and the exclusion of Maria Theresa and Anne appears in clause 15, Philip IV, *Testamento*, 22–37.

7. On French laws preventing women from receiving or passing on succession rights, see Hanley, "Family, the State, and the Law"; and Viennot, *L'invention de la loi salique*. Justification for exclusion is in clause 15, and Mariana's governorship if Margarita and Leopold succeeded is in clause 53, Philip IV, *Testamento*, 22–37, 66–67.

8. Printed versions of "copies of clauses" can be found in the Biblioteca Nacional in Madrid; for instance, see BNE VE 198.14. Reports of copies and distribution of the testament are in Pötting, *Diario*, 1:136. Emperor Leopold I received a copy of the testament a few weeks after Philip's death; see Pribram and Pragenau, *Privatebriefe*, 1:166–67. The wife of the English ambassador to Madrid from 1664 to 1666, Lady Anne Fanshawe, also reports accurately the lines of succession in her diary, revealing a thorough familiarity with the testament; see Fanshawe, *Memoirs of Anne, Lady Halkett and Ann, Lady Fanshawe*, 176. Louis XIV's intentions were deduced from Council of State deliberations and diplomatic correspondence from 1663 until Philip IV's death and immediately after; see, for example, diplomatic reports discussed in the Council of State deliberations, October 22, 1663; January 18 and July 8, 1664; and the rest of 1665; AHN E. leg. 2799. Also see Count of Lamberg to Castel Rodrigo, October 10, 1665, AGS E. leg. 2379, discussed below.

9. For the report of Louis XIV's reaction upon learning of Philip IV's death, see the Count of Lamberg to Castel Rodrigo,

October 10, 1665, AGS E. leg. 2379. False rumors of Carlos II's death were reported by the Spanish ambassador in Paris with a great sense of frustration; see AHN E. libros 129, 130, 139; and Mitchell, "Growing Up," 192.

10. Mariana's decree, September 23, 1665, AGS E. leg. 2683. On the financial situation at the beginning of the regency, see Aytona's memorandum to Mariana, February 2, 1666, ADM Hist. leg. 70; and Medina de las Torres in Council of State deliberation, August 11, 1666, AGS E. leg. 2538. For the 1667–68 income, see Kamen, *La España*, 467–68; and Sanz Ayán, *Banqueros*, 210–11.

11. The vice-chancellor of Aragon, Cristóbal Crespí de Valdaura, reported in his diary the confirmation of the marriage; see BNE ms. 5742, fol. 364r; and Mariana to Leopold I, September 23, 1665, AGS E. leg. 2378. Sums are confirmed in Aytona's memorandum, February 2, 1666, ADM Hist. leg. 70. Expectations of Mariana's regency among ministers of the Holy Roman emperor appear in the letter of the Count of Lamberg to the governor of the Spanish Netherlands, Marquis of Castel Rodrigo, October 10, 1665, AGS E. leg. 2379.

12. Leopold I to Mariana, October 18, 1665, AGS E. leg. 2378; Mariana to the Council of State, November 13, 1665, AGS E. leg. 2379; and Pötting to Mariana, January 10, 1666, AGS E. leg. 2381.

13. Lamberg to the Marquis of Castel Rodrigo, report sent to Madrid on October 10, 1665, AGS E. leg. 2379. For the Franco-Portuguese alliance, see Abreu y Bertodano, "Tratado secreto de liga ofensiva y devensiva entre Luis XIV, Rey de Francia, y Alphonso VI, Rey de Portugal, contra Carlos II, Rey Cathólico de las Españas," in *Colección de los Tratados de Paz*, 1:118–28. From Italy, see reports by the viceroy of Naples and governor of Milan, Don Luis Ponce, January 1666 n.d., AGS E. leg. 3100. For the League of the Rhine (1657) and French foreign policy in the post-Westphalian period to the Peace of the Pyrenees, see Ekberg, "Formulation of French Foreign Policy," 317–29. On Spain's diplomatic isolation, see Yetano Laguna, "Relaciones entre España y Francia," 203–72.

14. "Consultas" and reports sent by the Spanish ambassador in London; see the

Count of Molina, from October 1665, AGS E. leg. 2535; drafts of the treaty in AHN E. leg. 2797, exp. 20; and Abreu y Bertodano, "Tratado de Paz, y Comercio entre las Coronas de España, e Inglaterra, en que renovando el que se concluyó en el año de 1630, publicado, y puesto en execución en el 1660, se amplían sus Artículos y se añaden diez y seis secretos relativos a una Tregua con el Reyno de Portugal," in *Colección de los Tratados de Paz*, 1:1–27. Charles II's refusal to ratify it is explained by the English ambassador in Madrid, Sir Richard Fanshawe, discussed in the Council of State deliberations, July 9, 1666, AGS E. leg. 2538.

15. On Franco-Dutch relations in the post-1648 period, see Herrero Sánchez, *Acercamiento Hispano-Neerlandés*, 18–19, 36–44. On the discussions of the future of the Spanish Netherlands, see Rowen, *John de Witt*, 469; Hayley, *English Diplomat*, 45; Israel, *Dutch Republic*, 778; and Yetano Laguna, "Relaciones entre España y Francia," 204–14.

16. Mariana's instructions to Gamarra, January 21 and April 4, 1666, AGS E. leg. 8396. On the Anglo-Dutch wars, see Israel, *Dutch Republic*, 713–26, 766–825.

17. Council of State deliberation, March 31, 1666; see Peñaranda's opinion as well in AGS E. leg. 2381. For Peñaranda's and Montalto's opinions, see Council of State deliberation, September 25, 1666, AGS E. leg. 2538.

18. The *infanta*'s departure is discussed in the Council of State deliberation, March 31, 1666; for the counterproposal by Portugal, see AGS E. leg. 2381. On Mariana's preparations for the journey, see ADM Hist. leg. 70; and AGS E. leg. 2383. The Junta de Medios was presided over by Bartolomé de Legasa, one of the many royal secretaries Mariana relied on. Escudero, *Los secretarios*, 3:659–61. For the good-byes between mother and daughter, see Pötting, *Diario*, 1:199. Mariana expressed her feelings about her daughter in Mariana to the Countess of Harrach (in German), Madrid, May 5, 1666, Haus-, Hof- und Staatsarchiv AVA Wien, GHFA 321, unfoliated. I thank Professor Laura Oliván Santaliestra for providing me a copy of the letter. On Margarita's entourage and journey, see Labrador Arroyo, "Casa de Margarita," 2:1221–66.

19. On the Partition Treaty of 1668 between Louis XIV and Leopold I, see Bérenger, "Attempted Rapprochement," 137; Ribot García, "La repercusión en España," 55–96; and Ochoa Brun, *Diplomacia española*, 133.

20. On Leopold's rejection by Spaniards, see BNE ms. 8360, fols. 248v–249r. On money issues, see ADM Hist. leg. 70; and AGS E. leg. 2383. On Carlos II's childhood, see Mitchell, "Growing Up," 192–94.

21. Mariana to the Council of State, June 26, 1667, AGS E. leg. 2539. Medina de las Torres's opinion on Portugal had been circulated in manuscript form since January 1666; RAH ms. 9/1835. For foreign policy based on the principle of "reputation," see Elliott, *Olivares*, particularly 2:131–320; and Elliott, "Question of Reputation," 477.

22. On the Junta de Inglaterra, see AHN E. leg. 2797; and Council of State deliberations, 1666–67, AGS E. legs. 2538 to 2540.

23. These dynamics can be extrapolated from Pötting, *Diario*, and deliberations too numerous to be cited individually; see AGS E. legs. 2538–39. For Nithard's special vote on the independence of Portugal, see BNE ms. 22086(1) and Council of State deliberation, August 11, 1666, AGS E. leg. 2538.

24. Medina de las Torres, Council of State deliberation, August 11, 1666, AGS E. leg. 2538; other votes were recorded in Council of State deliberation, August 12, 1666, including Nithard's; AGS E. leg. 2538 and BNE ms. 22086(1). His dense disquisition is hard to read. He argued for peace for more than a hundred folio pages only to make a counterargument that Mariana should not cede Portugal on fol. 111 v.

25. Reports from Brussels and The Hague from July to December 1666 on France's mobilization of galleons and infantry and cavalry forces arrived regularly; AGS E. leg. 8397. Also see Molina to Mariana, February 21, 1666, AGS E. leg. 2536; paper by the English ambassador in Madrid read in the Council of State, October 22, 1666; Castel Rodrigo to Mariana, August 31, 1666, AHN E. leg. 2797; Hayley, *English Diplomat*, 61; Council of State deliberations of July 9, 1666; Castel Rodrigo's letter to Mariana from Brussels, August 31, 1666; Molina to Mariana, November 29, 1666; "Consultas de los tratados desde la primera

conferencia de Sandwich hasta el fin de año de 1666," AGS E. leg. 2538; and Fernández Nadal, *La embajada de Londres*, 147.

26. Molina to Mariana, March 10, 1667; Junta de Inglaterra meeting, May 18, 1667, AGS E. leg. 2539; and Abreu y Bertodano, "Tratado de Renovación de Paz, Alianza, y Comercio entre las Coronas de España y de la Gran Bretaña (May 23, 1667)," in *Colección de los Tratados de Paz*, 1:145–88. Although signed May 23, the treaty was confirmed in March, before the breaking of hostilities between Spain and France; Fernández Nadal, *La embajada de Londres*, 147.

27. Mariana's instructions to Esteban Gamarra in The Hague, copies of the same sent to Molina in London and Castel Rodrigo in Brussels, April 26, 1667, AGS E. legs. 8397; Molina to Mariana, April 22, 1667, AGS E. leg. 2539; and Summary of Molina's letter to Mariana, April 22, 1667, AGS E. leg. 2539. On the Peace of Breda, see Israel, *Dutch Republic*, 766.

28. Castellar to Mariana, January 16, 1666. The official announcement of the pregnancy was sent March 24, 1667, AGS E. leg. 2382. On Margarita's role in the court of Vienna, see Oliván Santaliestra, "La emperatriz Margarita," 837–908.

29. Lamberg (from The Hague) to Castel Rodrigo (Brussels), October 10, 1667, AGS E. leg. 2379; and de la Fuente to Mariana, April 29, 1667, which was written in Paris but arrived in Madrid from Brussels, AGS E. leg. 2382. For Louis XIV's call to other princes to join France and Portugal, see Abreu y Bertodano, "Manifiesto publicado por la Francia," in *Colección de los Tratados de Paz*, 1:131–33. For Louis XIV's declaration of war, May 17, 1667, see AGS E. leg. 3100.

30. Louis XIV to Mariana, May 7, 1667, AGS E. legs. 2382 and 3100 (copy).

31. Council of State deliberation, May 18, 1667, AGS E. leg. 2382; Anne of Austria's message to Philip IV (received by Mariana), in AHN E. libro 129, núm. 199; text of Louis XIV's declaration in AHN E. leg. 140; and "Tratado de los derechos de la Reyna Christianissima, sobre varios Estados de la Monarchía de España," summary in Abreu y Bertodano, *Colección de los Tratados de Paz*, 1:131–33.

32. Council of State deliberation, May 18, 1667, AGS E. leg. 2382.

33. Council of State deliberation, May 18, 1667, AGS E. legs. 2382 and 3100.

34. Pötting, *Diario*, 1:300.

35. Mariana to the Council of State, May 28, 1667, AGS E. leg. 2382.

36. Ibid.

37. Mariana to the Council of State, May 28 and August 9, 1667, AGS E. legs. 2382 and 2383. On fiscal reforms instituted during Mariana's regency and the rest of Carlos II's reign, see Sánchez Belén, *Política fiscal*, 1–54, 201–4, 259–60. On the economic situation, see Kamen, *La España*, 467. The reforms of the royal households are discussed in chapter 2; for the rest of the reign, see Luzzi Traficante, "La casa de Borgoña," 130–31. On the cost of the armada of Flanders during the War of Devolution, see Stradling, *Armada of Flanders*, 237. The regular silver fleets are mentioned in several deliberations, although the amount of silver received was not specified.

38. On the army of Flanders during the War of Devolution, see Rodríguez Hernández, *La Guerra de Devolución*, 131–38, 142, 154. On recruitment under Aytona, see Aytona to Mariana, January 30 and December n.d., 1666, ADM Hist. leg. 70. Also see Mariana's response to the Council of State, May 28, 1667, AGS E. leg. 2382.

39. Mariana's response to Louis XIV was read in the Council of State deliberation, May 28, 1667, AGS E. leg. 2382. Mariana commissioned the response to the jurist, Francisco Ramos del Manzano, who later became Carlos II's first teacher; AHN E. leg. 671 and AGS E. leg. 2382. For Manzano's treatise responding to the claim, see the summary of his response in Abreu y Bertodano, "Resumen de la respuesta dada por parte de España al Manifesto antecedente, publicado por Francia," in *Colección de los Tratados de Paz*, 1:133–38.

40. Mariana to Louis XIV (copy), May 22, 1667, AGS E. legs. 2382 and 3100.

41. Spanish ambassador in Vienna, Count of Castellar, to Mariana, May 30, 1667; and Council of State deliberation, June 21, 1667, AGS E. leg. 2382. On Habsburg relations during this period and Castellar's divisive presence in Vienna, see Ochoa Brun, "Estudio preliminar,"

XXVIII; and Ochoa Brun, *Diplomacia española*, 132–33.

42. Mariana to the Council of State, June 21, 1667, AGS E. leg. 2382.

43. Spanish ambassador in Vienna, Count of Castellar, to Mariana, May 30, 1667; Council of State deliberation, June 21, 1667, AGS E. leg. 2382; and Castellar to Mariana, June 21, 1667, AGS E. leg. 2383. On Habsburg relations during this period and Castellar's divisive presence in Vienna, see Ochoa Brun, "Estudio preliminar," XXVIII; and Ochoa Brun, *Diplomacia española*, 132–33.

44. Peñaranda, Council of State deliberation, July 9, 1667, AGS E. leg. 2383.

45. Mariana's response to the meeting of July 9, 1667, AGS E. leg. 2383.

46. Mariana to the Council of State, June 26, 1667, AGS E. leg. 2539.

47. On the transportation of the jewels, see 1667 n.d., AGS E. leg. 2688, and 1670, AGS E. leg. 2554. On embargoes and reprisals against French merchants, see Abreu y Bertodano, "Cédula Real, declarando la forma en que se ha de executar el embargo general de los bienes, y haciendas de los Franceses," in *Colección de los Tratados de Paz*, 1:251–52; and Mariana to the Council of State, August 9, 1667, AGS E. legs. 2383 and 3100. The fleets with the *barras de plata* (silver bars) are mentioned in AGS E. leg. 2686; AHN E. leg. 2797; Stradling, *Armada of Flanders*, 237; Sanz Ayán, *Banqueros*, 227; and Sánchez Belén, *Política fiscal*, 201–4, 259–60. For sums for the embassies of London and The Hague, see Mariana to the Council of State, August 9, 1667; and Fernández Nadal, *La embajada de Londres*, 151–52.

48. Mariana to the Council of State, August 9, 1667, AGS E. leg. 2383; and Rodríguez Hernández, *La Guerra de Devolución*, 140–43.

49. Mariana to the Council of State, August 31, 1667, AGS E. leg. 2686; de la Fuente to the Duke of San Germán, viceroy of Navarre, August 18, 1667, AGS E. leg. 2686; Stradling, *Armada of Flanders*, 237; and Rodríguez Hernández, *La Guerra de Devolución*, 208, 227.

50. Peñaranda, Council of State deliberation, September 17, 1667, AGS E. leg. 3100.

51. Hayley, *English Diplomat*, 101–3; Rowen, *John de Witt*, 626–27.

52. Rowen, *John de Witt*, 611, 633; Mariana to Gamarra and Castel Rodrigo by duplicate, May 28, 1667, AGS E. leg. 8397. Gamarra's report is discussed in the Council of State deliberation of August 13, 1667, AGS E. leg. 2541. Nithard's theological-political disquisition is in the Council of State deliberation, November 26, 1667, AGS E. leg. 2541. A draft can also be found in BNE ms. 22086(2). There was some opposition but not enough to change the approach. See Sánchez Belén, "Relaciones internacionales," 145. On potential subsidies to Charles II, see Lisola to Pötting, March 21, 1667, AGS E. leg. 2539; and Council of State deliberations of August 13, November 26, 1667, AGS E. leg. 2541, and January 11, 1668, AGS E. leg. 2542.

53. Mariana to the Council of State, November 26, 1667, AGS E. leg. 2541; Castel Rodrigo to Mariana, July 27, 1667, AHN E. leg. 2797, exp. 41; Abreu y Bertodano, "Tratado de Liga y Confederacion, ajustado por el Marques de Castel-Rodrigo en nombre de S[u] M[agestad] Catholica, y Werner Guillermo Blasperil en el del Elector de Brandemburg, por el cual se conviene en que S[u] A[lteza] Electoral ponga un Exercito de quatro mil Cavallos, y ocho mil Infantes, proveido de Artilleria, y las demas cosas necesarias para salir a campaña a ultimos del mes de Abril, a fin de oponerse a los progressos de las Armas del Rey Christianissimo . . . Brusselas, 6 de Noviembre, 1667," in *Colección de los Tratados de Paz*, 1:265–71; the original in AHN E. leg. 2797, exp. 47; and Pötting to Mariana, December 16, 1667, AGS E. leg. 2383. Plenipotentiary powers were sent October 6, 1667, AHN E. leg. 2797, exp. 45. On the league with Sweden, see Rowen, *John de Witt*, 698.

54. Valladares, *Rebelión de Portugal*, 215–16; and Council of State deliberation, October 24, 1667, AGS E. leg. 2541.

55. Instructions to the Marquis of Carpio drafted in December 1667 and draft of the clauses to be included in the Peace of Lisbon (drafted by Cardinal Aragón), AHN E. leg. 2797, exp. 46; Mariana to the Council of State, used to draft instructions for Sandwich, in AGS E. leg. 2541. The situation in Portugal and the

now accelerated process can be deduced from Sir Robert Southwell (Charles II's envoy to Portugal) to Sandwich; copy discussed in the Council of State, December 4, 1667; and Carpio to his father, Medina de las Torres, who reported the content of his letter to the Junta de Inglaterra, December 14, 1667, AGS E. leg. 2540.

56. On the situation in London, see Molina to Mariana, November 7, 1667, and December 31, 1667; Molina to Mariana, November 25, 1667, AGS E. leg. 2540; Hayley, *English Diplomat*, 149–52; and Rowen, *John de Witt*, 688.

57. Hayley, *English Diplomat*, 149–52, 162; Rowen, *John de Witt*, 687–88; Sonnino, *Origins of the Dutch War*, 13; and Molina to Mariana, November 25, 1667, AGS E. leg. 2540. A report Molina wrote on March 4, 1668, sheds some light on the convoluted negotiations, AGS E. leg. 2542; reports from The Hague, AGS E. leg. 8405.

58. Mariana to de Witt through Esteban Gamarra, her ambassador in The Hague; instructions to Gamarra, AGS E. leg. 8400; Molina to Mariana, March 4, 1668, AGS E. leg. 2542; Rowen, *John de Witt*, 689; and Abreu y Bertodano, "Carta de Louis XIV a sus aliados, en que les comunica los motivos que ha tenido para tomar la resolucion de passar al Franco Condado con un Cuerpo de Exercito . . . para inclinar a los españoles à la conclusion de la Paz," January 15, 1668, in *Colección de los Tratados de Paz*, 1:272–78.

59. For the remittance of silver, see Mariana to the constable of Castile, January n.d., 1668, AHNSN Frías, caja 82, docs. 41 and 43. On Brandenburg, see above.

60. Mariana to Gamarra, February 26, 1668, AGS E. leg. 8400.

61. Rowen, *John de Witt*, 698. The episode is much better disentangled by Hayley, *English Diplomat*, 157–72. Also see Castel Rodrigo's report on the meeting with Temple, January 31; Mariana received it on February 21, 1668; AHN E. leg. 2797, núm. 57.

62. Abreu y Bertodano, "Tratado de Alianza entre Carlos II., Rey de la Gran Bretaña, y en[tre] los Estados Generales de las Provincias Unidas, para procurar la Paz entre los Reyes Catholico, y Christianissimo: Hecho en la Haya à 23 de Enero de 1668," in *Colección de los Tratados de Paz*, 1:275–85.

63. Abreu y Bertodano, "Artículos separados," in *Colección de los Tratados de Paz*, 1:285–89.

64. Rowen, *The Ambassador*, 24; AGS E. leg. 8400; and AHN E. leg. 2797, doc. 51.

65. Hayley, *English Diplomat*, 165, 183–211; and Rowen, *John de Witt*, 697, 700–702.

66. Molina to Mariana, March 25, 1668, AGS E. leg. 2542.

67. Mariana's instructions to Gamarra, March 1668, AGS E. leg. 8400; Abreu y Bertodano, "Tratado de Empeño entre el Señor Rey Catholico, D[on] Carlos II y los Estados Generales," April 9, 1668, in *Colección de los Tratados de Paz*, 1:325–39; Rowen, *John de Witt*, 684; and Hayley, *English Diplomat*, 195.

68. Mariana's instructions to Gamarra, March 1668, AGS E. leg. 8400; and Hayley, *English Diplomat*, 196.

69. Abreu y Bertodano, "Accession del Rey de Suecia al Tratado de Alianza ajustado en La Haya el dia 13/23 de enero de 1668. Entre el rey de la Gran Bretaña, y los Estados Generales, para promover la Paz entre las Coronas de España y Francia, en que al mismo tiempo se renuevan los antiguos Tratados de Paz, y Confederacion entre las mismas Potencias; firmada en Westminster a 25 de abril del mismo año," in *Colección de los Tratados de Paz*, 1:352–62. The original is in AHN E. leg. 2797, exp. 59. See also Hayley, *English Diplomat*, 192–93.

70. Treaty of Aix-la-Chapelle, AHN e. leg. 2797, docs. 63/64, 66/67; Usunáriz Garayoa, *España y sus tratados*, 430–31; Louis XIV quoted in Sonnino, *Mémoires for the Instruction of the Dauphin*, 260.

71. Carlos II, *Testamento de Carlos II*, 43–51. For a clear analysis of Carlos II's decision in his last testament, see Ribot García, *Orígenes*, particularly 100–110.

72. Ribot García, "La repercusión en España," 55–96; for the Treaty of Aix-la-Chapelle, see Usunáriz Garayoa, *España y sus tratados*, 428–33.

73. On the composition of the army of Flanders, recruitment and fiscal policies, and Galicia's demographic boon, see the

groundbreaking study by Rodríguez Hernández, *La Guerra de Devolución*, 262–75; also see
Storrs, *Resilience*, 20–21.

74. See above, Philip IV to Sor María of
Ágreda on the Peace with the Dutch in 1648.

75. Mariana's letters to Gamarra from 1666 to
1668 seldom failed to report on the Portuguese
issue; AGS E. legs. 8396–8400.

Chapter 4

1. See the Malladas incident in BNE ms.
8345, fols. 136v–168r.

2. Examples of male relatives fighting
queen mothers who acted as regents during
minorities include Ludovico Sforza and
Bona of Savoy—respectively, uncle and
mother of the Duke of Savoy, Gian Galeazzo
Sforza (r. 1476–94). The problem of male
relatives—particularly uncles—during royal
minorities in France has been abundantly
documented during the several regencies of
Catherine d'Medici and more so during the
late medieval period. The behavior of male
relatives became one of the most important
foundations for the justification of female
regents in the French monarchy; see, for
example, Crawford, *Perilous Performances*,
13–23; Adams, *Life and Afterlife*, 56–57;
Lightman, "Sons and Mothers," 26–29; and
Cosandey, "Sucesión, maternidad y legado,"
485–96.

3. The literature on favoritism is long;
for an essential institutional context and as a
European phenomenon, see Tomás y Valiente,
Validos, 62; Bérenger, "Ministériat au XVIIe
siècle," 166–92; and Elliott and Brockliss, *World
of the Favourite*. For the *valido* in Spain as the
manager of royal patronage, see Feros, *Kingship*. For the favorite as a prime minister with a
program for the monarchy, see Elliott, *Olivares*;
and Elliott, *Richelieu and Olivares*. More
recently, see Escudero, *Validos*. On Nithard, see
Kalnein, *Juan José*, 115–78; Sáenz Berceo, "Juan
Everardo Nithard," 326–44; and Kamen, *Spain*,
329. Tomás y Valiente has challenged Nithard's
role as *valido*, but his assessment has had little
effect on narratives of Mariana's regency. See
below.

4. On the children of Emperor Charles V,
John of Austria (1547–1578), and Margaret of
Parma (1522–1586) and their significance in
Philip II's reign, see Parker, *Grand Strategy*,
38–39; on Ana Dorothea's political function
(she was the daughter of Emperor Rudolph II)
at the Descalzas Reales, see Cruz Medina,
"Illegitimate Habsburg," 97–117. Also see
Trápaga Monchet, "La actividad de Don Juan
José de Austria," 101–5.

5. Trápaga Monchet, "La actividad de Don
Juan José de Austria," 101–5; and Franganillo,
"La reina Isabel," 460.

6. I would like to thank Koldo Trápaga
Monchet for clarifying this issue.

7. On Don Juan's recognition and prerogatives, see Trápaga Monchet, "La actividad
de Don Juan José of Austria," 105–6. On Don
Juan's daughter, who was a resident at the Descalzas Reales, see Cruz Medina, "Illegitimate
Habsburg," 98, fn. 3. Dr. Alejandra Franganillo
confirmed the point about Queen Isabel;
email communication, January 5, 2016. On the
significance of the grandees for the political
life of the monarchy, see Elliott, *Imperial Spain*,
114–15.

8. Kamen, *Spain*, 139; Kalnein, *Juan José*, 44;
Trápaga Monchet, "La actividad de Don Juan
José of Austria," 537; Pötting, *Diario*, 1:287; and
Philip IV, *Testamento*, clause 57, pp. 69–71.

9. On Don Juan's melancholy and political
aspirations, see Pötting, *Diario*, entries of late
1665 and early 1666; and Trápaga Monchet, "La
actividad de Don Juan José of Austria," 508.

10. Don Juan's whereabouts from 1665 to
1667 are abundantly documented in Nithard's
memoirs. See, for example, BNE ms. 8344,
fol. 73v; and Mariana's royal decree of May 24,
1666, in 151r–v, and 8345, 58r.

11. Don Juan's proposal is discussed in the
Council of State deliberation of October 26,
1667; for Don Juan's progress, see Council of
State deliberation of December 31, 1667, AGS
E. leg. 2540, and discussion above. Mariana's
subtle change can be observed in the Council
of State deliberations, June 21, July 9, and
August 9, 1667, AGS E. legs. 2382 and 2539.

12. BNE ms. 8345, fol. 67r; AGS E. leg. 8399,
8400; and Mariana's royal decree, February 7,
1668, AGS E. leg. 2540.

13. BNE ms. 8345, fol. 78r, 82v–85v; Abreu
y Bertodano, "Plenipotencia dada al Señor D.
Juan de Austria," in *Colección de los Tratados*

de Paz, 1:319; BNE ms. 8345; and Trápaga Monchet, "La actividad de Don Juan José of Austria," 512–19.

14. Constable of Castile papers, AHNSN Frías, caja 82, docs. 41 and 43; Don Juan to Cardinal Aragón, February 6, 1668, copy of letter in BNE ms. 8345, fol. 99r, and also see 136v–138v; and Council of State deliberations, January 3 to June 27, 1668, AGS E. leg. 8400; Council of State deliberation, May 13, 1668, AGS E. leg. 2687.

15. BNE ms. 8345, fol. 137v. During the War of Devolution, Louis XIV's armies were about seventy thousand strong; he added twenty thousand more by 1670 and continued building the force. See Lynn, *Wars of Louis XIV*, 111. Kalnein also makes the connection between the execution of Malladas and Mariana's purpose for retaliating against Don Juan; see Kalnein, *Juan José*, 115.

16. Elliott, *Olivares*, 94–95.

17. Mariana to Don Pedro Fernández del Campo, July 26, 1666, AGS E. leg. 2538; and anon., "Papeles y cartas," n.f. Maura also sees Castrillo's resignation as Mariana's doing; see Maura, *Carlos II*, 1:324–25.

18. On Riquelme's intervention—he began to sweep vagabonds from Madrid streets, cracked down on crime, and tried to clean up government corruption—see Maura, *Carlos II*, 1:328–29; and "Papeles y cartas," n.f.; BNE ms. 8345, fols. 138r–140r.

19. BNE ms. 8345, fols. 138r–169v; Maura, *Carlos II*, 1:340–41. There are many manuscripts in the Biblioteca Nacional, the Real Academia de la Historia, and the Archivo Histórico Nacional and in the papers of the nobility in the Archivo Histórico Nacional, Nobleza Section (in Toledo), that document the conflict between Nithard and Don Juan.

20. "Papeles y cartas," n.f., AHNSN Frías, caja 82, docs. 58, 59, 60. Mariana's circular letter, August 7, 1668, and decree ordering Don Juan to go and stay in Consuegra are in AGS E. leg. 8401.

21. She specifically stated that the constable's appointment was to last until the arrival of a person of royal blood; AHNSN Frías, caja 82, docs. 62 and 69. There were many circulating papers; see, for example, "Grandes y ruidosas controversias acaecidas en la menor edad

del Señor Carlos II, entre la Señora Reyna Madre Da Ana María Teresa de Austria, el Señor Don Juan de Austria, hijo del Señor Don Felipe IV y el Padre Juan Everardo: Sobre manejo y gobierno de estos reynos," BNE ms. 11158; "Carta en que se da cuenta de una Junta que han tenido los Padres de la Compañía de Jesus refieriendo todas las maximas y disposiciones que para la conservación del Sr. Inquisidor en su Govierno conferian ser necesarias con muchas noticias de sus ocultos dictamenes que aqui se manifiestan," BNE ms. 12053, fols. 88r–111v; "Menor edad de Carlos II (1er tomo), a Favor de don Juan," BNE ms. 18208; "Menor edad de Carlos II (2do tomo), a Favor de Nithard," BNE ms. 18209; and "Versos satíricos sobre la Reina Mariana de Austria, D. Juan José de Austria y el P[adre] Everardo Nithard," ms. 12967²¹. For the back-and-forth between Mariana and Don Juan, see BNE ms. 18655. For fears of popular revolt, see Kalnein, *Juan José*, 143–62. For the utilization of libel as a political weapon during Mariana's regency, see Hermant, *Guerres de plumes*.

22. The description of the procession is based on Pötting, *Diario*, 1:393–94. On the Habsburg tradition of devotion to the Virgin of Atocha, see Schrader, *Virgen de Atocha*, 17.

23. The man was a captain named Pedro Pinilla. The fact that he obtained access to the queen almost immediately means that the story was deemed trustworthy. Mariana received the man briefly before leaving the palace. I base my account on the manuscript "Papeles y cartas," n.f.

24. Ibid.; Maura, *Carlos II*, 1:364; and Kalnein, *Juan José*, 116.

25. Text of the letter taken from "Papeles y cartas," n.f. It is also reproduced by Vermeulen, *A cuantos leyeren esta carta*, 113–28.

26. "Grandes y ruidosas controversias," BNE ms. 11158. Peñaranda tried to avoid voting on the controversial measure, excusing himself from the meeting. When Don Blasco de Loyola, obviously on Mariana's orders, went to Peñaranda's house to collect his vote, he refused to give it; see Maura, *Carlos II*, 1:365; and "Papeles y cartas," n.f., BNE ms. 8345. The open letter from Don Juan to Mariana was signed from Consuegra 21 de Oct[ubr]e de 1668, "Su mas humilde criado y Vasallo de V[uestra]

M[agestad] Don Juan." Numerous copies of this letter are spread throughout various archives. For a comparison of the extant copies (with a full transcription), see Vermeulen, *A cuantos leyeren esta carta*, 113–28.

27. Copies of Don Juan's letters can be found, for example, in BNE ms. 18433, fols. 25r–28v, and ms. 18655 núms. 17, 20, 21, and 24. Many of Don Juan's letters are reproduced in Nithard's memoirs (BNE mss. 8344–52); also see "Papeles y cartas," n.f.; Consultation of Council of Castile, November 18, 1668, AHN Consejos leg. 7178.

28. "Papeles y cartas," n.f.; Council of State deliberation, January 28, 1669, AGS E. 2688.

29. Council of Castile, consultation of December 18, 1668, AHN Consejos leg. 7178; and Kalnein, *Juan José*, 121–34.

30. Council of Castile, consultation of December 19, 1668, AHN Consejos leg. 7178.

31. Nithard's memoirs, BNE mss. 8344–52; and drafts and original papers in BNE mss. 8353–64.

32. For the inherent problem of using confessors' writings to study queens or Habsburg women, see Sánchez, *Empress, the Queen, and the Nun*, 137–55; and Cruz Medina, "Illegitimate Habsburg," 98.

33. On the Jesuits' influence with the Austrian and Spanish Habsburgs, see Bireley, *Religion and Politics*; and Lozano Navarro, *La compañía*. On the political influence of confessors, see Callado Estela, "Luis Aliaga," 27–46; Callado Estela, "El Confesor Regio," 317–26; and Sánchez, *Empress, the Queen, and the Nun*, 21. The Dominicans commissioned the paper, "Dudas políticas" (Political doubts), a thirty-six-point disquisition against Nithard's holding several official political appointments. There are several copies of this paper in various archives in Spain—for example, AHNSN Osuna, caja 571, doc. 145. According to the imperial ambassador, it circulated widely in Madrid and foreign courts; Pötting, *Diario*, 1:264. The feud between Nithard and the Dominicans was surely fueled by the orders' dispute over the Dogma of the Immaculate Conception of Mary—the Dominicans were against it; the Jesuits were for it—with Nithard playing a major role in advancing their case. On the feud between the orders (including the

Franciscans), see Bowman's MA thesis, "The Church Divided."

34. Peñaranda's opinion, Council of State deliberation, October 2, 1671, AGS E. leg. 3113. The appointment was not official. Nithard was already in Italy serving as extraordinary ambassador; he simply replaced the ordinary ambassador, who had been delayed. Council of State deliberation, July 14, 1676, recounts one of Nithard's major blunders with the Portuguese ambassador in Rome, which had members of the council up in arms; AGS E. leg. 3052. For Nithard's performance as a replacement for the Marquis of Carpio from 1672 to 1676, see Barrio Gozalo, *Roma*, 40–44; Sáenz Berceo, "Juan Everardo Nithard," 342; and Maura, *Carlos II*, 1:210.

35. Nithard, "Voto del confesor de la Reyna sobre si su Magestad puede ceder el derecho al Reyno de Portugal," BNE ms. 22086(1); last draft with the Council of State deliberation of August 11, 1666, AGS E. leg. 2538. On his ineffectiveness, see Pötting, *Diario*, 1:238, fn. 384. On discontent, see ibid., 1:201, fn. 328. Nithard was the subject of multiple and lengthy conversations between the imperial ambassador and Medina de las Torres. Also see Lozano Navarro, *La compañía*, 320.

36. Nithard's vote recorded in the Council of State deliberation of May 18, 1667. (Cardinal Aragón also voted with Nithard against imposing new taxes on the poor. See the same deliberation.) Mariana to the Council of State, May 28, 1667, AGS E. leg. 3100; and "Voto del Inquisidor General Confesor dela Reyna N[uest]ra Señora que Dios g[uar]de. sobre si es licito hacer su Magd liga ofensiva con el Rey de Inglaterra hereje, contra el Rey de Francia, Principe Catolico. Pone en las Reales manos de V[uestra] M[agestad] su voto y el de los demas theologos que intervieneron en la Junta que se tuvo en su posada sobre hacer liga con Inglaterra," BNE ms. 22086(2). On Nithard's proposed tax reforms, see Sánchez Belén, "Mirando hacia adelante," 167; Matilla Tascón, *La única contribución*, 22; and Kalnein, *Juan José*, 120–21. Nithard's testament indicates that he did not accumulate substantial wealth. The only major object he received from Mariana was a "golden crucifix decorated with numerous and valuable diamonds," which he

bequeathed to the Jesuits; see AHN Clero-Jesuits leg. 263.

37. On Medina de las Torres's influence, see Valladares, *Rebelión de Portugal*, 205; and Stradling, "Spanish Statesman," 9–10, 18, 29–30. On Peñaranda's role with England, see Council of State deliberations, AGS E (Estado England) legs. 2535–46. The deliberations during the summer of 1667 are also key to understanding the decision-making process. See chapter 3.

38. Tomás y Valiente, *Validos*, 71–72.

39. See Nithard's response in "Papeles y cartas," n.f., and a second one in BNE ms. 8346, fols. 276v–297r; and Escudero, *Administración y estado*, 615–19.

40. On rumors of Louis XIV's support of Don Juan, see Gerónimo de Quiñones to Don Pedro Fernández del Campo, December 9, 1669, AGS EK leg. 1395. Spaniards took advantage of the disorder in France during the Wars of Religion in the second half of the sixteenth century and the series of civil wars known as the Fronde (1648–52); Philip IV supported, for example, the Prince of Condé, one of the frondeurs.

41. On the handling of the pope's request, see Council of Italy deliberation, January 30, 1669, AGS E. leg. 3043; and Council of State deliberations, November 26, 1668, and January 31, 1669, respectively, in AGS E. legs. 2687 and 2688. Also see BNE ms. 11158, fol. 217r.

42. Council of Italy deliberation, January 30, 1669, AGS E. leg. 3043; Gerónimo de Quiñones to Mariana, December 9, 1668, AGS EK, leg. 1395; deliberation of the Council of State, January 12, 1668, AGS EK leg. 1396; and viceroy of Navarre, Duke of San Germán, to Mariana, January 23, 1669, AGS E. leg. 2688.

43. Decree written by the queen regent, addressed to the secretary of state, Don Pedro Fernández del Campo, reprinted in Tomás y Valiente, *Validos*, appendix 11, 176–77.

44. Maura, *Carlos II*, 2:8–9; and Council of Castile deliberation, April 6, 1669, AHN Consejos, leg. 7179; Peñaranda's letter to Don Juan, quoted in Maura, *Carlos II*, 1:386. I have drawn my own conclusions. On the demands about fiscal reforms, see Sánchez Belén, "La junta de alivios," 642, RAH ms. 9/3746.

45. Mariana to the Council of Castile, March 7, 1669, and June 8, 1669, AHN Consejos leg. 7179.

46. Royal decree, June 21, 1669, APR Adm. leg. 928; and "Cédula de Mariana de Austria aprobando la escritura de fundación de dos cátedras de Teología en la Universidad de Alcalá de Henares," AGS PTR leg. 39, doc. 107.

47. Aytona to Mariana, August 23, 1669, ADM Hist. leg. 68; and Álvarez-Ossorio Alvariño, "Las guardias reales," 1:439–46.

48. Álvarez-Ossorio Alvariño, "Las guardias reales," 1:449–50; and Mesa Gallego, "Itinerario biográfico," 74.

49. Council of Castile deliberation with Aytona's point-by-point rebuttal written for Mariana, ADM Hist. leg. 68; Mariana to the Council of Castile, April 6, 1669, AHN Consejos leg. 7179; RAH ms. 9/3746; and Mesa Gallego, "Itinerario biográfico," 75. The idea of using the guard to teach Carlos and inspire his love of martial arts was based on Juan de Mariana's tract *De Rege et Regis Institutione*, published in 1599; see Álvarez-Ossorio Alvariño, "Las guardias reales," 1:439.

50. Mesa Gallego, "Itinerario biográfico," 74; and Aytona to Mariana, August 23, 1669. The mathematics teacher had been brought from the Low Countries by the Marquis of Caraçena. The man asked for permission to return to his native lands, but Mariana denied the request; see ADM Hist. leg. 68. Numerous requests for employment can also be found among Aytona's papers.

51. Aytona's contributions are beginning to be noted, but his centrality in Mariana's regime has not been established until now. See, for example, the important study of Aytona's military treatise recently transcribed and edited with a preliminary biographical study: Mesa Gallego, "Itinerario biográfico," 41–76.

52. Aytona's memorandum on foreign policy, February 2, 1666. On fortifications, see Aytona to Mariana, January 30, 1666. On children's education, a project that Mariana wanted to implement, see Mariana to Aytona, n.d., 1667. On recruitment, see Aytona to Mariana, November 17 and 24, 1667; December 10, 17, 23, and 29, 1667; January 19, 1667; February 3 and 4, 1667; March 18, 1667; and May 19, 1668. On

the Council of War, Aytona provided Mariana with a profile of its members in 1668 (n.d.). On a commercial company with naval protection (*comercio armado*), see Aytona to Mariana, March 25, 1668, ADM Hist. leg. 70. Ramos del Manzano was appointed on June 5, 1667; see APR Personal, caja 867, exp. 33.

53. On Mariana's affinity with Magdalena de Moncada, see DBE Tomo 35:528; Malcolm, "Práctica informal," 38–48; Martínez Hernández, *Escribir*, 149. Aytona to Mariana, August 23, 1669, ADM Hist. leg. 68.

54. ADM Hist. leg. 68; and Mesa Gallego, "Itinerario biográfico," 76.

55. AHNSN Frías, caja 82, docs. 41–70; and Barbeito, *El Alcázar*, 177–89.

56. Estenaga y Echevarría, *Cardenal Aragón*. The executive command of the *coronelía* remained intact until it was reduced to the condition of an ordinary *tercio* in 1677.

57. Mariana's royal decree, October 18, 1669, AHN Consejos leg. 7179; and Estela, "Mecenazgo de los Marqueses de Mejorada," 472–74.

58. On Mariana's meetings with Villaumbrosa after Carlos II came of age, see Villaumbrosa to Mariana, December 11, 1675, Mariana, AGS E. leg. 8817. On the traditional Friday meeting between the king and the president of the Council of Castile, see Elliott, *Olivares*, 94–95.

59. On Mariana's regency portraits, see Llorente, "Imagen," 217–18. On Carlos II's increasing participation in court ceremonies, see Pötting, *Diario*, 1:46; and Mitchell, "Growing Up," 195–97. On the ambassadors, see Barozzi and Berchet, *Relazioni*, 339, 377, and 397. On the portraits of Mariana and Carlos during the minority and regency, see López Vizcaíno and Carreño, *Juan Carreño de Miranda*, 282–301, 320–37; and Philip IV, *Testamento*, clause 34, pp. 50–51.

60. Ramos del Manzano, *Reynados de menor edad*.

61. González de Salcedo, *Nudrición Real*, n.p.

Chapter 5

1. The collections from the Archivo de Simancas labeled Estado España, Estado Inglaterra, Estado Alemania, and Estado Negociaciones del Norte, which include

deliberations of the Council of State and diplomatic correspondence, are the main sources used in this chapter. Also important are the diplomatic instructions in the Archivo Histórico Nacional. These will be cited individually in what follows. Mariana's intervention in foreign policy ends on November 6, 1675, Carlos II's fourteenth birthday.

2. San Germán to Mariana, January 23, 1669; Osuna to Mariana, February 3, 1669, AGS E. leg. 2688; and Ochoa Brun, *Diplomacia española*, 97.

3. Mariana to Gamarra, June 21, 1669, AGS E. leg. 2540. On Savoy's place in the succession, see Philip IV, *Testamento*, clause 14, pp. 22–23.

4. Mariana learned of the Partition Treaty through her ambassador in The Hague, Esteban Gamarra. See Mariana to Gamarra, May 18, 1669, AGS E. leg. 2540; and Council of State deliberation, January 28, 1670, AGS E. leg. 2386. On the Partition Treaty of 1668, see Bérenger, "Attempted Rapprochement," 137; the text reproduced in Ribot García and Iñurritegi, eds., *Tratados de reparto*, 291–300; and Ribot García, "La repercusión en España," 79–85.

5. San Germán to Mariana, January 23, 1669; and Osuna to Mariana, February 3, 1669, AGS E. leg. 2688. Similar information came from Fuenterrabía, Rosellón, Barcelona, Gerona, Cerdaña, and Oran.

6. San Germán to Mariana, dispatches from January, March, and April, 1669; Osuna to Mariana, January 19, May 4, 1669; "Noticias que se han tenido por la parte de Gerona de Persona confidente en Perpiñan," AGS E. legs. 2688 and 2689; Mariana to the Duke of Alcalá, governor of Cadiz, February 1670; and Mariana to the governors of Guipúzcoa, Vizcaya, Quatro Villas, Asturias, Galicia, Duque de Alcalá, Melilla, San Miguel Ultramar, Larache, Gibraltar, Malaga, Oran, Ceuta, Cartagena, Valencia, Ibiza, Catalunia, Mallorca, San Felipe, Cerdeña, Canarias, and Marques de Santillana, March 15, 1670, AGS E. leg. 2690. See, for example, Juan Garces, an official from the island of Menorca, to Don Diego de las Torres, Mariana's secretary, requesting additional instructions, July 1670, AGS E. leg. 2691.

7. Marquis de la Fuente, Council of State deliberation, January 24, 1669, AGS E. leg. 2688; Mariana to Gamarra, August 7

and November 15, 1668, with copies of the instructions to Molina and the constable, AGS E. leg. 2540; Lonchay, *Correspondance,* 5:59, 68; Mariana to the constable, December n.d., 1668, AGS E. leg. 8401; Mariana to Gamarra, November 15, 1668, AGS E. leg. 2540; Mariana to the constable, January 10, 1669; Mariana to Gamarra, January 31, 1669, AGS E. leg. 8402; and Molina to Mariana, February 10, 1671, AGS E. leg. 2545. On inclusion of empire, Brandenburg, and "German princes," see also Westergaard, *First Triple Alliance,* lxii–lxiii; Mariana's instructions to the Count of Fernán Núñez, extraordinary ambassador to Stockholm, 1669, and ciphered instructions, March 2, 1672, AHN E. leg. 3455, exp. 1; Mariana's instructions to Baltasar de la Fuente, extraordinary ambassador to Copenhagen, March 8, 1674, AHN E. leg. 3457; the agreement on the subsidies in AHN E. leg. 2797, doc. 61, September 18, 1668; and Lonchay, *Correspondance,* 5:61.

8. Silver shipments in Sanz Ayán, *Banqueros,* 227; requests to Naples in Council of State deliberation, August 29, 1669, AGS E. leg. 2689. On fortifications, see Osuna's report for Mariana, February 1670, AGS E. leg. 2690; and Sánchez Belén, *Política fiscal,* 287.

9. Mariana received a good amount of jewelry as her own property and could dispose of it as she wanted; see Mariana's marriage capitulations, AGS PTR leg. 56, doc. 52, fol. 322v. On the shipment of the jewels, see constable to Don Pedro Fernández del Campo, November 25, 1668; and constable to Admiral Bartolome de Roys, November 25, 1668, AGS E. leg. 2688. Jewels are mentioned again in a Council of State deliberation, March 13, 1670, AGS E. leg. 2544. On the loans, see Sanz Ayán, *Banqueros,* 237–42; and "Relación delo que el Proveedor de la Armada Pedro del Vaus y Frias ha hecho en Amberes siendo embiado a ablar de orden del ex[celentísi]mo Señor Condestable de Castilla y de Leon a los hombres de negocios sobre quienes vinieron las letras para el apresto de los navios de Armada que estan en Flanders," Brussels, April 24, 1669, AGS E. leg. 2688. On Spain's improved financial situation relative to Philip IV's reign and before the 1680–86 fiscal reforms, see Sánchez Belén, *Política fiscal,* xii (on the deficit, 323). On

the general economic history of the reign, see Kamen, *La España,* 466–70; and Abreu y Bertodano, "Asiento octavo para la introduccion, y provision de Esclavos negros en las Indias," in *Colección de los Tratados de Paz,* 2:127–39, 217–37.

10. On the Low Countries, see Mariana to Council of State, December 30, 1668, AGS E. leg. 2687; and Storrs, *Resilience,* 20–21. On the Basque area, see Council of State deliberation, June 12, 1669, AGS E. leg. 2688. On Catalunia, see Mariana's royal decree, February 3, 1669; Osuna to Mariana, February 24, 1669; Council of State deliberation, March 3, 1669; Mariana's response, March 13, 1669, AGS E. leg. 2688; and "R[elaci]on de las art[iller]ia de Bronze y fierro[,] armas de Infant[er]ia y cav[aller]ia[,] Municiones y otros Pertrechos de Guerra que en prim[ero] de Diz[iembre] de este año de 1669 se alla en ser en la Plaza de Barz[elon]a y lo que debe haver en las demas de este Princip[a]do fronteras de Aragon y Valencia," AGS E. leg. 2690. On the tercios in Catalunia, see Osuna to Mariana, December 8, 1669; and Council of State deliberation, February, 7, 1670, AGS E. leg. 2690. On Navarre, see Mariana to Council of State, October 21 and November 3, 1669, AGS E. leg. 2689.

11. On Sardinia, see Revilla Canora, "El asesinato," 581; and AGS E. leg. 2687. On Mediterranean strategies in general, see Sánchez Belén, "Relaciones internacionales," 166–67. On the expulsion of the Jews of Oran, see Marques del Viso, a Spanish official in Oran, to Mariana, March 25, 1669, AGS E. leg. 2688; Sánchez Belén, "Expulsion de los judíos," 155–98; and Israel, "Jews of Spanish Oran," 235–55. On Ceuta's return to Spain, see "Treaty of Lisbon," in Usunáriz Garayoa, *España y sus tratados,* 416–17.

12. On confiscation of the ship *Unicorn* from the Dutch as well as arrests of Dutch smugglers, see Mariana to the Council of State, February 14, 1670, and Mariana to the Duke of Alcalá, February 16, 1670, AGS E. leg. 2690; and Hieronymus van Beverningk, Dutch ambassador in Madrid, to Mariana, July 8, 1671, AGS E. 2693. On the punishment for the counterfeiting act, see Mariana's royal decree, February 22, 1671, AGS E. leg. 2692; and

Mariana to the Council of State, October 22, 1672, AGS E. leg. 4128.

13. Mariana to Esteban Gamarra, February 19, 1669; Gamarra to Mariana, March 6 and 8, 1669; Mariana to the constable, January 10 and June 28, 1669, AGS E. leg. 8402; and Abreu y Bertodano, "Acto en que, en consequencia de la Garantia estipulada entre los Reyes de Inglaterra, y Suecia, y los Estados Generales de las Provincias Unidas, se especifican los socorros que se han de dar a S. M. Catholica por cada una de las tres referidas Potencias," and "Acto . . . entre los Reyes de Inglaterra, y Suecia, y los Estados Generales de las Provincias Unidas," in *Colección de los Tratados de Paz*, 1:415–19. On the subsidies and the ratification of the Triple Alliance as the League of Guarantee, see Pribram, *Franz Paul, Freiherr von Lisola*, 459–61; and Westergaard, *First Triple Alliance*, lxv.

14. Bishop of Bernis, France's extraordinary ambassador to Madrid, to Mariana, n.d.; and Monsieur Dupré, French envoy to Madrid, to Mariana, April 11, 1670, AGS E. leg. 2690. All of these communications went through the Marquis de la Fuente, who consulted Mariana personally on these matters. See Marquis de la Fuente to Diego de la Torre, April 23, 1670, AGS E. leg. 2690; and Mariana to the Duke of Osuna, November n.d., 1669, AGS E. leg. 2689.

15. These territories under dispute were the Fort of Linquer, the Village of Condé, and several towns in Nieuwpoort. On the back-and-forth over the mediation, see Don Marcos Alberto de Oñate to Mariana, February 7, 1670, AGS E. leg. 2544.

16. On the French point of view, see Sonnino, *Origins of the Dutch War*, 113–15. On England's point of view, see Hutton, "Making of the Secret Treaty of Dover," 297–318; and Lee, "Earl of Arlington and the Treaty of Dover," 58–70.

17. The course of the negotiations with Charles II can be elucidated from Mariana's instructions to Molina, June 1670, AGS E. leg. 2544, and Council of State deliberation of June 3, 1670, AGS E. leg. 2690, which served the basis for the instructions. Also see "Copia autentica en Frances y en Latin de la ratificacion hecha por parte del Rey de Inglaterra del acto de las fuerzas con que provisionalmente

han de asistir los de la triple alianza su f[ec]ha en Westminster a 7 de marzo de 1670," AHN E. leg. 2804, exp. 9; Marcos Alberto de Oñate, temporarily in charge of the embassy in London, to Mariana, February 7, 1670, AGS E. leg. 2544; and Abreu y Bertodano, "Tratado entre las Coronas de España, y de la Gran Bretañ, para restablecer la Amistad, y buena correspondencia en America: Ajustado en Madrid a 18 de Julio de 1670," in *Colección de los Tratados de Paz*, 1:498–513, and AHN E. leg. 2804, exp. 16.

18. Council of State deliberations, March 3, 1671, AGS E. leg. 2545, and June 5, 1671, AGS E. leg. 2692. On retaliations, see Mariana's royal decree, April 1671, AGS E. leg. 2692. Her orders were based on consultations from the Council of War, Indies, and State: Council of War deliberation discussed in State, July 1671, AGS E. leg. 2693. Medinaceli was granted the highest position in the king's household (see below) and eventually rose to the position of prime minister.

19. On the mending of the situation, see Manuel de Belfonte to Mariana, July 1671, AHN E. leg. 721; and Mariana to Godolphin (via Peñaranda), Council of State deliberation, November n.d., 1671, AGS E. leg. 2693. For the events in Panama and Portobelo and the punishments of the pirates, see Earle, *Sack of Panamá*, 236–45.

20. Molina to Mariana, April 9 and October 16 and 22, 1671, AGS E. legs. 2545 and 2546.

21. On Dutch ambivalence, see Herrero Sánchez, *Acercamiento Hispano-Neerlandés*, 192; Troost, *William III*, 71; Mariana's instructions to Manuel de Lira, AHN E. leg. 3456; "Minuta de ratificacion del Acto de Asistencias y socorros reciprocos ajustado con la Holanda, 20 de enero de 1672 en Madrid," AHN E. leg. 2804, exp. 21; and Abreu y Bertodano, "Acto, por el qual D. Manuel Francisco de Lira, Embiado Extraordinario de S. M. Catholica a Los Estados Generales, declara, y promete en Su Real nombre socorrerlos con todas las Tropas, y medios posibles siempre que sean invadidos" and "Acto Reciproco de los Diputados de los Estados Generales, en que ademas de las garantias estipuladas para la Paz de Aquisgran, prometen en nombre de S. A. P. socorrer a S. M. Catholica con todas las Tropas, y medios

posibles, en caso de ser acometido por la Francia en algunos de sus Paises, or plazas," in *Colección de los Tratados de Paz*, 1:557–60.

22. Pötting to Mariana, February 23, 1672; Mariana to Villars, the French ambassador in Madrid, Council of State deliberation, March 3, 1672; Mariana to the Marquis of Balbases, Spanish ambassador in Vienna; and Mariana to Leopold I, March 3, 1672, AGS E. leg. 2389.

23. Marquis of Fresno, current Spanish ambassador in London, to Mariana's secretary, Diego de la Torre, April 12, 1672, AGS E. leg. 2547. Peñaranda crafted Mariana's response for Godolphin; see Council of State deliberation, February 5, 1672, AGS E. leg. 2547.

24. On the beginning of the Dutch War, see Troost, *William III*, 71; Sonnino, *Origins of the Dutch War*, 192; and Ekberg, *Failure of the Dutch War*, 13. On the Spanish response, see Herrero Sánchez, *Acercamiento Hispano-Neerlandés*, 191–92. On the Partition Treaty of 1668, see Bérenger, "Attempted Rapprochement." Spielman argued that Leopold I never ratified it (Spielman, *Leopold I*, 56), but new archival evidence proves that he did: the copy is transcribed in Ribot García and Iñurritegi, eds., *Tratados de reparto*, 291–300, and had been ratified by Leopold in Vienna on February 28, 1668. See Council of State deliberation, January 28, 1670, AGS E. leg. 2386; Spielman, *Leopold I*, 57; and Balbasses to Mariana, March 23, 1672 (arrived April 11, 1672), AGS E. leg. 2389. On Balbases, see Ochoa Brun, *Diplomacia española*, 98–99.

25. Council of State deliberation, April 20, 1672, AGS E. leg. 2389. On Leopold I's neutrality agreement with France, November 1, 1671, see Usunáriz Garayoa, *España y sus tratados*, 437; Pötting to Mariana, July 4, 1672; and Council of State deliberation, July 9, 1672, AGS E. leg. 2390.

26. Spielman, *Leopold I*, 59–60; Council of State deliberation, July 9, 1672, AGS E. leg. 2390; "Liga entre el Emperador y el Elector de Brandemburg 23 de junio 1672," AHN E. leg. 2804, exp. 22; and Usunáriz Garayoa, *España y sus tratados*, 437. On the effect of Spanish subsidies on Leopold I's foreign policy, see Spielman, *Leopold I*, 59–60. On the increase of silver remittances from the New World and

loans, see Sanz Ayán, *Banqueros*, 227, 237–42, and table XIII, 491.

27. Villars to de la Fuente, August 19, 1672; de la Fuente's opinion, Council of State deliberation, August 23, 1672; and Mariana to the Council of State, August 23, 1672, AGS E. leg. 2390.

28. Mariana to the Council of State, October 18, 1672, AGS E. leg. 2390; and Israel, *Dutch Republic*, 796–824.

29. Mariana to Lira, January 19, February 19, 1673, AGS E. leg. 8409; Troost, *William III*, 71–93; Herrero Sánchez, *Acercamiento Hispano-Neerlandés*, 177–80, 192; and Israel, *Dutch Republic*, 802–3, 807–12. On Charleroy and French protests about Spain's intervention, see Fresno to Mariana, March 13, 1673, AGS E. leg. 2549.

30. Pötting, *Diario*, 2:338–39; Council of State deliberation, April 16, 1673, AHN E. leg. 2661, exps. 253–57; Council of State deliberation, April 18, 1673, AGS E. leg. 2391; Mariana's instructions to the Marques of Povar, May 13, 1673, AHN E. leg. 2661; and instructions to Don Pedro Ronquillo, June 10, 1673, AHN E. leg. 1632.

31. See particularly the Duke of Alburquerque's opinion, Council of State deliberation, April 18, 1673; and Mariana to the Council of State, AGS E. leg. 2391. On the reaction to Brandenburg's withdrawal, see Pötting, *Diario*, 2:343.

32. Mariana's instructions for Povar, May 13, 1673, AHN E. leg. 2661. For Ronquillo, see June 10, 1673, AHN E. leg. 1632; and Council of State deliberation, April 18, 1673, AGS E. leg. 2391.

33. Spielman, *Leopold I*, 72–73. On Lorrain's conflict with Louis XIV preceding the invasion, see Council of State deliberation, February 3, 1669, AGS E. leg. 2688; and Ronquillo to Mariana, August 9, 1673, AGS E. leg. 2392.

34. "Copia autentica del tratado de Alianza ajustado entre el Emperador y el Duque de Lorena y los Estados generales en la Haya, 1 de Julio 1673"; "Minuta de su ratificacion por el rey nuestro señor en Madrid a 1 de Agosto 1673 y copia del articulo separado secreto concerniente a los 15 [mil] talleres ajustados entre los S[eño]res Heusquerque y Brunink

en Viena a 1 de Agosto 1673"; and "Copia del
projecto de nueva confederacion entre S[u]
M[agestad] Ces[area] y los Estados generales y
dentro copia de los articulos secretos," AHN E.
leg. 2804, exps. 24 and 25; Abreu y Bertodano,
"Tratado de Alianza ofensiva y defensiva entre
el Emperador Lepoldo y el Señor Catholico
D. Carlos II . . ."; "Tratado de Alianza ofensiva,
y defensiva entre el Señor Rey Catholico
D. Carlos II y los Estados Generales de las
Provincias Unidas . . ."; "Tratado de Alianza
entre el Emperador Leopoldo y los Estados
Generales . . ."; and "Tratado de Alianza ofensiva y defensiva entre sus majestades Imperial
y Catholica, los Estados Generales, y el Duque
de Lorena . . . ," in *Colección de los Tratados
de Paz*, 1:592–601, 603–18, 624–36; Herrero
Sánchez, *Acercamiento Hispano-Neerlandés*,
195; and "Traduccion de projecto de Tratado
de Lorena con el S[eño]r Emperador, España,
Holanda, y Brandembourgh en la Haya a 19
de Febrero 1673," AGS E. leg. 8409.

35. For Mariana's war declaration and a
separate document prohibiting commerce,
see December 11, 1673, AGS E. leg. 2735. For a
longer, printed version, see Abreu y Bertodano,
"Declaración de Guerra de la Serenissima
Reyna Gobernadora de España contra los
Estados, Dominios, y Vasallos de la Francia, en
que refiriendo individualmente las infracciones
hechas por esta Corona a los Tratados de los
Pyrineos y Aguisgrán, prohibe, pena de la vida,
todo trato, y comercio con ella," in *Colección de
los Tratados de Paz*, 1:650–69.

36. Abreu y Bertodano, "Declaración
de Guerra de la Serenissima Reyna Gobernadora de España," in *Colección de los Tratados
de Paz*, 1:650–51.

37. Ibid., 1:652.

38. "Minuta de cartas," AGS E. leg. 2697; Lira
to Mariana, February 5, 1674; and Mariana to
Lira, February 14, March 19, March 27, April 10,
April 30, July 24, September 4, October 24, and
December 14, 1674, AGS E. leg. 8410.

39. Abreu y Bertodano, "Tratado de Alianza
entre el Señor Rey Catholico D. Carlos II y
el Elector de Saxonia, en que se estipulan los
socorros se se han de dar para defenderse
reciprocamente en caso de invasion:
Hecho en la ciudad de Egra a 25 de Agosto
de 1673"; "Tratado de Alianza entre sus

Magestades Imperial, y Catholica, y el Elector
de Treveris . . ."; and "Plenipotencias . . . al
Marques de los Balbasses," in *Colección de los
Tratados de Paz*, 1:587–91, 644–49, 2:43–45.

40. On Brandenburg's temporary defeat to
the French side and return to the opposite side,
see Ekberg, *Failure of the Dutch War*, xviii–xix;
Abreu y Bertodano, "Tratado de Alianza defensiva entre el Emperador Leopoldo,
S. M. Catholica, los Estados Generales, y los
Duques de Brunswick and Luneburg . . .";
"Tratado de Alianza defensiva, ajustado por
diez años entre el Emperador Leopoldo, S. M.
Catholica, los Estados Generales de las Provincias Unidas, y el Obispo de Osnabrug, Duque
de Brunswick, y Luneburg"; "Tratado . . . entre
el Señor Rey Catholico, los Estados Generales,
y el Obispo de Munster . . . en caso de ser invadidos"; and "Tratado . . . de mutua asistencia
entre el Señor Rey Catholico D. Carlos II, y los
Estados Generales de las Provincias Unidas, de
un parte; y Phelipe Guillermo, Conde Palatino
de Rhin, y Duque de Neuburg, de otra, con el
fin de restablecer la quietud pública," in *Colección de los Tratados de Paz*, 2:45–66, 123–27,
140–60, 183–92, 237–44 (treaty with Münster,
October 20, 1675, and with the elector palatine,
March 26, 1676); Marques de los Balbasses to
the emperor (copy), June 2 and 15, 1673; Mariana to the Council of State, September 10, 1673,
AGS E. leg. 2392; Sánchez Belén, "Relaciones
internacionales," 161; Storrs, *Resilience*, 25; and
Lynn, *Wars of Louis XIV*, 111.

41. Castel Rodrigo in Council of State delib-
eration, October 11, 1672, AGS E. leg. 2390;
Mariana's instructions to Conde de Fernán
Núñez, ambassador to Sweden, March 2, 1672,
AHNSN Fernán Núñez, caja 418, doc. 52; and
Mariana's instructions to Baltasar de la Fuente,
ambassador to Denmark, March 8, 1674, AHN
E. leg. 3457. On Sweden's switch to the French
side, see Hatton, "Louis XIV and His Fellow
Monarchs," 36; Ekberg, *Failure of the Dutch
War*, 77; and Abreu y Bertodano, "Tratado
de Alianza defensiva entre S[u] M[agestad]
Imperial, S[u] M[agestad] Catholica, el Rey
de Dinamarca, y los Estados Generales, A
fin de restablecer la paz, y quietud pública:
Ajustado en La Haya a 10 de Julio de 1674," in
Colección de los Tratados de Paz, 2:83–100. For
an excellent example of how the prince of a

small state at the head of a well-trained and substantial army could shape the course of war and diplomacy, see Helfferich, *Iron Princess*, which discusses the role of Amalia Elisabeth of Hesse-Cassel, who found herself at the head of an army during the Thirty Years' War.

42. Council of State deliberation, June 8, 1672; see, particularly, Cardinal Aragón's opinion; Mariana to the Council of State, August 5, 1672, AGS E. leg. 2547. On the beginning of the two wars, see Troost, *William III*, 71; and Sonnino, *Origins of the Dutch War*, 192. On the Spanish response, see Herrero Sánchez, *Acercamiento Hispano-Neerlandés*, 191–92. On England's anxiety about potential sanctions, see Arlington to Fresno, April 30, 1672, AGS E. leg. 2547; and Fresno to Mariana, October 9, 1673, AGS E. leg. 2549. On the Cologne conference and Sweden's interest in the settlement, see Ekberg, *Failure of the Dutch War*, 77–79. Mariana sent Lira as Spain's representative in Cologne; see her instructions drafted January 16, 1674, AGS E. leg. 8410.

43. Fresno to Mariana, October 9, 1673; Peñaranda's conference with Godolphin, reported to Mariana on December 11, 1673, AGS E. leg. 2549; Mariana's instructions to Fresno, December 20, 1673, AGS E. leg. 8420; and Mariana to Fresno, December 28, 1673, AGS E. 2550. On Spain and the United Provinces agreement, see "Artículo secreto que firmaron don Manuel de Lira y los Ministros de Holanda," AHN E. leg. 2804, exp. 25; and Abreu y Bertodano, "Tratado de Paz y Amistad entre el Sereníssimo Rey de la Gran Bretaña, y los Estados Generales de las Provincias Unidas, ajustado por mediacion de la Sereníssima Señora Reyna Gobernadora de España en Westminster a 9/19 de Febrero de 1673/4 con un Articulo Secreto, por el qual se obligan las Partes Contratantes a no dar ningun Socorro de Navios, dinero, o apresos Militares a sus respectivos Enemigos, ajustado el mismo dia, y año," in *Colección de los Tratados de Paz*, 1:618–22, 2:17–38.

44. On the implications of signing a separate peace, see Arlington to Fresno, March 5, 1674; Council of State deliberation, March 31, 1674; copies of treaties between England and the United Provinces; Mariana to the Council of State, March 31, 1674; Charles II to Mariana,

February 23, 1674, where he called her "guarantor and judge"; Arlington to Fresno, March 5, 1674; Council of State deliberation, March 5, 1674, AGS E. leg. 2550; and Mariana to the Marquis of Fresno, December 20, 1673, AGS E. leg. 8409.

45. On negotiations to get the Dutch to help in Messina, see Lira to Mariana, October 20, 1674. The armada was ready to be deployed to the Mediterranean in July 1675; AHN E. leg. 721.

46. On theater, see Campbell, *Theater of Negotiation*, 60, 146; Sanz Ayán, *Pedagogía de reyes*, 24; and Maura, *Carlos II*, 2:220–21. On building projects, see Barbeito, *El Alcázar*, 176–77. On Royal vacations, see APR Jornadas Administrativa, legs. 779 and 780. The Duke of Alburquerque, as *mayordomo mayor*, presented the budget to Mariana on November 26, 1674, she approved it November 30, and work started on December 1, 1674. The city of Madrid granted the subsidies to pay for the major expenses; see APR RCII, caja 92, exp. 2; CODOIN, 67:7.

47. On Valenzuela's trajectory, see Maura, *Carlos II*, 2:170–81; and AHNSN Osuna, caja 2026, doc. 24 (1). On Maria de Ucedo and her marriage to Valenzuela (July 24, 1661), see APR Personal, caja 1049, exp. 6.

48. Maura, *Carlos II*, 2:170–81; and AHNSN Osuna, caja 2026, doc. 24 (1).

49. *Relaciones* were similar to gazettes, an early form of journalism, produced and distributed by professional copyists. "Menor edad de Carlos II," CODOIN, 67:8. On the duties of palace mayors related to theatrical productions, see Sanz Ayán, *Pedagogía de reyes*, 41 and 52. On the court's transformation, see Kamen, *La España*, 534.

50. Anonymous arbitrista's paper published in late 1675, AHN E. leg. 912, fols. 106–12; and Medellín to Cardinal Aragón, November 1675, BNE ms. 2043, fol. 48r.

51. Barbeito, *El Alcázar*, 177–79, 183. The statue, cast by the Italian sculptor Pietro Tacca, is now in the Plaza del Oriente, in the space between the Palacio Real and the Opera House in Madrid.

52. "Menor edad de Carlos II," CODOIN, 67:8–9; and unknown writer to Pedro de Aragón (Cardinal Aragón's brother), November 1675, BNE ms. 2043, fol. 43r. The offices he

received before the end of the minority were Conservador del Consejo de Italia, Marques de Villasierra, Alcalde del Pardo, Superintendente de la Obras Reales de Palacio and Caballerizo Mayor of the Queen's Household; AHNSN Osuna, caja 2026, doc. 24 (1).

53. Pötting made a cryptic comment in his diary about a conversation he had with Mariana's *camarera mayor*, the Marquise of Baldueza, about the queen purposely postponing the formation of the king's household; Pötting, *Diario*, 2:349. See order dispatched by the contralor (comptroller), Don Francisco Mançano, April 16, 1675, and etiquette for Carlos II's household, APR RCII, caja 92, exps. 2 and 3.

54. APR RCII, caja 92, exp. 2; Medinaceli, APR Personal, caja 319, exp. 21; Maura, *Carlos II*, 2:210–12; and Kalnein, *Juan José*, 357.

55. They amount to nearly six hundred folio pages. BNE ms. 2043.

56. BNE ms. 2043, fol. 42r. On his appointment as the king's teacher on June 4, 1667, see APR Personal, caja 867, exp. 33.

57. BNE ms. 2043, fol. 32r.

58. Abreu y Bertodano, "Manifiesto de la Ciudad de Messina," in *Colección de los Tratados de Paz*, 2:100–104. On the Messina revolt, see Ribot García, *La revuelta antiespañola*; and Ribot García, *La monarquía de España y la Guerra de Mesina*; Mariana's orders to deal with the revolt, June 1674, AGS E. leg. 2698; and Council of State deliberation, July 1674, August 31, and October 19, 1674, AGS E. leg. 2699. On the impact of the revolt on the ongoing war with France, see Pötting to Castel Rodrigo, January 24, 1675, AHN E. leg. 1441; and Abreu y Bertodano, "Manifiesto del Rey de Francia, en que expressa los motivos que tuvo para conceder su proteccion a los Naturales de Messina, que la havian solicitado," in *Colección de los Tratados de Paz*, 2:180–82. On collaboration with the Dutch, see Lira to Mariana, October 20, 1674 (the armada was ready by July 1675), AHN E. leg. 721; and Council of State deliberation, March 17, 1675, AGS E. leg. 2700.

59. Mariana's royal decree naming Don Juan, April 1, 1675; Don Juan to the Marquis of Mejorada for Mariana, July 5, 1675; Council of State deliberation and Mariana's responses and orders, July 12, July 24, August 14,

August 22, August 31, September 7, October 15, and October 18, 1675; Don Juan to Mariana, July 28, July 30, August 10, 1675; Mariana's royal decree, October 20, 1675; and Ruyter to Mariana, October 6, 1675, AGS E. legs. 2700 and 2701. Admiral Ruyter lost his life in the War of Messina on April 29, 1676, but the Dutch continued to support Spain. Louis XIV abandoned the area in March 1678, and Spanish forces subdued the revolt soon after. This Carlos II reported to his mother, who was no longer in Madrid on April 13, 1678; see AHN E. leg. 2729.

60. Carlos II to Cardinal Aragón, October 11, 1675, in his own hand; Cardinal Aragón to Carlos II, n.d., but probably written on October 22, 1675, BNE ms. 2043, fols. 17r–v, 19r; and Carlos II to Don Juan, October 30, 1675, BNE ms. 12961.21.

Chapter 6

1. BNE ms. 2043, fol. 99r. On the king's crying, see Maura, *Carlos II*, 2:240–43; and Manescau Martín, "Don Juan José de Austria," 501. On Alburquerque's intervention, see Oliván Santaliestra, "Mariana de Austria," 278–79.

2. BNE ms. 2043, fol. 99r; Maura, *Carlos II*, 2:240–43; and Kalnein, *Juan José*, 363.

3. "Confederación del S[eño]r Don Juan de Austria, y los grandes de España," BNE ms. 18211; BNE ms. 2043, fol. 581r; Álvarez-Ossorio Alvariño, "El favor real," 422; and Kalnein, *Juan José*, 399–400.

4. Villaumbrosa to Carlos II, January 13, 1674; copy of memorandum, ADM Hist. leg. 159.

5. On queen mothers as regents in the French court and transition to emancipation, see Cosandey, "Puissance maternelle," 10. Lightman argues that in the French monarchy, the queen mother never lost power, during or after the regency; Lightman, "Sons and Mothers," 32.

6. On the administrative transition from Mariana to Carlos, see Mariana to the Council of State, November 6, 1675, AGS E. leg. 2700. For the official announcements of Carlos II's assumption of the government to foreign princes, see AHN E. leg. 2661, exps. 150–59. For the mention of the document requesting

Carlos II to extend his minority, see AHN E. leg. 912, fols. 106r–112v; and BNE ms. 2043, fol. 99r.

7. On Carlos II's attitude in the aftermath of the coup, see BNE ms. 2043, fols. 46v–47r. On Ramos de Manzano's exile to Barajas, see BNE ms. 2043, fol. 43. The reshuffling of the court is recounted by Pedro de Aragón in a letter to his brother, Cardinal Aragón, n.d., but between November 7 and 13, 1675, BNE ms. 2043, fols. 98r–100v.

8. Medinaceli's reaction to Mariana's rebuke in BNE ms. 2043, fol. 98r.

9. Ibid., fol. 140v.

10. Villaumbrosa to Mariana, November 28 and December 8, 11, and 13, 1675; and Mariana to Villaumbrosa, December 13, 1675, AGS E. leg. 8817.

11. BNE ms. 2043, fols. 71r, 76r, 97r–100r, 112v, 114v, 116v, 125r–126r, 129r–v, 139r, 248r–9v.

12. Philip IV, *Testamento*, clause 34, pp. 50–51; Llorente, "Mariana de Austria como gobernadora," 1808–9; Llorente, "Mariana of Austria's Portraits," 214–18; and Coolidge, *Guardianship*, 21–22.

13. Coolidge, *Guardianship*, 22; and Ruggiero, *Boundaries*.

14. "Sucesos varios," BNE ms. 9399, fol. 48v; Pedro de VillaReal (an official in the king's stables) to unknown recipient, Aranjuez, April 27, 1674, APR Adm. leg. 780; and Maria Theresa to the nuns in the Descalzas Reales, August 3, 1677, APRDR, caja 7, exp. 1.

15. Pötting, *Diario*, 2:388; and the emperor's proposal, November 25, 1674, AHN E. leg. 2799.

16. Council of State deliberations, December 30, 1674, to January 19, 1679, AHN E. legs. 2799 and 2796. The numerous alliances Mariana concluded between 1673 and 1675 are discussed above. On Carlos II's marriage to Maria Antonia, see Mitchell, "Marriage Plots," 91–93.

17. Council of State deliberations, December 30, 1674, and June 6, 1676, AHN E. leg. 2799.

18. Council of State deliberation, June 4, 1676; letters to foreign princes (copies), AHN E. leg. 2799; and Mitchell, "Marriage Plots," 91–93.

19. On bringing Maria Antonia to Madrid as an alternative solution to the marriage, see

Duke of Alburquerque's opinion, Council of State deliberation, December 30, 1674, and March 21, 1676; and Balbases to Carlos, December 9, 1676, AHN E. leg. 2799.

20. González de Salcedo, *Nudrición Real*, BNE R5175, 54–55.

21. "Novedades suzedidas desde el dia 6 de Nov[iemb]re del año de 1675," BNE ms. 10129, fols. 464r–76v, 465r; Villaumbrosa's memorandum to the king, January 14, 1677, ADM Hist. leg. 159; and "Historia Verdadera del coloquio que por espacio de una hora se hizo entre el serniss[imo]. señor Don Carlos 2º, monarca de las españas, de edad de deciseis años y el S[eño]r Don Juan de Autria de edad de 48 y un relig[ios]o saderdote teologo, y su, vasallo, de hedad de 67; de religioso 57, de la orden de N.P. S. Franc[isc]o estando todos tres enpie en un triangulo a 4 de Abril en el año 1677, en su Real Palacio luego escritta del mesmo religioso para memoria delos venideros y consuelo de sus vasallos, y para dar muchas gracias a Dios de averles dado tal y tan gran rey y señor detanta, Real Capacidad. Y para esperar de Dios por su medio muchos favores, y la restuaracion de su Catholica monarchia," RAH ms. 9/5135.

22. "Historia Verdadera," RAH ms. 9/5135, n.p.

23. Ibid.

24. On the medieval political theory of a contractual relationship between the king and his subjects and its application to the Habsburg Spanish monarchy, see Elliott, *Revolt*, 5, 10, 45, and 375.

25. Covarrubias Orosco, *Tesoro*, 778; and Álvarez-Ossorio Alvariño, "El favor real," 409–10.

26. Duke of Alba to Cardinal Aragón, n.d., BNE ms. 18655[25]; Pedro de Aragón to Cardinal Aragón, August n.d., 1676, BNE ms. 2043, fol. 354r; and Fernández Giménez, "Valenzuela," 367–68.

27. BNE ms. 2043, fols. 248r–9v; and Fernández Giménez, "Valenzuela," 367–69.

28. "Testamento de D. Fernando Valenzuela," AHNSN Osuna, caja 2026, doc. 24–21; Fernández Giménez, "Valenzuela," 372; Manescau Martín, "Don Juan José of Austria," 502; and Tomás y Valiente, *Validos*, 26.

29. "Confederación del S[eño]r Don Juan de Austria, y los grandes de España," BNE ms. 18211, fol. 19r. A list of nobles with the privilege of *grandeza* during Carlos II's reign (no specific year given) included thirty-six dukes, sixteen marquises, fifteen counts, and five Italian princes; APR RCII, caja 83, exp. 1.

30. BNE ms. 2043, fols. 540r–v; and "Novedades sucedidas," BNE ms. 10129, fol. 470v.

31. "Sucesos varios desde que salio de su menor edad el S[eño]r Carlos 2º hasta la muerte de don Juan de Austria principal objecto de este papel," BNE ms. 9399, fols. 52v–3r, 62r; and Álvarez-Ossorio Alvariño, "El favor real," 422. Maura, *Carlos II*, 2:327–28, calculates the force at sixteen thousand.

32. Villaumbrosa to Carlos II, January 13, 1677. There were several copies circulating of this well-thought-out paper—for example, in ADM Hist. leg. 159; and AHNSN Osuna, caja 4267, doc. 2, exp. 3.

33. Villaumbrosa to Carlos II, January 13, 1677, ADM Hist. leg. 159. The necessity of Carlos II's separation from his mother also mentioned in "Sucesos varios," BNE ms. 9399, fol. 64r.

34. Villaumbrosa to Carlos II, January 13, 1677, ADM Hist. leg. 159; and Oliván Santaliestra, "Mariana de Austria," 76.

35. Villaumbrosa to Carlos II, January 13, 1677, ADM Hist. leg. 159.

36. Vives, *Education of a Christian Woman*, 299–325; and Maltby, *Reign of Charles V*, 105. On the realities of widows' activities, see Fink De Backer, *Widowhood*, particularly 148–58.

37. Holograph note by Carlos II to the Duke of Medinaceli, n.d., ADM Hist. leg. 160, núm. 73.

38. BNE ms. 10129, fols. 470v–471r.

39. Ibid., fol. 471r; and Mariana to Sor Mariana de la Cruz, signed "Thursday 1677, from the palace," APRDR, caja 6, exp. 31, fol. 90.

40. "Novedades sucedidas," BNE ms. 10129, fols. 471v–5r.

41. Carlos II to his ministers, January 21, 1677, AHN E. leg. 2661, exp. 154.

42. "Diario de noticias," CODOIN, 67:79.

43. Ibid., vol. 67:72, 76, 79; and "Sucesos varios," BNE ms. 9399, fols. 64v–5r and 12,961.34, n.p.

44. "Prisión de D[on] Fernando Valenzuela en el Escorial, destierro que se decretaron y sucesos que siguieron al encargarse D[on] Juan de Austria de dirigir los negocios del Estado," BNE ms. 12961.34, n.p. On Valenzuela's wife, see "Diario de noticias," CODOIN, 67:73–74, 76–77. On the illegal procedures, see Valenzuela, "Testamento" (drafted in Mexico City, in 1689, when the man was dying), AHNSN Osuna, caja 2026, doc. 24 (1); Villaumbrosa to Carlos II, January 25, 1677, and June 8, 1677, AGS E. leg. 8817; "Decreto invalidando las mercedes," BNE ms. 12961.23, fol. 77; and Escudero, *Administración y estado*, 624.

45. "Diario de noticias," CODOIN, 67:73, 79–84, 89, 92; and BNE ms. 2289, fols. 38v–9r.

46. "Sucesos varios," BNE ms. 9399, fol. 64r. On Mariana's presence increasing the possibility of disorder, see "Diario de noticias," CODOIN, 67:82; and Suárez Quevedo, "Fiesta barroca y política," 66. On the formation of Mariana's household for Toledo, see APR RCII, caja 117, exp. 2.

47. Mariana to Carlos, February 18, 1677, transcribed in Maura, *Carlos II*, 2:355.

48. Philip IV, *Testamento*, clause 56, p. 69. Mariana had taken preemptive measures to secure her pension. Villaumbrosa to Mariana, February 22, 1675, AGS E. leg. 8817.

49. Mariana to Carlos II, March 1, 1677, transcribed in Maura, *Carlos II*, 2:357.

50. "Sucesos varios," BNE ms. 9399, fols. 66r–v.

51. Maria Theresa to the Descalzas Reales, March 2 and April 14, 1677, APRDR, caja 7, exp. 1.

52. "Diario de noticias," CODOIN, 67:79, 93, 97.

53. The preliminary list was given to Mariana on February 25, 1677. To reduce the numbers, many assumed several functions; see "Soldados de la guarda: Dos escuadras de soldados de la guarda, una de españoles y otra de alemanes, de a veinte y cinco soldados cada una incluso el Cavo," "Etiqueta de la servidumbre en Toledo de la Reina madre de Carlos II," APR RCII, caja 117, exps. 1 and 2.

54. Suárez Quevedo, "Fiesta barroca y política," 66–67, 71, 89.

55. Ibid., 62.

56. Cardinal Aragón to Pedro de Aragón, March 15, 1677, BNE ms. 2043, fol. 603r.

57. Mariana to Abbess Sor Juana del Espíritu Santo, 1678 (month is unclear); and Mariana to Sor Mariana de la Cruz, March 19, 1677, APR Descalzas C. 6, exp. 31, fol. 46r. Her migraines were a constant theme in her correspondence with Carlos as well. See the reports on the messages she received in "Sucesos varios," BNE ms. 9399, fol. 77v. Mariana left special gifts for abbesses and nuns in various convents in her testament; see Mariana's testament (copy) in AHNSN, Frías, caja 62, doc. 165, and another in BNE ms. 18735[13]. Other letters mentioning the nuns are in AHN E. leg. 2729.

58. Don Juan's strategies in the Descalzas Reales entailed his commissioning of art as a means to diminish Mariana's presence and strengthen his own. Art in the early modern period was a lot more than decoration and often played an affective role. See Goodman, "Conspicuous," 166, 169–72. A gazetteer reported that when the king asked a coach driver in how many hours he could take him to Toledo from Aranjuez, Don Juan decided at once to set the date of the trip to Aragon for the twenty-first; see Diario de noticias, 101. There are about twenty-five letters between Mariana and Harrach, from March 9 to August 10, 1677, that show the queen at her darkest hour. I thank Dr. Laura Oliván Santaliestra for providing this information, email communication April 29, 2010; and Oliván Santaliestra, "Mariana de Austria," 410–16.

59. On the transfer of the equestrian sculpture of Philip IV, see Barbeito, El Alcázar, 117, 178–80; and "Diario de noticias" (Friday, March 19, 1677), CODOIN, 67:101, 106. For a satirical text against Don Juan, see "Vision de Visiones que tuvo una Beata de la Legua," BNE ms. 18211. This one was written in 1677; for additional ones, see Kalnein, Juan José, 487.

60. The marriage announcement, June 16, 1677; Council of State deliberation, June 18, 1677, AHN E. leg. 2799; Oliván Santaliestra, "Mariana de Austria," 414; and Harrach's paper, "Al Señor Don Juan de Austria[,] el Embajador de Alemania," ADM Hist. leg. 159.

61. Council of State deliberations, June 18, July 2, and 8, 1677, AHN E. leg. 2799, and August 15, 1677, AHN E. leg. 2796. Studies of

Don Juan's tenure in office focused almost exclusively on his domestic policies rather than his foreign policy. His appeasement of France needs further elucidation.

62. Carlos II to Leopold I, July 30, 1677; Council of State deliberation, July 8, 1677; Cardinal Aragón's opinion, Council of State deliberation, July 8, 1677, and deliberation on August 2, 1677; Leopold I to Carlos II, September 30, 1677; copies of letters sent to Mariana on November 19, 1677, AHN E. leg. 2799; Carlos II to Leopold I, December 16, 1677, AHN E. leg. 2796. Maria Theresa to Sor Mariana de la Cruz, August 3, 1677, APRDR, caja 7, exp. 1.

63. On Don Juan as mother, see "Sucesos varios," BNE ms. 9399, fol. 68 v; and "Menor edad de Carlos II," CODOIN, 67:29.

64. Mariana's present to Carlos is mentioned in Maura, Carlos II, 2:403. On royal portraits as the embodiment of a person, see Goodman, "Conspicuous," 169.

Chapter 7

1. On Don Juan's political position in Carlos II's government from 1677 to 1679, see Maravall, Teoría española del estado, 305–6; Lynch, Spain, 245; Kamen, "Don Juan and the Regency," in Spain, 335; Manescau Martín, "Don Juan José de Austria," 509, 532–34; and Contreras, Carlos II, 166–67.

2. Unless otherwise noted, all references to the letters are from AHN E. leg. 2729. On Habsburg letter-writing practices, see the forthcoming volume De puño y letra: Cartas personales en las redes dinásticas de la Casa de Austria, edited by Bernardo José García García, Andrea Sommer-Mathis, and Katrin Keller (forthcoming 2019). The volume was based on an international congress held at the University of Vienna, December 2–3, 2015.

3. Nicolás Pertusato, one of the dwarfs portrayed by Velázquez in Las Meninas, maintained a close relationship with Mariana throughout his life; see Sánchez Portillo, "Algunas noticas de Nicolás Pertusato," 149–66. Also see Royal Household Records for Mariana's entourage in Toledo, APR RCII, caja 117, exp. 2.

4. APR RCII, caja 118, exp. 1; and Carlos to Mariana, April 13 (from Aranjuez), June 11, July 8, August 20, and October 1 (from El Escorial), 1678.

5. Carlos II holograph note to the Duke of Medinaceli, February 21, 1678, in ADM Hist., caja 1, núm. 74. It is reproduced in Paz y Meliá, *Series de los más importantes*, 195. For the official and formal document naming Medinaceli prime minister (February 1680), see ADM Hist. leg. 45, ramo 21, núm. 1; and Álamo Martell, "El VIII Duque de Medinaceli," 548. Álamo Martell mentions the official decree of 1680 based on a copy in the British Library, not the note of 1678 in the Medinaceli archive.

6. Mariana to Carlos, June 10, 1678. Valenzuela left Cadiz on July 14 and arrived in Manila on November 1679; see "Documentos, datos y relaciones para la Historia de Filipinas hasta ahora inéditos fielmente copiados de los originales existentes en archivos y bibliotecas, copiado fielmente por Ventura del Arco, Auditor de Marina y Oficial de la Contaduría General del Exercito," NL Ayer, ms. 1300, 11–18; Maura, *Carlos II*, 2:395–96; and Escudero, *Administración y estado*, 624.

7. Carlos to Mariana, June 11, 1678.

8. Mariana to Carlos, June 15, 1678.

9. Carlos to Mariana, June 19, 1678.

10. Carlos to Mariana, August 19, 1678, and May 15, 1679. Doña Francisca Manrique was listed as one of Mariana's ladies; APR RCII, caja 117, exp. 2.

11. The episode is described by Mancera in a letter to Jerónimo de Eguía, February 2, 1679. It will be discussed at length below; BNE ms. 2409, fols. 557r–558r.

12. Carlos to Mariana, September 4 and 27 and October 9, 1678.

13. Crawford, *Perilous Performances*, 3.

14. Mariana to Carlos, June 15, 1678.

15. Carlos to Mariana, May 19 and 21, June 11, and July 8 and 25, 1678.

16. Carlos to Mariana, September 27, 1678.

17. Mariana to Carlos, February 18, 1677, quoted in Maura, *Carlos II*, 2:355.

18. Carlos II to Leopold I, July 30, 1677; Council of State deliberation, July 8, 1677; Leopold I to Carlos II, September 30, 1677; copies of letters sent to Mariana on November 19, 1677, AHN E. leg. 2799; and

Carlos II to Leopold I, December 16, 1677, AHN E. leg. 2796.

19. Council of State deliberation, January 7, 1679; Medinaceli's opinion is recorded in the Council of State deliberation, January 11, 1679, AHN E. leg. 2796.

20. Carlos to Mariana, May 4, 1679, with a copy of the deliberation that took place in January 11. Medinaceli's opinion is recorded in the Council of State deliberation, January 11, 1679, AHN E. leg. 2796.

21. Carlos II's holographic responses to the Council of State deliberations, January 7 and 11, 1679; and Council of State deliberation, January 19, 1679, given to the king as a group, not individual opinions, AHN E. leg. 2796.

22. Carlos to Leopold I, January 22, 1679 (copy); the king wrote of his own hand. See also Medinaceli's opinion, Council of State deliberation, January 11, 1679, AHN E. leg. 2796.

23. Carlos to Mariana (copy), January 19, 1679, AHN E. leg. 2796.

24. Leopold to Carlos, March 4, 1679 (copy), Council of State deliberation, April 3 and 13, 1679, AHN E. leg. 2796.

25. Carlos to Mariana, January 23 and 28, April 2 and 17, and May 4, 1679; and Leopold to Carlos, March 4, 1679, AHN E. leg. 2796.

26. Carlos to Mariana, January 28, May 27, and June 12, 1679.

27. Villars, *Mémoires*, 28.

28. Carlos to Mariana, December 4, 1678; and Mancera to Jerónimo de Eguía, February 2, 1679, BNE ms. 2409, fol. 557.

29. Mancera to Eguía, BNE ms. 2409, fol. 557.

30. Carlos to Mariana, January 28, February n.d., 1679, and May 6 and 13, 1679.

31. Carlos to Mariana, May 11, 1679.

32. Carlos to Mariana, May 11 and 13, 1679.

33. Ibid.

34. Carlos to Mariana (from the palace of the Buen Retiro), May 15, 19, 1679; and Mariana to Carlos, September 13, 1679.

35. For the nature of Don Juan's ministry at the head of the monarchy, see Maravall, *Teoría española del estado*, 305–6; Lynch, *Spain*, 245; Kamen, *Spain*, 335; and Manescau Martín, "Don Juan José de Austria," 509. On Don

Juan's replacing of Mariana's men and for a sketch of his policies, see Manescau Martín, "Don Juan José de Austria," 512–22. On his economic and fiscal reforms, see Sánchez Belén, "Mirando hacia adelante," 170–73. For an overall assessment of his tenure as the king's main advisor, see Kalnein, *Juan José*, 441–99.

36. Don Juan's short tenure in office has been used to explain the poor results of his policies. His regime was not popular, as the abundant contemporary literature against his government shows. See Maura, *Carlos II*, 2:527–47 (part of appendix 2); "Sucesos varios," BNE ms. 9399, fols. 81v–83r; and Kalnein, *Juan José*, 493–95.

37. Villars, *Mémoires*, 28–29; and Carlos to Mariana, June 22, 1679.

38. "Sucesos varios," BNE ms. 9399, fol. 83r; and "Diario de noticias," CODOIN, 67:54.

39. Mariana to Carlos, September 18, 1679; and Carlos to Mariana, July 13, 14, and 19, 1679. The portrait was executed by Juan Carreño de Miranda (1614–1685), the court painter, and mentioned in the letters of June 9 and 29 and July 29. Mariana saw and approved the portrait and the jewel for Marie Louise sometime before July 14.

40. On etiquette for Don Juan when he became Carlos II's principal minister, see APR RCII, caja 79; "Sucesos varios," BNE ms. 9399, fol. 84r; and Maura, *Carlos II*, 2:473. On the collaboration between Mariana and Maria Theresa to bring forth the marriage, see Mitchell, "Marriage Plots," 96–98.

41. Philippe d'Orleans to Mariana, August 4, 1679, AHN E. leg. 2729; Maura, *Carlos II*, 2:475; and "Sucesos varios," BNE ms. 9399, fol. 84r.

42. Maura, *Carlos II*, 2:472; and "Sucesos varios," BNE ms. 9399, fol. 83v.

43. The preparations for the reconciliation are described in two letters Carlos wrote to Cardinal Portocarrero, August 10 and 13, 1679, AHN E. leg. 2729. Portocarrero acted as regent of the monarchy during the king's final illness in 1700 and played the principal role in drafting the king's last testament; see Bernardo Ares, *Cardenal Portocarrero*, 15–16; Moreno Prieto, "Cardenal Portocarrero," 223–25; and Ribot García, "Cardinal Portocarrero y la sucesión," 335–43.

44. Carlos to Cardinal Portocarrero, August 10, 1679; and Cardinal Portocarrero to Carlos, Toledo, August 15, 1679, AHN E. leg. 2729.

45. Carlos to Mariana, August 17, 1679.

46. Mariana to Carlos, September 13, 1679 (two letters).

47. Carlos to Mariana, September 18, 1679; and Maura, *Carlos II*, 2:481.

48. Mariana to Carlos, March 1, 1677, transcribed in Maura, *Carlos II*, 2:357.

49. Mariana to Carlos, September 18, 1679.

50. Carlos to Mariana, September 20, 1679; Duchess of Bejar to Mariana, September 18, 1679; and Mariana to the Duchess of Bejar, September 18 and 31, AHNSN Osuna, caja 3620, núm. 51.

51. "Sucesos varios," BNE ms. 9399, fols. 84v–85r; and Mariana to Carlos, September 19, 1679.

52. Mariana to Carlos, September 21, 1679.

53. "Sucesos varios," BNE ms. 9399, fol. 85r; and Barozzi and Berchet, *Relazioni*, 446.

54. Maria Theresa to Carlos, October 28, 1679, AHN E. leg. 2729.

Conclusion

1. On María Luisa's entry into Madrid, see Zapata Fernández de la Hoz, *La entrada en la Corte*. On Medinaceli, see Álamo Martell, "El VIII Duque de Medinaceli," 547–53. The diplomatic papers and royal household records refer to María Luisa (and later Mariana of Neuburg) as *reina reinante* and Mariana as *reina madre*.

2. Princess Juana of Austria, widow of the prince of Portugal and mother of the king of Portugal, founded the convent; she ruled the Spanish monarchy as governor from 1555 to 1559 and moved into the convent in 1570. See Cruz, "Juana of Austria," 116. Empress dowager Maria of Austria (1527–1603) lived there during the last years of her life. See Sánchez, *Empress, the Queen, and the Nun*, 29, 69–70, 89–90, 138, 146. On Mariana's adoption of the palace, see her letter to Carlos, November 29, 1679, AHN E. leg. 2729. On the palace of Uceda, see López Millán, "Don Luis de Haro y el palacio de Uceda," 313, 339. On the repairs, see APR Adm. General leg. 730.

264   NOTES TO PAGES 229–231

3. On Maria Antonia's marriage and the implication for the succession, see Council of State deliberation, August 17, 1690, AHN E. leg. 2805. On Mariana's support for Joseph Ferdinand, see her testament (copy) in AHNSN, Frías, caja 62, doc. 165, unfoliated.

4. Maximilian II of Bavaria to the nuns at Descalzas Reales, May n.d., 1696, APRDR, caja 6, exps. 31, 58. On the testament, see Ribot García, *Orígenes*, 24.

5. One of Mariana's many eulogies, BNE VE 119–16. On miracles reported as soon as Mariana died, see Baviera and Maura, *Documentos inéditos*, 550–51. On the "uncorruptibility" of Mariana's body, see APR RCII, caja 144; and Gómez Vozmediano, "En olor a santidad," 572.

6. Ribot García, "El rey," 39–40.

7. For a recent assessment of the state of the scholarship and with a warning about painting too rosy picture, see the excellent essay by Storrs, "Nuevas perspectivas sobre le reinado de Carlos II," particularly 19–20.

8. Storrs, *Resilience*, 25; Storrs, "Army of Lombardy," 373–74; and Lynn, *Wars of Louis XIV*, 191–265.

Archival Sources Consulted

Archivo Ducal Medinaceli (ADM), Toledo

Histórica legajos 45, 68, 69, 70, 159, 160

Caja 1

Archivo General de Simancas (AGS), Valladolid

Estado-Capitulaciones con la Casa de Austria, legajos 2378–2392

Estado-Embajada en La Haya, legajos 8396–8410

Estado-España, legajos 2683–2693, 2697–2700, 4128

Estado-Fondo Carlos II, legajos 8817–8821

Estado K (France), legajos 1395–1396

Estado Inglaterra, legajos 2531–2550, 2554

Estado Roma, legajos 3043, 3100, 3113, 3131, 3052

Patronato Real, legajos 39 (documento 107), 56 (documento 52–53), 57 (documento 153)

Archivo Histórico Nacional (AHN), Madrid

Estado, legajos 671, 674, 1441, 1632, 2653, 2661, 2729, 2779, 2796–2797, 2799, 2804, 4818, 3455–3457

Estado, libros 129, 130, 139, 140, 721, 912

Estado Clero-Jesuitas, legajo 263

Consejos, legajos 7178, 7179, 7259

Archivo Histórico Nacional, Sección Nobleza (AHNSN), Toledo

Fernán Núñez, caja 418

Frías, cajas 62, 82

Osuna, cajas 88, 127, 571, 2026, 3620, 4267

Archivo del Palacio Real (APR), Madrid

Admistrativa, legajos 730, 779–780, 928

Descalzas Reales (APRDR), cajas 6, 7

Personal: consulted by name

Reinados Carlos II, cajas 92, 117, 118, 144

Biblioteca Nacional de España (BNE), Madrid

Manuscripts 2409, 2043, 2289, 5742, 8344–8345, 8346, 8360, 9399, 10129, 11158, 12053, 12961, 18208, 18209, 18211, 18433, 18655, 18735, 22086(1), 22086(2)

Printed manuscripts VE 119–16, ER 3887, R5175

Real Academia de la Historia (RAH), Madrid

Manuscripts K9, 9/1835, 9/3746, 9/5135

Published Primary Sources

Abreu y Bertodano, José A. de, Francisco de Alesón, and Franciscus Accoltus, eds. *Colección de los Tratados de Paz, Alianza, Neutralidad, Garantía, Protección, Tregua, Mediación, Accesión, Reglamento de límites, Comercio, Navegación, etc. Hechos por los Pueblos, Reyes, y Príncipes de España con los Pueblos, Reyes, Príncipes, Repúblicas, y demás Potencias de Europa, y otras Partes del Mundo; y entre sí mismos, y con sus respectivos Adversarios; y juntamente de los hechos, directa, o indirectamente contra Bd.* 2 vols. Madrid, 1751.

Barozzi, Nicolò, and Guglielmo Berchet, eds. *Relazioni degli Stati Europei lette al Senato dagli Ambasciatori Veneti nel secolo decimosettimo: Raccolte ed annotate.* Series 1; Spain, vol. 2. Venice: Pietro Naratovich, 1860.

Barrionuevo, Jerónimo. *Avisos de don Jerónimo de Barrionuevo (1654–1658).* Biblioteca de Autores Españoles, vols. 221–222. Edited by Antonio Paz y Meliá. Madrid: Atlas, 1968.

Baviera, Adalberto de, and Gabriel Maura Gamazo, eds. *Documentos inéditos referentes a las postrimerías de la Casa de Austria en España*. Vol. 1. Madrid: Real Academia de la Historia, 2004.

Carlos II. *Testamento de Carlos II: Edición facsímil*. Edited by Antonio Domínguez Ortíz. Madrid: Editora Nacional, 1982.

Covarrubias Orosco, Sebastián de. *Tesoro de la lengua castellana o española*. 2nd ed. Edited by Felipe C. R. Maldonado. Madrid: Castalia, 1995.

"Diario de noticias de 1677 a 1678: Décima sexta parte de las misceláneas y papeles varios curiosos y manuscritos de D. Juan Antonio de Valencia Idiaquez." In *Collección de Documentos Inéditos para la historia de España*, vol. 67, edited by Marqués de la Fuensanta del Valle and José Sancho Rayón, 69–133. Madrid: Imprenta de Miguel Ginesta, 1877.

Diccionario Biográfico Español. 50 vols. Madrid: Real Academia de la Historia, 2011–13.

"Documentos referentes a D[on] Fernando Valenzuela." In *Collección de Documentos Inéditos para la historia de España*, vol. 67, edited by Marqués de la Fuensanta del Valle and José Sancho Rayón, 293–339. Madrid: Imprenta de Miguel Ginesta, 1877.

Ebben, Maurits, ed. *Un holandés en la España de Felipe IV: Diario del viaje de Lodewijck Huygens (1660–1661)*. Translated by Goedele de Sterck. Madrid: Fundación Carlos Amberes, 2015.

Fanshawe, Anne. *The Memoirs of Anne, Lady Halkett and Ann, Lady Fanshawe*. Edited by John Clyde Loftis. Oxford: Clarendon, 1979.

González de Salcedo, Pedro. *Nudrición Real (Texto impreso): Reglas o preceptos de como se ha de educar a los Reyes Mozos, desde los siete a los catorce años. . . . A la Reyna Nuestra Señora*. Madrid, 1671.

The History of the Treaty of Nimueguen with Remarks on the Interest of Europe in Relation to That Affair. Translated out of French. London: Printed for Dorman Newman at the King's Arms in the Poultrey, 1681.

"Inventario y tasación de los bienes de Fernando Valenzuela." In *Colección de Documentos Inéditos para la historia de España*, vol. 67, edited by Marqués de la Fuensanta del Valle and José Sancho Rayón, 135–292. Madrid: Imprenta de Miguel Ginesta, 1877.

The laws of Jamaica passed by the assembly, and confirmed by His majesty in council, Feb. 23. 1683: To which is added, A short account of the island and government thereof, with an exact map of the island. London, 1683.

Lonchay, Henri, Joseph Cuvelier, and Joshep Lefevre, eds. *Correspondance de la Cour d'Espagne sur Less Affaires des Pays-Bas au XIIe siècle*. Vol. 5. Brussels, 1935.

Martínez Hernández, Santiago, ed. *Escribir la corte de Felipe IV: El Diario del Marqués de Osera, 1657–1659*. Madrid: Ediciones Doce Calles, 2013.

Moncada, Guillén Ramón de. *Marqués de Aytona. Discurso Militar: Propónense algunos inconvenientes de la Milicia de estos tiempos, y su reparo. Estudio crítico*. Edited by Eduardo Mesa Gallego. Madrid: Ministerio de Defensa, 2008.

Núñez de Castro, Alonso. *Libro historico politico: Solo Madrid es corte, y el cortesano en Madrid*. Madrid, 1675.

Osorio, Juan Cortés. *Invectiva Política contra don Juan José de Austria*. Edited by Mercedes Etreros. Madrid: Editora Nacional, 1984.

Paz y Meliá, Antonio, ed. *Avisos de don Jerónimo de Barrionuevo (1654–1658)*. By Jerónimo Barrionuevo. Biblioteca de Autores Españoles, vols. 221–222. Madrid: Atlas, 1968.

———, ed. *Series de los más importantes documentos del Archivo y Biblioteca del ex[elentíssi]mo Señor Duque de Medinaceli*. Madrid, 1915.

Philip IV. *Testamento de Felipe IV: Edición facsímil*. Edited by Antonio Domínguez Ortíz. Madrid: Editora Nacional, 1982.

Pötting, Francisco Eusebio. *Diario del Conde de Pötting, Embajador del Sacro Imperio en Madrid (1664–1674)*. 2 vols. Edited by Miguel Nieto Nuño. Madrid: Biblioteca Diplomática Española, 1990.

Pribram, Alfred Francis, and Moriz Landwehr von Pragenau, eds. *Privatebriefe Kaiser Leopold I an den Grafen F. E. Pötting, 1662–1673.* 2 vols. Vienna: Historischen Kommission and Kaiserlichen Akademie der Wissenchaften in Wien, 1903.

Ramos del Manzano, Francisco. *Reynados de menor edad.* Madrid, 1672.

Seco Serrano, Carlos, ed. *Epistolario Español: Cartas de Sor María de Jesús de Ágreda y de Felipe IV.* Madrid: Biblioteca de Autores Españoles, 1958.

Sonnino, Paul. *Mémoires for the Instruction of the Dauphin.* New York: Free Press, 1970.

Tomás, Mariano. "Menor edad de Carlos II." In *Collección de Documentos Inéditos para la historia de España,* vol. 67, edited by Marqués de la Fuensanta del Valle and José Sancho Rayón, 3–68. Madrid: Imprenta de Miguel Ginesta, 1877.

Usunáriz Garayoa, Jesús Maria, ed. *España y sus tratados internacionales, 1516–1700.* Pamplona: Ediciones Universidad de Navarra, 2006.

Valencia, Don Juan Antonio de. "Diario de todo lo sucedido en Madrid desde el sábado 23 de enero de 1677, que entró S[u] A[lteza] el Ser[enísi]mo D[on] Juan de Austria, llamade de S[u] M[agestad], hasta el 15 de julio de 1678." In *Collección de Documentos Inéditos para la historia de España,* vol. 67, edited by Marqués de la Fuensanta del Valle and José Sancho Rayón, 69–133. Madrid: Imprenta de Miguel Ginesta, 1877.

Vilela Gallego, Pilar, ed. *Felipe IV y la Condesa de Paredes: Una Colección epistolar del Rey en el Archivo General de Andalucía.* Sevilla: Junta de Andalucía, 2005.

Villars, Marquis de. *Mémoires de la cour d'Espagne sous le regne de Charles II, 1678–1682.* London, 1861.

Vives, Juan Luis. *The Education of a Christian Woman: A Sixteenth-Century Manual.* Edited and translated by Charles Fantazzi. Chicago: University of Chicago Press, 2000.

Secondary Sources

Adams, Tracy. *The Life and Afterlife of Isabeau of Bavaria.* Baltimore: Johns Hopkins University Press, 2010.

Akkerman, Nadine, and Birgit Houben. *The Politics of Female Households: Ladies-in-Waiting Across Early Modern Europe.* Leiden: Brill, 2013.

Álamo Martell, Maria Dolores. "El VIII Duque de Medinaceli: Primer Ministro de Carlos II." In *Los Validos,* edited by Antonio Escudero, 547–71. Madrid: Dykinson, 2006.

Alcalá-Zamora y Queipo de Llano, José, ed. *Felipe IV: El hombre y el reinado.* Madrid: Real Academia de la Historia; Centro de Estudios Europa Hispánica, 2005.

Allen, Paul. *Philip III and the Pax Hispanica, 1598–1621: The Failure of the Grand Strategy.* New Haven: Yale University Press, 2000.

Álvarez-Ossorio Alvariño, Antonio. "El favor real: Liberalidad del Príncipe y Jerarquía de la República (1665–1700)." In *Repubblica e Virtù: Pensiero Político e Monarchia Cattolica fra XVI e XVII secolo,* edited by Chiara Continisio and Cesare Mozzarelli, 399–453. Roma: Bulzoni Editore, 1995.

———. "Las guardias reales en la corte de los Austrias y la salvaguarda de la autoridad regia." In *La Monarquía de Felipe II: La casa del rey,* 2 vols., edited by José Martínez Millán and Santiago Fernández Conti, 1:430–52. Madrid: Fundación Mapfre, 2005.

Aram, Bethany. *Juana the Mad: Sovereignty and Dynasty in Renaissance Europe.* Baltimore: Johns Hopkins University Press, 2005.

Aranda, Marcelo. "Instruments of Religion and Empire: Spanish Science in the Age of the Jesuits, 1628–1756." PhD diss., Stanford University, 2013.

Asch, Ronald G. "Introduction: Court and Household from the Fifteenth to the

Seventeenth Centuries." In *Princes, Patronage and the Nobility: The Court at the Beginning of the Modern Age, c. 1450–1650*, edited by Ronald G. Asch and Adolf M. Birke, 1–38. London: German Historical Institute, 1991.

Asch, Ronald G., and Adolf M. Birke, eds. *Princes, Patronage and the Nobility: The Court at the Beginning of the Modern Age, c. 1450–1650*. London: German Historical Institute, 1991.

Baltar Rodríguez, Juan Francisco. *Las Juntas de Gobierno en la Monarquía Hispánica (Siglos XVI–XVII)*. Madrid: Centro de Estudios Políticos y Constitucionales, 1998.

Barbeito, José Manuel. *El Alcázar de Madrid*. Madrid: Comisión de Cultura, Colegio Oficial de Arquitectos de Madrid, 1992.

Barrio Gozalo, Maximiliano. *La Embajada de España en Roma durante el reinado de Carlos II (1665–1700)*. Valladolid: Universidad de Valladolid, 2013.

Barrios, Feliciano. *El Consejo de Estado de la monarquía española (1521–1812): Estudio histórico-jurídico*. Madrid: Departamento de Historia del Derecho Español, 1983.

———. "El gobierno de la Monarquía en el reinado de Felipe IV." In *Felipe IV: El hombre y el reinado*, edited by José Alcalá-Zamora y Queipo de Llano, 137–54. Madrid: Real Academia de la Historia, 2005.

Bassegoda, Bonaventura. "La decoración pictórica de El Escorial en el reinado de Carlos II." In *Arte y Diplomacia de la monarquía hispánica en el siglo XVII*, edited by José Luis Colomer, 35–59. Madrid: Fernando Villaverde Ediciones, 2003.

Belcher, Gerald L. "Spain and the Anglo-Portuguese Alliance of 1661: A Reassessment of Charles II's Foreign Policy at the Restoration." *Journal of British Studies* 15, no. 1 (1975): 67–88.

Bérenger, Jean. "An Attempted Rapprochement Between France and the Emperor: The Secret Treaty for the Partition of the Spanish Succession of 19 January 1668." In *Luis XIV and Europe*, edited by Ragnhild M. Hatton, 133–52. London: Macmillan, 1976.

———. "Pour une enquête européenne: Le problème du ministériat au XVIIe siècle." *Annales* 29 (1974): 166–92.

Bernardo Ares, José Manuel de, ed. *El Cardenal Portocarrero y su tiempo (1635–1709)*. Valencia: CSED Editorial, 2013.

———. *La sucesión de la monarquía hispánica, 1665–1700. I: Lucha política en las Cortes y fragilidad económica-fiscal en los reinos*. Córdoba: Universidad de Córdoba, 2006.

Bertelli, Sergio. *The King's Body: Sacred Rituals of Power in Medieval and Early Modern Europe*. Translated by R. Burr Litchfield. University Park: Pennsylvania State University Press, 2001.

Bireley, Robert. *Religion and Politics in the Age of the Counterreformation*. Chapel Hill: University of North Carolina Press, 1981.

Bowman, Hayley R. "The Church Divided: The Dominicans, Franciscans, and Jesuits and the Immaculate Conception Controversy in Seventeenth-Century Spain." MA thesis, Purdue University, 2015.

Boyden, James M. *The Courtier and the King: Ruy Gomez de Silva, Philip II, and the Court of Spain*. Berkeley: University of California Press, 1995.

Brown, Jonathan. *Velazquez: Painter and Courtier*. New Haven: Yale University Press, 1986.

Brown, Jonathan, and John H. Elliott. *A Palace for a King: The Buen Retiro and the Court of Philip IV*. Revised and expanded ed. New Haven: Yale University Press, 2003.

Burke, Peter. *The Fabrication of Louis XIV*. New Haven: Yale University Press, 1992.

Callado Estela, Emilio. "El confesor fray Luis Aliaga y la expulsión de los moriscos." *Investigaciones Históricas* 34 (2014): 27–46.

———. "El Confesor Regio Fray Luis Aliaga y la controversia inmaculista." *Hispania Sacra* 68, no. 137 (2016): 317–26.

Calvi, Giulia. Introduction to "Women Rulers in Europe: Agency, Practice and the Representation of Political Powers (XII–XVIII)," edited by Giulia Calvi, 1–15. European University Institute Working Papers HEC no. 2 (2008).

———, ed. "Women Rulers in Europe: Agency, Practice and the Representation of Political Powers (XII–XVIII)." European University Institute Working Papers HEC no. 2 (2008).

Campbell, Jodi. *Monarchy, Political Culture, and Drama in Seventeenth-Century Madrid: Theater of Negotiation.* Aldershot: Ashgate, 2006.

———. "Women and Factionalism in the Court of Charles II of Spain." In *Spanish Women in the Golden Age: Images and Realities,* edited by Magdalena S. Sánchez and Alain Saint-Saëns, 109–24. Westport, CT: Greenwood Press, 1996.

Cárceles de Gea, Beatriz. "Juicio y debate del régimen polisinodial en las campañas políticas del reinado de Carlos II." *Pedralbes: Revista de historia moderna* 7 (1987): 103–23.

Carrasco Martínez, Adolfo. "Los grandes, el poder y la cultura política de la nobleza en el reinado de Carlos II." *Studia histórica: Historia moderna* 20 (1999): 77–136.

Castilla Soto, Josefina. "Tratados para la educación del rey niño." In *Carlos II: El rey y su entorno cortesano,* edited by Luis Ribot, 54–79. Madrid: Centro de Estudios Europa Hispánica, 2010.

Catterall, Douglas, and Jodi Campbell, eds. *Women in Port: Gendering Communities, Economies, and Social Networks in Atlantic Port Cities, 1500–1800.* Leiden: Brill, 2012.

Chenel, Álvaro Pascual. "El retrato de estado durante el reinado de Carlos II." Published PhD diss., Universidad de Alcalá, 2009.

Cobo Delgado, Gemma. "'Catorce veces el sol doró su edad de diamante.' Una fiesta

en honor a Mariana de Austria en el Nuevo Olimpo." In *"Venia Docendi": Actas del IV congreso internacional. Jóvenes investigadores Siglo de Oro,* edited by Carlos Mata Induráin and Ana Zúñiga Lacruz, 22–35. Pamplona: Universidad de Navarra, 2015.

Colomer, José Luis, ed. *Arte y Diplomacia de la Monarquía Hispánica en el siglo XVII.* Madrid: Fernando Villaverde Ediciones, 2003.

Contreras, Jaime. *Carlos II el Hechizado: Poder y melancolía en la corte del último Austria.* Madrid: Temas de Hoy, 2003.

Cook, Alexandra Parma. "The Women of Early Modern Triana: Life, Death and Survival Strategies in Seville's Maritime District." In *Women in Port: Gendering Communities, Economies, and Social Networks in Atlantic Port Cities, 1500–1800,* edited by Douglas Catterall and Jodi Campbell, 41–68. Leiden: Brill, 2012.

Coolidge, Grace E. "Families in Crisis: Women, Guardianship, and the Nobility in Early Modern Spain." PhD diss., Indiana University, 2001.

———. *Guardianship, Gender, and the Nobility in Early Modern Spain.* Aldershot: Ashgate, 2010.

Cordero Torres, José María. *El consejo de estado: Su trayectoria y perspective en España.* Madrid: Instituto de Estudios Políticos, 1944.

Coreth, Anna. *Pietas Austriaca.* Translated by William D. Bowman and Anna Maria Leitgeb. West Lafayette: Purdue University Press, 2004.

Cortés Echánove, Luis. *Nacimiento y Crianza de personas reales en la corte de España: 1566–1884.* Madrid: Consejo Superior de Investigaciones Científicas, 1958.

Cosandey, Fanny. "Puissance maternelle et pouvoir politique. La régence des reines mères." *Clio: Histoire, femmes et sociétés* 21 (2005). http://clio.revues .org/1447.

———. *La Reine de France: Symbole et pouvoir, XVe–XVIIIe siècle.* Paris: Gallimard, 2000.

———. "Sucesión, maternidad y legado." In *La Reina Isabel y las reinas de España: Realidad, modelos e imagen historiográfica. Actas de la VIII Reunión Científica de la Fundación Española de Historia Moderna (Madrid, 2–4 de Junio de 2004)*, edited by María Victoria López Cordón and Gloria Franco Rubio, 485–96. Madrid: Fundación Española de Historia Moderna, 2005.

Crawford, Katherine. *Perilous Performances: Gender and Regency in Early Modern France*. Cambridge: Harvard University Press, 2004.

Cruz, Anne J. "Juana of Austria: Patron of the Arts and Regent of Spain, 1554–59." In *The Rule of Women in Early Modern Europe*, edited by Anne J. Cruz and Mihoko Suzuki, 103–22. Urbana: University of Illinois Press, 2009.

Cruz, Anne J., and Maria Galli Stampino, eds. *Early Modern Habsburg Women: Transnational Contexts, Cultural Conflicts, Dynastic Continuities*. Aldershot: Ashgate, 2013.

Cruz, Anne J., and Mihoko Suzuki, eds. *The Rule of Women in Early Modern Europe*. Urbana: University of Illinois Press, 2009.

Cruz Medina, Vanessa de. "An Illegitimate Habsburg: Sor Ana Dorotea de la Concepción, Marquise of Austria." In *Early Modern Habsburg Women: Transnational Contexts, Cultural Conflicts, Dynastic Continuities*, edited by Anne J. Cruz and Maria Galli Stampino, 97–117. Aldershot: Ashgate, 2013.

Danvila y Collado, Manuel. *El poder civil en España*. 6 vols. Madrid: Imprenta y Fundición de Manuel Tello, 1885–86.

Dewald, Jonathan. *The European Nobility, 1400–1800*. Cambridge: Cambridge University Press, 1996.

Dickens, Arthur Geoffrey, ed. *The Courts of Europe: Politics, Patronage and Royalty, 1400–1800*. London: Thames and Hudson, 1977.

Dillard, Heath. *Daughters of the Reconquest: Women in Castilian Town Society, 1100–1300*. Cambridge: Cambridge University Press, 1984.

Domínguez Ortíz, Antonio. "Introducción." In *Testamento de Felipe IV*, transcribed and edited by Antonio Domínguez Ortíz, i–liv. Madrid: Editora Nacional, 1982.

Earenfight, Theresa, ed. "Absent Kings: Queens as Political Partners in the Medieval Crown of Aragon." In *Queenship and Political Power in Medieval and Early Modern Spain*, edited by Theresa Earenfight, 33–51. Aldershot: Ashgate, 2005.

———. *The King's Other Body: María of Castile and the Crown of Aragon*. Philadelphia: University of Pennsylvania Press, 2010.

———. "Partners in Politics." In *Queenship and Political Power in Medieval and Early Modern Spain*, edited by Theresa Earenfight, xiii–xxviii. Aldershot: Ashgate, 2005.

———. *Queenship and Political Power in Medieval and Early Modern Spain*. Aldershot: Ashgate, 2005.

Earle, Peter. *The Sack of Panamá: Captain Morgan and the Battle for the Caribbean*. New York: St. Martin's Press, 2007.

Eire, Carlos M. N. *From Madrid to Purgatory: The Art and Craft of Dying in Sixteenth-Century Spain*. Cambridge: Cambridge University Press, 1995.

Ekberg, Carl J. "Abel Servien, Cardinal Mazarin, and the Formulation of French Foreign Policy, 1653–1659." *International History Review* 3, no. 3 (July 1981): 317–29.

———. *The Failure of Louis XIV's Dutch War*. Chapel Hill: University of North Carolina Press, 1979.

Elliott, John H. "The Court of the Spanish Habsburgs: A Peculiar Institution?" In *Spain and Its World: 1500–1700. Selected Essays*, 142–61. New Haven: Yale University Press, 1989.

Elliott, John H. *The Count-Duke of Olivares: The Statesman in an Age of Decline*. New Haven: Yale University Press, 1986.

———. *Empires of the Atlantic World: Britain and Spain in America, 1492–1830.* New Haven: Yale University Press, 2006.

———. "A Europe of Composite Monarchies." *Past and Present* 137 (November 1992): 48–71.

———. *History in the Making.* New Haven: Yale University Press, 2012.

———. *Imperial Spain, 1469–1716.* London: Penguin, 2002.

———. "Philip IV of Spain: Prisoner of Ceremony." In *The Courts of Europe: Politics, Patronage and Royalty, 1400–1800,* edited by A. G. Dickens, 169–89. London: Thames and Hudson, 1977.

———. "A Question of Reputation? Spanish Foreign Policy in the Seventeenth Century." *Journal of Modern History* 55, no. 3 (September 1983): 475–83.

———. *The Revolt of the Catalans: A Study in the Decline of Spain, 1598–1640.* Cambridge: Cambridge University Press, 1963.

———. *Richelieu and Olivares.* Cambridge: Cambridge University Press, 1984.

———. "Self-Perception and Decline in Early Seventeenth-Century Spain." *Past and Present* 74 (February 1977): 46–61.

———. *Spain and Its World, 1500–1700: Selected Essays.* New Haven: Yale University Press, 1989.

Elliott, John H., and Laurence W. B. Brockliss, eds. *The World of the Favourite.* New Haven: Yale University Press, 1999.

Escudero, José Antonio. "Consultas al Consejo de Estado: Trámites irregulares en el reinado de Carlos II." In *Homenaje al dr. D. Juan Reglá Campistol,* 1:661–64. Valencia: Universitat de València, 1975.

Escudero, José Antonio. *Administración y estado en la España de los Austrias.* Madrid: Junta de Castilla y León, 1999.

———. *Los secretarios de estado y del despacho (1474–1724).* 4 vols. Madrid: Instituto de Estudios Administrativos, 1969.

———. *Los validos.* Madrid: Dykinson, 2006.

Estela, Margarita. "El mecenazgo de los Marqueses de Mejorada en la Iglesia y Capilla de su villa. Su altar-baldaquino y sus esculturas de mármol,

documentados." *Archivo Español del Arte* 288 (1999): 469–502.

Estenaga y Echevarría, Narciso. *El Cardenal Aragón (1621–1677): Estudio histórico.* 2 vols. Paris: Desfossés, 1929.

Fernández, Javier Santiago. *Política monetaria en Castilla durante el siglo XVII.* Valladolid: Junta de Castilla y León, 2000.

Fernández Giménez, María del Camino. "Valenzuela: Valido o primer ministro." In *Los validos,* edited by Antonio Escudero, 353–406. Madrid: Dykinson, 2006.

Fernández Nadal, Carmen María. *La política exterior de la monarquía de Carlos II: El consejo de estado y la embajada de Londres (1665–1700).* Gijon, Spain: Ateneo Jovellanos, 2009.

Feros, Antonio. "Images of Evil, Images of Kings: The Contrasting Faces of the Royal Favourite and the Prime Minister in Early Modern Political Literature, c. 1580–c. 1650." In *The World of the Favourite,* edited by John H. Elliott and Laurence W. B. Brockliss, 205–22. New Haven: Yale University Press, 1999.

———. *Kingship and Favoritism in the Spain of Philip III of Spain, 1598–1621.* Cambridge: Cambridge University Press, 2000.

Fichtner, Paula Sutter. "Dynastic Marriage in Sixteenth-Century Habsburg Diplomacy and Statecraft: An Interdisciplinary Approach." *American Historical Review* 81, no. 2 (April 1976): 243–65.

Fink De Backer, Stephanie Louise. *Widowhood in Early Modern Spain: Protectors, Proprietors, and Patrons.* Leiden: Brill, 2010.

Franganillo, Alejandra. "La reina Isabel de Borbón: Las redes de poder en torno a su casa (1621–1644)." PhD diss., Universidad Complutense de Madrid, 2015.

Gómez Vozmediano, Miguel Fernando. "'En olor a santidad.' La fallida beatificación de la Reina Mariana de Austria." In *La Reina Isabel y las reinas de España: Realidad, modelos e imagen historiográfica. Actas de la VIII Reunión Científica de la Fundación Española de Historia Moderna (Madrid, 2–4 de Junio de 2004),* edited by María Victoria López Cordón and Gloria Franco Rubio, 556–73. Madrid: Fundación Española de Historia Moderna, 2005.

González de la Peña, María del Val, ed. *Mujer y cultura escrita: Del mito al siglo XXI.* Gijón: Ediciones Trea, 2005.

Goodman, Eleanor. "Conspicuous in Her Absence: Mariana of Austria, Juan José of Austria, and the Representation of Her Power." In *Queenship and Political Power in Medieval and Early Modern Spain,* edited by Theresa Earenfight, 163–84. Aldershot: Ashgate, 2005.

Hanley, Sarah. "The Family, the State, and the Law in Seventeenth- and Eighteenth-Century France: The Political Ideology of Male Right Versus an Early Theory of Natural Rights." *Journal of Modern History* 78, no. 2 (June 2006): 289–332.

Hatton, Ragnhild M., ed. "Louis XIV and His Fellow Monarchs." In *Luis XIV and Europe,* edited by Ragnhild. M. Hatton, 16–59. London: Macmillan, 1976.

———. *Luis XIV and Europe.* London: Macmillan, 1976.

Hayley, Kenneth Harold Dobson. *An English Diplomat in the Low Countries: Sir William Temple and John de Witt, 1665–1672.* Oxford: Clarendon, 1986.

Helfferich, Tryntje. *The Iron Princess: Amalia Elisabeth and the Thirty Years War.* Cambridge: Harvard University Press, 2013.

———. *The Thirty Years War: A Documentary History.* Indianapolis: Hackett, 2009.

Hengerer, Mark. *Kaiser Ferdinand III. (1608–1657). Eine Biographie.* Vienna: Böhlau Verlag, 2012.

Hermant, Héloïse. *Guerres de plumes: Publicité et cultures politiques dans l'Espagne du XVIIe siècle.* Madrid: Bibliothèque de la Casa de Velázquez, 2012.

Hermosa Espeso, Cristina. "El Testamento de Felipe IV y la Junta de Gobierno de la minoridad de Carlos II. Apuntes para su interpretación." *Erasmo: Revista de Historia Bajo-Medieval y Moderna* 1 (2014): 102–20.

Herrero Sánchez, Manuel. *El acercamiento Hispano-Neerlandés (1648–1678).* Madrid: Consejo Superior de Investigaciones Científicas, 2000.

Hillgarth, J. N. "Spanish Historiography and Iberian Reality." *History and Theory* 24, no. 1 (1985): 23–43.

Höbelt, Lothar. *Ferdinand III (1608–1657), Friedenskaiser wider Willen.* Graz: Ares Verlag, 2008.

Hoffman, Martha K. *Raised to Rule: Educating Royalty at the Court of the Spanish Habsburgs, 1601–1634.* Baton Rouge: Louisiana State University Press, 2011.

Hortal Muñoz, José Eloy, and Félix Labrador Arroyo, eds. *La Casa de Borgoña: La Casa del Rey de España.* Leuven: Leuven University Press, 2014.

Hume, Martin Andrew Sharp. *Queens of Old Spain.* New York: McClure, Phillips, 1906.

Hutton, R. "The Making of the Secret Treaty of Dover, 1668–1670." *Historical Journal* 29, no. 2 (June 1986): 297–318.

Ibañez y García, Luís. *Historia de las Islas Marianas con su derrotero, y de las Carolinas y Palaos, desde el descubrimiento de Magallanes en el año 1521, hasta nuestros días, por el coronel de infantería D. Luís de Ibañez y García, Gobernador que fue de dichas Islas.* Granada: Paulino V. Sabatel, 1886.

Ingrao, Charles W., and Andrew L. Thomas. "Piety and Power: The Empress-Consort of the High Baroque." In *Queenship in Europe, 1660–1815: The Role of the Consort,* edited by Clarissa Campbell Orr, 107–30. Cambridge: Cambridge University Press, 2004.

Israel, Jonathan I. *The Dutch Republic: Its Rise, Greatness, and Fall, 1477–1806.* Oxford: Oxford University Press, 1995.

———. "The Jews of Spanish Oran and Their Expulsion in 1669." *Mediterranean Historical Review* 9, no. 2 (1994): 235–55.

Jordan Gschwend, Annemarie. "Mujeres mecenas de la casa de Austria y la infanta Isabel Clara Eugenia." In *El arte en la corte de los Archiduques Alberto de Austria e Isabel Clara Eugenia (1598–1633): Un reino imaginado*, 118–37. Madrid: Sociedad Estatal para la Conmemoración de los Centenarios de Felipe II y Carlos V, 1999.

———. "Los Retratos de Juana de Austria posteriores a 1554: La imagen de una princesa de Portugal, una Regente de España y una jesuita." *Reales Sitios* no. 151 (2002): 42–65.

Jurado Sánchez, José. *La economía de la corte: El gasto de la casa real en la edad moderna (1561–1808)*. Madrid: Instituto de Estudios Fiscales, 2005.

Jussen, Bernhard. "The King's Two Bodies Today." *Representations* 106 (Spring 2009): 102–17.

Kagan, Richard. "Prescott's Paradigm: American Historical Scholarship and the Decline of Spain." *American Historical Review* 101, no. 2 (1996): 423–46.

Kalnein, Albrecht Graf von. *Juan José de Austria en la España de Carlos II: Historia de una regencia*. Translated by Carlos Potayo. Lleida: Editorial Milenio, 2001.

Kamen, Henry. "The Decline of Spain: A Historical Myth?" *Past and Present* 91 (May 1981): 170–80.

———. *La España de Carlos II*. Barcelona: Biblioteca Historia de España, 2005.

———. *Spain in the Later Seventeenth Century, 1665–1700*. London: Longman, 1980.

Kantorowicz, Ernst. *The King's Two Bodies: A Study in Mediaeval Political Theology, with Preface by William Chester Jordan*. Princeton: Princeton University Press, 1997.

Keller, Katrin. *Hofdamen: Amtsträgerinnen im Wiener Hofstaat des 17. Jahrhunderts*. Vienna: Verlag, 2005.

———. "Ladies-in-Waiting at the Imperial Court of Vienna from 1550 to 1700: Structures, Responsibilities and Career Patterns." In *The Politics of Female Households: Ladies-in-Waiting Across Early Modern Europe*, edited by Nadine Akkerman and Birgit Houben, 77–99. Leiden: Brill, 2013.

Kent, Dale. "Women in Renaissance Florence." In *Virtue and Beauty: Leonardo's Ginevra de' Benci and Renaissance Portraits of Women*, edited by David Alan Brown, 25–47. Princeton: Princeton University Press, 2001.

Klapisch-Zuber, Christiane. *Women, Family, and Ritual in Renaissance Italy*. Chicago: Chicago University Press, 1987.

Labrador Arroyo, Félix. "From Castile to Burgundy: The Evolution of the Queens' Households During the Sixteenth Century." In *Early Modern Habsburg Women: Transnational Contexts, Cultural Conflicts, Dynastic Continuities*, edited by Anne J. Cruz and Maria Galli Stampino, 119–48. Aldershot: Ashgate, 2013.

———. "La formación de las Etiquetas Generales de Palacio en tiempos de Felipe IV: La Junta de Etiquetas, reformas y cambios en la Casa Real." In *La Casa de Borgoña: La Casa del Rey de España*, edited by José Eloy Hortal Muñoz and Félix Labrador Arroyo, 99–128. Leuven: Leuven University Press, 2014.

———. "La organización de la Casa de Margarita Teresa de Austria para su jornada al Imperio (1666)." In *Las Relaciones Discretas entre las Monarquías Hispana y Portuguesa: Las Casas de las Reinas (siglos XV–XIX)*, 3 vols., edited by José Martínez Millán and Maria Paula Marçal Lourenço, 2:1221–66. Madrid: Ediciones Polifemo, 2008.

Lane, Kris. *Pillaging the Empire: Global Piracy on the High Seas, 1500–1700*. New York: Routledge, 2017.

Langdon-Davies, John. *The King Who Would Not Die*. Englewood Cliffs, NJ: Prentice-Hall, 1963.

Lee, Maurice D., Jr. "The Earl of Arlington and the Treaty of Dover." *Journal of British Studies* 1, no. 1 (November 1961): 58–70.

Levin, Carole. *The Heart and Stomach of a King: Elizabeth I and the Politics of Sex and Power*. Philadelphia: University of Pennsylvania Press, 1994.

Lightman, Harriet L. "Sons and Mothers: Queens and Minor Kings in French Constitutional Law." PhD diss., Bryn Mawr College, 1981.

Liss, Peggy. *Isabel the Queen: Life and Times.* 2nd rev. ed. Philadelphia: University of Pennsylvania Press, 2004.

Llorente, Mercedes. "Imagen y autoridad en una regencia: Los retratos de Mariana de Austria y los límites del poder." *Studia histórica: Historia moderna* 28 (2006): 211–38.

———. "Mariana de Austria como gobernadora." In *Las relaciones discretas entre las Monarquías Hispana y Portuguesa: Las casas de las reinas (siglos XV–XIX),* 3 vols., edited by José Martínez Millán and Paula Marçal Lourenço, 3:1777–1810. Madrid: Ediciones Polifemo, 2008.

———. "Mariana of Austria's Portraits as Ruler-Governor and Curadora by Juan Carreño de Miranda and Claudio Coello." In *Early Modern Habsburg Women: Transnational Contexts, Cultural Conflicts, Dynastic Continuities,* edited by Anne J. Cruz and Maria Galli Stampino, 197–222. Aldershot: Ashgate, 2013.

López Álvarez, Alejandro. *Poder, lujo y conflicto en la Corte de los Austrias: Coches, carrozas y sillas de mano, 1550–1700.* Madrid: Ediciones Polifemo, 2007.

López Cordón, María Victoria. "La evolución de las damas entre los siglos XVII y XVIII." In *Las relaciones discretas entre las Monarquías Hispana y Portuguesa: Las casas de las reinas (siglos XV–XIX),* 3 vols., edited by José Martínez Millán and Maria Paula Marçal Lourenço, 2:1357–98. Madrid: Ediciones Polifemo, 2008.

———. "Mujer, poder y apariencia o las vicisitudes de una regencia." *Studia histórica: Historia moderna* 19 (1998): 49–66.

———. "Las mujeres en la vida de Carlos II." In *Carlos II: El rey y su entorno cortesano,* edited by Luis Ribot, 108–39. Madrid: Centro de Estudios Europa Hispánica, 2009.

———. *La Reina Isabel I y las reinas de España: Realidad, modelos e imagen historiográfica. Actas de la VIII Reunión Científica de la Fundación Española de Historia Moderna (Madrid, 2–4 de Junio de 2004).* Madrid: Fundación Española de Historia Moderna, 2005.

López Millán, Miguel Ángel. "'Esta casa no se acaba.' Don Luis de Haro y el palacio de Uceda." In *El mundo de un Valido: Don Luis de Haro y su entorno, 1643–1661,* edited by Rafael Valladares, 303–46. Madrid: Marcial Pons Historia, 2016.

López Vizcaíno, Pilar, and Ángel Mario Carreño. *Juan Carreño Miranda: Vida y obra.* Madrid: Cajasur, 2007.

Lozano Navarro, Julián J. *La compañía de Jesús y el poder en la España de los Austrias.* Madrid: Cátedra, 2005.

Luzzi Traficante, Marcelo. "La casa de Borgoña ante el cambio dinástico y durante el siglo XVIII (1680–1761)." In *La Casa de Borgoña: La Casa del Rey de España,* edited by José Eloy Hortal Muñoz and Félix Labrador Arroyo, 129–74. Leuven: Leuven University Press, 2014.

Lynch, John. *Spain Under the Habsburgs.* Vol. 2, *Spain and America, 1598–1700.* New York: New York University Press, 1984.

Lynn, John A. *The Wars of Louis XIV, 1667–1714.* London: Longman, 1999.

Major, J. Russell. *From Renaissance Monarchy to Absolute Monarchy: French Kings, Nobles, and Estates.* Baltimore: Johns Hopkins University Press, 1994.

Malcolm, Alistair. "Arte, diplomacia y política de la corte durante las embajadas del conde de Sandwich a Madrid y Lisboa (1666–1668)." In *Arte y Diplomacia de la Monarquía Hispánica en el siglo XVII,* edited by José Luis Colomer, 161–75. Madrid: Fernando Villaverde Ediciones, 2003.

———. "La práctica informal del poder. La política de la Corte y el acceso a la Familia Real durante la segunda mitad del reinado de Felipe IV." *Reales Sitios* 147 (2001): 38–48.

———. "Spanish Queens and Aristocratic Women at the Court of Madrid, 1598–1665." In *Studies on Medieval and Early Modern Women, 4: Victims or Viragos?*, edited by Christine Meek and Catherine Lawless, 160–80. Dublin: Four Courts Press, 2005.

Maltby, William. *The Reign of Charles V.* New York: Palgrave, 2002.

Manescau Martín, María Teresa. "Don Juan José de Austria, ¿Valido o dictador?" In *Los validos*, edited by Antonio Escudero, 447–546. Madrid: Dykinson, 2006.

Maravall, José Antonio. *La teoría española del estado en el siglo XVII.* Madrid: Consejo Superior de Investigaciones Científicas, 1944.

Martínez López, Rocío. "'La Infanta se ha de casar con quien facilite la paz o disponga los medios para la guerra.' Las negociaciones para la realización del matrimonio entre la Infanta María Teresa y Leopold I (1654–1657)." *Revista de Historia Moderna: Anales de la Universidad de Alicante* 33 (2015): 79–99.

Martínez Millán, José. "La corte de la monarquía hispánica." *Studia histórica: Historia moderna* 28 (2006): 17–61.

Martínez Millán, José, and Santiago Fernández Conti, eds. *La Monarquía de Felipe II: La casa del rey.* 2 vols. Madrid: Fundación Mapfre, 2005.

Martínez Millán, José, and Maria Paula Marçal Lourenço, eds. *Las relaciones discretas entre las Monarquías Hispana y Portuguesa: Las casas de las reinas (siglos XV–XIX).* 3 vols. Madrid: Ediciones Polifemo, 2008.

Matilla Tascón, Antonio. *La única contribución y el Catastro de la Ensenada.* Madrid: Servicio de Estudios de la Inspección General de Hacienda, 1947.

Maura, Gabriel. *Carlos II y su corte: Ensayo de Reconstrucción biográfica.* 2 vols. Madrid: Revista de Archivos, Bibliotecas y Museos, 1911 and 1915.

McGowan, Margaret, ed. *Dynastic Marriages 1612/1615: A Celebration of the Habsburgs and Bourbon Unions.* Aldershot: Ashgate, 2013.

Mesa Gallego, Eduardo de. "Itinerario biográfico." In *Marqués de Aytona: Discurso Militar. Propónense algunos inconvenientes de la Milicia de estos tiempos, y su reparo*, transcribed and edited by Eduardo de Mesa Gallego, 41–77. Madrid: Ministerio de Defensa, 2008.

Mínguez, Víctor. *La invención de Carlos II: Apoteosis simbólica de la casa de Austria.* Madrid: Centro de Estudios Europa Hispánica, 2013.

Mitchell, Silvia Z. "Growing Up Carlos II: Political Childhood in the Court of the Spanish Habsburgs." In *The Formation of the Child in Early Modern Spain*, edited by Grace E. Coolidge, 189–206. Aldershot: Ashgate, 2014.

———. "Habsburg Motherhood: The Power of Queen Mariana of Austria, Mother and Regent for Carlos II of Spain." In *Early Modern Habsburg Women: Transnational Contexts, Cultural Conflicts, Dynastic Continuities*, edited by Anne J. Cruz and Maria Galli Stampino, 175–96. Aldershot: Ashgate, 2013.

———. "Marriage Plots: Marriage Diplomacy, Royal Women, and International Politics at the Spanish, French, and Imperial Courts, 1665–1679." In *Women, Diplomacy, and International Politics Since 1500*, edited by Glenda Sluga and Carolyn James, 86–106. London: Routledge, 2014.

Molas Ribalta, Pere. "La duquesa de Cardona en 1640." *Cuadernos de Historia Moderna* 29 (2004): 133–43.

Morant, Isabel, ed. *Historia de las mujeres en España y América Latina II: El mundo moderno.* Madrid: Cátedra, 2005.

Moreno Prieto, María del Carmen. "El Cardenal Portocarrero como consejero de Estado (1677–1703). La documentación del Archivo Histórico Nacional." In *El Cardenal Portocarrero y su tiempo (1635–1709)*, edited by José Manuel de Bernardo Ares, 223–62. Valencia: CSED Editorial, 2013.

Muñoz Serrulla, Maria Teresa, and Karen Maria Vilacoba Ramos. "Del Alcázar a las Descalzas Reales: Correspondencia entre reinas y religiosas en el ocaso de la dinastía de los Austrias." In *La Reina Isabel I y las reinas de España: Realidad, modelos e imagen historiográfica. Actas de la VIII Reunión Científica de la Fundación Española de Historia Moderna (Madrid, 2–4 de Junio de 2004)*, edited by María Victoria López Cordón and Gloria Franco Rubio, 597–610. Madrid: Fundación Española de Historia Moderna, 2005.

Nader, Helen. *The Mendoza Family in the Spanish Renaissance, 1350–1550*. New Brunswick: Rutgers University Press, 1979.

Ochoa Brun, Miguel Ángel. "Estudio preliminar. La diplomacia española en el ocaso de la gran época." In *Diario del Conde de Pötting, Embajador del Sacro Imperio en Madrid (1664–1674)*, 2 vols., edited by Miguel Nieto Nuño, 11–33. Madrid: Biblioteca Diplomática Española, 1990.

———. *Historia de la Diplomacia Española: La Edad Barroca, II*. Madrid: Ministerio de Asuntos Exteriores, 2006.

Oliván Santaliestra, Laura. "La correspondencia de Mariana de Austria: Aspectos de cultura escrita de una regencia femenina." In *Mujer y cultura escrita: Del mito al siglo XXI*, edited by María del Val González de la Peña, 213–20. Gijón: Ediciones Trea, 2005.

———. "La dama, el aya y la camarera: Perfiles políticos de tres mujeres de la Casa de Mariana de Austria." In *Las relaciones discretas entre las Monarquías Hispana y Portuguesa: Las casas de las reinas (siglos XV–XIX)*, 3 vols., edited by José Martínez Millán and Maria Paula Marçal Lourenço, 2:1301–56. Madrid: Ediciones Polifemo, 2008.

———. "Discurso jurídico, histórico, político: Apología de las reinas regentes y defensa del sistema polisinodial, una manifestación de la conflictividad política en los inicios de la regencia de Mariana de Austria." *Cuadernos de historia moderna: Universidad Complutense* 28 (2003): 7–34.

———. "Giovane d'anni ma vecchia di giudizio: La emperatriz Margarita en la corte de Viena." In *La dinastía de los Austria: Las relaciones entre la Monarquía Católic y el Imperio*, 3 vols., edited by José Martínez Millán and Rubén González Cuerva, 837–908. Madrid: Polifemo, 2011.

———. *Mariana de Austria: Imagen, poder y diplomacia de una reina cortesana*. Madrid: Editorial Complutense, 2006.

———. "Mariana de Austria en la encrucijada política del siglo XVII." PhD diss., Universidad Complutense de Madrid, 2006.

———. "Modelo borgoñón en la Casa de las emperatrices hispanas (1629–73)." In *La Casa de Borgoña: La Casa del Rey de España*, edited by José Eloy Hortal Muñoz and Félix Labrador Arroyo, 547–73. Leuven: Leuven University Press, 2014.

———. "Pinceladas políticas, marcos cortesanos: El diario del conde de Harrach, embajador imperial en la Corte de Madrid (1673–1677)." *Cultura Escrita y Sociedad* 3 (2006): 113–32.

———. "The Representational Strategies of the Count-Duke of Olivares and Elisabeth of France: Equestrian Portraits, Guardainfantes and Miniatures (1628–1644)." In *The Age of Rubens: Diplomacy, Dynastic Politics and the Visual Arts in Early Seventeenth-Century Europe*, edited by Luc Duerloo and R. Malcolm Smuts, 213–34. Turnhout: Brepols, 2016.

Orr, Clarissa Campbell. *Queenship in Europe, 1660–1815: The Role of the Consort*. Cambridge: Cambridge University Press, 2004.

Orso, Steven N. *Art and Death at the Spanish Habsburg Court: The Royal Exequies for Philip IV*. Columbia: University of Missouri Press, 1989.

Palos, Joan-Lluís, and Magdalena S. Sánchez, eds. *Early Modern Dynastic Marriages and Cultural Transfer*. London: Routledge, 2016.

Parker, Geoffrey. *The Army of Flanders and the Spanish Road, 1567–1659*. 2nd ed.

Cambridge: Cambridge University Press, 2004.

———. *The Army of Flanders and the Spanish Road, 1567–1659: The Logistics of Spanish Victory and Defeat in the Low Countries' Wars*. Cambridge: Cambridge University Press, 1972.

———. *The Grand Strategy of Philip II*. New Haven: Yale University Press, 2000.

Parker, Geoffrey, and Simon Adams. *The Thirty Years' War*. London: Routledge, 1987.

Patrouch. "'Bella gerant alii.' Laodamia's Sisters/Habsburgs Brides: Leaving Home for the Sake of the House." In *Early Modern Habsburg Women: Transnational Contexts, Cultural Conflicts, Dynastic Continuities*, edited by Anne J. Cruz and Maria Galli Stampino, 25–38. Aldershot: Ashgate, 2013.

Patrouch, Joseph. "Dynastic, Imperial, International: Some Directions in Early Modern European Studies." *Sixteenth Century Journal* 40, no. 1 (2009): 217–19.

———. *Queen's Apprentice: Archduchess Elizabeth, Empress María, the Habsburgs, and the Holy Roman Empire, 1554–1569*. Leiden: Brill, 2010.

Peña Izquierdo, Antonio Ramón. *De Austrias a Borbones: España entre los siglos XVII y XVIII*. León: Editorial Akrón, 2008.

———. *La Casa de Palma: La familia Portocarrero en el gobierno de la monarquía hispánica (1665–1700)*. Córdoba: Universidad de Córdoba, 2004.

Pérez-Bustamante, Rogelio. *El gobierno del Imperio Español*. Madrid: Comunidad de Madrid, Consejería de Educación, 2000.

Pfandl, Ludwig. *Karl II: Das ende der spanischen machtstellung in Europa*. München: G. D. W. Callwey, 1940.

Pilo Gallisai, Rafaella. "Casi todos los hombres del Cardenal Moncada. La conjura del otoño (octubre de 1668–marzo de 1669)." In *La sucesión de la monarquía hispánica (1665–1725)*, edited by José Manuel de Bernardo Ares, 257–75. Madrid: Sílex Universidad, 2009.

Poska, Allyson. *Women and Authority in Early Modern Spain: The Peasants of Galicia*. Oxford: Oxford University Press, 2005.

Pribram, Franz A. F. *Franz Paul, Freiherr von Lisola und die Politik seiner Zeit*. Leipzig, 1894.

Raviola, Blythe Alice. "The Three Lives of Margherita of Savoy-Gonzaga, Duchess of Mantua and Vicereine of Portugal." In *Early Modern Habsburg Women: Transnational Contexts, Cultural Conflicts, Dynastic Continuities*, edited by Anne J. Cruz and Maria Galli Stampino, 59–76. Aldershot: Ashgate, 2013.

Rawlings, Helen. *The Debate on the Decline of Spain*. Manchester: Manchester University Press, 2012.

Redworth, Glyn. *The Prince and the Infanta: The Cultural Politics of the Spanish Match*. New Haven: Yale University Press, 2003.

Redworth, Glyn, and Fernando Checa. "The Kingdoms of Spain: The Courts of the Spanish Habsburgs, 1500–1700." In *The Princely Courts of Europe, 1500–1750*, edited by John Adamson, 43–65. London: Weidenfeld & Nicolson, 1999.

Revilla Canora. "Javier. El asesinato del Virrey Marqués de Camarasa y el Pregón General del Duque de San Germán (1668–1669)." In *De la Tierra al Cielo: Líneas recientes de investigación en Historia Moderna*, edited by Eliseo Serrano, 575–84. Zaragoza: Diputación de Zaragoza, 2013.

Ribot García, Luis. *El arte de gobernar: Estudios sobre la España de los Austrias*. Madrid: Alianza Editorial, 2006.

———. "El Cardinal Portocarrero y la sucesión de España." In *El Cardenal Portocarrero y su tiempo (1635–1709)*, edited by José Manuel de Bernardo Ares, 335–43. Valencia: CSED Editorial, 2013.

———. "Carlos II: El centenario olvidado." *Studia histórica: Historia moderna* 20 (1999): 19–44.

———, ed. *Carlos II: El rey y su entorno cortesano*. Madrid: Centro de Estudios Europa Hispánica, 2009.

——. *La monarquía de España y la Guerra de Mesina (1674–1678)*. Madrid: Actas, 2002.

——. *Orígenes políticos del testamento de Carlos II: La gestación del cambio dinástico en España. Discurso leído el día 17 de octubre de 2010*. Madrid: Real Academia de la Historia, 2010.

——. "La repercusión en España del tratado de reparto de la Monarquía de 1668." In *Tiempo de cambios: Guerra, diplomacia, y política internacional de la Monarquía Hispánica (1648–1700)*, edited by Porfirio Sanz Camañez, 55–96. Madrid: Actas, 2012.

——. *La revuelta antiespañola de Mesina: Causas y antecedentes (1591–1674)*. Valladolid: Universidad de Valladolid, 1982.

——. "El rey ante el espejo: Historia y memoria de Carlos II." In *Carlos II: El rey y su entorno cortesano*, edited by Luis Ribot, 12–52. Madrid: Centro de Estudios Europa Hispánica, 2010.

Ribot García, Luis, and José María Iñurritegui, eds. *Europa y los tratados de reparto de la Monarquía de España, 1668–1700*. Madrid: Biblioteca Nueva, 2016.

Rodríguez Hernández, Antonio José. *España, Flandes y la Guerra de Devolución (1667–1668): Guerra, reclutamiento y movilización para el mantenimiento de los Países Bajos españoles*. Madrid: Colección Adalid, 2007.

Rodríguez-Salgado, M. J. "The Court of Philip II of Spain." In *Princes, Patronage and the Nobility: The Court at the Beginning of the Modern Age, c. 1450–1650*, edited by Ronald Asch and Adolf M. Birke, 205–44. London: German Historical Institute, 1991.

Rowen, Herbert H. *The Ambassador Prepares for War: The Dutch Embassy of Arnauld de Pomponne, 1669–1671*. The Hague: Martinus Nijhoff, 1957.

——. *John de Witt, Grand Pensionary of Holland, 1625–1672*. Princeton: Princeton University Press, 1978.

Rufino Novo, José. "La Casa real durante la regencia de una reina: Mariana de Austria." In *Las relaciones discretas entre las Monarquías Hispana y Portuguesa: Las casas de las reinas (siglos XV–XIX)*, 3 vols., edited by José Martínez Millán and Maria Paula Marçal Lourenço, 1:483–547. Madrid: Ediciones Polifemo, 2008.

Ruggiero, Guido. *The Boundaries of Eros: Sex, Crime, and Sexuality in Renaissance Venice*. New York: Oxford University Press, 1985.

Ruiz, Teofilo F. "Unsacred Monarchy: The Kings of Castile in the Late Middle Ages." In *Rites of Power: Symbolism, Ritual, and Politics Since the Middle Ages*, edited by Sean Wilentz, 109–44. Philadelphia: University of Pennsylvania Press, 1985.

Ruíz Rodríguez, Ignacio. *Don Juan José de Austria en la monarquía hispánica: Entre la política, el poder y la intriga*. Madrid: Dykinson, 2007.

——. "Juan José de Austria y Aragón." In *Los validos*, edited by José Antonio Escudero, 407–46. Madrid: Dykinson, 2006.

Saavedra Vázquez, María del Carmen, ed. *La decadencia de la monarquía hispánica en el siglo XVII: Viejas imágenes y nuevas aportaciones*. Madrid: Biblioteca Nueva, 2016.

Sáenz Berceo, María del Carmen. "Juan Everardo Nithard, un valido extranjero." In *Los validos*, edited by José Antonio Escudero, 323–52. Madrid: Dykinson, 2006.

Sahlins, Peter. *Boundaries: The Making of France and Spain in the Pyrenees*. Berkeley: University of California Press, 1989.

Salas Almela, Luis. *The Conspiracy of the Ninth Duke of Medina Sidonia (1641): An Aristocrat in the Crisis of the Spanish Empire*. Leiden: Brill, 2013.

Sánchez, Magdalena S. *The Empress, the Queen and the Nun: Women and Power at the Court of Philip III of Spain*. Baltimore: Johns Hopkins University Press, 1998.

——. "A House Divided: Spain, Austria, and the Bohemian and Hungarian Successions." *Sixteenth Century Journal* 25, no. 4 (1994): 887–903.

———. "Sword and Wimple: Isabel Clara Eugenia and Power." In *The Rule of Women in Early Modern Europe*, edited by Anne J. Cruz and Mihoko Suzuki, 64–79. Urbana: University of Illinois Press, 2009.

Sánchez, Magdalena S., and Alain Saint-Saëns, eds. *Spanish Women in the Golden Age: Images and Realities*. Westport, CT: Greenwood Press, 1996.

Sánchez Belén, Juan Antonio. "La expulsion de los judíos de Orán en 1669." *Espacio, Tiempo, y Forma Serie IV: Historia Moderna* 6 (1993): 155–98.

———. "La junta de alivios de 1669 y las primeras reformas de la regencia." *Revista de la Facultad de Geografía e Historia* 4 (1989): 639–68.

———. "Mirando hacia adelante: Las reformas económicas y fiscales en el reinado de Carlos II." In *La decadencia de la monarquía hispánica en el siglo XVII: Viejas imágenes y nuevas aportaciones*, edited by María del Carmen Saavedra, 165–81. Madrid: Biblioteca Nueva, 2016.

———. *La política fiscal en Castilla durante el reinado de Carlos II*. Madrid: Siglo XXI de España, 1996.

———. "Las relaciones internacionales de la monarquía hispánica durante la regencia de doña Mariana de Austria." *Studia histórica: Historia moderna* 20 (1999): 137–72.

Sánchez Gómez, Rosa Isabel. "Formación, desarrollo y actividades delictivas del regimiento de 'La Chamberga' en Madrid durante la minoria de Carlos II." *Torre de los Lujanes* 17 (January 1991): 80–96.

Sánchez Portillo, Paloma. "En torno a las Meninas: Algunas noticias de Nicolás Pertusato." *Anales de historia del Arte* 12 (2002): 149–66.

Sánchez Ramos, Valeriano. "El poder de una mujer en la corte: La V marquesa de los Vélez y los últimos Fajardo (segunda mitad del s. XVII)." *Revista Velezana* 25 (2006): 19–65.

Sanz Ayán, Carmen. *Los Banqueros de Carlos II*. Valladolid: Universidad de Valladolid, 1989.

———. *Pedagogía de reyes: El teatro palaciego en el reinado de Carlos II*. Madrid: Real Academia de la Historia, 2006.

Sanz Camañes, Porfirio. *La monarquía Hispánica en tiempos del Quijote*. Madrid: UCLM, 2005.

Schrader, Jeffrey. *La Virgen de Atocha: Los Austrias y las imágenes milagrosas*. Madrid: Ayuntamiento de Madrid, 2006.

Serra, Eva. "The Treaty of the Pyrenees, 350 Years Later." *Catalan Historical Review* 1 (2008): 81–99.

Sevilla González, María del Carmen. "La Junta de Gobierno de la minoridad del rey Carlos II." In *Los validos*, edited by José Antonio Escudero, 583–616. Madrid: Dykinson, 2006.

Simón Palmer, María del Carmen. *La Cocina de palacio, 1561–1931*. Madrid: Castalia, 1997.

Sonnino, Paul. *Louis XIV and the Origins of the Dutch War*. Cambridge: Cambridge University Press, 1988.

———. *Mazarin's Quest: The Congress of Westphalia and the Coming of the Fronde*. Cambridge: Harvard University Press, 2008.

———. *Mémoires for the Instruction of the Dauphin*. New York: Free Press, 1970.

Spielman, John P. *Leopold I of Austria*. New Brunswick: Rutgers University Press, 1977.

Starkey, David. "Court, Council, and Nobility in Tudor England." In *Princes, Patronage and the Nobility: The Court at the Beginning of the Modern Age*, edited by Ronald Asch and Adolf M. Birke, 175–203. London: German Historical Institute, 1991.

Storrs, Christopher. "The Army of Lombardy and the Resilience of Spanish Power in Italy in the Reign of Carlos II (1665–1700). (Part I)." *War and History* 4, no. 4 (1997): 371–97.

———. "Nuevas perspectivas sobre le reinado de Carlos II (1665–1700)." In *La decadencia de la monarquía hispánica en el siglo XVII: Viejas imágenes y nuevas aportaciones*, edited by María del Carmen Saavedra Vázquez, 17–37 Madrid: Biblioteca Nueva, 2016.

———. *The Resilience of the Spanish Monarchy, 1665–1700*. Oxford: Oxford University Press, 2006.

Stradling, R. A. *The Armada of Flanders: Spanish Maritime Policy and European War, 1568–1668*. Cambridge: Cambridge University Press, 1992.

———. *Philip IV and the Government of Spain, 1621–1665*. Cambridge: Cambridge University Press, 1988.

———. "A Spanish Statesman of Appeasement: Medina de las Torres and Spanish Policy, 1639–1670." *Historical Journal* 19, no. 1 (March 1976): 1–31.

Suárez Quevedo, Diego. "Fiesta barroca y política en el reinado de Carlos II. Sobre el triunfal destierro a Toledo de Mariana de Austria (1677)." *Madrid: Revista de arte, geografía e historia* 3 (2000): 57–100.

Tercero Casado, Luis. "A Fluctuating Ascendancy: The Spanish Party at the Imperial Court of Vienna (1631–1659)." *Libros de la Corte* Monográfico 2, año 7 (2015): 54–67. Portal de revistas electrónicas UAM (Universidad Autónoma de Madrid), https://revistas.uam.es/librosdelacorte/article/view/1617/1690, accessed November 24, 2017.

———. "La jornada de la Reina Mariana de Austria a España: Divergencias políticas y tensión protocolar en el seno de la casa de Austria (1648–1649)." *Hispania: Revista Española de Historia* 71, no. 239 (2011): 639–64.

Thompson, I. A. A. "The Institutional Background to the Rise of the Minister-Favorite." In *The World of the Favourite*, edited by John H. Elliott and Laurence W. B. Brockliss, 13–25. New Haven: Yale University Press, 1999.

Tomás y Valiente, Francisco. *Los validos en la monarquía española del siglo XVII*. Madrid: Siglo XXI de España Editores, 1982.

Tracy, James. *Emperor Charles V, Impresario of War: Campaign Strategy, International Finance, and Domestic Policy.* Cambridge: Cambridge University Press, 2002.

Trápaga Monchet, Koldo. "La reconfiguración política de la monarquía católica: La actividad de Don Juan José de Austria (1642–1679)." PhD diss., Universidad Autónoma de Madrid, 2015.

Troost, Wout. *William III, the Stadholder-King.* Translated by J. C. Grayson. Aldershot: Ashgate, 2005.

Valladares, Rafael, ed. *El mundo de un valido: Don Luis de Haro y su entorno, 1643–1661*. Madrid: Marcial Pons Historia, 2016.

———. *La Rebelión de Portugal, 1640–1680.* Valladolid: Junta de Castilla y León, Consejería de Educación y Cultura, 1998.

———. "El Tratado de Paz de los Pirineos: Una revisión historiográfica (1888–1988)." *Espacio, Tiempo, y Forma Seria IV: Historia Moderna* 2 (1989): 125–38.

Van Wyhe, Cordula. "The Making and Meaning of the Monastic Habit at Spanish Habsburgs Courts." In *Early Modern Habsburg Women: Transnational Contexts, Cultural Conflicts, Dynastic Continuities*, edited by Anne J. Cruz and Maria Galli Stampino, 243–74. Aldershot: Ashgate, 2013.

Varela, Javier. *La muerte del rey: El ceremonial funerario de la monarquía española (1500–1885).* Madrid: Turner Libros, 1990.

Vermeulen, Anna. *A cuantos leyeren esta carta: Estudio histórico-crítico de la famosa carta de don Juan José de Austria, fechada en Consuegra el 21 de octubre de 1668.* Leuven: Leuven University Press, 2003.

Viennot, Eliane. *La France, les femmes et le pouvoir: L'invention de la loi salique (Ve–XVIe siècle).* Paris: Perrin, 2006.

Vilacoba Ramos, Karen María. "Cartas familiares de una reina: Relaciones epistolares de María Teresa de Francia y las Descalzas Reales." In *Mujer y cultura escrita: Del mito al siglo XXI*, edited by María del Val González de la Peña, 199–212. Gijón: Ediciones Trea, 2005.

Villa-Urrutia, W. R. *Relaciones entre España y Austria durante el reinado de la Emperatriz doña Margarita, Infanta de España, esposa del Emperador Leopoldo I.* Madrid: Imprenta y Estereotipia de Ricardo Fé, 1905.

Weiss, Sabine. *Zur Herrschaft geboren: Kindheit und Jugend im Haus Habsburg von Kaiser Maximilian bis Kronprinz Rudolf.* Vienna: Tyrolia-Verlag, 2008.

Weissberger, Barbara F. *Queen Isabel I of Castile: Power, Patronage, Persona.* Woodbridge: Tamesis, 2008.

Westergaard, Waldemar, trans. and ed. *The First Triple Alliance: The Letters of Christopher Lindenov, Danish Envoy to London, 1668–1672.* New Haven: Yale University Press, 1947.

Wilentz, Sean. "Introduction: Teufelsdröckh's Dilemma: On Symbolism, Politics, and History." In *Rites of Power: Symbolism, Ritual, and Politics Since the Middle Ages*, edited by Sean Wilentz, 1–10. Philadelphia: University of Pennsylvania Press, 1985.

———, ed. *Rites of Power: Symbolism, Ritual, and Politics Since the Middle Ages.* Philadelphia: University of Pennsylvania Press, 1985.

Wunder, Amanda. "Women's Fashions and Politics in Seventeenth-Century Spain: The Rise and Fall of the Guardainfante." *Renaissance Quarterly* 68, no. 1 (Spring 2015): 133–86.

Yetano Laguna, María Isabel. "Relaciones entre España y Francia desde la Paz de los Pirineos (1659) hasta la Guerra de Devolución (1667)." PhD diss., Universidad Nacional de Educación a Distancia, Facultad de Geografía e Historia, Madrid, 2007.

Yun Casalilla, Bartolomé. "De centro a la periferia: La economía española bajo Carlos II." *Studia histórica: Historia moderna* 20 (1999): 45–75.

Zaggia, Massimo. "Culture in Lombardy, 1535–1706." In *A Companion to Late Medieval and Early Modern Milan*, edited by Andrea Gamberini, 190–213. Leiden: Brill, 2015.

Zanger, Abby E. *Scenes from the Marriage of Louis XIV: Nuptial Fictions and the Making of Absolutist Power.* Stanford: Stanford University Press, 1997.

Zapata Fernández de la Hoz, Teresa. *La entrada en la Corte de María Luisa de Orleans.* Madrid: Fundación de Apoyo a la Historia del Arte Hispánico, 2000.

———. "El nuevo mundo en el arte efímero del Madrid del siglo XVII." In *Actas del Congreso: Madrid en el contexto de los hispánico desde la época de los descubrimientos*, 2:1249–65. Madrid: Universidad Complutense Madrid, Departamento del Arte Moderno, 1992.

———. "El viaje de las reinas austriacas a las costas españolas. La travesía de Mariana de Austria." In *España y el mundo mediterráneo a través de las Relaciones de Sucesos (1500–1750)*, edited by Pierre Civil, Françoise Crémoux, and Jacob S. Sanz Hermida, 341–65. Salamanca: Universidad de Salamanca, 2008.

Act of Guarantee, 147–48, 158
Act of Reciprocal Assistance Against France, 150–51
Aguilar, count of, 133, 183, 188–89
Alba, duke of. *See* Álvarez de Toledo y Mendoza, Fernando
Alburquerque, duke of. *See* Fernández de la Cueva, Francisco
Alcalde de Corte, 117
Alcázar (Madrid), 31, 53–54, 195–96, 227
    Carlos II's departure from, 186–87
    Mariana alone in, 188
    renovations of, 164
Alcázar (Toledo), 190, 194
Alexander VII, Pope, 63, 71
Álvarez de Montenegro, Pedro, 167, 168–69, 173, 189
Álvarez de Toledo, Mariana Engracia, marquise of los Velez, 61
Álvarez de Toledo y Mendoza, Fernando, duke of Alba, 63–64, 181
Ana Dorothea of Austria, Sor, 111
Angulo, Isidro de, 201
Anne of Austria, infanta of Spain, queen of France, 76, 78–79, 80, 89, 192
Aragon, Crown of, 2, 68, 128–29, 195
    queen lieutenancy in, 13
    support for Don Juan, 122
Aragón, Pascual de, Cardinal, viceroy of Naples, 70–71, 93, 133, 168–69, 174, 188
Aragón, Pedro of, 181
Aragon, vice-chancellor of, 189
Aragon, vice-chancellor of. *See* Crespí de Valdaura, Cristóbal
Aranjuez, palace of, 162, 193
arbitristas, 164, 173
Arlington, earl of. *See* Bennet, Henry
Army of Flanders, 76–77, 231
    funding for, 94, 102
    rebuilding of, 80, 92–93, 106–7
Asiento de Esclavos, 145
Auersperg, Johann Weikhard, 152

Austria. *See* Holy Roman Empire: Imperial Court
aya, 60, 61
    See also Álvarez de Toledo, Mariana Engracia
Aytona, marquis of. *See* Moncada, Guillén Ramón de

Balbases, marquis of. *See* Spínola, Pablo
Baldueza, marquise of. *See* Ponce de León, Elvira
Baltasar Carlos, prince of Asturias
    death of, 27–28
    as heir to Spanish monarchy, 67
    as Mariana's fiancé, 27
Barrionuevos, Jerónimo, 37
Battle of Villaviciosa, 4, 44, 77
Bejar, duchess of, 223
Bennet, Henry, earl of Arlington, 87, 99
Beverningk, Hieronymus van, 146
Bohemian Revolt, 24
Bonaventure, Ferdinand, count of Harrach, 42
Bourbon dynasty, 230
    rivalry with Habsburgs, 78
    as rulers of Spain, 6
Bracamonte y Guzmán, Gaspar de, count of Peñaranda, 29, 69–70, 83, 128, 134, 148
    criticism of Leopold I, 95–96
    and foreign policy, 141
    influence of, 125
    opinion of Nithard, 123–24
    and Portugal debate, 44, 85
    and Portuguese war, 90
Braganza dynasty, 4, 26, 36
Brandenburg, elector of, 152, 153, 159
Bretel de Grémonville, Jacques, 95, 151
Buen Retiro, palace of, 32, 171, 186–87, 188

Cadiz, Spain, 97
Calderón, María Inés, 111
camarera mayor, 59–60
    authority of, 61
    See also Ponce de León, Elvira

Candia, duchy of, 144
Caraçena, marquis of, 42
    and Portuguese war, 91
Caribbean region, 149
Carlo Emanuel II, duke of Savoy, 143
Carlos II, king of Spain
    assertions of independence, 173–74,
        214, 224, 226
    birth of, 41–42
    consoling mother after Margarita's
        death, 154
    criticisms of, for Mariana's exile, 192
    under a curatorship, 176–77
    devotional acts, 118–19
    and Don Juan, 168–69; amnesty to
        supporters, 189; support for,
        214–15
    education of, 132, 135
    emancipation, 15–16, 162, 168–69, 170
    fear of his mother, 179, 184, 187–88
    first public procession, 118–19
    historiography of, 6–8, 230
    in Philip IV's testament, 47–48, 78
    portraits of, 135, 140
    preservation of the Spanish Nether-
        lands for, 106
    lack of autonomy, 172
    loved by his subjects, 118–19
    love for his mother, 185, 186, 198, 206,
        208, 215
    marriage negotiations; for Maria
        Antonia, 177–79, 196–97; for
        Marie Louise, 200, 209, 210,
        211–12, 217–18
    during regency, 15, 48, 130–31, 132, 135,
        140
    relationship with Mariana, 207
    and royal guard, 131
    as ruler of Portugal, 85
    selection of successor, 229–30
    separation from Mariana, 187–88
    as showing maturity, 180, 185
    tenth birthday of, 135
    transition to adulthood, 174–76
Carpio, marquis of, 100
Carreño de Miranda, Juan, 135
Castellar, count of. See Cueva, Baltasar de la
Castel Rodrigo, marquis of. See Moura Corter-
    real, Francisco de
Castile, admiral of, 166, 188
Castile, kingdom of, 2, 13, 126

Castillo, Antonio del, 46
Castrillo, count of. See Haro Sotomayor y
    Guzmán, García de
Catalina Micaela of Austria, infanta of Spain,
    duchess consort of Savoy, 78
Catalonia
    French threat to, 144
    revolt, 3–4, 26
    support for Don Juan, 122, 126
Catherine of Braganza, infanta of Portugal,
    queen of England, 42
Cerda, Antonio de la, seventh duke of Medi-
    naceli, 80
Cerda, Juan Francisco de la, eighth duke of
    Medinaceli, 149, 166, 173–74, 184, 201,
        209–10
    as president of Italy, 216
    as prime minister, 227
    rise of, 202
Charles II, king of England, 39, 42
    and invasion of the United Provinces,
        142, 148
    Mariana's alliance with, 98–99, 101, 105,
        149, 151
    mediation in peace of Spain with
        Portugal, 87–88, 91, 98, 100
    negotiations with Louis XIV, 142, 148
    neutrality of, in War of Devolution,
        87
    role in Triple Alliance, 101, 103, 105
    See also England; Second Anglo-Dutch
        War; Third Anglo-Dutch War;
        Treaty of Madrid; Peace of
        Westminster
Charles IV, duke of Lorraine, 17, 40–41, 156
    See also Quadruple Alliance
Charles V, Holy Roman Emperor, 19, 49, 236
    n. 18
    retirement of, 185, 194
childhood, royal, 20–24, 132
    definitions of, 13
Claudia Felicitas of Tyrol, archduchess of
    Austria, Holy Roman Empress, 112, 156
Clement IX, Pope, 127
Cologne, 153
Committee of Theologians, 124
Condé, prince of, 38, 40
Confederación, 178, 182–84, 216, 219–20
Conference of Lille, 148, 149, 150
constable of Castile. See Fernández de Velasco,
    Íñigo

coronelía. *See* royal guard

correspondence, among Habsburgs
    between Carlos II and Leopold I, 210
    between Mariana and Carlos II, 200–206, 210, 214–15, 217, 221
    between Mariana and Leopold I, 95–96
    in "own hand," 94, 96, 200

Cortes, 124, 195
    Portuguese, 100
    Spanish, 92

Council of Aragon, 68, 86, 127

Council of Castile, 68, 71, 86, 116, 122, 127–29, 130–31, 134

Council of Indies, 86

Council of Italy, 63–65, 69, 86, 163

Council of State, 77
    and Carlos II's marriage, 197, 209, 211
    Carlos II's role in, 174–75
    divided by Don Juan, 121
    dynamics of, 73, 108
    history of, 71, 72
    Mariana's postregency role, 175, 197
    Mariana's supervision of, 47, 73
    members of, 134, 141
    and Portugal debate, 85–87
    records of, 9, 56
    role in political system, 75, 134, 141–42
    strengthening of, 73
    and *validos*, 72
    war deliberations, 155
    and War of Devolution, 90–91, 94

Council of War, 73, 86, 130, 132

councils, system of, 55–56

court, Spanish Habsburg, 15–16, 29–30, 31–33
    dynamics of, 108, 121, 141, 175, 181, 202
    entertainments, 31, 142, 163–65
    exchange economy of, 57–58
    expenses, 58–59
    fashion, 36
    hierarchy of, 55, 64
    Mariana's centrality at, 32, 44
    offices, 53–54, 55, 57

Crespí de Valdaura, Cristóbal, vice-chancellor of Aragon, 47, 50, 66, 70, 134

Cruz, Mariana de la, Sor, 187, 192, 194–95

Cueva, Baltasar de la, count of Castellar, 88, 94, 95, 143, 152

curatorship, 54–55, 176
    See also under Mariana of Austria

De la Fuente, marquis. *See* Teves y Tello de Guzmán, Gaspar de

D'Embrun, archbishop of, 89

Denmark, 159–60

Descalzas Reales. *See* Royal Convent of the Descalzas Reales

De Witt, Johan, grand pensionary of Holland, 82, 88, 98
    assassination of, 154
    negotiations with, 101–2, 103
    and Triple Alliance, 104

Dohna, Christopher von, 103

Dominicans, 123, 129, 167, 250 n. 33

Don Juan of Austria, 5, 108, 109–10, 128, 213
    accomplishments of, 42, 111–12
    ambition of, 16, 112–15, 184
    banishment of, 117
    and Carlos II, 179, 183, 188, 214–15
    as Carlos II's main advisor, 197–200, 202, 205, 213, 215–17, 219–20
    and Council of State, 94, 113
    death of, 221–22
    flight of, 119
    funeral of, 222–23
    and governorship of Low Countries, 113–15, 117, 120–21
    historiography of, 232
    illegitimacy of, problems caused by, 111–12, 218
    lack of support for, 126
    manifestos against, 196, 213
    and Mariana, 94, 108, 109, 111–15, 119–21, 168–69, 192, 195–96, 216
    and 1669 coup, 109, 118, 120–21, 127–28
    and 1675–76 coup (see also *Confederación*)
    opposition to, 200, 216–19
    political strategies, 189–90, 199–200, 216, 261 n. 58
    public opinion of, 196, 198, 200, 216, 219
    rejection by Philip IV, 46
    as viceroy of Aragon, 128–29

Doria, Pagan, 80

Dutch Republic. *See* United Provinces

Dutch War, 11, 156–60, 177
    See also Franco-Dutch War; Third Anglo-Dutch War

Eguía, Jerónimo de, 201, 213

Eighty Years' War, 82

Eleonora Gonzaga, Holy Roman Empress
    Dowager, 22
emoluments, 57–59, 92
empress consorts, 22
England
    alliance against France, 98
    as "heretics," 99, 124
    as mediator with Portugal, 82, 85, 88
    support of, in Portuguese war, 87
    treaties with, 87, 148–49, 231
    and United Provinces, 150; alliance
        with, 103; peace with, 98
    See also Charles II; Second
        Anglo-Dutch War; Third
        Anglo-Dutch War; Treaty of
        Madrid
Escorial, El, 31, 183, 189

Fanshawe, Richard, 83
favorites, royal, 5, 6, 10, 66
    See also validos
favoritism, 10, 72, 110, 236 n. 13, 248 n. 3
    See also valimiento
Felipe Próspero, infante of Spain, 39, 41–42
Ferdinand Bonaventure I, count of Harrach,
    33, 177, 195, 196–97
Ferdinand I, Holy Roman Emperor, 19
Ferdinand II, Holy Roman Emperor, 24–25
Ferdinand II, king of Aragon, 2, 68
Ferdinand III, Holy Roman Emperor, 19, 23,
    25, 27, 39, 78, 140
Ferdinand IV, king of the Romans, 20, 29, 39
Fernández de Córdoba, Catalina, duchess of
    Cardona, 70
Fernández de la Cueva, Francisco, duke of
    Alburquerque, 86, 166, 167, 170, 183
Fernández del Campo, Pedro, marquis of
    Mejorada, 74, 134–35
Fernández de Velasco, Íñigo, duke of Frías,
    constable of Castile, 114, 115, 117–18, 133
Fernández Portocarrero, Luis, Cardinal, 220,
    263 n. 43
Fernando, Cardinal-Infante, 25, 111, 114
Fernando Tomás, infante of Spain, 40, 41
First Battle of Nördlingen, 25–26
France
    alliances against, 156, 231
    armies of, 89, 115
    league with Portugal, 89, 96, 157
    regency in, 13–14, 248 n. 2
    rituals on king's majority, 15–16, 172–73

Spanish-born queens of, 78
    See also Franco-Dutch War; Franco-
        Spanish War; Louis XIV; War
        of Devolution
Franche-Comté, 102, 105, 158
Franco-Dutch War, 142, 151
Franco-Spanish War, 3, 26–27, 38
Franz Eusebius, count of Pötting, 42, 91, 112,
    152, 154
Franz Paul, baron of Lisola, 42, 87, 88
Frederick V, elector palatine, king of Bohemia,
    24
Fresno, marquis of, 161

galanteos, 61–62
Galicia, 97, 107
Gamarra, Esteban, 83, 102, 143, 150
Godolphin, William, 148
Gómez de Sandoval, Francisco, duke of
    Lerma, 72, 129
González, José, 67–68
González de Salcedo, Pedro, 116, 140, 179
governess. See aya; Hofmeisterin
governor of the monarchy, 55
governorship, 55
    Habsburg women governors, 13, 49, 67
    rights, 14
grandees, 53–54, 182–83, 240 n. 2
guardainfante, 34, 36, 88
guardamayor, 62
guardianship, 8, 13, 16, 49, 175–76
Guzmán, Gaspar de, count-duke of Olivares, 3,
    26, 66, 72–73, 130

Habsburg dynasty, 2–3, 4, 19–20, 66
    alliances, by marriage, 78
    Austrian branch, 19–20, 24–25, 39, 42,
        152–53, 229
    and Austrian succession, 43, 84–85, 156
    dynastic bloc, 25
    and female power, 8, 13, 21–22, 25,
        49–50, 240 n. 1
    intradynastic conflict, 26–27, 29, 94–96
    intradynastic marriage, 20, 25, 27,
        42–43
    military bloc, 153
    rivalry with Bourbons, 11, 78, 230
    Spanish branch, 19–20, 25–26, 43
    and Spanish succession, 84–85, 229
    unity of, 88, 152–53, 177, 197
Haro, Luis de, 38, 40, 66–67, 73, 130

Haro Sotomayor y Guzmán, García de, count
     of Castrillo, 45, 69–70, 116
Harrach, countess of. *See* Lamberg, Johanna
     Theresia
Harrach, count of. *See* Ferdinand Bonaven-
     ture I
Hedwig Eleonora, queen regent of Sweden, 98
Henrietta of England, duchess of Orleans, 148
     (*see also* Secret Treaty of Dover)
Hofmeisterin, 22, 23
     See also Trautson, Susanna Veronika
          von
Holland. *See* United Provinces
Holy Roman Empire, 20, 197
     armies of, 152
     Imperial Court, 20, 22–23; anti-
          Spanish sentiment, 211;
          expectations of Mariana's
          regency, 81; reception of Mar-
          garita, 84
     See also Habsburg dynasty: Austrian
          branch; Leopold I
house, vs. chamber, 60–61
household, royal
     Carlos II's, 142, 162–63, 165–66
     expenses, 58–59, 92
     and female power, 21–22, 60–63
     as gendered, 60–64
     hierarchy of, 59–60
     inner chamber, 60–61
     king's, 45, 48
     Mariana's, 31–33, 55, 59–60, 61–62;
          power dynamics, 63–64; ties to
          Austria, 32–33
     Philip IV's, 57, 58–59
     queen's, 240 n. 2
     reforms, 57–60, 61, 74, 92

Iberian Union, 36, 41, 107
Immaculate Conception, 23–24, 250 n. 33
inner chamber. *See under* household, royal
Innocent X, Pope, 28
Isabel I, queen of Castile, 2, 68
Isabel of Avis, Holy Roman Empress, 49, 236
     n. 18
Isabel of Bourbon, queen of Spain, 32, 67, 111
Italy, 81

Jamaica, 148–49
Jesuits, 23, 123, 129, 216, 250 n. 33
Jews, expulsion from Oran, 146

John of Austria, 111
Joseph Ferdinand of Bavaria, 229, 230
Juana of Austria, princess of Portugal, 49, 236
     n. 18, 263 n. 2
Junta de Alivios, 129
Junta de Gobierno, 9, 10, 56–57, 64–70, 123,
     127, 173
     as consultative body, 65, 68
     diminishing role of, 72–74
     formation of, 47–48
     and Malladas execution, 117
     members of, 69–70, 134
     precedents for, 67–68
     rationale for establishing, 65–67, 68
     representation in, 68
Junta de Inglaterra, 74, 85, 123
Junta de Represalias, 149
Junta de Teólogos, 99
juntas, 66

kings
     as minors, 14–16, 135, 140; control of,
          54–55
     powers of, 55–56
     qualities of, 184–85
     "two bodies" theory, 14–15
     See also individual rulers
king's guard. *See* royal guard
"king to king" negotiations. *See under* Portugal

Lamberg, Johanna Theresia, countess of
     Harrach, 32–33, 42, 196
Lamberg, Johann Maximilian, 81
League of Guarantee, 153
League of the Rhine of 1657, 81–82
Leopold I, Holy Roman Emperor, 2, 4, 20,
     39–40, 78, 80–81, 112
     against war with Portugal, 43
     as diplomatic ally of Spain, 77, 99,
          152–53, 156, 177, 196–98, 231
     discord over Margarita's departure,
          44
     and Franco-Dutch War, 158
     after Margarita's death, 154–56
     and Mariana, 22–23, 94, 96, 152, 192
     Mariana's influence on, 152, 154, 156
     as military ally of Spain, 43, 77, 81,
          84–85, 94, 152–53, 156, 158–59,
          197, 231
     and negotiations of Maria Antonia's
          marriage, 177, 197, 209–11

Leopold I (*continued*)
  negotiations to marry Margarita,
    42–43
  neutrality agreement with France, 95,
    152, 255 n. 25
  and Partition Treaty, 106, 143
  in Spanish succession, 43, 78–79, 156
Leopold Wilhelm, archduke of Austria, gover-
    nor of Spanish Netherlands, 114
Lerma, duke of. *See* Gómez de Sandoval,
    Francisco
letrados, 73–74, 75, 167
Lionne, Hugues de, 38
Lira, Manuel de, 150, 154, 158, 163
Lisola, baron of. *See* Franz Paul
lits. See France: rituals on king's majority
Los Velez. *See* Álvarez de Toledo, Mariana
    Engracia
Louis XIV, king of France, 11, 76, 98, 142–44
  armies of, 115, 159, 161
  as consort of Maria Theresa of Austria,
    infanta of Spain, 4
  deceptiveness of, 79–80, 89–90, 157–58
  deference to Mariana, 219
  denunciation of, by Spain, 91, 93, 101,
    157
  and Don Juan, 113–14, 121, 126, 127, 218
  as good son, 192
  and Mariana, 90, 93, 151
  Mariana's strategies against, 82, 84, 87,
    91–92, 94, 96–97, 103–5, 141,
    143–44, 151, 156–57, 167
  naval strategies, 144
  negotiations with Carlos II, 197 (see
    Marie Louise of Orleans)
  negotiations with Charles II, 87, 100,
    142, 148–49, 161 (see also Secret
    Treaty of Dover)
  negotiations with Leopold I, 84, 95, 152
  provocations by, 143–44, 147
  and Spanish Netherlands, 79, 82, 87,
    96, 101–2, 105, 115, 141, 232
  strategies against Spain, 38, 100–102,
    142, 147–49, 218
  as threat to Spain, 4, 11, 68, 76–77, 84,
    87, 89–90, 140, 142–44, 168, 192
  Triple Alliance, against, 105–6, 115,
    142, 147
  Quadruple Alliance, against, 142,
  and United Provinces, 82, 149–51
  See also War of Devolution

Low Countries, 25, 105
  Dutch support for Spanish claims
    to, 150
  See also Spanish Netherlands
Loyola, Blasco de, 45, 47, 74

Madrid, Spain, 31, 58, 130–31
Malladas, Joseph, 109, 115, 116–17
Mancera, marquis of, 201, 212–16
  banishment, 214
  as *mayordomo mayor*, 205–6, 213
  pardon of, 221
  resignation, 213
Manzano, Ramos del, 135
Margaret of Austria (1480–1530), princess of
    Asturias, duchess of Savoy, governor of
    the Netherlands, 135
Margaret of Austria (1584–1611), archduchess
    of Austria, queen of Spain, 20–21
Margaret of Parma, illegitimate daughter of
    Emperor Charles V, governor of the
    Netherlands, duchess of Florence,
    Parma, and Piacenza, 111
Margarita of Austria, infanta of Spain, Holy
    Roman Empress, 59, 77, 95
  birth of, 34
  death of, 154
  as heiress, 41
  marriage, 42–43, 80, 84, 143
  in Philip IV's testament, 78–79
  pregnancy, 88
  in Vienna, 84–85
Maria Antonia of Austria, archduchess of
    Austria, electress of Bavaria, 154, 186,
    196–97
  death of, 229
  as fiancée to Carlos II, 177–79, 209–12,
    259 nn. 16, 19, 264 n. 3
  as heiress to Spanish monarchy, 178,
    229
  as Mariana's granddaughter, 209, 229
  marriage, 229 (*see also* Maximilian II
    Emanuel of Bavaria)
María Luisa. *See* Marie Louise of Orleans
Mariana of Austria
  authority of, legal and constitutional,
    8, 14, 45, 47–48, 54–57, 72,
    115–16, 117
  and birthing an heir, political and
    international implications of,
    36–38

bridal journey, 29–31
childhood, 20–24
conflicts with Don Juan; in 1669, 110,
    126–28; in 1675, 16, 170–71,
    173, 187–90; *see also* Mariana:
    exile of
as curator, 16, 47, 54–56, 65–66, 169,
    173, 175, 236 n. 20
death of, 230
descriptions of, 5–6, 31–32, 49–50
diplomatic strategies, 11–12, 80–84,
    87–89, 94–97, 100–101, 106, 146,
    150, 151–54; alliances, 81–82,
    107–8, 156, 231–32; alliances,
    by marriage, 80–81, 94, 209,
    229–320; in exile, 209, 217
double Habsburg heritage, 20, 140
education; cultural, 22–23; political,
    23–24
exile of, 16, 171–72, 190–98; benefits
    of, 199–200; political influence
    during, 209, 217; public opin-
    ion of, 191–92
fiscal policies, 92, 96–97, 102, 107, 129,
    145
as governor, 8, 13–14, 16, 47–50, 55–56,
    60, 64–66, 79, 81, 135, 141, 169,
    175, 208, 219–20, 223 (*see also*
    Junta de Gobierno; portraits:
    of Mariana, as governor)
historiography of, 5, 10, 122, 230–33,
    232–33
as imperial daughter, 19–20, 28–29, 48
international power of, 142, 146, 151, 161
legacy of, 5, 169, 197, 227–33, 229,
    230–32
marriage negotiations of, 27–29
military strategies, 80, 91–92, 97,
    106–7, 145–46; alliances, 80, 81,
    98–105, 102, 158–60
as Philip IV's fiancée, 28–30
as Philip IV's wife, 30–31
political agency of, sources to study, 9
political roles of, evolution, 48–49
political system, 70–75, 133–35
postregency role, 16, 170, 172, 193, 199,
    223, 227
pregnancies of, 34, 37–38
as queen consort, 29–34, 36–42,
    44–45
readiness for childbearing, 28–29, 33

reconciliation with Carlos II, 200,
    203–6, 212–18, 219–20, 222–23
as regent, 5–8, 15–16, 49–50, 53–75,
    76–108, 109–40, 141–62
restitution to Carlos II's court of,
    223–24, 227, 229
as tutor, 14, 16, 47, 49, 54–56, 60–61,
    65–66, 79, 81, 94, 135, 140,
    175–76, 178, 223, 240 n. 3
as widow, 49, 50, 227
See also Don Juan: and Mariana;
    Leopold I: and Mariana; Louis
    XIV: and Mariana; portraits:
    of Mariana
Mariana of Neuburg, queen of Spain, 229
Maria of Ágreda, Sor, 27
Maria of Austria (1527–1603), archduchess of
    Austria, infanta of Spain, Holy Roman
    Empress, 236 n. 18, 263 n. 2
Maria of Austria (1606–1646), infanta of
    Spain, Holy Roman Empress, 19, 21, 25,
    26–27, 78
Maria of Ucedo, 189, 204, 205–6, 213
Maria Theresa of Austria, infanta of Spain,
    queen of France, 33, 76
    exclusion from succession, 78–79
    and Franco-Spanish War, 89
    as heiress to Low Countries, 89–90
    as heiress to Spanish monarchy, 27,
        36, 38
    and Mariana's exile, 192, 212
    marriage, 4, 40, 41; negotiations, 38,
        39–40
    relationship with Mariana, 212, 218,
        224
    renunciation of Spanish inheritance,
        41, 76, 78, 90, 232
Marie Louise of Orleans, niece of Louis XIV,
    queen of Spain, 197, 200, 209, 227. *See*
    María Luisa
Maura y Gamazo, Gabriel, 6, 7, 65, 66
mayordomo mayor, 59, 61–64, 132, 213
    authority of, 63
    See also individual *mayordomos*
Maximilian II Emanuel of Bavaria, elector
    of Bavaria, 229, 230, 264 n. 4. *See also*
    Maria Antonia of Austria: marriage
Mazarin, Cardinal, Jules, 39, 40, 41
Medellín, count of, 173, 216
Medinaceli, eighth duke of. *See* Cerda, Juan
    Francisco de la

Medinaceli, seventh duke of. *See* Cerda,
 Antonio de la
Medina de las Torres, duke of. *See* Núñez de
 Guzmán, Ramiro
Mediterranean region, conflicts in, 144,
 145–46, 147, 161
Mejorada, marquis of, 189
Mejorada, marquis of. *See* Fernández del
 Campo, Pedro
Méndez de Haro, Luis, 32, 38, 40, 66–67, 73,
 130, 132, 229, 242 n. 43, 263 n. 2
Messina, revolt of, 167–68, 170, 201
Milan, Italy, 30
minority, royal, 12–16, 45
Molina, count of. *See* Tobar y Paz, Antonio de
Molinet, Baltasar, 63
Moncada, Guillén Ramón de, marquis of
 Aytona, 58, 63, 64, 70, 85, 110, 121,
 131–34
  death of, 133
  on Junta de Gobierno, 71
  and Malladas execution, 117
  as *mayordomo mayor*, 132
  political roles of, 132
  and Portugal debate, 86
  and royal guard, 129–30
  and royal household reforms, 58–59,
   64, 74, 92, 132
Moncada, Maria Magdalena de, 33, 132
Moncada Aragón, Luis Guillermo de, duke of
 Montalto, 125, 241 n. 22
  conflicts with Mariana, 61–63
  as *mayordomo mayor*, 58, 61–63
  and Portuguese war, 83, 90–91
Mondejar, marquis of, 215
Montalto, duke of. *See* Moncada Aragón, Luis
 Guillermo de
Monterrey, count of, 153, 173–74
Morgan, Henry, 149
motherhood
  Mariana as example of, 192, 217
  politics of, 172, 198, 206–8, 209–10
  power of, 179–81, 184, 187, 206–8
  principle of, 224, 226
Moura Corterreal, Francisco de, marquis of
 Castel Rodrigo, 29, 87, 134, 155, 160
  as *caballerizo mayor*, 133
  on Council of State, 133
  and foreign policy, 141
  as governor of the Spanish Netherlands, 77, 81, 87, 96–97, 102

  as military leader, 92, 93
  and Triple Alliance, 102, 104

Naples, 145
Naples, viceroy of. *See* Aragón, Pascual de
Navarra y Rocafull, Melchor de, duke of
 Palata, 134
Navarre, viceroy of. *See* Tuttavilla, Francisco
 de
Netherlands, female governorship of, 13, 53, 111
Nithard, Everard, 6, 84, 122–26
  as ambassador to Rome, 124
  conflict over, 75, 109–10, 118–22
  conspiracies against, 115, 119
  dismissal of, 109–10, 122, 127–28
  historiography of, 232
  and historiography of Mariana, 5, 10,
   122–23
  as inquisitor general, 71–72, 123
  justification of alliance with England,
   99, 124
  lack of support for, 121, 125–26
  and Malladas execution, 117
  Mariana's opinion of, 124–25
  as Mariana's teacher, 23
  memoirs, 9–10, 122–23
  as not *valido*, 110, 124, 125
  and Portugal debate, 85, 86, 124
  role in Mariana's regime, 110, 125
  symbolic function of, 124–25
Núñez de Guzmán, Pedro, count of Villaumbrosa, 134–35, 167, 174–75, 184–86
Núñez de Guzmán, Ramiro, duke of Medina
 de las Torres
  influence of, 125
  omission from Junta de Gobierno,
   70, 72
  opinion of Nithard, 123
  and Portugal debate, 44, 85–86
  and Portuguese war, 91
  and royal household, 58

Olivares, count-duke of. *See* Guzmán, Gaspar
 de
Osuna, duke of. *See* Tellez Girón, Gaspar
Ottoman Empire, 144, 152
Oviedo, bishop of. *See* Valladares Sarmiento,
 Diego de

Panama City, 149
Pardo, El, palace of, 163

Parliament of England, 87, 100
parliaments. *See* Cortes
Partition Treaty, 106, 143, 152
pasquinades, 118, 133
Pastrana, duke of, 64, 133
Patiño, Bernardo, 119
patronage, royal, 22, 49, 53–54, 57–58, 126, 131,
　　134, 205
Peace of Breda, 98
Peace of Münster, 82
　　See also Westphalian congress
Peace of Nijmegen, 209
Peace of Westminster, 161
Peace of Westphalia, 3, 29, 30, 40, 152
　　See also Westphalian congress
Peñaranda, count of. *See* Bracamonte y
　　Guzmán, Gaspar de
Pertusato, Nicolás, 201
Peter, duke of Beja, regent of Portugal, king of
　　Portugal, 100
Philip II, king of Spain, 19, 66
Philip III, king of Spain, 3, 25, 72
Philip IV, king of Spain, 1, 3, 4, 9, 10, 11, 14
　　confidence in Mariana, 46, 53, 65
　　death of, 11, 45–47
　　and Don Juan, 42; deathbed snub, 46,
　　　112; recognition of, 111
　　and early military commitments,
　　　25
　　establishment of Junta de Gobierno,
　　　64–68
　　focus on Portugal, 38, 42, 43–44
　　funeral, 48
　　Mariana as substitute for, 56, 64
　　as Mariana's father-in-law, 27
　　as Mariana's fiancé, 28–30
　　as Mariana's husband, 19, 30–31
　　reforms of, 26
　　role in Leopold I's election, 95
　　royal guard of, 130
　　statue of, 164–65, 195–96
　　succession of, 3
　　successors, 78–79
　　testament, 13, 15, 16, 17, 44–47, 53,
　　　54–57, 64–67, 72
Philippe Charles, duke of Anjou, 143
Philippe I, duke of Orleans, 218–19
pirates, 144, 146, 147, 149
Ponce de León, Elvira, marquise of
　　Baldueza, 61, 62, 154, 166, 241 n. 17, 258
　　n. 53

portraits
　　of Carlos II, 135, 198, 217
　　of kings, conventions of, 56, 135
　　of Mariana, 1, 7; as child, 20–21; as
　　　governor, 56, 135; as queen
　　　consort, 34; as queen mother,
　　　227; as widow, 50
　　significance of, 198
Portugal
　　allies of, 42
　　debate over, 85–87, 96
　　and Franco-Spanish War, 36, 38, 40
　　independence of, 77, 90–91, 102, 231, 232
　　internal conflicts, 100
　　"king to king" negotiations, 83, 85, 88
　　Louis XIV's support for, 76
　　negotiations with, 99–102
　　peace with, 102, 107
　　truce offers to, 82, 83, 88
　　war with, 3–4, 11, 38, 43–44, 76–77, 81, 99
Pötting, count of. *See* Franz Eusebius
Povar, marquis of, 155

Quadruple Alliance, 17, 142, 156, 231
queen mothers, 13, 14, 15, 180, 227, 240 n. 6
　　political power of, 56, 172–73
queens
　　consort, 12, 23, 28, 227 (*see also* empress
　　　consorts)
　　historiography of, 12, 232–33
　　proprietary, 12–13
　　regent, 12–16
　　See also individual rulers
queenship studies, 12–13, 232–33
Quiñones, Gerónimo de, 127
Quiroga, Diego de, 25

Ramos del Manzano, Francisco, 132, 167,
　　168–69, 173, 189
regency
　　definition, 12
　　end date of, 15–16
　　examples of, 140
　　as feminine office, 13
　　in France, 13–14
　　among Habsburgs, 13–14
　　and "king's two bodies" theory, 14–15
　　in Spain, 13–14
　　as special form of queenship, 12–13
　　and transitions of power, 14–15, 49–50,
　　　172–73

Regency Council. *See* Junta de Gobierno
Reluz, Francisco, 219–20
reputation, policy of, 85, 86
retirement, 50, 166, 177, 185–86, 190, 192, 194,
    197, 239 n. 58
    See also Mariana of Austria: exile of
Richelieu, Cardinal, Armand Jean du Plessis,
    25, 41
Riquelme de Quirós, Diego, bishop of Plasen-
    cia, 116
Ronquillo, Pedro, 155–56
Royal Convent of the Descalzas Reales, 25, 33,
    44, 195, 201, 261 n. 58, 263 n. 2
royal guard, 121, 129–31, 183–84
    dismissal of, 188
royal minority. *See* minority, royal
Ruyter, Michiel de, 161, 168, 177

Salic Law, 13
Sandwich, earl of, 100
San Germán, duke of. *See* Tuttavilla, Francisco
    de
Sardinia, 146
Savoyard dynasty, 143
Second Anglo-Dutch War, 83, 88, 89, 98
secretaries, 73–74, 201
Secret Partition Treaty, 106, 143, 152, 244 n. 19,
    252 n. 4, 255 n. 24
Secret Treaty of Dover, 148
Seven Divisions of Law, 68
Sicily, 167–68
Siete Partidas. *See* Seven Divisions of Law
silver, from New World, 92, 96, 145, 153
Spanish monarchy, 2–3, 19–20
    allies, 98–105, 151–54, 158–60; gaining
        of, 107–8; lack of, 77
    armies of, 26, 44, 77, 107, 159, 231
    and commerce, 146 (*see also* silver,
        from New World)
    as composite monarchy, 15, 26, 68, 231,
        235 n. 2
    composition of, 2
    and Dutch War, 156–60
    and female inheritance, 4, 27,
        78–79
    as global conglomerate, 13
    political system, 8–9
    regency in, 13–14
    resilience of, 6
    role in European politics, 11–12
    succession, 4, 43, 78–79, 84–85

    transition of power, 68; Mariana to
        Carlos II, 169, 170–72, 174;
        Philip IV to Mariana, 45–49, 50
    Union of Arms, 26, 130
Spanish Netherlands, 76–77, 79, 82, 87–88
    defense of, 96, 232
    Don Juan's planned cession of, 197
    French desire for, 115, 141, 232
    and Triple Alliance, 105
Spínola, Pablo, marquis of Balbases, 152, 153,
    159
Sweden, 105
    alliance with, 98, 99; end of, 159–60
    subsidies to, 145, 146–47, 159–60

taxes, 92, 124, 145
Tellez Girón, Gaspar, duke of Osuna, viceroy
    of Catalonia, 121, 127, 145–46
Temple, William, Sir, 87, 102–3
Terranova, duchess of, 221
Teves y Tello de Guzman, Gaspar de, marquis
    de la Fuente, 80, 134, 153
    as ambassador to France, 89, 97
    and foreign policy, 141
Third Anglo-Dutch War, 18, 151
    Mariana's mediation, 161
Thirty Years' War, 3, 24–26
Tobar y Paz, Antonio de, count of Molina,
    99
    and Portuguese war, 87–88
Toledo, Spain, 190, 193–95, 203
    Mariana's entry into, 193–94
Toledo y Colonna, Victoria de, countess of
    Siruela, 22
Trautson, Susanna Veronika von, 22, 23
Treaty of Aix-la-Chapelle, 104–6, 115, 158 (*see
    also* War of Devolution)
Treaty of Lisbon, 102
Treaty of Madrid, 148–49, 232
Treaty of Peace and Commerce, 82, 87–88, 98
Treaty of the Pyrenees, 4, 40, 79, 103, 105, 150
    violation by Louis XIV, 42, 76, 90,
        93–94, 157
Triple Alliance, 98, 100, 102–5, 231
    dissolution of, 142
    formation of, 102–3
    preservation of, 144, 146–48
    secret clauses, 103, 104
    role in preserving Spanish Nether-
        lands, 104–6
    threats to, 115, 142, 145

See also Treaty of Aix-la-Chapelle;
Moura Corterreal, Francisco
de, marquis of Castel Rodrigo:
as governor of the Spanish
Netherlands; Mariana of
Austria: diplomatic strategies;
War of Devolution
tutorship, 176
of Mariana, for Carlos II, 54–55, 135
rights, 14, 240 n. 6
Tuttavilla, Francisco de, duke of San Germán,
viceroy of Navarre, 80, 97, 127, 143, 146
Twelve Years' Truce, 25

Ucedo y Prada, Maria Ambrosia de, 163
Union of Arms. *See under* Spanish monarchy
United Provinces, 3, 12, 17, 25, 39, 82–83
alliance against France, 98, 103–4
alliance with England, 100, 103 (*see also*
Triple Alliance)
independence of, 3
and Spain, collaboration with, 98,
100–102, 107, 150–51, 153, 154,
159, 160–61, 168, 177, 231, 232
as traditional French allies, 39
regime change, 154
See also Act of Reciprocal Assistance
Against France; De Witt,
Johan; Franco-Dutch War;
Mariana of Austria: diplomatic
strategies; Quadruple Alliance;
Second Anglo-Dutch War;
Third Anglo-Dutch War; Triple
Alliance

Valenzuela, Fernando, 6, 142, 162–65, 171–72,
184
building program of, 164
and Don Juan's vengeance, 189
elevation to grandeeship, 182
exile of, 203
historiography of, 232
and historiography of Mariana, 5, 10
Mariana's advocacy for, 204
Mariana's patronage of, 164, 171–72

as organizer of court entertainments,
142, 162–63
role in Carlos II's court, 181–84
See also Maria of Ucedo; *Confederación*
validos, 10, 26, 32, 66–67, 72–74, 133, 175, 181
definition of, 110, 125
See also favorites, royal
valimiento, 10, 72
lack of, in Mariana's court, 133
See also favoritism
Valladares Sarmiento, Diego de, bishop of
Oviedo, 116, 119, 129, 134
Velasco, Leonor de, 33
Velazquez, Diego, 34, 36
Velez, los, marquise of. *See* Álvarez de Toledo,
Mariana Engracia
Villars, Pierre de, 143, 216–17, 218, 219
Villaumbrosa, count of. *See* Núñez de
Guzmán, Pedro
Vives, Juan Luis, 50

Wallenstein, Albrecht von, 25
War of Devolution, 11, 77, 89–96, 113, 232
"alternatives" solution of Louis XIV, to
end, 101–2, 103–5
financing of, 92
justification for, 89–90, 93
Mariana's response to Louis XIV,
93–94
outcomes of, 105
peace mediations, 98
response to Louis XIV, 93–94
significance of, 105–6
and Spain, military innovations, 107
as uniting Spanish court, 90–91
See also Army of Flanders; Treaty of
Aix-la-Chapelle
War of Restoration. *See* Portugal: war with
War of the Spanish Succession, 6
Westphalian congress, 26, 29, 36
See also Peace of Münster; Peace of
Westphalia
widowhood, 49, 50, 185–86
William of Orange, Statdholder of Holland,
king of England, 154